THE DAY
DIXIE DIED

THE DAY DIXIE DIED

THE BATTLE OF ATLANTA

GARY ECELBARGER

THOMAS DUNNE BOOKS

St. Martin's Press ≋ New York

THOMAS DUNNE BOOKS.
An imprint of St. Martin's Press.

THE DAY DIXIE DIED. Copyright © 2010 by Gary Ecelbarger. All rights reserved.
Printed in the United States of America. For information, address St. Martin's Press,
175 Fifth Avenue, New York, N.Y. 10010.

www.thomasdunnebooks.com
www.stmartins.com

Design by Meryl Sussman Levavi

Library of Congress Cataloging-in-Publication Data

Ecelbarger, Gary L., 1962–
    The day Dixie died : the battle of Atlanta / Gary Ecelbarger.—1st ed.
        p. cm.
    Includes bibliographical references and index.
    ISBN 978-0-312-56399-8
    1. Atlanta Campaign, 1864.   2. Atlanta (Ga.)—History, Military—19th century.
I. Title.
    E476.7E25 2010
    973.7'37—dc22

                                                                        2010032480

First Edition: November 2010

10 9 8 7 6 5 4 3 2 1

To
Craig, Kurt, Jon, and Karla
from
your brother

CONTENTS

LIST OF MAPS

LIST OF ILLUSTRATIONS

ACKNOWLEDGMENTS

This work is the product of several years of research and could not have been achieved without the assistance of those at the local, state, and national historical depositories and without the aid of historians and biographers whose interests dovetailed with mine. Their numbers run into the scores; for example, each historical society and archive listed in the bibliography employed as many as five who directly assisted me. They proved as knowledgeable as they were dedicated, and I found them indispensable to producing this book. The same holds for the authors of all the books cited. Their works held pearls necessary to tell my story, many of which I would never have found on my own. Collectively, I salute them and thank them for their time and effort spent on me.

Specifically, I wish to highlight a few talented people who made this work possible. No book about a Civil War battle or campaign can convey the author's interpretation without a decent set of troop-movement maps to guide the reader through the author's narrative. George Skoch is the cartographer of this book and his outstanding maps are the first ones ever published to interpret the Battle of Atlanta in more than one or two phases. His maps capture the battle in stages ranging from thirty to ninety minutes and it was a genuine thrill to see each of them for the first time. I thank Mr. Skoch for his talent, his patience, and his professionalism.

Dr. Stewart Bennett of Blue Mountain College proved indispensable to this work. His Ph.D. thesis interpreted the Battle of Atlanta, and he generously provided primary source material that filled in the gaps of my own research. More than that, Stewart became a favorite sounding board to field my questions and assess my interpretations while sharing his own take on the battle in whole and in parts. His knowledge, generosity, and warm friendship will never be forgotten. I also thank historian Steven E. Woodworth—not only for his expertise on the Army of the Tennessee, but also for connecting me with Dr. Bennett.

Keith Bohannan is a valuable Civil War historian and the expert of all things Georgia. I thank him for all the times he directed me to source material I had not previously considered and for sending me some archival gems from his own research. I also thank historian Scott Patchan for sharing his expertise on the Civil War in 1864 and for his skills in research and battlefield interpretation. All of my trips to Atlanta have been with Scott as well as other research trips to several other states where we collected source material specific to the battle and campaign for Atlanta. Nearly twenty years of friendship with Scott have proven invaluable to my understanding of this pivotal period of America's past. Rod Gainer, another historian and yearslong friend, critiqued some of my manuscript chapters for which I am grateful.

I thank Ed Knappman (New England Publishing Associates) for representing this work and finding it a great home. I am also grateful for those who produced this book at Thomas Dunne Books, particularly Rob Kirkpatrick for acquiring the project and overseeing its publication, Bob Berkel for line editing the manuscript, and to Margaret Smith for guiding it through all the necessary steps to produce the final product.

I close with acknowledging my wife, Carolyn, for her numerous sacrifices made to afford me the countless hours necessary to research and write this history. Her selflessness in this regard is but one reason why she always has and always will own my appreciation, my respect, and my love.

AUTHOR'S NOTE

Most historians and Civil War buffs concur that the war was won for the Union and lost for the Confederacy in the West. The meaning here generally refers to a military theater bordered by the Appalachians in the east and the Mississippi River in the west. In the spring and summer of 1864 the theater boundary expanded southeastward as the opposing armies that had spent the two previous years battling in Kentucky, Mississippi, and Tennessee waged war within 250 miles of the beaches lining the Atlantic coast. This book isolates one battle of the summer of 1864 that had a greater impact on that outcome than previously recognized.

The fact that two Western armies fought in the East symbolizes the difficulties a historian must overcome to present this history as clearly as possible. Understanding the Battle of Atlanta presents challenges to even the most voracious readers of military history. The aggravating similarity in the names of the opposing armies—the Army of Tennessee versus the Army of the Tennessee—is guaranteed to confuse readers and sometimes even writers. Add to this the facts that there are several brigade and division commanders surnamed "Smith," that opposing forces clashed against each other from opposite directions in consecutive days, and that aside from "Sherman," "Hood," and perhaps "Cleburne" most of the personalities involved in the battle are unknown to those with a general interest in the Civil War as well as to those well versed in Eastern campaign battles. There are hundreds of Civil War aficionados who can rattle off the names of Sickles, Hancock, Ewell, and Longstreet as the surnames of corps commanders at Gettysburg, but will be reduced to scratching their heads when asked to name just one corps commander active in the Atlanta campaign, let alone any of the six Union and Confederate corps commanders at the Battle of Atlanta. Nor would it be surprising to see the Eastern theater buffs respond with a vacuous stare when asked to name the general in charge of the victorious army at the close of the Battle of Atlanta.

Aside from the lack of recognition of the participants opposing each other at Atlanta on July 22, 1864, challenges to interpretation exist that are not unique to this battle or theater for that matter. Oftentimes Confederate brigades, divisions, and corps are identified by a proper name taken from an earlier war commander no longer in charge of the unit. For example, Cheatham's Division (note the capitalization of the unit) fought in the Battle of Atlanta commanded by Brigadier General George E. Maney. Major General Benjamin Franklin Cheatham—for whom the division was named—fought in the battle as a corps commander, not in charge of the corps for which his old division served, but, instead, at the helm of Hood's Corps that had a vacancy when its namesake commander, General John Bell Hood, ascended to command the entire Army of Tennessee in this battle. One can imagine the tedium and confusion reading the following phrases that would pepper the battle narrative, "General Cheatham, in charge of Hood's Corps," and "Cheatham's Division, under General Maney." Furthermore, referring to these two specific commands by their capitalized names renders ambiguous the phrase "Cheatham's command" or even "Hood's men." Other named units, such as Granbury's Brigade and Hindman's Division, fought in the Battle of Atlanta without their namesake commanders; Generals Granbury and Hindman were nursing wounds that kept them from this battle. To constantly refer to these commands by their absent commanders will guarantee confusion for both writer and reader.

This book was written with the deliberate attempt to avoid the aforementioned pitfalls in comprehension. To prevent confusion between the nearly identical names of the opposing armies, the Confederate Army of Tennessee is more frequently called "Hood's army" while the Union Army of the Tennessee retains its name throughout the narrative to distinguish it from the other two Union armies surrounding Atlanta. Additionally, all of the Union corps—and only the Union corps—are identified by a Roman numeral (e.g., XV Corps). All Union and Confederate regiments are designated by their number and state (e.g., 5th Arkansas, 11th Iowa); whenever the terms "Artillery," "Cavalry," or "Infantry" do not immediately follow the numeric and state designations, it can be assumed that the unit referred to is infantry.

For other bodies of troops, Union and Confederate brigades and divisions as well as Confederate corps, identification in the narrative will usually be in reference to its commander on the Atlanta battlefield and not by its numeric designation or—in the case of Confederate units—by a name of a commander no longer in charge of the body of troops. Therefore, the four Tennessee brigades commanded by General Cheatham from 1862 until four days before the battle are not referred to as Cheatham's Division, but instead are called Maney's division after the general in charge of them on July 22, 1864. Not only does this method eliminate the confusion of misidentifying any of the divisions Cheatham led as a corps commander, for other units it prevents the introduction of superfluous commanders who had nothing to do with the Battle of Atlanta. So, Clayton's division replaces Hindman's Division, and James A. Smith's brigade replaces Granbury's Brigade. For consistency's sake, nearly every brigade, division, and corps identified by its commander is depicted in lower case letters. (The exceptions are the Orphan Brigade, a prominent Kentucky force, and the Florida Brigade, which are identified by capitalization.) For the sake of consistency, lower-case designations also apply to brigades, divisions, and corps still led by the same commander for which they earned a proper name. Thus, Cleburne's division replaces Cleburne's Division and Lowrey's brigade is used instead of Lowrey's Brigade. A complete Order of Battle for the Battle of Atlanta is listed in the Appendix; in it can be found the original names of these units for the Confederate side and the numeric designation of divisions and brigades on the Union side.

It seems impossible to keep up with the Smiths during the battle of Atlanta. No fewer than six generals and colonels with that ubiquitous surname led troops during this bloody day of battle—four Confederates and two Union. Every time one of these commanders appears and reappears in the story he will be identified by his full name or at least the initials of his first and middle name to make it absolutely clear to the reader which Smith is described. Fortunately, no Smith was directly opposed by a Smith during the battle. Equally as fortunate, the chronological and geographical flow of the battle allows for separate chapters to isolate the battle to smaller and sometimes uniform bodies of troops. For example, chapters 4 and 5 describe two Confederate divisions against troops from one Union corps. Chapter 7 isolates two other Confederate divisions against three new Union divisions, and chapter 8 introduces an entirely new Confederate corps attacking Union troops who had not been mentioned in earlier chapters because they are active here for the first time. This "natural" isolation of portions of two large armies brings the reader into chapters describing action varying in length between thirty to ninety minutes where no more than one-third of the opposing armies are fighting each other.

It is the intention and hope of this author that these deliberate decisions provide the reader with a more appreciative and less frustrating battle "experience" than one would normally expect given all of these impediments to comprehension. If the reader still finds himself enveloped by the fog of war with the multitude of personalities and military units associated with the Battle of Atlanta, the troop movement maps and the Order of Battle should serve as a beacon to help guide him through the action of July 22, 1864.

THE DAY
DIXIE DIED

BATTLE OF ATLANTA LITHOGRAPH

This Kurz and Allison view was released in the late 1880s and depicts an embroidered view of the battle, including the death of General McPherson below the U.S. flag. (*Courtesy of the Library of Congress*)

INTRODUCTION

"THE DISSATISFACTION WITH MR. LINCOLN GROWS TO ABHORRENCE"

J uly was a terrible month for Abraham Lincoln, certainly his worst month thus far in 1864 and one of the most troublesome periods of his entire presidency. It started out well enough. After gratefully accepting the resignation of his thorny secretary of the treasury, Salmon P. Chase, Lincoln swiftly and smoothly sent in the nomination of Senator William B. Fessenden to the U.S. Senate as Chase's replacement (it was confirmed the same day). As satisfied as he was to be rid of the troublemaking Chase, the resignation underscored the brewing problems in Lincoln's cabinet. Three of the initial seven members of the Lincoln cabinet did not successfully complete the first term of his presidency with him and two more—Attorney General Edward Bates and Postmaster General Montgomery Blair—were growing so cantankerous and dissatisfied with the administration that their service would also end before the year did (Blair was gone by September; Bates would resign in November).

The month turned sour beginning in the second week. The Civil War was brought to Lincoln's doorstep when Confederate General Jubal Early carried his Shenandoah Valley campaign to the northern outskirts of Washington, D.C. The threatening Confederate tide ebbed on July 12 with the timely arrival of Major General Horatio G. Wright's VI Corps of the Army of the Potomac, who were Union troops detached from their Petersburg, Virginia, campaign. General Early wisely turned tail and hustled back to the west side of the Blue Ridge Mountains, chased by Wright's corps that had come to Washington to rid the area of the menace.

According to John Hay, one of the President's personal secretaries, Lincoln was never concerned for the safety of Washington during the peak of Early's offensive, seeing that as an opportunity to severely damage his army. Two days after the threat receded Lincoln sarcastically reported to Hay, "Wright telegraphs that he thinks the enemy are all across the Potomac but that he has halted & sent out an infantry reconnaissance, for fear he might come across the rebels & catch some of them." Hay entered into his diary that night, "The Chief is evidently disgusted."[1]

Indeed he was and America was disgusted with him. Obviously, the Confederate States of America had no love for the president, but the North—those states that elected Lincoln with a clear majority of the Electoral College in 1860 (although he only received 39 percent of the popular vote nationwide)—had grown more and more disillusioned with his job performance. They displayed that anger first in the off-year election of 1862, stripping Lincoln of twenty-two Republican seats in the U.S. House of Representatives. A promising 1863 had given way to an 1864 that was growing more alarming and frustrating for the North with each passing day. Indeed, June and July of 1864 had inaugurated the summer of America's discontent.

"The dissatisfaction with Mr. Lincoln grows to abhorrence," vented a native Kentuckian since removed to Cincinnati. His opinion was somewhat tainted as he had been a friend of Chase, but his connections to his birth state explained much of his observation. Lincoln suspended the writ of habeas corpus in Kentucky and established martial law throughout that Border State. Anti-Lincoln fervor was displayed in newspaper editorials, private letters, and public displays across the states of the Union. It came from prominent men and ordinary citizens, from people who had always opposed Lincoln to those who had supported him in years—and months—past. All shared their disapproval of the way the president was handling his duties as commander in chief.[2]

Collapsing support for the president had many contributions to it, none bearing more negative influence than the current state of the Civil War. So much promise in March of 1864 had turned to anger, frustration, and despair four months later. On March 6, 1864 Ulysses S. Grant was commissioned as a lieutenant general, a rank last bestowed upon George Washington, and made general in chief of all the Union armies in the field. Grant moved across the Alleghenies, leaving the Western theater, where he had won all of his laurels, behind to work directly with the Army of the Potomac, officially still commanded by Major General George Meade. Grant submitted a plan for simultaneous movements on four fronts. The objective was to apply overwhelming pressure upon the Confederacy and prevent shifting of troops from one harried war front to another. Grant would move with Meade's army to take on Robert E. Lee and the Army of Northern Virginia in central Virginia; Grant's former department, the Military Division of the Mississippi, would carry forward where it left off in Chattanooga the past autumn and battle General Joseph Eggleston Johnston's army with an objective to destroy the army while penetrating as deep into Georgia as possible. A third front placed an army on the Yorktown Peninsula, the scene of a major Union campaign failure in 1862, to attempt to take Richmond while guiding up the James River. The fourth front was another war-long headache for the Union: the Shenandoah Valley. There a Union force would drive southward to strike and destroy the rail lines at Staunton, Virginia, and the hub at Lynchburg, Virginia.

Grant's plans called for all of the movements to commence in the first week of May, and Lincoln wholeheartedly approved it. The president understood that while all fronts were important, the two most vital ones were the Georgia theater and, of course, the operation against General Lee and his elusive army. That the president considered the other elements as less crucial appears to have initiated a problem with Grant's operation. Lincoln was responsible for selecting the commanders of those theaters. Here, the president's performance was mediocre and had a foreboding history just a few months before. A fifth front began its operation in the winter of 1863–1864. The objective was to move up the Red River from Louisiana into Texas, combine with a southward moving Union force in Arkansas and, after they cleared the region in short order, the combined force was expected to head southeastward all the way to Mobile Bay on the Gulf Coast of Alabama. Against Grant's wishes, Lincoln chose Major General Nathaniel P. Banks to head that operation. Banks was a political general with a scant record of military success at Port Hudson in 1863, a victory that failed to neutralize his stunning defeat in the Shenandoah Valley in the spring of 1862. Yet, Lincoln insisted upon Banks, and the general delivered another failure by abandoning the Red River operation, which terminated the thrust to Mobile.

Lincoln's choice for the Yorktown Peninsula army, appropriately called the Army of the James, was Major General Benjamin "the Beast" Butler, another controversial political general with little military ability. Unlike Banks, Butler's operation began very smoothly and nearly reached Richmond before the summer. A skilled Confederate defense, however, not only halted him, it kept him stagnant throughout the summer, leading to the oft-repeated statement "The Beast is bottled up on the James." Lincoln's third horrible choice, both in foresight and hindsight, was Major General Franz Siegel to head the army in the Shenandoah. The fact that the Confederate Shenandoah army under Jubal Early reached the gates of Washington in July is evidence of how poor that choice turned out to be. All three of those hand-picked commanders were failures that led to fiascos. They signaled a huge threat to the success of Grant's grand plan.

To no one's real surprise, Grant was forced to fight for every mile of Virginia terrain against Robert E. Lee in an operation known as the Overland campaign. From May through July, he successfully pushed Lee's army back from the Rapidan River to the trenches of Petersburg where both sides dug in for a siege. Grant's siege of Vicksburg the previous year lasted six weeks with the capture of the entire army there on the Fourth of July. Nevertheless, Lee was the best general in the South with a much bigger army; by the middle of July 1864 the duration of the Petersburg siege already exceeded Vicksburg's with no end in sight. Still, that was not a military failure because Lee was trapped and unless he could break out or receive reinforcements, Grant could lock him in so tightly that he could starve Lee's army out. "I begin to see it: you will succeed," Lincoln declared as Grant started the siege, but what the president understood the voters could not.[3]

Public perception throughout the North saw that in an entirely different light, a light that failed to reveal the overall progress but only exposed the most unseemly and appalling aspect of a military campaign—the casualties. Grant had successfully ground Lee down, inflicting nearly 35,000 casualties upon him, but he did so while losing 65,000 killed, wounded, and missing men. The enormity of those losses was shocking; adding in the losses in all theaters from May through mid-July revealed that Lincoln's armies lost over 100,000 soldiers (including captured) in just ten weeks—an average of 1,500 soldiers every single day! As Americans stared stunned at the lengthy lists that marred their hometown papers, they collectively asked, "What do we have to show for this sacrifice?"

To achieve victory, Lincoln needed to provide more soldiers to offset those atrocious losses and to buttress the armies in the field. On July 18, he issued a proclamation calling for 500,000 more volunteers, boldly adding that a draft would begin in September to guarantee the number of recruits should the requisite number of volunteers fall short. The proclamation was met with disdain and derision. Adam Gurowski told his diary:

> July 18.—A new call for 500,000 men. Lincoln ought to make his *whereas* as follows:
>
> *Whereas,* my makeshift and of all foresight bereaved policy—
>
> *Whereas,* the advice of a Seward, of a Blair, and of similar etc's—
>
> *Whereas,* my Generals, such as McClellan, Halleck, and many other pets appointed or held in command for political reasons, have occasioned a wanton slaughter of men; *therefore*
>
> *I,* Abraham Lincoln, the official Juggernaut, call for more victims to fill the gaps made by the mental deficiency of certain among my commanders as well as by the rebel bullets.[4]

Gurowski was a Radical Republican; his cynical entry underscored how many felt about the history of Lincoln's mistakes in prosecuting a war that most of them supported, and many of them still did, but no one seemed to approve the current state of affairs in the summer of 1864. That was a dire time for Lincoln; he was up for reelection, that time under a new ticket. War-supporting Democrats joined political forces with Republicans to form the National Union Party for that election. At their national convention held at Baltimore in June, Lincoln was nominated for reelection on the first ballot. The ticket was complete with the choice of Governor Andrew Johnson, a Tennessee War Democrat, as his running mate. That convention met and chose Lincoln in June, but Republican dissention grew so quickly that it began to boil over in the middle of July. Horace Greeley, the influential editor of the *New York Tribune*, was the most prominent former Lincoln supporter to bolt the ranks by seeking another candidate "to save us from utter overthrow" and preserve the

Union. "Mr. Lincoln is already beaten," insisted Greeley that summer. "He cannot be elected."[5]

Lincoln floundered in attempting to put together a peace commission to meet with Confederate emissaries at Niagara Falls. He also allowed two loyal citizens to meet with President Jefferson Davis in Richmond. In both instances Lincoln clung to his ideals, insisting that the war should end in the field and negotiations could compromise on differences between North and South, but the two Union causes must stay in place: The rebellious Southern states must return to the United States of America without their "peculiar institution." Lincoln insisted there must be no Confederacy and slavery must end throughout the land. Negotiations broke down on both fronts over that, so the war would continue.[6]

But for how long? Lincoln was coming closer and closer to the realization that he would lose the November 8 election (in a month he would be certain of it). He lamented that the public was not realistic about the time required to succeed in a campaign, complaining to an aide, "they expect too much at once." Lincoln had been guilty of the same expectations two years before, but by then he was reconciled to allow Grant's campaign to wind down in 1865. "As God is my judge," Lincoln declared in the summer of 1864, "I shall be satisfied if we are over with the fight in Virginia within a year. I hope we shall be 'happily disappointed,' as the saying is, but I am afraid not—I am afraid not."[7]

News from the Shenandoah Valley bode ill that Lincoln would be "happily disappointed" at an end to the war in Virginia before the election. On July 20, the Union forces in the Shenandoah Valley were beaten again by Jubal Early's army. Butler remained bottled up on the James River, and Grant's siege of Lee at Petersburg had produced no discernable gains. That left one general as the only glimmer of hope for Lincoln: Major General William T. Sherman and his Atlanta campaign. Like Grant, Sherman had made significant progress against the Confederate army that was defending northern Georgia against his advance. In two months Sherman had advanced almost 100 miles into Georgia, sparring and maneuvering at the cost of 20,000 Union casualties during that time. Those losses were significant, but were less than a third of what Grant and Meade had suffered during their simultaneous campaign against Lee.

Sherman oftentimes appeared as the antithesis of General Grant. Sherman was taller, thinner, and redheaded. He knew the South, had

MAJOR GENERAL WILLIAM TECUMSEH SHERMAN, U.S.A.

Taken at Atlanta within three months of the battle, this image captures the head of the Military Division of the Mississippi on horseback. Sherman commanded three Union armies numbering nearly 100,000 soldiers in July of 1864. *(Courtesy of the Library of Congress)*

lived in the South, and was very accustomed to Southern customs. He tolerated the institution of slavery but was absolutely intolerant of secession. Sherman was very excitable and rather emotional; the stress of the Civil War (and his chain-smoking) made him appear more than ten years older than his forty-four years of life. His friends called him "Cump" (a shortened version of his middle name, Tecumseh) and the rank and file under him called him "Uncle Billy." He accepted both and basked in the adoration of peers and subordinates, but hated newspaper reporters with a passion and worked hard to expel them throughout his military district.

Sherman earned the command of the army group for his dedicated service and steady ascent over two years of successful campaigns west of the Appalachians. His Civil War career, however, prior to 1864 had been far less stellar. Sherman proved to be a less-than-spectacular battlefield tactician as a division commander, a corps commander, and an army commander, but his tactical flaws were not appreciated at the time, while his seniority and friendship with General Grant secured a series of field promotions. He rose to a position where he excelled when he took over the Military Division of the Mississippi in March of 1864. Sherman was a master of maneuver and logistics, working wonders with a single-track railroad between Chattanooga, Tennessee, and Marietta, Georgia, to feed and supply a military population equivalent to the ninth largest city in the country. Those skills placed all three of his armies south of the Chattahoochie River and within 6 miles of Atlanta on the morning of July 20, 1864.

Sherman succeeded at maneuvering three distinct armies through the rough terrain of northern Georgia, partially perhaps because he thought of them as one. Indeed, he referred to his command in the singular "my whole army." His enemy, both rank and file, respected his swiftness. Earlier in July, the opposing pickets exchanged some friendly banter across the Chattahoochie:

"Hello, Yank, who is your Commanding General?"
"Sherman. Who is yours?"
"Well, I believe Sherman is ours too. Whenever he moves, we move too."

Less than two weeks after that verbal exchange, Sherman moved both armies southward by crossing that river and pushing the Confederates into Atlanta as he proceeded to surround it. "I think I shall succeed," Sherman wrote his wife, "at all events you Know I never turn back." Although the line referred to his July 9 prediction of crossing the Chattahoochie, Sherman could easily have offered the same line verbatim in describing his intention for Atlanta.[8]

Lincoln grew particularly hopeful during July's third week about the potential end of the campaign, anticipating that Sherman's grand offensive would result in the Confederates abandoning Atlanta without a fight or a siege. By July 20, however, that hope diminished when he learned that the Confederate army remained to defend it. Given his belief that no dramatic improvements would occur in the other theaters, Atlanta was the key to the future course of the Civil War. It was all linked to his reelection. If General Sherman could seize that vital business center, rail hub, and symbol of the South, it would overturn a great deal of the dour news that had permeated the North regarding the conduct of the war. That could be the first solid success of Grant's four-pronged grand strategy. The newly acquired manpower obtained through volunteers and drafted recruits would buttress the armies in the other theaters and produce visible results as well, but that would likely only occur after November 8. Atlanta had to be conquered well before that to boost Lincoln's chances for reelection and guarantee the prosecution of the war to its end— the submission of the Confederate armies in the field. Lincoln feared that his loss to a Peace Democrat (they would choose their nominee at the end of August) would end the war on completely different terms. It would be a negotiated peace in which the Southern states would either form their own nation or would come back into the Union with slavery preserved.

Lincoln's hopes were pinned to Atlanta, a city that owed its existence to the very factor that made it a prized military objective: railroads. When the Western & Atlantic (W&A) Railroad was completed with its terminus at the sleepy little town of Marthasville in 1845, no one could predict how that Georgia hamlet would thrive from its new lifeline. Nine years and three more railroads later, the renamed city of Atlanta then competed with the largest urban areas of the South. By 1860 its population approached 10,000 souls with blacks comprising about 1 out of 5 of the residents. The city flourished from the four crossing ribbons of iron, transporting textiles and foodstuffs from all over the country to and from markets in the North, South, East, and West. In addition to the wealth they accumulated by trading and by railroad employment, Atlanta residents reaped the harvest of living at the center of regional markets whose products were hauled to the iron crossroads.[9]

Naturally, Atlanta was a valuable depot for the Southern states during the Civil War, rolling out troops and supplies throughout the entire Confederacy. Grant's instructions to Sherman early in April to "get into the country as far as you can, inflicting all the damage you can against their war resources" made Atlanta the objective point of the campaign without even having to name it. That Sherman received those instructions

THE CAR SHED IN DOWNTOWN ATLANTA 1864.
The great 300-foot depot on the Georgia Railroad highlights the importance of the city as the junction of four rail lines and how prized it was as
the objective of Sherman's summer campaign. *(Courtesy of the Library of
Congress)*

in Chattanooga and embarked on a campaign one month later that carried three Union armies through northern Georgia along the line of the
W&A Railroad made Atlanta a prized possession at the terminus of that
lifeline. With Grant stymied well south of Richmond, the focus fell upon
Atlanta, where opposing lines of battle stood within 6 miles of the city.
In July of 1864 it had become the symbol for both the life of the Confederacy and the preservation of the Union. Richmond was the capital of
the Confederacy, but Atlanta was the heart of the South.[10]

On July 20, the *Atlanta Daily Appeal*, a newspaper one day from extinction, printed a prediction—one that would be carried by newspapers

throughout the North, including the urban centers of Philadelphia and New York:

> The greatest battle of the war will probably be fought in the immediate vicinity of Atlanta. Its result determines that of the pending Northern Presidential election. If we are victorious the Peace party will triumph; Lincoln's Administration is a failure, and peace and Southern independence are the immediate results. While we are not disposed to underestimate the importance of holding Atlanta as a strategic position, yet the fate of the city itself is a question of minor import when compared with other necessary national results.

> Everything—life, liberty, property and the independence of the South, the security of our homes, wives, mothers and children all depend upon the courage and heroism of the men whose toils may now be terminated by a brilliant victory. Never before were such incentives to valor placed before an army whose courage requires no stimulant, whose gallantry has never been questioned.[11]

In the middle of July readers of the plea in the *Appeal* both in the North and the South could come to a consensus on one point: Atlanta was the key. James Russell Lowell, a renowned poet and editor of the era, identified it as "the real campaign" for Lincoln's election. A big battle appeared inevitable at Atlanta; its result would determine the fate of a nation.[12]

★ ★

1

∽

CLOSING THE VISE

A brass-laden brigade band blared forth a spirited rendition of "The Star-Spangled Banner" as the blue-clad soldiers of the Army of the Tennessee marched westward toward Atlanta, the objective point of an arduous and angst-filled campaign. The army had begun that trek in Chattanooga seventy-five days and 100 miles earlier. Since then they had crossed three rivers; fought three battles and skirmishes nearly every day between them; all the while enduring hardships from both anticipated and unexpected sources. Six days earlier, 15 men in one division were killed or wounded by a single lightning strike during a violent storm blanketing the Chattahoochie River valley, a freakish bolt that did not discriminate between foot soldiers, artillery men, or mule drivers. Thousands more fell dead or wounded from Confederate lead, iron, and steel over the two months prior to that deadly storm. But on Wednesday morning, July 20, 1864, Atlanta and ultimate victory stood just 6 miles away from the surviving Union soldiers.[1]

The army was not surprised to be so close to its campaign destination. Named for a major river—as were most Union armies in the field—the Army of the Tennessee, in the haughty words of one of its members, expected "nothing but victory" at the completion of its campaign. The soldier trumpeted that boast the previous autumn, a prediction borne out by ultimate success in the field. It was a statement that proved true in every major campaign in which the army participated before that: at Fort Donelson, Shiloh, and Corinth in 1862; and at Vicksburg and Chattanooga in 1863. This was the army previously commanded by the two most important generals in the Union: Ulysses S. Grant and William Tecumseh Sherman. With only a smattering of setbacks on battlefields and two and a half years of continuous victories in military campaigns—including the surrender of Confederate armies at Fort Donelson, Tennessee, and Vicksburg, Mississippi—the collective opinion of soldiers within the Army of the Tennessee was that the capture of Atlanta was inevitable. They expected nothing less, for they laid claim to be the most successful army on the continent.[2]

In Georgia the Army of the Tennessee was not operating alone. Since the fall of 1863 it moved and fought as a collective unit called the Military Division of the Mississippi. The district was named for a major river as were the three armies under its umbrella—the Army of the Tennessee, the Army of the Cumberland, and the Army of the Ohio. Major General William T. Sherman led that army group, a command of seven infantry corps, nearly two corps of cavalry, and 250 cannons. It was a formidable Union force approaching 100,000 officers and men.[3]

Sherman had taken over many of the duties left by Ulysses S. Grant, who had departed during March of 1864 to head east as a lieutenant general in charge of all the Union armies in the field. Sherman's promotion carried him from the immediate command of the Army of the Tennessee, a position he had taken once Grant was chosen to head the armies in the Western theater in the fall of 1863, to overall command of the Military Division of the Mississippi. Consequently, throughout the Atlanta campaign of the spring and summer months of 1864, command of the Army of the Tennessee belonged to Sherman's replacement—Major General James Birdseye McPherson.

McPherson was the darling of all the Union armies in the field—at least in the eyes of the two men who mattered the most: Grant and Sherman. He came to Grant's army in the winter of 1861–1862 (several months before it was officially called the Army of the Tennessee) and served initially as his chief engineer. By the end of 1862 McPherson had risen from lieutenant colonel to major general and held the helm of Grant's XVII Corps. The corps was active and successful throughout the Vicksburg campaign and even though "Mac" was overlooked for promotion after Grant was elevated, he was awarded command of the Army of the Tennessee upon Sherman's ascension to Grant's position in March of 1864.

MAJOR GENERAL JAMES BIRDSEYE MCPHERSON, U.S.A.
The third commander of the Army of the Tennessee, McPherson overcame a shaky start at Resaca at the initiation of the Georgia campaign to bring his army to the outskirts of Atlanta in the third week of July. Engaged to marry a Baltimore belle named Emily Hoffman, his wedding was postponed by the campaign for Atlanta. *(Courtesy of MOLLUS-Massachusetts, USAMHI, Carlisle Barracks, Pa.)*

The command of an army was the appropriate reward and a seemingly perfect fit for McPherson, the ultimate "A" student of the Army of the Tennessee. McPherson had graduated first in his West Point class of 1853, a class including the likes of Major General John M. Schofield (in charge of the Army of the Ohio), Major General Philip Sheridan (soon to be in charge of the Union forces in the Shenandoah Valley), and Confederate General John Bell Hood, who stood in his path to Atlanta. Schofield claimed that McPherson was not overly inventive, but "his was the most completely balanced mind and character with which I have ever been intimately acquainted. . . ." The stress of war had begun to prematurely gray the beard of the thirty-five-year-old Ohioan, but McPherson was otherwise the model of health and fitness. McPherson fit his uniform well. He stood erect, close to the 6' mark, fully bearded with a pleasant face. McPherson was attractive in intellect, personality, and appearance.[4]

He was also taken. McPherson was engaged to Emily Hoffman, a Baltimore belle whom he met at a party in San Francisco during the spring of 1859. Miss Hoffman was twenty-five years old when he met her, young and beautiful, blessed with dainty features and striking blue eyes. It appears that they fell in love at first sight, but the war postponed their wedding, which they had planned for 1861. Just three days after he sailed away from her in August of that year, McPherson poured his heart and soul out to her. "You cannot imagine how much I miss you, though each hour is adding to the distance which separates us," he wrote en route to New York from San Francisco. "But I thank Heaven every day and hour of my life, dearest Emily, that there are invisible cords stronger and more enduring than any ever made by hands which bind me to you; cords which will withstand the fury of the tempest, the rude shock of battle, and the allurements of an active, exciting life, and cause me to return to you with a heart overflowing with love and devotion."[5]

Active campaigning kept the two lovers apart for nearly three years. McPherson confessed to Sherman his love for her while the generals wrapped up affairs in Vicksburg late in the winter of 1864. In an effort to help out his friend, Sherman arranged for McPherson "to steal a furlough" late in March of 1864. McPherson arranged to travel to Baltimore to the Hoffman home where he planned to marry Emily. That was a coup in itself because the Hoffman family—particularly Emily's mother—were passionate Southern sympathizers who swallowed their aversions to allow a Union army commander into their home to wed one of their own. But telegrams sent by Sherman interrupted McPherson's plans while traveling north—one announcing his promotion to army command and the other ordering him to northern Alabama to help plan the Georgia campaign. When the frustrated and heartbroken McPherson arrived from the postponed wedding, Sherman empathized. "Mac," he told him, "it wrings my heart but you can't go now." Sherman followed up by personally writing to Emily Hoffman to smooth over the ruffled feathers and to assure her that McPherson was worth the wait.[6]

The problem for McPherson was that his performance at the initiation of the Atlanta campaign did not exemplify a confident commander. McPherson's letters home reveal his own self-doubts at the time, confessing to his mother, "I have a much greater responsibility than I desire."[7] His overbearing sense of caution captured him at a moment when the Union needed a risk taker for a swift and victorious end to the campaign. That was exhibited at the opening of the campaign, just west of the town of Resaca on May 9. Instructed to hustle his army through Snake Creek Gap and cut the rail line in the rear while Sherman's other two armies demonstrated in the gaps of Rocky Face Ridge against General Joseph E. Johnston's Army of Tennessee (Confederates named their armies for regions, not rivers), McPherson marched the Army of the Tennessee (at that time consisting of two corps totaling 25,000 men) through the mountain pass and placed the men within striking distance of the Western & Atlantic Railroad and the town of Resaca, several miles south of Johnston's Confederates and guarded by only 4,000 troops. McPherson had at least 6,000 men deployed on the hills overlooking that poorly defended locale.

If McPherson deployed and charged his men upon Resaca that day, brushing away the overmatched force there and taking control of the railroad and the town, the Southerners would have been trapped in a vise closing upon them from the north and south without a good avenue for escape. The campaign could have—and perhaps should have—ended with McPherson's offensive, but he vacillated and eventually gave in to his caution, pulling his men back several miles into the gap rather than charging them one mile upon the town. It was a very costly decision, for General Johnston was able to use the railroad and pull his Confederate army unimpeded down to Resaca where they fought three hard days to keep possession of the town from May 13–15. He escaped southward to fight again and again, playing the game of maneuver with Sherman all the way to the outskirts of Atlanta. General Sherman realized McPherson's error even before the battle began. "Well, Mac," said Sherman upon greeting McPherson three days after the latter's cautious decision and one day before the battle, "you have missed the opportunity of a lifetime."[8]

Indeed he did miss a golden opportunity, but the incident would not sway McPherson from that proclivity. He never admitted that as a mistake at all and would continue to prefer caution over what he deemed as recklessness. Although the opening "inaction" at Resaca irked Sherman and caused him to label McPherson as "timid," the fact was that McPherson had a strong case to not commit his men to an assault against a region he knew to be defended, but was unaware of the strength of that defense.

The cavalry that was supposed to be his eyes as well as the force that actually cut the railroad never reached his advance. Approaching darkness that day convinced McPherson to follow Sherman's written contingency "to draw back four or five miles, to Snake Creek Gap, make it secure, and wait for orders." That is exactly what he did. His West Point classmate, John Schofield, felt compelled to defend his friend against Sherman's allegations. "McPherson was a subordinate in spirit as well as in fact, and cannot fairly be charged with timidity for not attempting what he was not ordered to do, and what, in fact, was no part of the plans of his superior so far as were indicated in his orders."[9]

Affected by Sherman's rebuke to open the campaign, McPherson and his army had performed well since then, beginning with the Battle of Resaca where they seized and held hills formerly belonging to the Confederates and forced Johnston to withdraw over the Oostanaula River. Two weeks later the XV Corps inflicted over 1,000 casualties upon an ill-fated assault by a division of Confederates at the Battle of Dallas, Georgia, the only Union victory in five days of battles in a region called the "Hell Hole." McPherson and his army continued to flank and press throughout the month of June, suffering a rare and temporary setback at Kennesaw Mountain on June 27.

The constant maneuvering, skirmishing, and battling gained McPherson more experience. By July 20 he was veteran of eight battles and at least twice as many skirmishes in his past fourteen months as a corps and army commander. His army was not big, but it was formidable and had made an impact throughout the past two months in Georgia. The Army of the Tennessee fought and marched the first half of the campaign with merely five divisions of the XV and XVI Corps. The XVII Corps completed its detached duties in Alabama and arrived in June, boosting McPherson's strength to 30,000 officers and men, and 1,750 artillery horses pulling 96 cannons (by comparison the Army of the Cumberland had nearly twice as many men and 35 more cannons).[10]

Still, the compactness of the Army of the Tennessee enabled it to serve as the most mobile component of Sherman's department. It was known as the "Whip-Snapper"—the army that conducted the huge sweeping marches while the other two held the Confederates in place. Throughout the campaign of maneuver against Johnston in Northern Georgia, Sherman ordered the Army of the Tennessee to conduct the flanking marches designed to get around the Confederate front and attack the sides and rear to prevent the ungodly casualties seen 500 miles north with Grant combating Lee head on in the battles of the Wilderness, Spotsylvania, and Cold Harbor. The cunning Johnston never allowed his flank to be completely turned but it certainly was not for a lack of trying on Sherman's part. The Army of the Tennessee was counted on at times to march over 15 miles a day on consecutive days, and instantly deploy into battle formation and fight at a moment's notice—no mean feat.

The "Whip-Snapper" role served those soldiers of the Old Northwest well. It is exactly how they found themselves 6 miles east of Atlanta on July 20 and closing in minute by minute. Just three days earlier they stood on the north bank of the Chattahoochie River, set to embark upon another grand sweep to challenge the Confederate defense of Atlanta from the east as the other two armies struck from the north and northeast. On July 17, McPherson crossed his army over the Chattahoochie at Roswell, 21 miles northeast of Atlanta, on a bridge constructed by the XVI Corps several days before. The Federals covered close to 20 miles that day and spent the following day destroying the Georgia Railroad between the stunning monolith called Stone Mountain and the railroad town of Decatur. Here, McPherson was acting on Sherman's directive to prevent the Confederates from bringing in any reinforcements and provisions on the rail line to strengthen the army protecting Atlanta. That was the second of four rail lines leading into Atlanta that was under Union control and McPherson's army made sure the Georgia Railroad was a dead line. Truman G. Tuttle of the 26th Iowa briefly explained to his hometown newspaper how he and his comrades accomplished the mission, "We took up the ties, piled them in cords with the rails across and then fired the ties, then bending the rails and making them useless."[11]

The head of McPherson's army marched into Decatur on Tuesday night, July 19, and continued to proceed unabated through the town the following morning. "This is a very old, dilapidated, wooden town, of perhaps 400 inhabitants," determined an Iowan in the ranks; "it was certainly the most forlorn looking place we have seen for a long time." An Illinois soldier concurred about the miserable appearance of Decatur but was buoyed by a specific attraction in the town. "I saw a couple of right pretty girls," he wrote, but he had no time to talk to them. Even before noon most of the army had cleared through Decatur and proceeded westward to Atlanta, guiding along the Georgia Railroad.[12]

An Illinoisan in Decatur caught a rare glimpse of the high command of the Army of the Tennessee, a sighting he recorded in his diary:

> In afternoon Gens. Dodge & McPherson & Logan conversed together in the streets of the town. Dodge rather nervous—McPh. cool as could be & smiling as ever & Logan silent and twirling his moustache, which is long enough to reach behind his ears.[13]

The foot soldiers of the Army of the Tennessee exhibited strong faith and trust in their generals. Solid at brigade and division commands, the army's three corps commanders all had proven records of success throughout the Georgia campaign and the Vicksburg campaign before it. That was particularly fortunate for the army, for none of the corps commanders had solid military education or experience prior to the war. Only Major General Grenville Dodge of the XVI Corps could claim that he was a cadet—but not at West Point (instead from Norwich University). He had no military experience between his education and the war, serving as a civil engineer. Major General John Logan of the XV Corps was a company officer during the Mexican War, but his unit stayed in Santa Fe and never went to the battle front. He and Frank Blair (XVII Corps) were renowned politicians prior to 1861, not military men. Nevertheless, all three were outstanding corps commanders and all three had a strong bond with General McPherson.

It all went so smoothly for the Union rank and file that more than a few began to harbor the notion that McPherson could march unopposed into Atlanta that very Wednesday. That was Sherman's expectation. At noon he received a cavalry report insisting that the Confederate army had evacuated Atlanta and that demoralized Confederate militia was all that remained there. That afternoon Sherman learned that report was totally erroneous. The Army of the Ohio was victimized by an artillery barrage as they crept toward Atlanta. Southern prisoners brought inside Union lines confirmed that a corps opposed them. General Thomas and the Army of the Cumberland came under attack at 4:00 P.M. in an engagement called the Battle of Peachtree Creek. Two different corps of Confederate infantry battled the army for hours, launching attacks up the center and attempting to strike the flanks of the Army of the Cumberland.[14]

Unable to advance from the north and northeast, Sherman counted on General McPherson and the Army of the Tennessee to find a weakness in the Confederate defense. Sherman accounted for all of the corps belonging to the Confederate Army of Tennessee. McPherson's men should not be opposed by a significant force, but Sherman's intelligence had failed him before and it surely would again. However, one bit of intelligence became very important to him and confirmed rumors that had trickled into the lines. Sherman had known since Tuesday, July 19, that Joseph Eggleston Johnston no longer was in charge of the Army of Tennessee. He had been ousted by Confederate President Jefferson Davis two days earlier. "It is true Johnston is relieved and gone east," Sherman assured a subordinate; "I have seen a copy of his order of farewell to his troops. Hood is in command and at Atlanta."[15]

General John Bell Hood had become the fourth commander of the Army of Tennessee in seven months, rising from corps command where he had led throughout the Atlanta campaign. Hood had earned laurels for one facet of warfare—he was a tenacious combat officer. Hood made his mark and a name for himself in the Army of Northern Virginia fighting under General Robert E. Lee in 1862 and 1863 where he sparkled on the offensive at Gaines's Mill, Manassas, Antietam, Gettysburg, and Chickamauga. Whether the battle was a Confederate win or loss, Hood's attacks were memorable for their ferocity and impact. On three battlefields, Hood's assaults were so decisive as to produce or assure a Confederate victory. No one leading troops for the North or the South, whether serving in the East or the West, hit an opponent harder than John Bell Hood.

That fearless skill on the offensive fueled Hood's meteoric rise of four grades from colonel to brigadier general to major general to lieutenant general and to the top Confederate rank of general—all in just a little over two years. He could also claim the youngest age to earn his final two ranks, having celebrated his thirty-third birthday at the end of June. On the other hand, Hood's aggressiveness paid a heavy toll on his body. His right arm had been shattered by shrapnel at Gettysburg. He was able to keep it from the surgeon's amputating saw, but the limb was limp and lifeless. His entire left leg was gone—including the thigh—a necessary loss to save his life after a Yankee bullet shattered his femur at Chickamauga. Nearly 8 out of every 10 soldiers who had their leg surgically removed at the hip like Hood did died from complications of the procedure.

GENERAL JOHN BELL HOOD, C.S.A.

Taking command of the Army of Tennessee on July 18, 1864, Hood was one of the most aggressive generals in the Civil War. That reputation was earned while Hood served under General Robert E. Lee in the Army of Northern Virginia. *(Courtesy of MOLLUS-Massachusetts, USAMHI, Carlisle Barracks, Pa.)*

Hood's death-defying feat was only matched by his ability to resume command in just six months.

When Hood returned from his Chickamauga wound to field duty in March he left the Army of Northern Virginia and came to the Army of Tennessee in Dalton, Georgia. He was welcomed into the army for leading an assault in Longstreet's command at the Battle of Chickamauga that turned the Union flank and achieved the Confederate victory that day. That assault produced the grievous leg wound that made Hood a hero, albeit a crippled one. Although fitted with an artificial leg, Hood could only walk with crutches, which were difficult to use because of his useless arm. Aides needed to tend to his personal needs. They also needed to strap him to his saddle where he remained for hours as he led the corps he earned for his years of sacrifice and achievement. Ironically, it was

General Johnston who put a good word in to bring the hero into his army, "Hood is much wanted here."[16]

Hood's war wounds did not appear to diminish his zeal for carnage and mayhem but the troops he commanded could not match up to the awesome performances of his Texas brigade in 1862 and the divisions he commanded in 1863. He counterpunched fluidly at Resaca, Georgia, preserving Johnston's right flank in mid-May, but the punch was landed too weakly by one of his divisions to roll up the Union flank as Johnston had intended. Hood severely punished part of Thomas's army for haphazard attacks made upon his corps at New Hope Church, Georgia, ten days later. Hood's offensive prowess was entirely lacking at Kolb's Farm, Georgia, in the third week of June. There, Hood's two-division assault was easily brushed away by a division of the Army of the Cumberland, which inflicted 1,500 casualties upon Hood while suffering relatively few losses (250) on the defensive. Either Hood was losing his touch, or the subordinate division and brigade commanders failed to share his passion for the assault, or other circumstances, such as a stronger and wary opponent, were conspiring to neutralize his forte on those Georgia killing fields.

None of that mattered by July, for according to President Davis, Johnston "failed to arrest the advance of the enemy to the vicinity of Atlanta" and the War Department had lost confidence in him. Again, Hood's Chickamauga wound appeared to aid him in the decision to replace Johnston. Hood had convalesced from his amputation for a time in Richmond late in 1863, where the blond-haired hero was treated well. There he continued to woo "Buck" (Sally Buchanan Preston), a South Carolina belle who caught Hood's eye and heart back in 1862. She loved to flirt, but she did not love Hood. Still, he managed to get a tacit acceptance of his marriage proposal, an agreement that would disintegrate within a year. Perhaps Hood had an inkling of her teasing nature. He found an outlet to his needs by frequently visiting a young prostitute, a teenager who must have been aware of Hood's courtship with the beautiful "Buck" when she wrote, "I wondered why he came here, when he could get all he wanted free."[17]

Hood's dalliances with the fairer sex did not prevent him from endearing himself to the person that mattered the most in Richmond: President Jefferson Davis. He had met Davis frequently during his convalescence and grew beyond his 6'2" frame in the President's already approving eyes.

Physically, Hood was no longer the imposing figure that helped Lee defend Richmond in 1862. His shoulders no longer appeared so broad and his chest was not as thick, both a consequence of that crippled right arm. The uniform was always ill-fitting, making Hood appear like "a raw boned, country-looking man" or "like a raw backwoodsman." Moreover, his face remained long and sad, although his booming voice was still melodious and rich in tone, and those blue eyes still were as penetrating as ever, kindly and expressive all at the same time. The few photographs taken of him darkened his features when in actuality his tawny beard and brown hair were so light as to be described as blond.[18]

Hood could not impress Davis with his brilliance because he was not a brilliant man. He ranked in the bottom fifth of his West Point class of 1853, far below General Schofield and forty-three notches below James McPherson (the head of that class), but Hood's battlefield performances outshone the class star. That and his heroic injuries impressed Davis who sent Hood to Georgia in 1864 with a rank of lieutenant general, the youngest commander in the Confederacy to hold that distinction. On July 17, Hood was promoted again to the highest Confederate rank of general, although that was noted to be a temporary rank, it was one sure to stand if Hood could somehow save Atlanta and expel the opposition from its tightening grip on the beleaguered city. In choosing him, President Davis did not consider Hood's unproven skills as a strategist or whether or not he could handle the reams of paperwork and communicate well with his subordinates—all traits required for success by army commanders. None of that seemed to matter at that point. Davis cast his lot with Hood because he knew he would attack and not retreat. Hood's promotion sent a message to him, his subordinates, and his opponents that the army was not going to give up Atlanta without a fight.

On Wednesday, July 20, Hood spent his third day as commander of the Army of Tennessee doing exactly what was expected of him by his president—attacking the enemy to keep them from closing in upon Atlanta. He inherited General Johnston's command on July 17, a force that could rightfully boast seven weeks earlier to be one of the largest armies ever fielded by the Confederacy in the three-year-old war. Back then the army approached 80,000 officers and men present for duty, but Johnston lost significant numbers of troops as he ceded 100 miles of Georgia to General Sherman. He lost a higher percentage of men killed, wounded, and captured on the defensive than did Sherman, who had sparred with him since early May. The addition of Georgia militia failed to significantly offset those losses; still, Hood inherited a significant and skilled force that numbered close to 63,000 soldiers in his infantry, cavalry, artillery, and militia. Hood's Army of Tennessee was the largest Confederate army on the continent on July 20, 1864, larger than Robert E. Lee's dwindling numbers facing the Union Army of the Potomac 450 miles north of them at Petersburg, Virginia.[19]

The Army of Tennessee was torn between its ardor for its former commander and its dissatisfaction with the conduct of the campaign to that point. Grumbling within the ranks was palpable over the previous month as Johnston continued to fall back through northern Georgia. Most soldiers who wrote an opinion were distraught to see Johnston go, but Hood was not considered a source of despair for those writing within days of the command change. Quite the contrary, he was a source of hope for a change of direction and fortune. One soldier claimed that all were "perfectly satisfied" with Hood as their new commander. He could hardly speak for everyone, but even some Johnston men, like Captain Samuel Kelly, confessed that he did not object to Hood's ascent to command "and hope it is for the best." It was the most ardent Johnston supporters who were dumbfounded by his dismissal and also distraught at Hood's ascent to the top of the command. "Hood is the most unpopular Gen'l in the Army and some of the troops are swearing that they will not serve under him," revealed Lieutenant Robert Gill of the 41st Mississippi the day he learned that Johnston was gone. That same day (July 18) Martin Van Buren Oldham scrawled in his diary, "Hood's fighting quality, as demonstrated by his total disregard for human sacrifice, does by no means suit the men." That Tennessee soldier well realized why Hood replaced Johnston, closing his daily entry by easily predicting, "Gen. Hood will probably teach the army other tactics than fortifying."[20]

Hood sensed the low morale and insisted that battle victories were the perfect antidote. Charged with the responsibility to protect Atlanta from Union invasion, Hood saw the adverse outcome as inevitable unless he could deliver a devastating blow to Sherman. The first opportunity arose Wednesday July 20 as Hood studied Thomas's Army of the Cumberland as it crossed Peachtree Creek, a northwesterly flowing tributary of the Chattahoochee. "Feeling it impossible to hold Atlanta without giving battle, I determined to strike the enemy while attempting to cross this stream," reported Hood, stressing that his objective was "to crush Thomas' army before he could fortify himself, and then turn upon Schofield and McPherson." To destroy Thomas he planned on hitting him with two of his corps to drive him over Peachtree Creek and trap him between the stream and the Chattahoochee River while the third Confederate corps—his former command—kept Schofield in place northeast of Atlanta. If he failed to destroy or irreparably wound the Army of the Cumberland, Hood realized his chances to turn the campaign around would suffer severely.

He failed. The Battle of Peachtree Creek began at 4:00 P.M. (three hours later than initially planned), and despite some early success against the center of Thomas's army, Hood's two attacking corps failed to throw the enemy across Peachtree Creek. Vigorous assaults were initiated by the corps of Major General Alexander P. Stewart, but Hood seethed that his other attacking corps, commanded by Lieutenant General William J. Hardee, "failed to push the attack." Two hours and fifteen minutes later, Hood called off the battle when he rightfully convinced himself that the opportunity for success had come and gone. Thomas's defense cost him 1,500 killed and wounded men, attesting to the vigor of the Southern attack, but Hood's casualties reached 2,500 without appreciable gain on the battlefield.[21]

Unknown to General Hood was that by initiating the Battle of Peachtree Creek, he upset Sherman's plans for General Thomas to order his troops to "push hard for Atlanta, sweeping everything before them." Sending that message to Thomas half an hour before Hood launched his attack, Sherman was looking for a quick and simultaneous assault upon the outer defenses of Atlanta. With Thomas under continuous assaults throughout the late afternoon, and Schofield opposed by a larger corps of Confederates, Sherman looked to McPherson to break the stalemate. Based on the limited number of troops Hood had to protect Atlanta, Sherman realized that of the three armies under his command, the Army of the Tennessee must be opposed by the fewest number of Southerners and the lowest number of cannons. No one could blame Sherman if McPherson's earlier vacillation at Resaca invaded his thoughts. If it did, that would be McPherson's opportunity for redemption.[22]

McPherson's army advanced from Decatur, Georgia (due east of Atlanta), with two corps marching westward on parallel roads. The XV Corps followed the line of the Decatur road and the Georgia Railroad while the XVII Corps attempted to keep pace on a more tortuous farm road off the left flank of the XV Corps. The undersized XVI Corps, all of four brigades, took up the reserve role and marched in the rear. McPherson's supply train, over 1,000 wagons, remained in an established park near Decatur.[23]

Early in the afternoon McPherson's men struck a line of Confederates who opened fire upon them with a battery from a belt of woods a half mile west of a north-south road known for the Clay residence off to the side of it. Major General Frank Blair's corps, the XVII, was hit by that barrage. Blair's men faced off against Hood's cavalry corps, approximately 2,500 horse soldiers commanded by Major General Joseph Wheeler. Wheeler was a Georgian and only twenty-seven-years old but had come under enemy fire so often in the war that he would eventually tally three wounds, sixteen horses shot out from under him, and thirty-six staff officers who caught lead probably intended for him.

To counter Wheeler's guns, Blair called up two batteries, the 15th Ohio and 1st Minnesota Light Artillery. A heavier-than-expected artillery duel followed in that sector, one that imbued a lasting effect on the artillerists engaged. Thomas D. Christie, a Minnesotan working one of the cannons, declared, "I never want to see shells fly thicker than they did at us there. . . . Four of our fancy horses were killed, & another wounded, three of them by our shell, which burst under the Limber, throwing splinters & gravel right in the Captain's face." In less than an hour the two Union batteries overpowered the lone Confederate battery and Blair's men knocked Wheeler's defenders back to a ridge line 2 miles east of Atlanta, dominated by a treeless eminence known as Bald Hill.[24]

Wheeler was attempting to make a stand as Hood launched the Battle of Peachtree Creek. Hood's army was essentially arrayed in an arc that partially ringed Atlanta and covered approaches north and east. (If Atlanta was the center of the face of the clock, the Confederate army was aligned from 11 o'clock to 3 o'clock.) Wheeler was Hood's right flank, a position made more important as the afternoon waned while Hood battled Thomas on his left. If Wheeler was driven into Atlanta, Hood risked the threat of one of Sherman's armies at his rear as he attempted to drive two others away from his front. Furthermore, Wheeler protected the right flank of Hood's infantry—Hood's old corps commanded by Major General Benjamin Franklin Cheatham—that extended to the east-west Georgia Railroad to prevent the advance of the Army of the Ohio against it.

If Wheeler was forced from the ridge south of Cheatham and the railroad, Hood's army could be rolled up counterclockwise from the railroad. That not only was unacceptable; it would be disastrous to Hood's defense of the city. Trying to oversee the battle on each side of his arc of defense, Hood was unable to spare any infantry from his three corps to support Wheeler. He sent up more cavalry to boost his numbers up to 3,500. It was up to his cavalry chief to hold on and stave off the Union infantry and artillery opposing him. Wheeler got his men on the high ground, but he was outnumbered two to one by the available troops of Blair's corps, and five to one if the generally unopposed XV Corps was sent after Wheeler. If General McPherson pushed his attack like Sherman expected him to, Wheeler stood no chance against the weight of Union manpower and the strength of artillery fired by the Army of the Tennessee. Throwing Wheeler back into Atlanta would open the ground for McPherson to claim, place artillery on those enticing heights, and unravel Hood's entire defense. "If we can soon dislodge the enemy from the hill," wrote McPherson to Sherman that afternoon, "I will press my whole line forward and ascertain the exact state of affairs." That was the moment to redeem the lost opportunity at Resaca back on May 9.[25]

McPherson refused to throw caution to the wind, and he was hampered by those unforeseen circumstances on battlefields that conspired against the armies fighting there. His army crawled at the time when Sherman desired a full, hard press against any enemy troops in front. By the middle of the afternoon, McPherson was advancing close to 20,000 troops (with at least 5,000 more in reserve) within striking distance of an opponent of under 4,000 men yet it appeared he was doing as little as possible to strike. It was Resaca all over again with nearly the same number of troops opposing each other.

The XV Corps infantry enjoyed an unimpeded advance with its right moving on the Decatur road and Georgia Railroad (two routes so close that at times they occupied the same roadbed). Yet, McPherson never called upon any of its divisions or brigades to assist the XVII Corps. Only the artillery saw activity that day. As soon as he caught a view of the buildings in Atlanta just two and a half miles west of him, Major General John A. Logan ordered one of his batteries to unlimber and symbolically fire the first shots into the city. The cannons chosen belonged to Captain Francis H. De Gress's Battery H, 1st Illinois Light Artillery. De Gress deployed his 4 Parrott rifles on elevated ground and sent twenty-pound rounds arcing into Atlanta. The shells exploded in the square in front of City Hall and at the great railroad depot (called the Car Shed). Twenty-five years later came the claim that De Gress's battery killed a young girl near the corner of Ellis and Ivy Streets, a tragedy that escaped the newspapers and diaries in Atlanta during the summer of 1864.[26]

While De Gress's artillerists hurled rounds unopposed, another XV Corps battery was horrified—"for one mortal hour" as described by its captain, William H. Gay—as Confederate artillerists attached to Cheatham's corps harassed it with converging fire from a mere 500 yards. For reasons unknown, Gay had been ordered not to return fire, so there his silent guns stood as 7 men and numerous horses in his Iowa battery were killed and wounded. "It was indeed a trying hour," lamented Captain Gay.[27]

Union Brigadier General Walter Q. Gresham personally suffered a more trying hour than did Captain Gay. His day started out cheerfully. Writing a short letter from Decatur to his worried wife back home, Gresham assuaged her with optimism, "Be of good cheer. A good time is coming. We will soon be through."[28] General Wheeler's stubborn stand stole Gresham's cheer. Gresham's division of two brigades belonged to the XVII Corps; it was the principal engaged force throughout the afternoon of July 20. General Blair with another division at hand had yet to provide Gresham any assistance, nor did General McPherson who had two more corps at his disposal. Slowly Gresham had gained ground throughout the sweltering afternoon, but was unable to push Wheeler's dismounted cavalry from Bald Hill and the ridge line running northward from it. He sent one brigade under the command of Colonel Benjamin F. Potts forward in line of battle to a point about 400 yards east of that hill. Potts advanced his men to the cover of the banks of a creek ravine where he halted his men and awaited orders.

Gresham had a trying time that late afternoon and although his 50 killed and wounded men were much smaller losses compared to most battles, he was suffering the only significant casualties of the day for the Army of the Tennessee. Seeking an end to the harassment, he rode up behind the ravine hiding Potts and his brigade, dismounted and walked toward his skirmish line in front of the Confederate battery. He never made it. A rebel bullet tore into his lower left leg and shattered his tibia, dropping Gresham immediately. He was quickly tended to and borne from the field on a litter. Gresham's leg was saved from amputation, but his Civil War career ended that day.[29]

Gresham's wound should not have ended the day's action. Replaced temporarily but immediately by Colonel William Hall, who had commanded the Iowa brigade in the division, the division remained in position and was soon reinforced by elements of Brigadier General Mortimer Leggett's division, which Blair ordered up to support Hall's left. One brigade arrived and protected the Iowa flank by extending it and facing southward. McPherson rode upon the scene urging Blair to drive the Confederates off the hill. Leggett rode back to his command to prepare them for the assault. At the same time an officer was sent forward to scout out the extent of Wheeler's line atop Bald Hill. He returned shortly and notified the generals that the line of enemy troops abruptly stopped just south of the hill. An aide to General Leggett rode up to the commanding generals, saluted them, and asked, "General Blair, General Leggett wishes to know if he shall attack the enemy in his front."[30]

McPherson was instantly consumed by the caution that last overtook him at Resaca ten weeks earlier. He was swiftly arriving to the conclusion that there was not enough daylight for him to complete the job on July 20. He needed much more than the expected two hours that remained. The general practice adopted by both sides throughout the war was not to fight after dark; the few times that was attempted had proved ineffective and sometimes disastrous. Night time was for preparing for morning action, perhaps for some skirmishing and marching, but usually for rest and repose. McPherson decided to postpone his assault of Bald Hill until Thursday morning. Wheeler had figuratively dodged another bullet; Hood's right was preserved.[31]

As afternoon waned to evening, Sherman could not hide his frustration. He was surprised to learn rather late of Hood's attacks on Thomas and accepted the fact that Thomas could not counterpunch with only a few hours of daylight remaining. Directly in front of him, a Confederate division also showed its artillery strength against the Army of the Ohio. Shortly after 6:00 P.M. Sherman asserted, "I will push Schofield and McPherson all I know how," but two hours passed without the push he so desperately sought. Sherman assured General Thomas that he would urge McPherson onward, "but [I] think the opportunity on that flank if it did exist is now past."[32]

By nightfall the opportunity had indeed passed and Sherman was forced to plan for tomorrow. He fielded a report from McPherson, describing the day's events with a dispatch that read as an elaborate excuse. McPherson described the wounding of General Gresham, the difficulty of advancing along the terrain, and an enemy armed with Enfield carbines and four pieces of artillery, but McPherson also admitted that he endured a day that ended with very light casualties, and that only enemy cavalry opposed his left flank. (Several hundred militia were in supporting distance of Wheeler but were not ever called upon.) The dispatch revealed a day of failure, for from the moment of first contact with Wheeler, McPherson had barely deployed one of his three corps against it and at the end of the day Wheeler had remained on his high perch, most certainly destined to be reinforced overnight.[33]

Sherman soaked up the events of the day and realized that Hood was going to be as tough a fighter as defined by his reputation. That made the results of the day so unsettling, so unsatisfying. Receiving McPherson's excuse-laden dispatch made matters worse, but Sherman swallowed most of his disappointment and let the rest flow from his pen in the form of a mild reprimand, a way of putting in writing his Resaca exclamation, "Well Mac, you missed the opportunity of a lifetime!" He rebuked McPherson by writing, "I was in hopes you could have made a closer approach to Atlanta," highlighting the expectation that he opposed a weaker force and shorter earthworks than would be revealed by daylight, when Hood's reinforced right would come into view. He ordered McPherson to press the Confederate right, in front of his army, reinforced or not, in an attempt to gain ground for easy artillery range to the inner works ringing Atlanta. Sherman also revealed that because of the expected heavy losses Hood suffered in the Battle of Peachtree Creek, "I would not be astonished to find him off in the morning, but I see no signs looking that way yet."

Nor would he. Hood was not going to abandon his defense and Sherman knew it. Hood's reputation, his past history, and his demeanor suggested just the opposite—a fact Sherman could not avoid in passing while writing McPherson's attack order, "Hood proposes to Hold Atlanta to the death."[34]

"Death" was destined to be the operative word.

2

PRELUDE

General McPherson's decision to delay the assault of Bald Hill until dawn of July 21, although sensible in allowing time to reconnoiter and organize an attack force, appears to have cost the Army of the Tennessee an easy and relatively bloodless victory. Unknown to McPherson, a weak line of defense covered that hill and ridge, a force ill-prepared to fend off an infantry attack. Major General Joseph Wheeler managed close to 3,000 horse soldiers—fifteen regiments organized in three brigades—on that line to fend off an army of 25,000 soldiers should they attack him. Some of Wheeler's men acted like true infantry by instinctively digging into the high ground and making a primitive structure of earthworks that night. The attack Wheeler feared did not materialize in strength but that failed to quell his anxiety over the more than 8 to 1 mismatch he faced.

A stream of messages was exchanged between Wheeler and army headquarters, regarding the tenuous position he held. Receiving Wheeler's pleas for infantry support, Hood promised his cavalry chief that he would reinforce him in two separate messages that evening, emphasizing to Wheeler to "communicate this to the men and *urge them to hold on.*" Those reinforcements never came as Wednesday gave way to Thursday, but McPherson saved Wheeler a great deal of aggravation and even more casualties by not pressing him that night.[1]

Major General Patrick Cleburne took charge of the defense of Bald Hill at 2:30 A.M. on Thursday, July 21. Cleburne was the star of Hood's army, at least by standards of accomplishments and by potential. It certainly helped to have the strongest and most successful brigades with talented brigadier generals commanding them. Cleburne had enlisted in the war as an Arkansan, but his Irish birth marked him as one of only two foreign-born major generals in the entire Confederacy. Cleburne excelled as a combat officer, either when pegged to protect a position on a battlefield or to attack it. He was Hood's most experienced and reliable division commander, having led at that level for two years. He had been overlooked every time an opening was present at corps command—most recently when General Cheatham was picked to head Hood's corps four days earlier. Perhaps Cleburne's incredible and ill-received suggestion to arm slaves and muster them into the Confederate service (circulated in a written memorandum back in January) factored into the decision to hold him at division command. Regardless, no division commander on the continent was more savage and successful than Pat Cleburne.[2]

His division, recently reduced from four brigades to three by realignment, had been in reserve during the Battle of Peachtree Creek. Cleburne's command suffered close to 100 losses in that role, mostly as a result of distant artillery fire (except for the wounded and the families of the dead, those losses would be deemed inconsequential relative to the heavily engaged divisions that day). After pulling back southward into Atlanta that night, Cleburne deployed his three brigades in a long, loose line that advanced 2,500 yards eastward, his left moving along the Georgia Railroad. They marched as quietly as possible so as to not attract enemy skirmish fire.

The clandestine movement was not perfectly concealed and casualties mounted before Thursday's light of dawn revealed the Georgia landscape. Colonel Samuel Adams of the 33rd Alabama (a regiment with a "Boy Company" composed of at least a score of teenaged soldiers) positioned his command and was inspecting his regiment on foot when one of McPherson's skirmishers perceived his form and figured out that he was an officer. The Yankee aimed his rifle at Adams and fired. It was a perfect shot, one that tore into his chest. Adams clasped his hands over his breast, dropped to the ground, and was dead before he could receive any medical attention. The loss of Adams, regarded as a top colonel of the division, was an ill foreboding for Cleburne and his command.[3]

The southernmost of Cleburne's three brigades would be the most active that day. Brigadier General James A. Smith led the brigade. Smith had about 1,500 men in six regiments, half of them consolidated units from two former distinct regiments. The brigade was a mix of infantry and dismounted cavalry; all were Texans except the 5th Confederate Infantry, a force formed from two consolidated Tennessee regiments. Before morning's first light, Smith reinforced the Confederate cavalry on the hill and the rise of ground from where it protruded. There he dug in the best he could, ordering his regiments to carve out some earthworks to protect them from the Army of the Tennessee, already entrenched half a mile east of them. The Confederate brigade stood at the southernmost position of Hood's infantry deployment, with its right up on Bald Hill and its left extending north of the knob.[4]

Union artillerists were determined to overturn the Confederate defense. At 7:00 A.M. Captain Henry H. Griffiths, chief of artillery for the 4th Division of the XV Corps, chose his former battery to harass Cleburne's men. Griffiths may have seen an opportunity for redemption here, for the 1st Iowa Battery had suffered from hard luck in recent weeks. Their guns had been temporarily captured at the Battle of Dallas late in May, and only were recovered due to the daring exploits of corps commander "Black Jack" Logan. On July 20, just one day earlier, the Iowans suffered two killed and five wounded artillerists when a Confederate battery opened on their right flank. "I was ordered to remain in this position, and not to fire till further orders," complained Captain William Gay, who had inherited Griffiths's battery when the latter was promoted. Those orders never came, inducing Gay to ruefully claim that "for one mortal hour the enemy poured a well directed fire into our silent battery."[5]

On the morning of July 21 Captain Gay received the necessary instructions to exact his revenge. The 1st Iowa Battery was composed of ten-pounder Parrott rifles. These cannons, though not as deadly as De Gress's twenty pounders, were considered devastatingly accurate when deployed within 2,000 yards of their intended target. Gay unlimbered his battery from high ground a mere 800 yards northeast of Bald Hill. With no opposing fire against his right flank, Gay had 3 of his guns rolled out of the Union works in an open field where he ordered his men to open upon the Confederate left protruding northward from Bald Hill.[6]

Screaming solid shot and exploding shells interrupted the work by the Texans and Tennesseans, who could no longer complete their earthen fort. Gay lauded his gunners for "causing the enemy great discomfort," but that was about as severe an understatement as one could make. "Their artillery are killing our men very fast," acknowledged Captain Samuel T. Foster of the 24th Texas, who observed eighteen members of a company of the 18th Texas take cover in a little ditch they had dug to rest and escape the metal maelstrom above them. Foster and several others near him watched in horror as an Iowa round soared into the excavation and exploded, killing or crippling all but one of the ditch dwellers. "Knocked one man in a hundred pieces," recounted Captain Foster, "one hand and arm went over the works and his cartridge box was ten feet up in a tree."[7]

The terror spread to nearly every company on Bald Hill. Solid shot and shrapnel did not discriminate. It killed Confederates out in the open; it killed those hugging the ground; it killed those in position prepared for it; and it killed those in the rear eating their breakfast. For about five minutes, the Texans endured a hell on earth. Forty men were killed and 100 wounded in less than 300 seconds. General Smith, the brigade commander, paid grudging respect to the Iowa battery, "I have never before witnessed such accurate and destructive cannonading."[8]

By killing, maiming, and terrorizing so many Texans in such a short span with cannon fire and by impeding their defense construction, the Iowa gunners had effectively softened the defense on Bald Hill for an infantry assault. "We worked steadily under that murderous fire, digging trenches and throwing up breastworks," recalled James Turner of the 6th Texas, "but before our works were more than half completed, heavy masses of infantry appeared in our front." The attacking foot soldiers hailed from Major General Frank Blair's XVII Corps. He sent Brigadier General Mortimer Leggett's division out to take Bald Hill away from Cleburne's division.[9]

General Leggett would be so indelibly linked to the hill that it would bear his name in the aftermath. Leggett was a distinctive man in McPherson's army. He was neither tall nor short, but his athletic build—particularly his broad shoulders—drew attention, as did his moon-shaped face that was distinguished by his wild, unruly hair and thick beard. Born into a Quaker family, Leggett eventually turned to Presbyterianism and took his religion to heart by shedding all visible vices. He did not drink coffee or tea and he never smoked or drank liquor. As unusual as the lack of those habits appeared for a general, there was no mistaking Leggett's combativeness. He was a first-class warrior, earning his division command

BRIGADIER GENERAL MORTIMER DORMER LEGGETT, U.S.A.
Leggett was a tough division commander in the XVII Corps. His successful assault and subsequent defense of Bald Hill was the reason that the height was renamed Leggett's Hill. The hill was essentially destroyed in the latter half of the twentieth century by interstate highway construction. *(Courtesy of the Library of Congress)*

for his aggressiveness throughout the Vicksburg campaign of May 1863 as a brigadier. Leggett was given the post of honor to lead the first brigade into the captured city of Vicksburg on the Fourth of July. One year later, Leggett was "awarded" the opportunity to take Bald Hill with his division.[10]

He was already in position before he received the order that morning because he was prepared to attack the night before. Leggett spent the night in the belt of woods between the opposing lines with his brigade essentially deployed to wake up and assault at a moment's notice. His division consisted of three uneven brigades of eleven regiments and a battalion, 4,000 infantrymen and three batteries of artillery. Directly opposite Bald Hill was Leggett's largest brigade, two Wisconsin and three Illinois regiments commanded by Brigadier General Manning F. Force (a fourth Illinois regiment under his command was in reserve and not on the field). South of them were the three Ohio regiments of Colonel Robert K. Scott's brigade, and facing south, perpendicular to Scott's left flank, was the tiny brigade of Colonel Adam G. Malloy (consisting only of the 17th Wisconsin Infantry and Worden's Battalion).[11]

General Blair's attack orders were expected at dawn, but they had to be improvised as the division commander, Brigadier General Giles Alexander Smith, replacing the injured General Gresham, familiarized himself with his new duties. The orders arrived and were acted upon closer to 8:00 A.M. Leggett's attack was not ideally formed. One regiment, the very large 12th Wisconsin Infantry, had never "seen the elephant," although they had been in service for three years but had joined Leggett's command less than two weeks earlier. They occupied the front attack line of Force's brigade, while more experienced and battle-tested men would be supporting them in the second line. No adjustment was made to switch positions, perhaps due to the Wisconsin colonel's affecting plea to Leggett, "Now, General, if you have any fighting to do, give us a chance."[12]

The 12th would get that chance, sharing the frontline with the 16th Wisconsin on its left while three Illinois regiments formed behind them. The back-line units had been chewed up during the Vicksburg campaign, so much so that two of the regiments had requested to consolidate into one unit, the same structure of necessity adopted within many Southern brigades. The union request had been denied just a few days before the battle, assuring that the two relatively untested Wisconsin regiments well outnumbered the total of the three Illinois regiments behind them.[13]

Leggett had what one contemporary called a "great propulsive power over his men." Never was it more necessary to display that magical power than then. The attackers heard the bellowed orders, "Trail arms! Forward, march!" They paced westward through the protective woods and entered a clearing. Before a destructive fire could be thrown in their faces, the bluecoats disappeared from view. Force's men reached a creek with steep walls and lined with tall grass on both banks. Veering to the left (southwest) as they splashed through the brook, the Wisconsin men reappeared on the opposite bank and attracted fire—but not just from Confederate infantry. Two batteries from Arkansas and Mississippi unlimbered on the ridge north of Bald Hill during the eight o'clock hour, just in time to place 8 twelve-pound smoothbores in position to fire exploding shells and spew canister at the lines of approaching bluecoats. "My shot struck the enemy in the flank, enfilading his whole line," wrote Captain Thomas J. Key of the Arkansas battery.[14]

Scores of Yankees were mowed down in the open, but suddenly most of the frontline attackers disappeared again when they thankfully received orders to take cover in the tall grass once they completed the climb up the west bank. "It was indeed refreshing and comforting to 'lie down' at such a time," admitted one of the Badgers, "—especially so when we heard the little leaden messengers of death whizzing over us on their way to the rear." The next order barked by General Force, however, ended their respite, "Fix Bayonets!"[15] By attaching those small steel spears to their rifles, the soldiers were preparing for the old style of warfare, the way the patriots of the Revolution fought when they got close enough to the British.

The unmistakable sound of metal sliding against metal emanated across the quarter-mile lines as the prone infantryman affixed their bayonets to the muzzles of their guns. The anticipated order to charge sent them forward again. As Confederate gunners loaded and fired and infantry and cavalry blazed away, the three blue lines (skirmishers, Wisconsin, and Illinois) rushed one-quarter mile up the slope of the creek valley and up the eastern side of Bald Hill. Three lines quickly became two as the skirmishers in front were absorbed into the Wisconsin line. "Our men fell in bunches," claimed one in the frontline. Bunches soon became dozens; dozens grew to scores. Still, Force's brigade pressed on, their general directly behind the first line and his adjutant behind the second—the only two on horseback. "The Rebs kept firing volley after volley at us, and our boys kept dropping all the way up the hill," recalled a member of the 16th Wisconsin.[16]

Enough of them stayed afoot to overwhelm the first line of Southerners on the crest of the hill. The assault was too much for the Confederate cavalry assigned to protect Cleburne's southern flank, consisting of part of three brigades of Wheeler's horse soldiers. Alabama cavalry regiments under the command of Brigadier General William W. Allen, Georgians commanded by Brigadier General Alfred Iverson, and a mixed brigade of Alabama and Mississippi cavalry under the direction of Brigadier General Samuel W. Ferguson had fanned out along the defended ridge line. Dismounted to fight like infantry, those cavalry were not experienced as skirmishers. The sight of the onrushing blue wave with their silvery bayonets held high and gleaming in the morning sun was awesome and terrifying at the same time. The Confederate cavalry fired—and then they fled. Ferguson's brigade was the first to buckle under the pressure, exposing the right flank of the other two brigades and the infantry behind it. Magnifying a small panic, one regimental commander warned the Texans to follow them rearward or "you will all be captured." In less than five minutes the equivalent of a cavalry division—2,000 horse soldiers—had peeled away leaving Cleburne's infantry alone to face the onslaught.[17]

The sight of the rout spurred on the Union attackers, but most of Brigadier General James A. Smith's Texans behind the fleeing cavalrymen remained, as did the two artillery batteries supporting them. What they viewed satisfied even the most hard-bitten veterans about their romanticized visions of combat. "Line after line of the enemy came into sight," remembered William J. Oliphant of the 6th Texas, "and as the blue columns advanced toward us in perfect formation, with bright flags flying and bayonets flashing in the sunshine they presented what, under different circumstances might have been a beautiful spectacle." The Texans and their artillery support marred the beauty of that spectacle. Together they pummeled the assaulting Union infantry. The Texans on the right initially fell back amid the confusion created by the panicked cavalry. They rallied and realigned to face southward, perpendicular to the main line to cover the southern portion of the hill vacated by the fleeing cavalry.[18]

As the Texans faced the void, the Yankees filled it. The 16th Wisconsin Infantry, the southernmost attacking regiment, chased after the fleeing Alabamans and Georgians and Texans who had abandoned the southern crest of Bald Hill. Corporal James G. Wray of the 16th Wisconsin vividly recalled what he saw atop that hill:

> As we went up in the works I saw most of the Rebs get up out of the ditch and run away. Their works were a ditch about three feet wide and the same depth, with the dirt thrown up in front about two feet high so that a man could stand upon the ditch and see over the front. A few laid down in the ditch and let us capture them. [Henry] L. Phillips of our company must have been looking at the Rebs who were running away, for when he jumped over the works he landed on top of a Reb, and from the scramble they made I think it was quite a shock to both of them.[19]

The impetus of the Union charge carried them to the crest of the hill. "[W]e found ourselves on a level field, with nothing larger than a cornstalk for protection," asserted a Wisconsin soldier, "but onward we went through the most murderous fire that any men were ever in, cutting our men down by the dozens; but we carried the works, jumping right in among them, and charging some fifty rods after them." The Badgers descended the hill on its western side and soon struck a second line of works that pinned them down in front as Smith's Texans blazed into their flank and rear.[20]

General Force quickly recalled the Wisconsin men back to the hill where his brigade lines had united as they attempted to force the Confederates to abandon the high ground entirely. The grapple that ensued was so intense as to defy the type of distance fighting the opposing lines had grown accustomed to, particularly over the past two years. According to a witness, "Bayonets and musket butts, sabers and revolvers, even fists and feet were used in that dreadful struggle." North and South fought hand to hand on the hilltop. At one point a Wisconsin soldier cursed at a wounded Texan at his feet. The dispute ended when—according to Captain Foster of the 24th Texas—Private Joel Harrison of his company "ran up to [the] Yank . . . put the muzzle of his gun to his back and blew him up."[21]

The slugfest produced an appalling number of dead and wounded men without an early and appreciable result. The casualty tallies over a very short time reflected the grisly nature of the contest waged on and near that hill. The 16th Wisconsin suffered over 130 casualties in fifteen minutes—nearly a quarter of the regiment that initiated the charge. The 12th Wisconsin on their flank fared worse with the loss of 150 officers and men. The Illinois men in the second line suffered nearly 50 casualties in those first fifteen minutes. After losing 140 members of his brigade to Union artillery before the infantry charge, General Smith counted an additional 45 men who were placed hors de combat.[22]

The action waged back and forth for possession of the high ground, but Force's brigade had gained enough of a toehold to attempt to secure the position against Rebel counterassaults. As the two Southern batteries rolled westward to a safer position, a Union battery began its ascent to the unfinished earthworks. That additional show of strength failed to dissuade Cleburne's men from giving up the field altogether. Cleburne had committed Smith's brigade in the contest, but regiments from his other two brigades reinforced the Texans as they attempted isolated rallies to reclaim their lost ground. The consolidated 24th/25th Texas lost its commander, Lieutenant Colonel William N. Neylund, with a thigh wound during their second charge; however, they recovered and redoubled their efforts with Major William Taylor taking over. They temporarily gained 200 yards of breastworks on the hill—originally held by Wheeler's cavalry—but were forced to abandon it again before significant reinforcements from the rest of Cleburne's division arrived.[23]

To prevent friendly-fire catastrophes during the fight for Bald Hill, Captain Gay's Iowa Battery had not fired during the charge of Force's brigade. No longer threatened by those deadly rounds, the Confederates opposite the northern portion of Bald Hill brazenly assaulted Force's right flank, supported by a large body of Southerners firing from the shelter of trees north and west of the knoll. The 20th Illinois became the unlucky recipient of that cross fire. To minimize their losses the Illinoisans flattened themselves on their stomachs to escape a certain death. While prone they took cover behind the ready-made earthen bank created by Cleburne's men and attempted to entrench on the eastern side of it.[24]

General Blair would have to win it with more infantry. South of General Force, a couple of Ohio regiments from Leggett's 2nd Brigade encountered no opposition and would survive the day with only 2 casualties (the remaining regiment from Leggett's 2nd Brigade and his regiment and battalion in the 3rd Brigade stayed in reserve). To this point General Blair had held his 4th Division from the fight, the force that lost its leader the evening before when General Gresham went down with his incapacitating wound. To keep control of Bald Hill he needed to commit them and so attack orders were sent to its brand new commander.[25]

At 8:00 A.M. on July 21 Brigadier General Giles A. Smith had been in charge of Gresham's division for a grand total of six hours. General Smith was disadvantaged by not only commanding a division not containing his old brigade, but also one in an entirely different corps from the XV Corps where he had commanded since 1862. He stepped into his new role that morning in less-than-perfect health. Coughing up blood during a winter-long convalescence, Smith apparently believed the hemorrhaging from his lungs was due to a bullet wound in his chest (received at Chattanooga). He was unaware that he had begun the slow decline to death from tuberculosis.[26]

Notwithstanding the newness of his command and his failing health, Giles Smith was up to the task. Back in 1863, assistant secretary of war Charles A. Dana performed an extensive evaluation of the Army of the

Tennessee and its commanders for Secretary Stanton. Dana was impressed with Giles Smith (a colonel at that time), so much so as to inform his boss, "There are plenty of men with general's commissions who, in all military respects, are not fit to tie his shoes." The accolade was impressive and Smith's performance on the field of battle after it was made merely strengthened it.[27]

Smith had been shocked to learn how quickly General Force had captured Bald Hill but not surprised at all to receive the orders to support him. He first relieved Colonel William Hall who had commanded the division in the interim between Gresham and Smith. The division consisted of two brigades (a third brigade had been detached to guard a railroad). North of Force's attackers, General Smith deployed his new division with the Iowa brigade, presumably back under the command of Colonel William Hall, on the right flank of Force and Colonel Benjamin Franklin Potts's brigade of Ohio, Illinois, Iowa, and Indiana men on the right of the Iowans.

Oddly, after Giles Smith replaced him at the division helm, Colonel Hall did not resume command of his Iowa brigade from where he originated, leaving those duties to Colonel John Shane of the 13th Iowa. The Iowans had already advanced a short distance to support Force's attack when General Giles Smith changed their mission to take the enemy works northwest of Bald Hill. Shane organized his attack with two regiments in front and the remaining two supporting them. The charge started shortly after 8:00 A.M. with the 15th Iowa on the left and the 13th Iowa on the right. They trudged over a slough and ascended a ridge through the immense cornfield, stalks 3 feet high. Each step by Shane's men appeared to be contested by Confederate infantry, but the terrain protected the Iowans. As one of them explained, "We were sheltered by a hill in our front, or we would have been cut to pieces."[28]

The real challenge faced the Iowans once they reached the spine of that ridge. Thankfully, their left flank was held by Force's brigade with their tenuous claim on the frowning hill, but the Iowans received the same ugly greeting that had met the north flank of Force's brigade. One of the Texans opposing them recalled, "As the enemy came nearer, our boys looked into each others [sic] eyes for a moment and there was a determination written upon every face to die rather than yield an inch. Suddenly the command 'fire' was given and a sheet of flame ran along our line." Confederate infantry and artillery assailed them in front and flank. The searing lead and iron forced them on their stomachs to shoot from a prone position. "I never heard such a rain of bullets as passed over us and among us!" declared a soldier in the 15th Iowa. His regiment attached itself to the left flank of Force's brigade as it extended up the northern slope of Bald Hill. Although that position provided succor to the 20th Illinois on the hill and allowed General Force to shift his right to fire obliquely at Cleburne's men in the woods, the Iowa brigade could not complete their mission. Stuck on the spine of the ridge, the brigade found it impossible to attempt the final 100 yards to dislodge the Southerners.[29]

Colonel Potts's brigade had advanced north of the Iowans and without protection on their right flank, they buckled and retreated. That exposed the Hawkeyes to a withering fire against their right flank. Their position was deemed untenable. By 8:45 A.M. Colonel Shane received permission to pull his brigade back 500 yards to their earthworks where he returned the regiments back to the command of Colonel Hall. Shane's half-hour brigade attack was costly; he calculated that 1 out of every 4 men in three of his regiments were killed or wounded in that bloody thirty minutes (only the 11th Iowa escaped that destruction). In particular, Jacob Easterly of the 13th Iowa proved to be a lead magnet. He had been wounded in four engagements prior to July 21, including a slight wound the day before, but on Thursday just north of Bald Hill, Private Easterly was struck seven times. He survived the ordeal but his fighting days were over.[30]

Although on its face it appeared that nothing was gained, Giles Smith saw the glass half full. "Although the enemy's works in my front were not carried, the main object of the assault, viz, enabling General Leggett to hold his position . . . was accomplished," Smith reported. His point had merit, for within that half hour, considerable firepower buttressed the blue wall on the crest of Bald Hill when a Union battery rolled up onto the crest— Battery H, 1st Michigan Light Artillery, commanded by Captain Marcus D. Elliott. That was the "Black Horse Battery," identified by the jet-black horses that pulled the black steel guns. Elliott had 4 of his 6 rifled Rodmans with him. They unlimbered and opened fire on Cleburne's men, which seemed to trigger the Iowa battery several hundred yards north of them to resume the work it initiated earlier that morning. The character of the fight was permanently altered by the deployment of the Union cannons. "We could do nothing during the remainder of the day but to

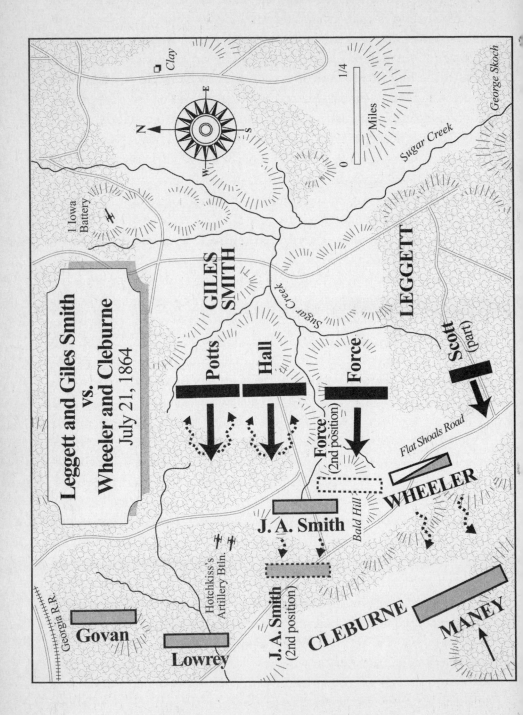

Leggett and Giles Smith
vs.
Wheeler and Cleburne
July 21, 1864

GILES SMITH

LEGGETT

Potts

Hall

Force

Scott
(part)

Force
(2nd position)

J. A. Smith

WHEELER

Bald Hill

Flat Shoals Road

Hotchkiss's
Artillery Btln.

J. A. Smith
(2nd position)

CLEBURNE

MANEY

Govan

Lowrey

Georgia R.R.

1 Iowa
Battery

Clay

Sugar Creek

Sugar Creek

Miles

1/4

0

George Skoch

lie and take that terrible fire, and to fire back whenever any thing to shoot at came within range," complained William Oliphant of the 6th Texas.[31]

By 11:00 A.M. most of the killing was done for the day—but not all. The action surrounding Bald Hill produced over 1,000 casualties on July 21. In the first three hours of that incessant action, General Blair had sacrificed 700 soldiers to seize and hold the hill while General Cleburne lost close to 300 men defending against the first assault and then trying to win back the height (most of those losses came from the Texas brigade). Captured Confederates were rounded up and herded over to General Blair's headquarters to be reprimanded by the Union corps commander. "They had a large flag over his tent," recalled a Georgian captured from Wheeler's cavalry. "He made us a speech and told us what bad boys we were and that we ought to honor the flag, but I felt more like cutting his throat than listening to his speech."[32]

Cleburne refrained from attempting any more fruitless assaults to reclaim the high ground. The cannons on Bald Hill were much too foreboding for such an endeavor. Instead, both sides settled in to engage in combat by firing at distances no closer than 150 yards. One of the Iowans noted that "Heavy cannonading was kept up all day and the skirmishing was incessant." On Bald Hill, the Wisconsin and Illinois men could only concur. "I don't know how many guns they had," remembered a Badger, "but the shells were screaming in the air all the while." A Confederate counterpart complained about the unnerving and unyielding barrage of infantry and artillery. "The carnage during the day was awful," he continued, "our loss was very heavy and the ground was slippery with blood."[33]

After being knocked off that hill, General Cleburne appeared concerned that General McPherson might attempt to advance his entire army into Atlanta that very day. He realized that his 4,300 men and Wheeler's cavalry would not be able to stop McPherson's advance without more manpower. Sending a request in the morning to General Hood for aid, the response was satisfying. Another division of troops from Hardee's corps— the one commanded by Brigadier General George Maney—was ordered eastward with his all-Tennessee command to extend southward from Wheeler's right flank. They began to file into position in the first two hours of the afternoon. Cleburne was also promised additional infantrymen to buttress Wheeler's skittish horse soldiers. Hood intended to create a 10,000-man defense to assure that Atlanta was safe from that eastern threat.[34]

On Bald Hill, the Union defenders did not escape the horrors of bullets, shot, and shell; however, relatively few fell in the afternoon and evening hours compared to the casualties incurred during the morning assault. Private Edwin M. Truell of the 12th Wisconsin hobbled on Bald Hill with a Minié ball in his foot, a wound received in the morning charge through the cornfield. Somehow Truell kept up with his company and helped to lay claim to Bald Hill, personally capturing three Confederates in the process. While he was on the high ground, a second Rebel bullet hit Truell in the lower leg, close to the first hole. Refusing to be escorted to the rear, Truell descended the hill on his hands and knees to the creek bottom, dressed and bandaged his own wounds there, and then crawled back up the hill to join his company where he tended to wounded comrades. It was late in the evening before Truell was finally convinced to consider his own needs and was taken to a field hospital. He subsequently lost his leg to amputation, but gained the Congressional Medal of Honor for his selfless performance on July 21.[35]

Both sides suffered casualties from climate in addition to enemy metal. The hot weather withered soldiers on July 21, not discriminating between Blue and Gray although one would expect Wisconsin men in particular to be more brutalized by the stifling heat and humidity of a Georgia summer. Even those acclimated to the summer conditions of the South told their diaries how "verry warm" and "excessively warm" that day felt. Cleburne's assistant adjutant general remembered the day as "fearfully hot" and added that "it truly seemed that a modern Joshua had appeared and commanded the sun to stand still." Sunstroke wiped out men from both sides. It found ways to throw obstacles into the paths of success for the opposing field commanders. General Force, for example, was not personally affected by the heat, but his generalship was impaired when one of his aides was removed from the field by sunstroke. Those that stayed on their feet were still affected by the ill effects of temperatures that must have risen well into the 90s that day, and perhaps flirted with the 100-degree mark.[36]

Securing the highest ground between Atlanta and Decatur allowed General Blair to form a line of XVII Corps troops from the hill. He could not extend northward as that ground would be contested for the remainder of July 21, but the region south of the hill was beyond the Confederate flank. Two of Leggett's regiments encountered no resistance when they moved with Force's brigade on their left. Scouts in those advanced positions notified General Blair that Southern troops appeared to be shifting to outflank his Bald Hill defense on the left. (What they saw were the Tennesseans from General Maney's division marching in, south of Cleburne and Wheeler's men.) Blair could not allow the hill to be surrounded on three sides.

The Flat Shoals Road, also known as the Old McDonough Road (not to be confused with McDonough Road south of Atlanta), ran southeastward from Bald Hill. That road was a prominent thoroughfare for the region and served as a perfect line on which to form a defense. With Force's men atop the hill—and still engaged in a death struggle to keep it in their possession—Blair claimed that ground by shifting Giles Smith's troops south of Bald Hill during Thursday's afternoon hours. Giles Smith's division would be the new left flank of the Army of the Tennessee. Smith aligned Potts's brigade on the Flat Shoals Road with his right connecting with Leggett's left flank. South of Potts's men, the Iowa brigade under Colonel Hall continued the Union left along the bed of the road. By midafternoon 4,500 soldiers extended the Union line for half a mile down the road. They spent the rest of the daylight hours entrenching to secure their defense.[37]

Northwest of Bald Hill, General Cleburne was unaware that the Union flank continued to grow and strengthen. Nor was he interested in Blair's activities south of Bald Hill, for his division was still engaged in a death struggle with Leggett's troops on the hill. Wave after wave of counterassaults had failed, forcing Cleburne to adopt the tactic of defensive fighting from breastworks his division constructed in the woods. Union cannon fire continued to swell the casualty list in the most gruesome manner. William W. Royall of the 18th Texas Cavalry crouched behind an earthwork next to Bill Simms, also from Company K. A cannonball glanced off the breastwork in front of the two Texans and careened into Simms, decapitating him. The severed head flew into the chest of Royall and knocked him on his back as it sprayed him with gore. The horrified survivor recalled, "In the evening when we left the breastworks our clothes were sprinkled with blood and men's brains and the bottom of the breastworks were nearly half covered with blood."[38]

Obviously affected by the brutality of the day, General Cleburne assessed July 21 as "the bitterest" fighting of his life. Back at Confederate army headquarters, General Hood had devised a plan for the following day that was destined to enhance that bitterness for the sake of ultimate victory.[39]

3

∽

THE PLAN

During the sultry midafternoon hours of July 21, 1864, all indications and circumstances suggest that John Bell Hood planned to defend Atlanta to fend off attacks from General Thomas from the north, General Schofield from the northeast, and from General McPherson in the east. Two of Hood's three infantry corps, under Generals Stewart and Cheatham, were deployed to face off against Thomas and Schofield, while over half of Hardee's corps had dug in 2,500 yards east of Atlanta in a one-mile line extending southward from the Georgia Railroad. That Hood assured more support for Hardee's line in a 2:30 P.M. dispatch promising that night to "fill the vacancy between Cleburne and Maney with infantry" strengthens the argument that the commanding general was not planning to conduct a tactical offensive for the rest of July 21 or even July 22 for that matter.[1]

Dramatically, Hood changed his mind and pulled the trigger not for a simple head-on attack plan for July 22, but one unlike any seen in the Western theater of the Civil War to date. Brewing factors led to the abandonment of his defensive posture, ones that not only involved the limited strength of his own defense but also the potential vulnerability of his opponent. Hood was relieved that Wheeler and Cleburne were able to stymie the advance of McPherson's army (Hardee's assistant adjutant general proclaimed it was a result of "a combination of good luck, audacity, and hard fighting").[2] But McPherson's position added a threat from the east and potentially was a source of vulnerability to the Macon & Western

Railroad, unprotected and only 8 miles south of McPherson's left flank. The capture of that railroad would place the next rail line west of it, the Atlanta & West Point Railroad, in jeopardy for Hood. Alternatively, if Sherman gave McPherson permission to strike the main northward rail line above the East Point depot, a point merely 7 miles from the Union left flank, then the common line to those two railroads would be severed and all railroads to and from Atlanta would be owned and controlled by General Sherman. Even without a major battle, that would be "checkmate" for Hood and his army defending the Gate City.

Hood was determined to stop McPherson before his old West Point classmate could get fairly started. Hood's army was down 2,500 men from the ill-fated assault against the Army of the Cumberland on July 20. Although he failed to trap General Thomas against Peachtree Creek, or in the least force him to cross back over it, Hood had temporarily paralyzed Thomas from launching any attack against him from Atlanta's northern environs. McPherson was not likely to attack imminently after the casualties he suffered to claim Bald Hill. Hood felt like he had less than twenty-four hours to act, for even if the armies did not attack him, they could reinforce their positions with deep trenches and high earthworks, and plant several batteries to harass Atlanta.

What were his options? Attacking Thomas again, even if Hood committed all three corps, was the least attractive one. The Army of the Cumberland was the largest of the three armies in Sherman's military district. Schofield's Army of the Ohio was the smallest, but it also was the safest with his left flank covered by the Army of the Tennessee (although Hood noted a significant degree of separation between Schofield's right and Thomas's left). McPherson's army had garnered a steady two-and-a-half-year record of success, primarily when it was commanded by General Grant. Since Sherman and McPherson had taken over, the record had been spotty. Arkansas Post and Kennesaw Mountain had been setbacks for the Army of the Tennessee. Could Hood deal it another blow?

Hood set his sights southeastward, toward McPherson's left flank. Wheeler's and Cleburne's engagement against the Army of the Tennessee had defined McPherson's exact position for Hood. More specifically, he looked behind McPherson at Decatur, where he learned the vast supply wagons of the Army of the Tennessee tarried, lightly guarded. If Hood could somehow get around that flank and behind the Union army, the element of surprise would roll up that force in a panic. Because McPherson's army was smaller than Thomas's force, Hood reasoned that he could surprise it and rout it with his cavalry and one of his three infantry corps. Rolling up the Army of the Tennessee also removed it as an immediate threat to the vital rail lines south (Atlanta & West Point Railroad) and southeast (Macon & Western Railroad) of Atlanta.

Hood looked at the rout of McPherson's army as an indirect means to accomplish the objective of sending Thomas and Schofield back to and over Peachtree Creek. Rather than isolate and annihilate the Army of the Tennessee by turning both of its flanks inward, Hood determined not to assault the right of McPherson's position until the left had been so routed and rolled up as to disorganize the opposite flank as well. One Confederate corps could remain between Thomas's army and Atlanta while the other shifted eastward to intensify the rout. Here, General Hood also had troops in the form of the Georgia militia, potentially 3,000 additional troops to reinforce the attackers once the rout was on. Therefore, Hood's plan covered the contingency of protecting Atlanta from a southward thrust while simultaneously he removed the eastern threat and opened up the Georgia Railroad at the same time. The ultimate goal was to create a mass panic and roll all the armies in Sherman's district—all 100,000 men—back to Peachtree Creek and severely wound Sherman's entire campaign in the process.

The plan was audacious—reminiscent of what Hood had witnessed in the Eastern theater with the exploits of Robert E. Lee and Stonewall Jackson. General Lee, like Hood, had replaced Joseph Johnston while the latter had his back against a major objective point for the Union. Back in 1862 that objective was Richmond and Robert E. Lee had successfully erased Johnston's retrograde steps with the Army of Northern Virginia. First he stopped Union momentum at the gates of Richmond by completing the Battle of Fair Oaks/Seven Pines. Three and a half weeks later he pushed Major General George McClellan and his Army of the Potomac back down the Yorktown Peninsula in a series of near-daily clashes called the Seven Days battles. By the second day of July the threat to Richmond was removed as McClellan was licking his wounds on the banks of the James River. A few weeks later he and his army were returning to Washington while Lee was already fighting a second campaign in central Virginia.

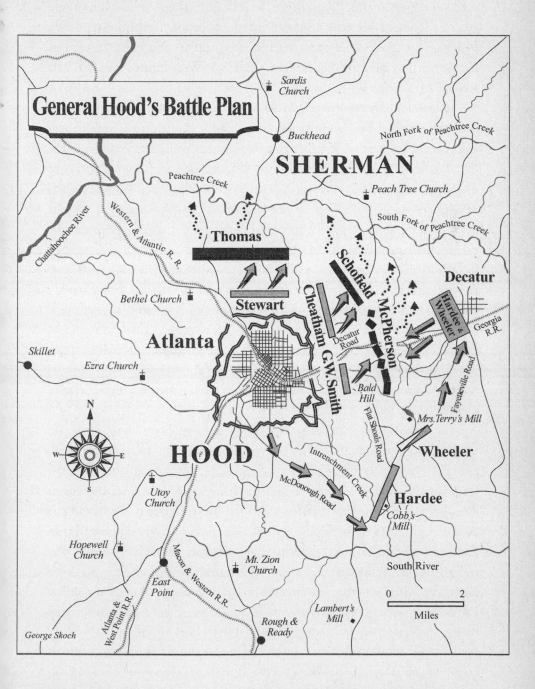

General Hood's Battle Plan

Sardis Church

Buckhead

North Fork of Peachtree Creek

SHERMAN

Peachtree Creek

Peach Tree Church

South Fork of Peachtree Creek

Chattahoochee River

Western & Atlantic R. R.

Thomas

Bethel Church

Stewart

Atlanta

Skillet

Ezra Church

Cheatham G.W. Smith

Schofield

McPherson

Decatur

Hardee & Wheeler

Georgia R.R.

Decatur Road

Bald Hill

Mrs. Terry's Mill

Fayetteville Road

Flat Shoals Road

HOOD

N

W E

S

Utoy Church

Intrenchment Creek

McDonough Road

Wheeler

Hardee

Cobb's Mill

Hopewell Church

Macon & Western R.R.

East Point

Mt. Zion Church

South River

0   2

Miles

Atlanta & West Point R.R.

George Skoch

Rough & Ready

Lambert's Mill

The lesson Hood learned from Lee in that experience was the importance of aggression and a sustained offensive. Hood's losses at Peachtree Creek and at Bald Hill on July 20–21 should not postpone or delay a major assault on July 22, based on the experiences around Richmond in the early summer of 1862. Back then General Lee sacrificed nearly 8,000 soldiers at the Battle of Gaines's Mill, yet fought the pivotal Battle of Glendale less than seventy-two hours later, which began to force McClellan permanently away from Richmond at the cost of another 3,600 Confederate casualties. The very next day, while those Federals were retreating, Lee attacked them again at Malvern Hill, losing more than 5,600 men. The entire Seven Days campaign cost Lee 20,000 soldiers—over 20 percent of his army—to achieve his goal of driving McClellan away from Richmond. General Hood had participated in that campaign as a brigade commander and nothing he bore witness to back then dissuaded him from the concept of sacrificing men in his own army two years later to drive the Yankees from the gates of Atlanta.[3]

Hood witnessed Lee accomplish that feat with subpar commanders, others who were inexperienced to lead men at that stage of the war, and even with one legendary commander—Stonewall Jackson—who was so mediocre throughout that campaign as to be fairly inconsequential to its successful outcome. Hood's Army of Tennessee consisted of regiments, brigades, divisions, and corps composed of vastly more battle-tested men and commanded by more experienced colonels and generals than those who were subordinate to Lee back in the summer of 1862. The problem facing Hood is what faced him, for at the brigade, division, and corps level, the Army of the Tennessee in the summer of 1864 was superior to the Army of the Potomac as it existed in the summer of 1862, and the Western army had a record of success in every campaign in which those units participated to support that favorable comparison. For General Hood to measure up to the legendary Lee in his first campaign as an army commander, he and his army would have to overcome and rout an army that had never lost a campaign. The loss of 3,000 Confederate soldiers over the past two days would not dissuade him from attempting that feat.

To achieve his goal, Hood wished to repeat the ingredients of a previous success. Stonewall Jackson secured his legendary status on May 2, 1863 at the Battle of Chancellorsville. On the second day of that battle he marched his entire corps clandestinely on a wilderness road that eventually

placed them on the unsuspecting right flank of the Army of the Potomac. Late that afternoon, he charged his men on that open flank and
proceeded to roll it up during the evening hours. Jackson was mortally
wounded that night, but his immortality as a Confederate icon was established in the process, for that famous flank march and subsequent
surprise assault secured Robert E. Lee's most audacious victory of the
entire war. Hood wished to supplant Lee's mark with an equally audacious plan with more salvaging results.

In his words, General Hood hoped that the assault upon McPherson's
left flank and rear "would result not only in a general battle, but in a signal
victory to our arms." During the waning afternoon hours of July 21 Hood
called in his four infantry and cavalry corps commanders, and Major General Gustavus Smith, in charge of the Georgia militia. At Hood's headquarters they all gathered and listened to his battle plan for the following
morning. No one voiced an objection to the outlines of what Hood was
expecting and all accepted their respective missions. Hood pegged Lieutenant General William J. Hardee to be his Stonewall Jackson for that flank
march. Hood personally was not fond of Hardee and still justifiably blamed
him for tactical blunders that weakened his punch at the Battle of Peachtree
Creek. For that reason alone, Hardee was a reluctant choice. Still, few corps
commanders in the war were considered more dependable than William
Joseph Hardee, a general whose very nickname was "Old Reliable."

Hardee was a forty-eight-year-old Georgian with a distinguished military career prior to the Civil War that included two brevets for gallantry
in Mexico. Hardee's reputation and acumen were so solid that an infantry-
tactics manual he authored was used as a standard text for training troops
from the North and the South. Hardee was not spectacular during the
first three years of the Civil War, but he was solid enough to be awarded
a lieutenant generalship in 1862 and had led a wing or a corps for two
years. During the previous November, after Braxton Bragg resigned for
his abysmal performance at Chattanooga, Hardee commanded the army
in the interim for the winter. President Jefferson Davis offered the command of the Army of Tennessee to Hardee, but Hardee turned down the
offer and disappointed his president, who was forced to settle on Joseph
E. Johnston, a man Davis loathed.

Hardee was friendly to General Johnston throughout the spring and
early summer campaign in Georgia, but when talk brewed in Richmond

LIEUTENANT GENERAL WILLIAM JOSEPH HARDEE, C.S.A.

Nicknamed "Old Reliable," Hardee was ordered to conduct an overnight march to gain the flank and rear of McPherson's army and attack it with his entire corps. That mission was reminiscent of Stonewall Jackson's at the Battle of Chancellorsville nearly fifteen months earlier. *(Courtesy of the Library of Congress)*

that Johnston needed to be removed, Hardee again seemed the most available and obvious replacement. Hardee had grown disillusioned with how frequently Johnston had backpedaled with the army. Here, he was in agreement with General Hood, but Hood (with the help of Braxton Bragg) conspired behind the scenes to give President Davis the impression that Hardee shared the same mindset as Johnston. Regardless, Davis had been burned once when he offered Hardee the army and he decided against offering it to him again. The command went to Hood. Hardee generally kept his feelings to himself in the first five days he served under Hood; his later writings suggest he was resentful because of Hood's ascendency over him. The ill feeling was reciprocated on July 20 when Hood firmly believed that Hardee was anything but reliable in his lackluster performance at the Battle of Peachtree Creek.[4]

Under the best circumstances, Hood would have preferred to bestow the honor of the flank march to Major General Alexander P. Stewart and his corps, but Stewart's men were the farthest northwest of all of Hood's corps from McPherson's army and would require the greatest distance (and time) to conduct the required march. Hood also justified Hardee over Stewart because he "commanded the largest corps, and [his] troops were comparatively fresh as they had taken but little part in the attack of the previous day."[5] Here Hood was wrong for Hardee's men had indeed fought at Peachtree Creek, losing about 1,000 men compared to Stewart's 1,500. Cleburne's division was also taking losses that very day near Bald Hill and brought Hardee's casualty totals over the past two days much closer to Stewart's aggregate losses. Conversely to Hood's line of thinking, two of Stewart's three divisions were actually fresher than two of Hardee's.

More puzzling perhaps was Hood's decision not to spearhead that very important movement with the most rested troops of his army—his own former corps, commanded by General Cheatham. By the late afternoon of July 21 Cheatham's corps may have been the largest of Hood's army with over 14,000 officers and men present for duty. Those men were undoubtedly fresh, for they had only been minimally engaged on July 20 and July 21. Hood dismissed any consideration for using them for the flank march by claiming, "I selected Hardee for this duty because Cheatham had, at that time, little experience as a corps commander." True as that statement was, it cannot be overlooked that Cheatham was one of the most experienced division commanders to take over a corps in the history of the Army of Tennessee. Moreover, Hood did not apply that logic to himself as a general who "had, at this time, little experience as" an army commander. Given that Hood knew those troops better than any other and had achieved some success in previous battles during the Atlanta campaign, his insistence to forgo his former command in favor of a more fatigued corps led by a commander who disappointed him the previous day was the weakest branch of his decision tree.[6]

With Hardee chosen to lead the flank assault, Hood explained to all of his chief subordinates that the other key to the success of the attack was Wheeler's cavalry. Wheeler had approximately 7,500 men under his command, but half of them probably were not available that night. Still, adding Wheeler's force magnified the size of the flank and rear assault to 17,000–18,000 foot and horse soldiers. As their movement around the flank commenced, the remaining Southern infantry was ordered to pull back and entrench in a stronger ring of works clockwise one mile north and east of Atlanta. That was to commence after dark; i.e., overnight on July 21–22. Then Hardee and Wheeler were to move out together on the flank march overnight, obtain the flank and rear of the Union army, and attack "at daylight"—about 5:30 A.M.—"or as soon thereafter as possible." Once Hardee and Wheeler succeeded in forcing back McPherson's left flank, Cheatham was told to use his corps "to take up the movement from his right and continue to force the whole from [Cheatham's] right to left down Peach Tree Creek." In other words, Cheatham was to serve as bellows to a fire started by Hardee and Wheeler, stoking the flames of the rout. General Gustavus Smith was also instructed to assist Cheatham with his militia.[7]

Those instructions revealed a unique and ambitious battle plan, one that has been misinterpreted and misunderstood for nearly 150 years. It is clear from Cheatham's role—and to a lesser extent, Smith's—that Hood was not attempting to isolate the Army of the Tennessee from the rest of Sherman's department. The destruction of McPherson's army east of Atlanta was not the goal. If it was, Hood would have instructed Cheatham to assault the Union right flank as soon as he heard Hardee's attack upon the left, or shortly thereafter, with the goal of turning the flank southward as Hardee was turning his northward. That Hood ordered Cheatham to pick up the anticipated rout by attacking from right to left (south to north) with his three divisions contradicts any notion that Hood was attempting to trap the army between Bald Hill and the Georgia Railroad to destroy it there. Because McPherson and Schofield were adjacent to each other, Hood essentially saw that as one entity, a four-corps army slightly separated from General Thomas's three-corps army. Benjamin Cheatham's and Gustavus Smith's mission to send the panic created by Hardee northward assured that Schofield would be extricated from his position with the rout of McPherson. It was Hood's hope that that would instigate Thomas's departure from his position north of Atlanta.

General Alexander P. Stewart would mop up the whole, but Hood forewarned him that his position was pivotal as he faced the Army of the Cumberland, which would necessarily make him the last engaged force against McPherson. As Hood explained, "General Stewart, posted on the left, was instructed not only to occupy and keep a strict watch upon

Thomas, in order to prevent him from giving aid to Schofield or McPherson, but to engage the enemy as soon as the movement became general; i.e., as soon as Hardee and Cheatham succeeded in driving the Federals up to Peach Tree Creek and near his [Stewart's] right." With those instructions Hood was expecting Schofield to be routed with McPherson, treating them as a single entity, and hoping that the Union catastrophe would also infect the Army of the Cumberland.[8]

It was a heady plan crafted by a commander seeking a large objective with economy of force, all the while covering as many contingencies as he could in the process. In its conception the apparent flaw existed where Hood wanted the surprise to commence. An attack by 17,000–18,000 soldiers pushing westward from Decatur would not assure that the Army of the Tennessee would be rolled up from south to north, for the assault was destined to strike the army in the rear of its center. If McPherson's men were not instantly shocked and routed by the presence of Hardee and Wheeler behind them, they could about-face and make a stand facing toward that attack. By attempting to imitate the Lee-Jackson model of Chancellorsville, Hood lost sight of the fact that Stonewall succeeded because he struck and collapsed the flank of the Army of the Potomac, not the rear, rolling it up from west to east in the process. Hood was banking more on the element of surprise than the position of his attack to accomplish the same goal.

To assure the highest chance for ultimate success, Hood made sure that each commander knew and understood their respective roles, but also the overall plan and the mission of the other "brother corps commanders" [Hood's term] at the headquarters meeting. Hood's command style was comprehensive, "I hoped each officer would know what support to expect from his neighbor, in the hour of battle." Hood repeated the orders and discussed them with each and all his commanders until their comprehension met his satisfaction.[9]

Hood had stressed an attack as close as possible to dawn to assure that the Union army would be surprised and to provide enough daylight to accomplish the broad objective "to press the Federal Army down and against the deep and muddy stream in their rear." The timing was entirely dependent on General Hardee and Wheeler to reach the flank and rear during the night hours of Thursday–Friday. Hood had mapped out the route they were required to take. From Atlanta the troops were required

to march southward on McDonough Road, turn sharply left on Fayetteville Road near South River, cross Intrenchment Creek at Cobb's Mill
and continue northeastward toward Decatur (see map on p. 51). The distance from Atlanta to Decatur straight eastward along the road or railroad between the locales is 6 miles. The distance by following that huge
"V" of roads around the Union left flank lengthened the distance
between Atlanta and Decatur to 15 miles (and up to 3 miles longer for
troops that were positioned north or east of Atlanta at the commence-
ment of that grand march).[10]

Hardee's and Wheeler's mission in the plan was to cover the 15 miles
by the break of dawn. That gave them roughly eight hours to cover the
route with a minimum of 17,000 men. At Chancellorsville in 1863,
Stonewall Jackson moved 28,000 men on a 12-mile flank march, but his
grand march and deployment took ten hours and he covered it entirely in
daylight. Hood's expectations for Hardee would have made Jackson
blush: add 3 to 6 more miles to Jackson's immortal march and launch the
attack in two fewer hours—and do it all between sunset of July 21 and
sunrise of July 22. Hood had no qualms about the task he set before
Hardee. Darkness notwithstanding, Hood maintained the route was
laid out well and that Wheeler's cavalry knew the roads enough to guide
the troops along it.

Within a few hours of the close of that meeting, Hardee's corps began
to pull in to Atlanta and initiate the march southward through the town
toward the flank. As Major General William H. T. Walker's division
passed down Peachtree Street, its commander stopped at Hood's headquarters to pay the commanding general a visit. Walker was described by
a contemporary as "a fierce and very war-like fireater" who wore his pas-
sions on his sleeves. He was a proud Georgian, telling an Atlanta newspaper reporter that he would prefer to die than to see Atlanta fall without a
desperate fight to defend it. He went on to add that he "would hang his
head in shame to see Georgia overrun by the enemy, and her men failing
in their duty."[11]

Rail thin and appearing as pale as well as frail, Walker's acerbic nature
was an offshoot of his sickly appearance. He had a good reason to appear
that way. Few participants in the campaign, North or South, had survived
as many severe bullet wounds as Walker had over a twenty-seven-year career since graduating West Point in 1837. He was—according to a witness—

"literally shot to pieces" in the Seminole War and took two more bullets in the Mexican War. Walker still carried much of the pain of those war wounds (and some of the lead), well deserving his nickname: "Shot Pouch." He hated some of his peers and superiors seemingly as much as he hated the North. He was one of the few officers in the Army of Tennessee who reserved judgment on Hood's replacement of Johnston, merely stating that time will tell if Hood has "the capacity to command armies." That time had come and despite the setback at Peachtree Creek, Walker was pleased at Hood's aggressiveness, a trait that matched his own mindset. He entered Hood's headquarters to tell him so. Hood remembered the conversation well. He recalled that Walker "wished me to know before he entered the battle that he was with me in heart and purpose and intended to abide by me in all emergencies." Walker's brief visit instilled him with vigor, an enthusiasm he neither could, nor would, attempt to suppress. His aide claimed that when Walker returned to his command from Hood's headquarters, he "was aglow with martial fire from that moment."[12]

Hood received a second set of visitors to his headquarters. Between 10:00 P.M. and midnight, General Hardee, General Cheatham, and (probably) General Wheeler paid Hood a visit for a vital mission—to alter Hood's plan. Hardee had arrived at the conclusion that the late start and the requisite distance conspired against Hood's plan to reach Decatur by dawn. The head of the column could make it there by dawn, but several hours after that would be required for the tail of the army to complete the mission and for the entire column of 17,000–18,0000 soldiers to deploy for the big attack. It was readily apparent to Hardee that Hood's plan was much too ambitious. Hardee advised Hood to shorten the march for the foot soldiers in an effort to save time while still accomplishing the objective to strike the army from behind—but from the southeast instead of directly east.

The commanding general had no choice but to change his plan based on the location and condition of the flanking troops and the late hour. Hood agreed with the adjustment but strove to maintain the element of surprise by stressing to attack as close to dawn as possible. He gave Hardee discretion to shorten the length of the flank destination and strike the flank and the rear of McPherson's army. Wheeler would continue to extend to Decatur for the purpose of a rearward surprise and to bag the Union supply wagons.[13]

Hood was hardly satisfied with making that concession, but in doing so he not only rendered the impossible plausible, he also improved the chances for the outcome he sought. By focusing on the southern flank of McPherson's army, Hardee was equally as likely to surprise it as he did by striking it directly from behind. Hitting the rear of the flank at nearly the same time that Wheeler struck the supply wagons at Decatur improved the chances of success for both directions. More than that, Hardee's new position would certainly force the Union defenders northward, the direction Hood relied upon to send Sherman's entire department to the banks of Peachtree Creek. If the rout was not immediate and McPherson chose to fight, the flank strike prevented an enfilading fire on each side of Hardee's attacking lines; that overlapping musketry and cannon fire on the Confederate flanks was more likely to occur if he had driven directly into McPherson's center from the rear. It also minimized the initial resistance that could possibly be formed against an attack that angled in behind the flank. In its conception, the adjusted plan was nearly perfect.

The generals departed headquarters and returned to their moving columns to transform the concept into reality. The first two divisions of Hardee's corps, Major General William Bate's three brigades followed by Major General William H. T. Walker's three brigades, had followed Wheeler's horse soldiers out of Atlanta close to 9:00 P.M., having already marched 3 miles from the northern environs to clear the last houses of the city in the southern sector (a distressing march due to the Union shells continuously lobbed into the city). All singing and chatter dissipated once the soldiers left Atlanta, replaced by determined if not tired men "bent forward silently to the all night march before us."[14]

As the column snaked down McDonough Road it lengthened considerably. A clear night with a waning but nearly full moon provided little succor to men marching blindly into the wilderness, forced to trust their side-by-side partners and the cadence of the tramping feet in front of them as they marched four abreast down McDonough Road. The only advantage noted by the disappearance of the sun was that the march was not conducted in uncomfortably hot weather, but a late afternoon shower the previous day still failed to tamp down the road dust that eventually found its way onto the faces, into the eyes, and between the teeth of the rearward soldiers in the column. Not until the vanguard reached Cobb's

Mill almost six hours later was most of the flanking force on the road—a gray serpent more than 8 miles long.[15]

The pace of one and a half miles per hour seemed very slow for soldiers and their officers accustomed to cover twice that distance over the same period in daylight, but it actually was admirable considering that the overnight march thus far was conducted at the same speed as the daytime one led by the immortal Stonewall Jackson at Chancellorsville. Nonetheless it was too slow to comply with Hood's mission for the entire column to be in position at daybreak. Hardee realized that by 3:00 A.M., if not sooner. His leading division under General Bate had halted at Cobb's Mill with the rest of the infantry strung out 8 miles behind him. Most of Wheeler's men were farther advanced than Hardee's corps. They could reach their Decatur destination according to the timetable of the original instructions, but the infantry was not going to strike at daylight or even three hours after daylight. The rear of the infantry column— Cleburne's exhausted division—had not been able to free itself from its fifteen-hour contest with the XVII Corps until 10:00 P.M. and had not begun to march out of Atlanta until 1:00 A.M. The rear of Cleburne's division was less than 2 miles from Atlanta and some of the artillery batteries slated to partake in the flank attack had not left Atlanta yet. Most of those men were in no condition to fight without some rest.[16]

Hardee ordered Bate to halt near the crossing of Intrenchment Creek at Cobb's Mill. The entire column lurched and completely stopped, inducing soldiers to drop along the roadside and sleep. Hardee allotted them a two-hour respite while he and his generals labored to improve the chances for success. They gathered at the house of the mill proprietor, William Cobb. There they talked to Cobb and a neighbor—a mill worker named Case Turner—and impressed them as guides for their column. Here the generals first learned of the obstacles that stood between them and the enemy army: expansive woods, a thick underbrush of briars, and a huge millpond northeast of them.[17]

Dawn had already begun to break across the Georgia landscape when Hardee commenced moving his men forward again. They remained hidden in the woods south of McPherson's left flank. As Bate resumed his division's march northeastward along the Fayetteville Road toward Decatur his men were beginning to gain the rear of the unsuspecting Army of the Tennessee, but the Confederates then could see each other and the inescapable consequence of trudging on dusty roads. "When morning came," recalled a Kentuckian, "we looked like the imaginary Adam 'of the earth earthy,' so completely were we encased in dust." The head of the column was then guided by Case Turner, who led Walker and Bate northeastward on the Fayetteville Road, while William Cobb remained with Cleburne's division near his mill.[18]

Hardee moved on for 3 miles from Cobb's Mill on an arrow-straight and very level segment of the Fayetteville Road. As the flank commander felt his way cautiously up the road, his army was constantly slowed and annoyed by lurches and abrupt stops. "Halts came," complained an artillerist in the van, "the men jamming up against each other each time (for they were sleepy) just like cars on a freight train." Hardee continued on in that fashion until he reached the house of a widow of a man named Parker, who was murdered on the streets of Decatur the previous summer. Parker's little farmhouse stood on the right of the road near a grove of peach trees. A soldier noted, "How sweetly tranquil the little home seemed in dewy, dusky dawn. No sound, no moving thing, not even a dog, all like within it and around it, wrapped in peaceful slumber." The residence marked the end of the road march of Hardee's infantry and artillery through the wilderness southeast of Atlanta.[19]

As 7:00 A.M. came and went General Hardee had clearly grown impatient with the slowness of the march. He ordered Bate to move by aligning with his back parallel to the Fayetteville Road. Here the formation commenced 2 miles southeast of Bald Hill, but only Bate's men had begun to form over the next hour due to the position of the rest of the soldiers behind (southwest) of him. As the time approached 8:00 A.M. Hardee called in his division commanders and cavalry commander, General Wheeler, for a brief meeting. All were annoyed at how slow everything was developing as the time seemed to fly by, but they were certain that they had planted themselves behind McPherson's flank.[20]

As Hardee attempted to place his corps into battle formation in the woods, he was oblivious to impeding factors that conspired to delay his attack and interfere with its intended success. Although they were concealed in the woods, the light of morning penetrated between the trees for division, brigade, regiment, and company commanders to notice that their respective commands had shrunk considerably overnight. Straggling was atrocious; in some commands numerical strength was down by nearly half. The 13 miles covered by the troops in the front over the past twelve hours was not fatiguing enough to explain how so many men were missing from the ranks, particularly since the rearward ranks had marched less than 10 miles in eight hours. "I never saw as much straggling from our Corps since we have been moving," wrote an appalled Tennessean in his diary. It appears that the combination of thick, deep woods and darkness yielded the opportunity for thousands of foot soldiers to fall out of line, sleep longer than the two-hour respite allowed, or shirk the inevitable battle by hiding behind trees or in the underbrush. Hardee's column, which should have been able to put 14,000 officers and men into battle formation, was down closer to 11,000 troops readily available. When the sun disappeared the previous night so apparently did discipline and duty.[21]

Despite the fact that the battle Hood wanted at dawn was late by four hours and counting, the flank march of Hardee and Wheeler had still gone undetected. However, each passing hour gave the Union defenders time to strengthen their hard-fought position from the previous day. Not only did the capture of Bald Hill secure a line on the Flat Shoals Road angling southeast from it, it also had rendered the defense created by Cheatham's corps indefensible. Cheatham's men had dug in on high ground bisected by the Georgia Railroad a mile north of Bald Hill. Shortly after dawn, Cheatham ordered the men back to a new line of defense a mile closer to Atlanta.

The relinquished ground, along with reports that Hood's army had headed down to the East Point station (XVII Corps pickets had inched close to Atlanta and had witnessed the southward movement shortly after midnight) misinformed General Sherman into believing that Atlanta had been abandoned. He sent orders to all three of his army commanders to pursue Hood and cut off his army before they reached the trains. Within an hour of sending the missives, Sherman rescinded the instructions when the faulty intelligence was corrected and he became convinced that Hood had merely pulled back to a stronger ring of defense north and east of Atlanta. It had not dawned on him that the troops seen moving through Atlanta might actually be heading southeastward to turn his flank.[22]

Once the ground north of Bald Hill was abandoned by Cheatham's corps, XV Corps troops moved forward to claim it within the first daylight hours of Friday, July 22. They set about "reversing" the Confederate works by digging a ditch on the east side of the earthen walls (created by Confederates who had dug out a trough on the western side), strengthening the breastwork, and throwing abatises on the Atlanta side. South of Bald Hill, XVII Corps troops, who had taken up positions there the previous afternoon, strengthened the earthworks they began creating more than twelve hours earlier.

As the morning waned, the position of the Army of the Tennessee morphed into a distinct fishhook shape. All but one brigade of General Blair's XVII Corps occupied strong works from Bald Hill southward for half a mile with 9 cannons interspersed in the southern sector. Colonel Hall's Iowa brigade formed the hook eastward across the Flat Shoals Road. North of Bald Hill, for 2 miles, stood the three divisions of Major General John A. Logan's XV Corps. His men had been reversing works and digging in all the way across the Georgia Railroad with infantry and westward-facing artillery covering the north, center, and southern sector of his corps. Brigadier General Thomas Sweeny's division of Major General Grenville Dodge's XVI Corps had extended Logan's right northward the night before, linking McPherson's army with Major General John Schofield's Army of the Ohio, but when the XV Corps moved half a mile closer to Atlanta, Sweeny's men were squeezed out of their line; most of them had stood in reserve since daylight.

Dodge's only other division on the field was dispersed. One brigade of the 4th Division, under Colonel John W. Sprague, was 3 miles behind the Union line at Decatur, where they had remained to cover the wagon park in the absence of appreciable numbers of cavalry, which Sherman had sent off on a mission deeper into Georgia. The other brigade, under the leadership of division commander Brigadier General John W. Fuller, occupied a reserve position half a mile behind (east of) the left of General Frank Blair's XVII Corps. Fuller's men, separated from the army line by a substantial body of woods, bivouacked in the rolling fields that drained into Sugar Creek east of them.[23]

The fact that a Union infantry brigade was stationed at Decatur already threw an unexpected obstacle into Hood's plan, for the adjustment that then would place only Wheeler's cavalry at Decatur increased the chance that Wheeler would have to fight for that position (compared to the original plan with Hardee and Wheeler together at Decatur that guaranteed an easy brush-back of that overmatched opponent). The adjustment still favored Hood's attackers because the left flank of the XVII corps was certain to be overwhelmed by simultaneous assaults in flank and rear. Nevertheless, Hood was about to be victimized by the same circumstances that upset the grand plans of greater and lesser generals: His opponent was about to change the appearance of his flank.

General McPherson was never comfortable with the position of his left flank. According to his assistant adjutant general, Lieutenant Colonel William E. Strong, "McPherson was confident our army would be attacked." He repeated that concern several times that morning, convinced that he was vulnerable behind his flank from an attack from the woods and would only be satisfied if he did something about it. McPherson rode a line from the rear of his XVII Corps, traversing the tiny cart paths running eastward. He neither saw nor heard any evidence of Wheeler's and Hardee's flanking movements (the Confederates were quiet enough and deep enough in the woods not to give away their intention). The silence failed to quell McPherson's uneasiness.

Riding 2 miles north to Dodge's headquarters, McPherson told his corps commander that he had a better place for Sweeny's division than the reserve spot they currently occupied near the Georgia Railroad. Dodge received the verbal order to move Sweeny's men eastward down the railroad, turn right, and march southward on a road that passed by the Clay house and across the west branch of Sugar Creek, and there occupy a position east of Fuller's men. McPherson's adjustment essentially would turn his fishhook formation into an "L" with a substantial gap at the junction of the two lines of the letter. Once Dodge's men reached their new destination, McPherson's new line would mollify him somewhat about the safety of his flank and rear.[24]

As eleven o'clock came and went, Sweeny's division began its hour-long march to its newly assigned positions. If General Sherman had the final say, as his rank suggested he would, McPherson's L would be turned into a sideways T. Sherman scribbled a message to McPherson, instructing him to abandon his new formation and leave the original line with the XV and XVII Corps in their current formations. "Instead of sending General Dodge to your left," wrote Sherman, "I wish you would put his whole corps at work destroying absolutely the railroad back to and including Decatur." That would place Fuller's lone brigade and Sweeny's two brigades, about 5,000 men, along the 3-mile length of Georgia

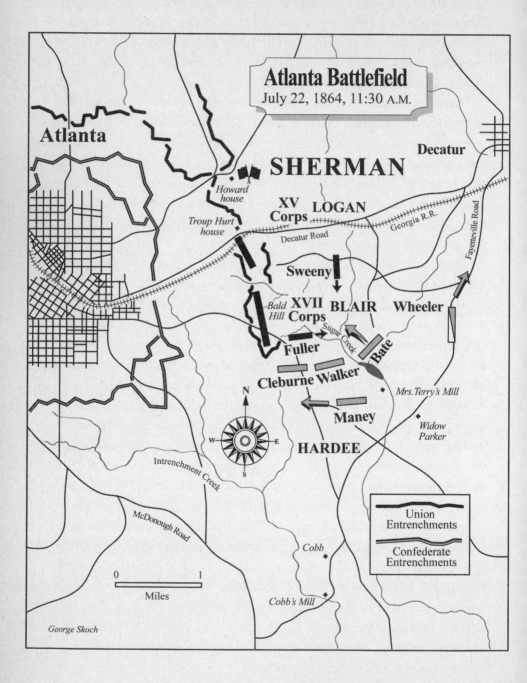

Atlanta Battlefield
July 22, 1864, 11:30 A.M.

Atlanta

Decatur

SHERMAN

XV Corps

LOGAN

Georgia R.R.

Fayetteville Road

Decatur Road

Howard house

Troup Hurt house

Sweeny

Bald Hill

XVII Corps

BLAIR

Wheeler

Fuller

Sugar Creek

Bate

Cleburne

Walker

Mrs. Terry's Mill

Maney

Widow Parker

HARDEE

N

W — E

S

Intrenchment Creek

McDonough Road

Cobb

Union Entrenchments

Confederate Entrenchments

0   1

Miles

Cobb's Mill

George Skoch

Railroad from the XV Corps to the position of Sprague's brigade at Decatur. Sherman's priority was to twist every heat-softened rail (dubbed "Sherman's Neckties") around the young trees and burn every rail tie. Sherman unknowingly assured Hardee his best opportunity to roll up the army with the rear of Blair's XVII Corps completely open for the hidden Confederate assault.[25]

That was exactly what McPherson feared even without the knowledge of 17,000 Confederates moving around that flank. McPherson did not reverse his orders to Dodge, nor did he halt them from the mission he had put them upon. Instead he allowed Sweeny's division to continue its march and he rode northward to Sherman's headquarters to argue his intention. Neither the district commander nor his subordinate army general realized that the threat upon the flank of the Army of the Tennessee was not only real, it was imminent.[26]

During the final hour before noon, General Hardee finished aligning his corps for the assault that Hood was hoping would change the momentum of the Atlanta campaign. The march had been one of the most annoying endeavors for the Southerners and their commanders, particularly during the six hours that transpired since the break of dawn. Wheeler's cavalry vedettes assured General Hardee that his advance was in the rear of McPherson's left flank. Apparently, Wheeler's patrols had spied Fuller's lone brigade just west of Sugar Creek oriented southward toward the woods. By 11:00 A.M. on the northeast Fayetteville Road Wheeler's cavalry separated from Hardee at the Widow Parker's house. Although the Confederate cavalry served as decent guides for Hardee's infantry, their separation and subsequent advance to Decatur was universally welcome, for reinforcing companies and regiments of horse soldiers had been constantly trotting down McDonough Road and the Fayetteville Road and forcing the infantry off the paths. After the cavalry had passed the foot soldiers stepped back onto a churned up line of march marred by the annoying hoofprints and refuse created by half-ton horses.[27]

Some scattered companies of cavalry remained behind to guide Hardee's advance northwestward from the roadbed to the rear of the enemy. The corps was ordered to "dress to the left" and guide upon General Cleburne's division, whose left was anchored upon the Flat Shoals Road angling directly toward the curved fish hook in Blair's formation. General Walker's division extended the corps line eastward, followed by Bate's division and Maney's men, representing the right side of Hardee's line as it extended across the Fayetteville Road. Hardee ordered his 2-mile double line forward and they stepped northwestward to battle an unsuspecting enemy 2 miles away.

The Confederates were forced to fight a battle merely to maintain cohesion as they attempted to negotiate through all the intervening oaks and thick underbrush overgrown with briar patches. Worse than that was the combination of man-made and natural disaster confronting Walker, Bate, and Maney: Mrs. Terry's Mill Pond. Hardee had been alerted to its presence back at Cobb's Mill, but he was clearly undersold about that dammed-up segment of Sugar Creek. It looked more like a small lake than a pond. It jutted across their path for nearly 500 yards at its base and ran northwest for half a mile. The center of the pond was 10 feet deep and although the muddy banks were much shallower, they were covered with debris and brushwood embedded into the muck and mire.[28]

The abominable obstacles throughout Hardee's front tried his patience. He decided upon another major adjustment. Hardee ordered Maney's division to shift from the extreme right to the left of his corps. With them would move most of a brigade of Bate's division, reducing the latter to fewer than 2,000 officers and men. Left of Bate advanced Walker's division, a portion of it stalled by a tremendous thicket of briars. Walker rode up to Hardee to get permission to bust the alignment in an effort to skirt the obstacle, but before he could complete the request, Hardee curtly interrupted. "No, Sir! This movement had been delayed too long already. Go and obey my orders." Walker rode away boiling over in a rage over how roughly he was dressed down in front of his staff and subordinates. Hardee must have recognized that and quickly tried to neutralize the aftermath when he sent a staff officer to Walker with verbal regrets for his "hasty and discourteous language," promising to meet up with Walker for a face-to-face apology once he was freed up from immediate corps duties. Walker, however, was hardly placated. A staff officer heard him mumble through clenched teeth about Hardee's behavior, "He must answer for this."[29]

Walker's rage that forenoon was hurled at his luckless guide, Case Turner, who failed to inform Walker about a 300-yard bulge in the mill pond as they traversed the western side. Not willing to hear any explanation about that surprise from Mr. Turner, Walker drew his pistol and threatened to shoot the poor guide. A staff officer intervened and the column continued. The incidents and arguments underscored the strain endured by Hardee's infantry as it finally neared the point of attack at 11:30 A.M. It would attack at much less strength than intended. At least a quarter of the infantry had straggled deep in those woods and was not with their companies as they began to align for the assault. Making matters worse was the repositioning of Maney's division from east to west. They would not be able to participate in the initial assault as they shifted to the left of Hardee's line (it was enough for them just not to get in the way of Cleburne's and Walker's men). With Maney's division temporarily out of the formation, Hardee would have no more than 9,000 ready for the opening attack out of a corps with 14,000 officers and men present for duty the previous evening.[30]

Still, 9,000 should be more than enough to swallow up an unsuspecting flank with far fewer men to protect it. Confident that his position matched with what was discussed with General Hood the previous night, Hardee wrote out the dispositions of his divisions and sent a courier galloping back to Atlanta to give that message to General Hood. The aide found Hood temporarily headquartered east of the Atlanta Hotel in the large open square near the depot of the Georgia Railroad. Hood read the dispatch from Hardee, found the position on his map, and pointed to it as he turned to Brigadier General William W. Mackall (his chief of staff) and proclaimed, "Hardee is just where I wanted him."[31]

At least that is what Hardee maintained was told to him by General Mackall. Regardless, Hardee was finally in the right spot but certainly at the wrong time. Yet chances were still so good for the Confederacy that the time might not matter after all. Noon approached as did two opposing forces from two different directions. Sweeny's men continued their march southward toward the fields east of Sugar Creek. Hardee's Corps struggled to keep its alignment as its right flank also approached the Sugar Creek valley from the southeast while its center guided along the banks of the stream. Between those moving forces was high open ground; it was an outstanding position to align infantry and artillery. The success of Hood's plan and the outcome of the Atlanta campaign depended upon which side was first to claim and hold that ground.

4

BEHIND THE LINES

The blazing Georgia sun rose steadily overhead as General McPherson and his staff dismounted at district headquarters at the Augustus Hurt house on the knoll half a mile north of the unfinished brick summer home of Hurt's brother. The white, double-frame house was General Sherman's headquarters and was rarely recognized by his army group as the Hurt home. Instead, it had taken on the name of its current resident, Thomas Howard, whose distillery stood nearby. Sherman occupied the house ostensibly to be centrally located within his three armies and indeed he was, for the Army of the Tennessee was entrenched to his right, south of the house; the Army of the Ohio surrounded him and was also in front of the house while the Army of the Cumberland extended off to his right, west of the home.

McPherson found Sherman on horseback in front of the "Howard house" shortly past 11:00 A.M. The two walked back to the home, stood on the steps, and discussed the prospects of battle that Friday. McPherson's mission was to convince Sherman to rescind his order for the XVI Corps troops to tear up the Georgia Railroad. He convinced Sherman that his pioneers could accomplish that task and that he needed Dodge's troops to protect his left flank and rear that he was convinced was going to be attacked. Sherman chose not to argue or override his subordinate. "We agreed that we ought to be unusually cautious," remembered Sherman of that meeting, recognizing that Hood was inevitably going to strike them somewhere along his lines. He permitted McPherson to use those troops to cover the flank with the agreement that they would be dispatched to tear up several miles of the railroad later in the afternoon if the attack did not take place.[1]

The two parted company after that brief meeting ended around 11:15 A.M. McPherson conducted a spirited ride from Sherman's headquarters southward down the lines of his army, briefly talking to brigade and division commanders as he conducted his personal inspection. At 11:30 A.M. McPherson returned to the right flank of the Army of the Tennessee. Coalescing around him were Generals Logan and Blair, a few of their division commanders and their respective staff personnel—close to 20 mounted soldiers. They all dismounted for lunch in a small grove of oaks just south of the railroad, several hundred yards behind the line occupied by the northernmost divisions of the XV Corps. McPherson had come to the conclusion that it was then safe to comply partially with Sherman's request. He had orders written out to General Dodge of the XVI Corps to send one of his three available brigades northeastward to tear up the Georgia Railroad halfway between Decatur and the current Union line.[2]

No officers of the XVI Corps dined at McPherson's mess. Shortly after 11:30 A.M., Major General Grenville Dodge felt confident and comfortable enough with his repositioned corps to share a meal with one of his subordinates. Of the three corps commanders of the Army of the Tennessee, Grenville Dodge was the only one who could claim a military education. He was a graduate of Norwich University in the late 1840s (a military academy in Vermont considered the V.M.I. of the North) where he endured the tough training of a military cadet while obtaining a top-notch education in civil engineering. Dodge's reputation in engineering and railroads had quite an impact on Abraham Lincoln who had met with Dodge in 1859 and early in 1863 about where to run the Transcontinental Railroad. Dodge influenced Lincoln to set the terminus at Council Bluffs—close to where he lived—and Dodge's reputation and experience were destined to place him as the chief engineer in charge of the Union Pacific Railroad.[3]

The war, however, got in the way of any significant progress on the railroad, and Dodge, who was commissioned major general one month earlier in June of 1864, was dedicated to the Union cause more than the Union Pacific. He rode to the tent of General Fuller, who commanded the 4th Division of the XVI Corps, and the two sat down for an early lunch, the canvas above shielding them from a scorching midsummer sun. They

MAJOR GENERAL GRENVILLE MELLEN DODGE, U.S.A.

Promoted one month before the Battle of Atlanta, Dodge bore the brunt of the first ninety minutes of the battle with his XVI Corps, an undersized unit with only three brigades positioned behind the main army line and an additional brigade detached at the town of Decatur. After the war, as the chief engineer of the Union Pacific Railroad, Dodge had an instrumental role in the construction of the Transcontinental Railroad. *(Courtesy of the Library of Congress)*

had barely begun their meal when their ears picked up the sound of distant skirmish fire. Both generals dropped their utensils to listen. "There must be some rebel cavalry raiding in our rear," surmised Dodge.[4]

The rattling of musketry was much closer to Dodge's troops than to Dodge himself. His men had just completed their movement from the

main line to the rear of the XVII Corps as instructed. Fuller's lone brigade had just stopped in their position when they heard the scattered
shots emanating from the woods east and south of them. Convinced the
sporadic gunfire was intended for game animals, an Ohioan remarked
that someone would have fresh meat for dinner. James Thompson of the
39th Ohio knew better. "Yes," he responded to his naïve friend, "you will
find it is two-legged meat in a few minutes."[5]

Members of Brigadier General Elliott W. Rice's brigade (one of two
brigades in General Thomas Sweeny's division) had just completed their
2-mile march from the right flank of the XV Corps line. They halted in
the byroad in the brush, waiting for orders to tell them where they were
to be placed, when enemy bullets whistled across the road. Without any
protection against that unexpected enfilade fire, those that had knap-
sacks and blankets dropped them in the roadbed and then crouched behind that makeshift breastwork. No casualties were recorded here, but an
Iowan worried that the bullets "began to come thick and fast."[6]

The regiments of Rice's brigade were hustled into an empty field, open
ground bordered on the west and south by a wide belt of timber. The
dominant features of the field were a ridge and a stream. The ridge dropped
westward and southward to the treeline of the woods while Sugar Creek
coursed southward in an impressive valley. The Iowans and Indianans of
Rice's brigade negotiated across the creek and aligned on the far side, facing the woods 800 yards east of them.[7]

Confederate soldiers crowded those woods. General Bate's division
conquered the dense undergrowth and the undulating landscape those
woods carpeted. He had maneuvered around and through Mrs. Terry's
millpond, an obstacle that had cost the command an additional hour to
clear. Ordered to shift to the Confederate right "resisting every impedi-
ment and, if possible, overrun the enemy," Bate complained of no time to
reconnoiter and a dangerously short field of vision. "I was ignorant of
what was in my front but believed the enemy was without defenses," he
explained, deciding to move as rapidly as possible to strike the Federals
before they had time to dig in. Near the western edge of the woods, Bate's
skirmishers announced their presence with small arms fire wreaking
havoc on Dodge's unprepared men.[8]

Bate did not expect to encounter any infantry here; that was the
Union rear, but Dodge's corps had interposed between the Confederate

attackers and the backs of the XVII Corps at the most serendipitous moment. Perhaps Bate was unaware of the unexpected prize if he was successful at brushing away the 4,000 men of the XVI Corps. Some of the Army of the Tennessee's wagon train was here. Those wagons had just begun to roll northward with the arrival of Dodge's men, but were still easily within striking distance of Bate's division.[9]

Back at Fuller's headquarters, a staff officer galloped up, dismounted, and entered the tent to inform Dodge that the Rebels were massing in force in the woods. "General Dodge forgot his dinner," noted a member of the headquarters mess, but he did not forget the time. He made sure to note that the battle had opened with his corps "at two minutes after twelve." Dodge instructed Fuller to post his regiments before mounting his horse and trotting westward to the position of his 2nd Division and its acerbic leader, Brigadier General Thomas W. Sweeny.[10]

Born in Ireland on Christmas Day back in 1820, the forty-three-year-old Sweeny was denigrated by a contemporary as "a little, ordinary man with a weak voice." Sweeny could easily be distinguished within a gaggle of officers by his armless right sleeve pinned to his coat. The telltale reminder of his Mexican War experience underscored his fearless conduct in battle, for he had also survived an arrow through his neck in an 1852 Indian fight and two more less-prominent battle wounds in the first three years of the Civil War, including a musket ball embedded in his thigh. There were at least as many close calls with enemy bullets as there were scars from them. Two years earlier at the Battle of Shiloh, a bullet grazed the side of his face and deprived him of half of his mustache. Without emotion, Sweeny's first reaction was to curse, "That's a ____ rough razor to shave a man with."[11]

Notwithstanding his unimposing appearance, General Sweeny stood out as one of the most blunt and abrasive offices in Sherman's department. An underling claimed that Sweeny delivered his orders in three languages, "English, Irish-American, and profane." He tended to lapse into the last of those tongues more frequently when excited, delivering the profanity-laden orders in staccato, "making it decidedly unpleasant for the person addressed." The feistiness of "Fightin' Tom" fit into the stereotype of his Irish birth, as did his disdain for peers with British blood coursing through their veins. That did not bode well for General Fuller, born in England. Yet, as in most cases, stereotyping Sweeny in that manner was a disservice. True, he disliked Fuller, but he apparently had *no* friends in the officer corps of the Army of the Tennessee.[12]

Sweeny's past leadership experiences in Missouri, Tennessee, and Mississippi taught him to react reflexively to the desultory sounds of enemy pickets. Taking advantage of the vocal cords of his burly orderly— whose voice reminded one of "a big gray timber wolf"—Sweeny relayed orders to send out infantry skirmishers from each of his two brigades to replace the cavalry pickets that had instigated the opposing skirmish fire minutes earlier. Approximately 100 Iowa and Indiana infantrymen fanned out eastward toward the body of woods 800 yards away. No sooner did the skirmishers reach the timber than they tumbled back out, overwhelmed by a large body of Confederate infantry charging westward toward Sweeny's soldiers. Sweeny sat mounted next to his orderly between the skirmish line and the hill when Confederate lead pattered around them. Sweeny swiftly sent another aide galloping back to his division to get them under arms and he trotted back to the hill where his men would be deployed. Writing to a friend a week later, Sweeny claimed, "I examined the ground as I returned, though fired on constantly by the skirmishers, and knew where to put every gun and regiment."[13]

The noon-hour sounds of skirmish fire rippled northward to General McPherson's lunch spot in the grove of oaks behind the XV Corps line. The generals had just completed their meal and were relaxing with lit cigars when the distinct rifle fire could be detected from the south. McPherson had just sent an orderly off in the direction where the XVI Corps stood to inform Dodge that he should send General Fuller's four regiments half way to Decatur to tear up the railroad. As soon as the courier rode southward out of sight of them, an incoming shell from that direction crashed through the tops of the oaks above the generals, sending leaves and tree limbs in an all-too-familiar shower near them. Undaunted by the close call, General Logan turned to McPherson and quipped, "General, they seem to be popping that corn for us." Sensing the sounds of Dodge's return fire, McPherson, Logan, and Blair called for their horses. As McPherson mounted up, he already knew that the repositioning of Fuller would have to wait. The Battle of Atlanta had begun.[14]

The Confederate attackers hailed from Bate's division, mostly from two of his brigades. One of those brigades was commanded by Brigadier General Joseph H. Lewis. That was the "Orphan Brigade," five Kentucky regiments originally led by General John C. Breckinridge, the former vice president and a presidential candidate in 1860. Named for their inability to return home to the border state of Kentucky—else risk capture by Unionists—many members of the Orphan Brigade never made the attempt to visit their homes for the duration of the war. General Lewis had led the Kentuckians throughout the spring and summer in Georgia, bloody seasons for the Orphans who lost heavily at Resaca and particularly at the battle of Dallas, Georgia, on May 28 where more than 50 percent of the brigade was killed or wounded in an ill-fated charge against a heavily entrenched opponent. Lewis was left with fewer than 700 men in the entire brigade at the point of attack against Sweeny's division on July 22.[15]

Close to the same paltry numbers existed in Brigadier General Jesse J. Finley's Florida Brigade, the other force in Bate's division joining in the noontime assault. The third brigade of Bate's division—Brigadier General Thomas B. Smith's mixed brigade of Tennesseans and Georgians—was a nonfactor that day (most of them likely stood in the reserve line and never were engaged on July 22). Finley's Floridians, though, made their presence known, for their left flank had the most unfortunate luck to beeline toward the only impenetrable position in the thin line of Sweeny's division—the 6 guns of Lieutenant Seth M. Laird's 14th Ohio Light Artillery.[16]

Laird's position was fortuitous for the Union. Less than half an hour earlier, Lieutenant Laird had been ordered on the knoll in the field by General Fuller, whose division he supported. When Laird asked Fuller if there would be time to unhitch and water his horses in Sugar Creek, Fuller assured him, "Oh yes. We may stay here half the afternoon." Fuller was half right. Indeed they would be staying the afternoon, but if the horses had time to be led down to the brook for a drink, they would not be rejoining the cannons before the rebel assault against their position.[17]

The Floridians jumped out of the woods and joined the assault of the Kentuckians, likely far enough off the flank for the Orphan Brigade not to even notice. "We opened at once with shell, firing as rapidly as possible," Laird reported, "yet on they came." One of the Florida regiments approached closer than the others, its color bearer jumping into a ravine within 50 yards of the battery. That intrepid but reckless flagman left the protection of the ravine and crawled closer and closer to the muzzles of the 3-inch-ordinance rifles—so close as to cause his flag to billow out upon every discharge of the guns.[18] Unable to advance directly into the teeth of a seemingly impenetrable artillery position, the Florida men shifted northward to their right where the Kentuckians had already initiated their assault as the extreme right of the Confederate line. "It is supposed we have gone far enough to our right to overlap the left of the enemy & thus turn his flank," surmised Sergeant John W. Green of the 9th Kentucky Infantry. As the Orphan Brigade pickets drove back the Federal skirmishers the rest of the Confederate attackers closed up with their skirmish line, absorbing them into the line of battle. Then all pushed forward.[19]

The bull rush of the Kentuckians was so sudden and swift that the Iowa and Indiana skirmishers had no chance to return to their lines. They were saved from immediate capture by General Sweeny's orderly, whose booming voice could still be heard amidst the din of the Rebel yell. He split the skirmishers in the center by sending the Iowans northward and the Hoosiers southward. The Kentuckians immediately filled the breech as they poured out of the woods. First to emerge was the 5th Kentucky, followed immediately by the 2nd and 9th Kentucky. The only obstacle impeding their advance was a troublesome rail fence that separated the woods from the field. It was high enough to trap one Blue Grass soldier, who was left dangling on the west side by his canteen strap (the canteen was lodged across the fence). Fortunately for him, a Yankee bullet hit the strap and cut him free to join his company mates in their charge toward the Union line.[20]

The Orphan Brigade rushed out directly in front of the eastward facing XVI Corps troops of Rice's 1st Brigade. A veteran of several battles—and a victim of seven battle wounds over that span—General Rice was fighting the battle with a deep emotional injury; his brother Samuel, a general serving in the Red River campaign, died two weeks earlier from a bullet that shattered his leg. Nevertheless, Rice was awestruck at the gallant rush of the Kentuckians. "They burst forth from the woods in truly magnificent style," raved Rice, mesmerized by the Confederate battle flags "proudly flaunting in the breeze." His infantry was not in an optimum position to stop them. With only three of his four regiments in line (the 52nd Illinois was not up yet), the command had not had time to construct works. Rice admitted, "My position being in an open field, I could only rely on the bravery and endurance of my command."[21]

Although the attackers and defenders were roughly equal in number at that part of the field at noon that Friday, Sweeny's force had a decided advantage. Their two batteries made all the difference. Adding their fire-power to Laird's Ohio battery were 6 cannons of Battery H, 1st Missouri Light Artillery, as they stood on the rise occupied by Rice's brigade, wedged between the 2nd and 7th Iowa Infantry. Lieutenant Andrew T. Blodgett was in charge of those guns, all Napoleons. The smoothbore cannons, designed to throw twelve-pound rounds, proved to make the difference in the initiation of the contest. As the Kentuckians poured out of the woods the cannons belched out half a dozen shells directly at them. Fortunately for the Confederates, the rounds all struck 20 yards in front of the attackers, bounced over their heads and exploded well behind them. Manning their pieces without the protective cover of entrenchments in a large open field, the gunners did not escape injury. One sergeant and two of his underlings dropped with wounds early, reducing the number of men on that piece by nearly half. Another section commander went down with a bullet through his neck, but he refused to leave his guns. Eight men and eight horses were either killed or wounded by the Confederates, a testament to the close-range firing in the short-lived charge.[22]

General McPherson and his staff entered the open field in time to wit-ness the attack of Bate's brigades. They took position on a knoll well be-hind the artillery positions, and north of Fuller's line. "The scene at this time was grand and impressive," lauded Lieutenant Colonel William E. Strong of McPherson's staff. "It seemed to us that every mounted officer of the attacking columns was riding in front of, or on the right or left of the first line of battle." The staff officer noted that Bate's assaults had Confed-erate artillery support posted on high ground and in the woods, but it was no match for the two Union batteries wreaking havoc upon the Floridians and Kentuckians. The Confederates, continued Strong, "showed great steadiness, closed up the gaps, and preserved their alignments; but the iron and leaden hail that was fairly poured upon them was too much for flesh and blood to stand, and before reaching the centre of the open fields, the columns were broken up and thrown into great confusion."[23]

Scores of Kentuckians and Floridians were victimized by shrapnel and bullets ripping through and embedding in their bodies, but the rest kept coming. "Balls flew thicker than I ever experienced," remembered a Confederate. "It seemed I was among a swarm of bees." To General Rice, the rebel charge then was desperate with those in the rear urging the

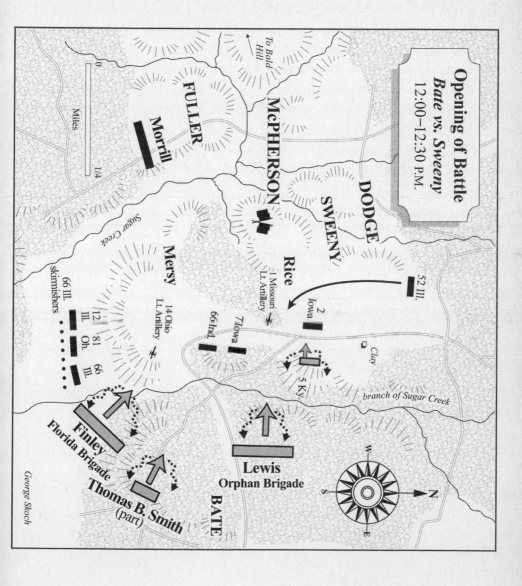

Opening of Battle
Bate vs. Sweeny
12:00–12:30 P.M.

FULLER

Morrill

McPHERSON

SWEENY

DODGE

52 Ill.

Rice

1 Missouri
Lt. Artillery

Sugar Creek

Mersy

66 Ill.
skirmishers

12
Ill.

81
Oh.

66
Ill.

14 Ohio
Lt. Artillery

2
Iowa

7 Iowa

66 Ind.

Clay

5 Ky.

branch of Sugar Creek

Finley
Florida Brigade

Thomas B. Smith
(part)

Lewis
Orphan Brigade

BATE

To Bald
Hill

0 ¼
Miles

George Skoch

frontline ranks to keep moving. Even so, the desperation was matched within his ranks. On his right, eight companies of close to 400 men from the 66th Indiana had fired so many bullets at the Confederates that they had run out. That happened at the worst possible time—right as the Floridians advanced against them. They left the line, replaced by the 7th Iowa, carrying more than 2,000 rounds of lead to fire.

According to a lieutenant in the 6th Florida Infantry, Bate's men charged "to within gunshot of the Yankees." Rice boasted that his thin line of troops "stood like a fence of iron" in that moment of desperation. He claimed that a crisis point was approaching fast—"one or the other must soon succumb." At that moment the 52nd Illinois, the lone reserve unit in Rice's brigade, entered the fray and added fresh firepower to the line. The only protection for the Union troops was a short pile of fence rails hastily stacked in front of them to serve as a rudimentary breastwork.[24]

Onward rushed the Kentuckians and Floridians to within 200 yards as Lieutenant Blodgett ordered his sergeants (each of them commanded a section of 2 guns) to load canister. The round was essentially a can filled with iron balls, used only in close range encounters. The can was obliterated once it left the barrel sending dozens of the metal balls on errant paths of destruction. Blodgett ordered them to fire the canister at point-blank range. With perfect compliance, the gunners pulled the lanyards and the cannons belched forth the lethal rounds. The canister-spewing cannons simulated hundreds of infantrymen firing shotguns at the Orphan Brigade. Moreover, for the Kentuckians that effect was magnified twofold, for the Iowans and Illinoisans wedged between the batteries loosed a synchronized volley on command. The effect was devastating. According to a Confederate, the volley was "unusually destructive." Of the Orphan Brigade, 135 men were killed or wounded by the infantry fire and artillery blasts.[25]

The Florida Brigade fared worse than the Kentuckians, for they appeared to head directly into the teeth of Laird's 14th Ohio battery. Blodgett's artillery was effective against the Kentuckians, but Laird's battery devastated the Floridians. "Our guns are burning hot," complained one of his gunners, "but still we pour the shell and [canister] in to their ranks. . . . We slaughter them as they come up and drive them back in confusion." More Florida men dropped with gaping wounds in their arms, legs, and torsos. "An effort was made to advance," explained a Confederate, "but the confusion and destruction rendered it futile." An Iowan with a frontline view marveled at the tenacity of the Rebels, "They would waver, fall back, form and come again, only to be hurled back again with greater slaughter." Lieutenant Laird seamlessly filled the void created by the sick captain of the battery. Laird coolly rode his horse to each end of his artillery line, directing his gunners to shoot to the best advantage. "We slaughter them as they come up and drive them back in confusion," declaimed an Ohio artillerist, noting, "They do not attempt it again."[26]

Realizing he could not dislodge Rice's brigade, Lewis ordered the Orphan Brigade and Finley commanded his Florida men to return to the protection of the woods. The Confederates found their quarter-mile march back to the woods a most harrowing experience. "As we turned our back upon them," recalled Sergeant John W. Green, "they poured the shot into us & caused many of our dear boys to bite the dust." The Iowans watched three color bearers of the 5th Kentucky drop in succession, with no further attempt to rescue the flag. John McKee of the 2nd Iowa told his diary, "Their colors fell repeatedly, and finally I saw one stand fall and no one picked them up and then the whole line faltered and fell back in confusion." One of McKee's regimental comrades, J. A. Cease of Company C, rushed out and retrieved the flag and brought it back to Rice's line.[27]

General Bate brought up Captain Cuthbert H. Slocomb's Washington, Louisiana, Battery of smoothbore cannons, but they came up late. After they left the road, the cannons could not be rolled between the trees of the dense woods. Artillerists became temporary axmen as they blazed a trail to the destination point, which was reached after Bate's infantry assault was thwarted. Slocomb's battery deployed behind Bate's line—"where we ought to have been the entire time," complained one of the artillerists. There they fired a few rounds without any discernable effect. Blaming General Bate for the lack of coordination between infantry and artillery, as well as their poor position, a member of the battery insisted that they "were not in a position to do any execution."[28]

General Bate decided against forcing his men to charge again, lamenting that "the condition of my command did not justify a renewal of the assault." The condition of his command was deplorable. Two of his brigades were wrecked. The total casualties were never tallied in official correspondences, but the private letters of the soldiers suggest how devastating it all was. Gervis Grainger of the 6th Kentucky insisted that "not more than" half of the regiment re-formed behind a hill; his company was down to a handful of members. Letters from Union soldiers in Rice's brigade claimed scores of killed and captured Confederates, "there being hardly a grease spot left of the Kentucky Brigade," portrayed an artillerist to his brother.[29]

The Confederates did not disagree. "The most of the division was captured," lamented a soldier in the 6th Florida Infantry. Although that was overstated, his claim that Finley's brigade was down to fewer than 400 men was not, and the reason that they had even that many could be attributed to the immense straggling that took perhaps more than 300 men in each brigade out of the fight—the equivalent of two regiments. "Our Regiment went into the fight on the 22nd with ten good large companies and they are now consolidated," he wrote four days after the battle, insisting that the ill-fated attack reduced the regiment to five very small companies. Bate lost about 500 officers and men killed, wounded, and captured—more than 40 percent of his attacking strength. With nearly sixty years of reflection, a lieutenant in one of the Kentucky regiments considered that assault as "the most ill-conceived and unsatisfactory executed plan of battle of the whole war in which I participated." Sensing the loss of valuable officers throughout the brigade, the lieutenant seethed, "The whole thing was disappointing and to me really disgusting."[30]

Rice and his men had saved the Union left. His unprotected flank position had been sniffed out by Hardee and assaulted, and it should have cost his brigade dearly—particularly given that the attack was a complete surprise. Regardless, he escaped with 3 men killed and 30 wounded in his four infantry regiments of perhaps as many as 1,500 officers and men. The low casualties can be primarily attributed to the firepower of the 12 cannons of Laird's and Blodgett's batteries. Laird tallied 650 rounds of ammunition fired for the entire day—most of them were expended within half an hour after deploying on the hill. Similar to Blodgett, Laird reported 2 men killed and 6 injured, but "2 of the 6 were wounded but slightly and continued to do duty." One of those two, Henry Everingham, continued to man his gun after his wound, but could be forgiven if he was overly jittery about it. A rebel ball skimmed the top of his head, carrying away the hair and some scalp all the way from the forehead to the crown.[31]

No further attacks would emanate from the woods west of Rice's brigade. The artillery blasts had been so effective as to neutralize the two active brigades of Bate's division. Minutes after noon—barely half an hour after they made their appearance—Bate's division was out of the fight. They had the opportunity to roll up a weak flank of the Army of the Tennessee. Sweeny's defense consisted of four infantry regiments—no more than three of them in the line at one time—in a high open field without protective entrenchments. At full strength, Bate's three brigades would have outnumbered Rice's brigade by two to one, but Bate's division was hampered by straggling and by history. Nine weeks was not enough time to erase the appalling memory of the Battle of Dallas where the Kentucky and Florida brigades were chewed up in front of Union works at the cost of more than 1,000 casualties. The third brigade of the division, Brigadier General Thomas B. Smith's command of Tennessee and Georgia regiments, found a way to escape the assault at Dallas and appears to have done so again. It appears most of them never left the woods, reducing Bate's entire attack to as few as 1,200 armed soldiers—numbers barely exceeding those of Rice's lone brigade. The anemic and uncoordinated assault by two weakened Confederate brigades was so efficiently repulsed by Blodgett's and Laird's batteries that the casualties incurred by Rice's infantry amounted to a mere 3 percent of his entire command.[32]

Adding to the problems of that Confederate division was the disintegration of the relationship between the soldiers and their commander, one that had dissolved into a mutual distaste and distrust. Worse than that was that the unit no longer had pride or confidence. A mere four days after their failure to roll up the XVI Corps, Lieutenant Hugh Black of the 6th Florida could no longer control his bitterness. "Old General Bates [sic] has not made anything by keeping me here," he railed, "for him and his Division has the name of being the poorest fighters in the Army—which they are."[33]

The hard-luck battle history of General William Bate had added another sorry chapter on that field 3 miles east of Atlanta. Not long after their failure to roll up the Union left, one of his soldiers revealed the understated cause for their failure in the campaign. "Strange to say Gen. Bate possessed neither the affection or respect of the men and undoubtedly has the falsest reputation of anyone I know," surmised Sergeant Washington Ives of the 4th Florida Infantry. "He is always applauded by men of his own staff and no one else. The Floridians and Kentuckians

MAJOR GENERAL WILLIAM BRIMAGE BATE, C.S.A.

As the division commander who opened the battle of Atlanta, Bate attacked General Sweeny's division of Dodge's XVI Corps with a Kentucky and a Florida brigade. His quick repulse initiated a series of piecemeal Confederate failed assaults against the Union left and rear. *(Courtesy of MOLLUS-Massachusetts, USAMHI, Carlisle Barracks, Pa.)*

despise him on account of the [way] in which he acted at Dallas on the 28th of May." No commander on the Atlanta battlefield was more hated by his men than William Bate by his division; whether deserved or not, the quick retreat of Bate's assaulting brigades against Rice's line was the product of that toxic relationship.[34]

No one in Dodge's corps knew of the troubles brewing in Bate's division, but they did know that they had been at the right place in the nick of time. There was no time for back-slapping congratulations. Bate's attack was indeed a quick one and a weak one, but he merely initiated a battle that would be waged for eight more hours, one marked by several more attacks—all of them deadlier and longer in duration that the noontime fight behind the Union line.

5

REPULSE

A s the weak noontime assault against the Union left ebbed back to the woods 800 yards east of the Yankee line, the Battle of Atlanta shifted 90 degrees on its axis to a north-south contest. The remaining two brigades of Dodge's XVI Corps on the Atlanta battlefield west of Decatur were not blessed with the same serendipity as Rice's brigade of Sweeny's division. Both of those brigades faced southward, forming a right angle with Rice's brigade as they extended westward across the open field. (Laird's 14th Ohio Light Battery formed the apex.) Sweeny's other brigade was commanded by Colonel August Mersy, whose command consisted of three available regiments from Illinois and Ohio, while the only brigade on the field from Fuller's division was his former brigade, one he commanded less than a week prior, but was then led by Colonel John Morrill. That brigade was slightly larger than Mersy's with four regiments from Missouri, Illinois, and Ohio. Together, those two brigades contained 3,000 officers and men present for duty.

Assaulting that southward-facing Union force was Major General William H. T. Walker's division, approximately 4,000 butternut-clad soldiers in three brigades of fourteen regiments, all but two of them from Georgia. Brigadier General Hugh W. Mercer led four Georgia regiments for the entire campaign as did Brigadier General States Rights Gist, but he led a mixed brigade of Georgians and South Carolinians. The third brigade had lost its commander (Brigadier General Clement H. Stevens) to a mortal wound at the Battle of Peachtree Creek. That left Colonel

George A. Smith of the 1st Georgia (Confederate) Infantry as the rank-ing officer, forcing him from a regiment of fewer than 200 officers and men to handle a brigade five times as numerous.[1]

If Walker's attack was intended to be in concert with Bate's assaults, the terrain killed that plan. The woods threw out the alignment of the division so that it not only would attack after Bate was repulsed, it would also advance with each brigade moving independently of the other two. Colonel George A. Smith's brigade was the only one of Walker's prepared to attack. Gist's brigade still had not arrived upon Smith's left flank and General Mercer's brigade lagged in the rear. That reduced the firepower to about 1,200 rifles toted by the Georgians in Smith's six regiments.

"We had orders to push through a swampy branch to reform under the hill and charge a battery," recalled Colonel James Cooper Nisbet of the 66th Georgia years after the fact. The swampy branch was a tributary of Sugar Creek, the moat that separated Blue from Gray in that sector of the field. The battery was Laird's Ohio battery, which had not been ori-ented in Walker's direction, but rather had been pummeling the Floridi-ans of Bate's division for the past fifteen minutes. Fortunately for the Georgians, all of the rounds belched from the barrels of Blodgett and Laird had spewed east and southeast, away from Colonel George Smith's line of attack. Smith's men, formed in two lines for battle, stretched east to west for nearly a third of a mile. The 66th Georgia marched at the western end of the line and the 1st Georgia Confederate—George Smith's own regiment—anchored the right flank closest to Laird's cannons.[2]

Even so, the attack by the Georgians would receive the complete at-tention of General Dodge, General Fuller, and General Sweeny. All were on the field inside the angle formed by the three brigades of the XVI Corps. Dodge would take no chances with his corps, personally aligning the regiments of Sweeny's division. Years afterward a captain in the 52nd Illinois noted that Dodge performed "as if he was [sic] a brigade com-mander or a mere colonel, cutting red tape all to pieces." It was Dodge who shifted regiments within Rice's brigade to the heavily pressed sec-tion on the right of the command, and it was Dodge who aligned Mersy's brigade perpendicular to Rice's, posting from east to west the 66th Illi-nois, the 81st Ohio, and then the 12th Illinois—all to the east of the southward flowing branch of Sugar Creek. General Fuller extended the line on the opposite side of the creek with three of his regiments in front and one in reserve.[3]

Dodge was worried; he had every reason to be. Notwithstanding the successful repulse of Bate's division, Dodge fretted that the Confederates east of him would renew their assault. They had progressively moved northward, threatening the northern (left) flank of Rice's brigade, anchored by the 52nd Illinois. A more ominous threat emerged on his right, beyond the western flank of Fuller's 1st Brigade under Col. John Morrill. Dodge could sense Confederates massing in the woods (likely viewing the brigade commanded by States Rights Gist) and knew well he had not enough troops to fill the yawning half-mile gap between his corps and the XVII Corps. "Where I stood just at the rear of the Sixteenth Army Corps," recalled Dodge decades later, "I could see the entire line of that corps, and could look up and see the enemy's entire front as they emerged from the woods, and I quickly saw that both of my flanks were overlapped by the enemy." Dodge sent a courier off to find General Giles A. Smith near Bald Hill and deliver his request for Smith to fill the gap between the XVI and XVII Corps by refusing his flank, i.e., bending the defensive line backward to consolidate his forces to prevent an outflanking maneuver. Until that was done, Dodge was determined to hold his ground with his three brigades and two batteries.[4]

All of that personal attention by General Dodge did not sit well with Thomas Sweeny. It was Sweeny who had met the immediate threat by the Orphan Brigade just before Dodge trotted onto the contested field. Then with Dodge interfering within his division, Sweeny stewed at the impropriety and how weak that all made him look in front of his brigade commanders and the rank and file of his regiments. With a brewing distaste for General Dodge (one that rivaled the lack of respect Bate's division held for their commander), as well as a malignant hatred of General Fuller—whose command was not tweaked as much by Dodge—Sweeny would never forgive either of them. An altercation between Sweeny and his Union nemeses was inevitable, but it would wait until the contest was over.[5]

So with Sweeny relegated to the status of an unessential commander—called a supernumerary—Dodge and Fuller handled the assault on the southward portion of the command. Their frontline of five regiments covered half a mile, interrupted by the creek and its valley. Sweeny's brigade commander, Colonel August Mersy, and Fuller's brigadier, Colonel John Morrill, would have minimal impact on the performance of their men with Dodge and Fuller involved. The brigadiers also grabbed the attention of the highest command of the Army of the Tennessee as General McPherson witnessed the fight in the rear of his army from a knoll west of Dodge's three deployed brigades.

The six Georgia regiments were then matched against a nearly equal number of Union regiments, but the bluecoats outnumbered the Southerners here by nearly 50 percent. Even though Confederate Colonel George A. Smith's men did not initially have to contend with artillery as had the Orphan Brigade and the Florida Brigade, one of the Union regiments—the 66th Illinois—carried an advantage over the Southerners. Two hundred and twenty members of the regiment used four months of a soldier's salary to purchase sixteen-shot Henry repeating rifles; perhaps 180 of them faced off against the Georgians of Smith's brigade. The best trained soldier with a single-shot rifle required half a minute to load, fire, and then reload his weapon. In the same time, the Henry-toting Illinois soldiers could empty their chambers of all the rounds they contained. By weaponry alone, one of those Illinois soldiers was worth 15 Georgians on the Atlanta battlefield.

Two companies of the 66th Illinois fanned out in front of Mersy's line. They contested every inch made by the eastern wing of George Smith's brigade from the moment it left the cover of the woods. Making matters worse for Smith was how nature impeded cohesion of his regiments even on open ground. The southern flowing branch of Sugar Creek separated his regiment from the rest of the brigade, forcing it to advance without support on its left (States Rights Gist had yet to bring up his command). That bottomland also had its share of thickets and briar bushes, shredding the clothes and skin of the Southern foot soldiers.[6]

The entire Georgia line halted in the field to fire. They did not keep up the advance as had Bate's men, but were sent back to the wood line by the combination of Union infantry fire by Mersy's and Morrill's brigades, and from artillery fire from Laird's gunners, who shifted some of their pieces from the southeast to the south to counter the new threat. It was then near 12:30 P.M., and Bate's Southerners in the eastern woods no longer pressured the Union artillery, allowing a few precious minutes for

Laird's gunners to reorient their pieces to rake the advance of Walker's division.[7]

General Dodge had determined that the next advance by the Georgians would be their last. He ordered Mersy's brigade, under Sweeny, and Morrill's brigade, under Fuller, to "fix bayonets." No longer would Yankees trade volleys with their Rebel opponents at a shouting distance; instead, they would be thrusting their weapons into the bodies of their enemy.

A strong premonition of death overtook Captain Charles Lane of Company K, 81st Ohio. He asked his commander, Lieutenant Colonel Robert Adams, if the enemy was truly in force in those woods in front of them, and Adams affirmed that they were. Lane then pulled a picture of his little boy, Charlie, from his pocket and with tears tumbling down his cheeks he held the image in front of Adams's face. Not knowing why Captain Lane, whom he deemed "one of our bravest and best officers," chose that moment to show the picture of his namesake son to him, Adams merely complimented the boy, puzzled at the captain's agitated and emotional state.[8]

Tumbling out of the woods, the five Georgia regiments east of the creek surged toward the guns and the Yankee infantry protecting them. At that point they were coming uncomfortably close. A member of Laird's battery complained that they had not the time to relish in the repulse of "the detestable grey jackets" from Bate's division because Mercer's division then "came rolling up in our front and to the right in three lines." One of Mersy's men admitted, "We saw their strength was not to be despised," while another sensed those Confederates approached with "the purpose of overpowering us by mere brute force, and their impetuous or rather blind fury brought them within a few paces of our lines." Riding to and fro behind Mersey's prone men, Dodge looked for an opportunity to counterpunch. That opportunity arose in front of the western end of Mersy's brigade where one or two Georgia regiments advanced too far in front of the others, exposing an inviting flank. Without hesitation Dodge bellowed for the 81st Ohio and 12th Illinois to rush forward and "strike the enemy."[9]

The timing of the Union counterpunch was perfect for them. The two Yankee regiments rose from their bellies to their feet and shocked the Georgians in front of them with a synchronized charge. Henry Van

Sellar, the lieutenant colonel of the 12th Illinois, matter-of-factly reported that his regiment "drove them from the valley, killing and wounding a respectable proportion of them." The 81st Ohio had equal success and a greater impact. Thomas J. Shelley of Company D stated, "Just then our troops raised a yell, rushed forward, and drove the enemy from the field in great disorder." The Confederates were wholly unprepared for the old-style bayonet charge. Colonel Smith, the Georgia brigade commander, went down with a wound after his horse was killed from underneath him. Regimental and company commanders attempted to continue pushing their men forward, but to no avail.

The Ohioans claimed to scoop up three flags during their charge, but it appears only one was taken. It belonged to the 1st Georgia (Confederate) and was brought back by a member of the 81st Ohio after he pried it from the hands of the dead Georgian, who had attempted to rally his regiment around it. It was quick, momentous, but devastating to the attackers as well as the recipients. Among the dead of the 81st Ohio was Captain Charles Lane, the father of "Charlie," whose premonition of death was fulfilled when a bullet struck him in the head during the bayonet charge.[10]

The sudden and unexpected rush of several hundred soldiers stunned the Georgians and sent them fleeing to the woods. The sight of it electrified Morrill's brigade on the other side of Sugar Creek. After they had attached their bayonets, Fuller ordered the 39th Ohio and 27th Ohio to lie down in the open field, telling them to withhold their fire until the Rebels came within 60 yards. Enjoying an unobstructed, panoramic view east of him, General Fuller witnessed the desire of his division soldiers to emulate the success of Sweeny's. "The cheer of this regiment [the 81st Ohio] and its gallant charge was so contagious," explained Fuller, "that the men of the 39th Ohio rose to their feet, fired a volley and went for the Johnnies on the double-quick." To the right of the 39th Ohio, the 27th Ohio did likewise. The failure to wait for orders to charge dismayed General Fuller, who preferred the Georgians in front of him to be well into the fields before they were preyed upon. Instead, they had barely cleared the woods, well behind their advancing comrades east of the creek, when Morrill's Buckeyes unleashed their surprise. "This movement was executed too soon to give us very many prisoners," Fuller complained.[11]

Notwithstanding the impetuous movement, the two Ohio regiments

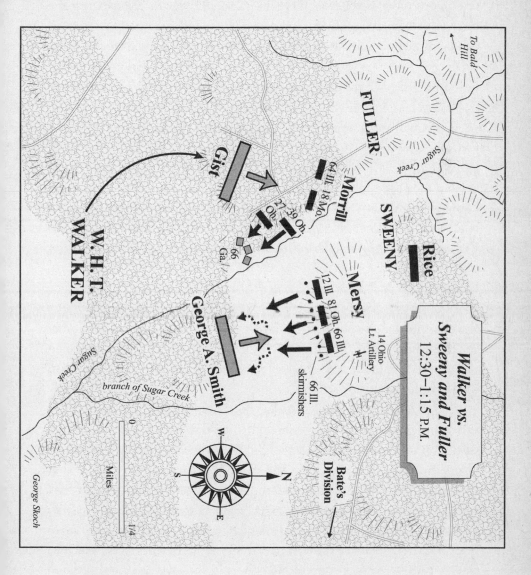

W.H.T. WALKER

Gist

FULLER

Morrill

64 Ill. 18 Mo.

27 Oh. 39 Oh.

66 Ga.

SWEENY

Rice

Mersy

12 Ill. 81 Oh. 66 Ill.

14 Ohio Lt. Artillery

George A. Smith

branch of Sugar Creek

66 Ill. skirmishers

Sugar Creek

To Bald Hill

Sugar Creek

Walker vs.
Sweeny and Fuller
12:30–1:15 P.M.

Bate's Division

0   Miles   1/4

George Skoch

were initially as successful as Sweeny's men across the creek. Colonel Nisbet and the 66th Georgia were the victims of that success. As the next ranking officer of the Georgia regiments, Colonel Nisbet inherited the brigade after Smith's injury 500 yards east of him but he probably never was informed of that for he remained isolated with his regiment on the west side of Sugar Creek. Emerging from a thicket just as the Ohioans fired and charged, Nisbet and his Georgians were stuck and could not avoid the inevitable. They were surrounded by dozens of soldiers, all shouting "You are my prisoner!" Shocked and helpless, Nisbet surrendered. Scores of Georgians accompanied their colonel as prisoners of war.[12]

The remaining Confederates of the brigade were then commanded by Colonel William J. Winn of the 25th Georgia—their third leader in thirty minutes. Winn disappeared with his men in the thicket, no longer able to fight, while the Ohioans who disrupted their formation west of Sugar Creek continued southward to chase after them. The Yankees reached a low wooden fence that fringed the briar-laden woods; both lines of attack somewhat scattered into the thicket despite the entreaties of their officers to maintain order. Colonel Mendal Churchill attempted to keep formation of his 27th Ohio as he oversaw them climbing over the fence and negotiating through the briars. "I was on the point of giving the order to move forward," he entered into his diary, "when a column of the enemy was seen emerging from the wood on our right flank with banners unfurled, preceded by a heavy line of skirmishers and bearing down on our right and rear."[13]

The elation of the conquerors disintegrated, for the Ohioans had then exposed themselves to a counterpunch. That left hook came in the form of Georgia and South Carolina infantry. Those were the four regiments commanded by a man with the most unique birth name in the war—Brigadier General States Rights Gist, who was born during South Carolina's nullification crisis of 1832. Gist's father named him as a symbol of the state's resolve, one that was enacted twenty-eight years later when South Carolina became the first of eleven Southern states to secede from the United States. General Gist was an experienced, brave, and resilient commander. The day before the battle, Gist was struck in the back by an enemy bullet, a glancing shot that hit him close to his spine, but did not lodge within him. The general shrugged it off; a surgeon dressed the wound, and he was back in the saddle almost immediately.[14]

Late to deploy, Gist's brigade would become the second of three engaged from Walker's division. His late arrival still managed to be a timely one. Catching the Ohioans exposed in advance of their line, Gist's men tore into them with ragged volleys. Although the 39th Ohio was the weaker of the two regiments (a substantial amount of it was occupied with Georgia prisoners) they were on the inside of the assaulted line. The 27th Ohio was to their right and bore the brunt of Gist's wrath.

"We were not in a situation to offer serious resistance," confessed Colonel Churchill. He refused his right flank by bending his most western companies northward in a right angle with the rest of the regiment to protect all from being devoured in the field. On came the Rebels, angling to the northeast and threatening to separate those Ohioans from the rest of the brigade up on the hill 200 yards behind them. Watching from a knoll north of the action, General Fuller despaired at seeing several Ohioans leave the ranks and he determined to do what was necessary to prevent skulking. One member of the 27th Ohio made the mistake of heading to the rear by crossing Fuller's path; the general chased him down in a foot race and struck him hard with the flat of his sword. The astonished soldier spun around to face Fuller and then tore open his coat to show his commander a bloody chest wound as evidence that he was not shirking his duty but had been sent back for treatment. Before Fuller could acknowledge his mistake, the Buckeye collapsed to the ground from the shock caused by his injury.[15]

Despite his tardiness—it was then past 1:00 P.M.—Gist was better suited to roll up Dodge's corps from west to east. That thrust was less impeded than that waged by the Orphan Brigade and Finley's Floridians from the opposite direction nearly an hour earlier. Not only were fewer regiments in Gist's way, they were separated in groups of two, not facing toward their attackers, and at that time entirely without artillery support. Blodgett's and Laird's batteries facing east and south stood well away from the Georgians and Carolinians. Gist had the opportunity to take out those menacing batteries from the rear.[16]

The 18th Missouri and 64th Illinois stood directly behind the Buckeyes, positioned near the creek on their left. Seeing Gist's Confederates fanning out on their right, Colonel Morrill ordered the 64th Illinois westward to a body of woods 300 yards from the Missourians, facing southwest directly at Gist's approaching brigade. Many of those Illinois men, like their Prairie State brethren in Mersy's brigade, carried Henry repeaters, private purchases aided by Governor Richard Yates of Illinois (the unit's nickname was the "Yates' Sharpshooters"). Unfortunately for those Yankees, the strength of their weaponry was muted by their formation. The right wing of the regiment completed its perpendicular change of direction without difficulty, but not so for the inside companies. The appearance of Confederates in the field forced the left wing to abandon its attempt to extend the regimental line southward; instead they reformed behind the right-hand companies and reduced the firepower of the regiment by 50 percent.[17]

Gist's left-hand regiments found the going tough against Illinois men who could fire sixteen rounds without reloading, but the main threat to the brigade was from Gist's right-hand regiments who were in a position to wipe the 27th Ohio from existence. General Fuller found himself in a predicament. Separated from General Dodge and Sweeny's division by Sugar Creek, Fuller recognized that his men would face the crisis alone. Fuller was amazed at what was unfolding in front of him, "the extraordinary spectacle presented itself of our men rushing across the field in one direction, while the rebels on their right were marching steadily the opposite way." While Winn's Georgians stayed out of sight deep in the woods south of the two Ohio regiments, Gist's men spread out as they approached the fields west of Fuller, threatening both his flank and his rear.[18]

Lieutenant Colonel Mendal Churchill of the 27th Ohio was shot in the abdomen, a blow that staggered him but did not knock him off his feet. Regardless, Churchill understood that a gut shot was usually a mortal one. "I fully believed," he wrote, "that the ball had gone straight through me; I thought 'abdomen, dead man' . . . [and] turned the command over to Captain [Frank] Lynch next in rank." To his overwhelming relief, as Churchill was escorted to the rear he pulled up his shirt above his pants and watched the leaden ball that had struck him drop harmlessly to his feet (it had struck a metal button that had pushed inward and penetrated the skin, but caused no injury to vital organs). Churchill hurried back to his regiment at about the time that Captain Lynch dropped with two severe wounds.[19]

As Churchill returned to his regiment, General Fuller immediately attempted to secure its right flank. He ordered out the 18th Missouri, who hustled to those western woods to extend the Union line southward and block the Confederate surge against them. Lieutenant Colonel Charles S. Sheldon aligned all of his Missouri companies at the edge of the woods and directed his men to fire three volleys. The Confederates had just reached a wooden fence bordering the woods when they were raked by the Union men from Missouri. The volleys proved too hot for the Southerners and they fell back into the woods. The Missourians were trapped. No sooner did they form in their new position than they saw the 64th Illinois buckle to their right. Within minutes Lieutenant Colonel Sheldon was temporarily out of the fight with a wound that required immediate attention.[20]

General Fuller was about to experience his entire right cave in, but he was less aware of the troubles of the 64th Illinois than he was of his former command, the 27th Ohio. He had sent orders for both Ohio regiments in the southern sector of the field to swing around and return to their original line on the hill. That required the regiments to turn their backs upon their foe, a realization that did not sit well with the Ohioans. The 39th Ohio managed to complete the maneuver, but the 27th Ohio did not. Since they were on the outside of the formation, they were forced to attempt the maneuver on the run. They also kept stopping, turning, and firing toward Gist's Georgians and Carolinians. Both factors caused a loss of their formation and a serious threat of the loss of the regiment as the Confederates closed to within 100 yards of them. The confused-looking mass of Ohioans withered under the devastating fire delivered from such a short range. Close to a third of the regiment melted away in the field—more than 100 men killed and wounded on the spot.[21]

General Fuller rushed forward to save his old regiment. He hurried down the hill to rally the men. "There was no time to explain anything," Fuller noted, "for the rebels were coming on in fine style, not more than 100 yards away." Fuller grabbed the regiment's flag and shocked the Ohioans by running toward the Confederates with it. The general was not acting out a death wish; he stopped abruptly, wheeled toward his men, stuck the flag staff into the ground. Pointing with his sword, he directed the 27th Ohio to form on the line he had just marked.

The Ohioans responded with a shout as they ran toward General Fuller to align on each side of that flag. Churchill ordered another charge and with their bayonets gleaming from the ends of their barrels, the bluecoats rushed forward. As experienced by the luckless 66th Georgia fifteen minutes earlier, Gist's men were caught off guard. With no time to reload or attach their bayonets, they refused to attempt hand-to-hand combat with a rejuvenated opponent charging toward them and quickly returned to the cover of the woods. That counterpunch freed up the harassed flank of the 18th Missouri, who could then adjust to the threat to their front and the right recently vacated by the 64th Illinois.[22]

General Gist refused to lose the momentum. Whether or not he understood how poorly defended the Union flank was, Gist saw to it that all of his soldiers were committed into the fight. He personally led his reserve companies forward. Gist was a commanding figure astride his beautiful horse, both to the Confederates rallying by him and the Federals opposing him. Gist was much too conspicuous to his enemy, watching him wave his hat and urge on his men. Nonetheless, the Union artillery had begun to train their muzzles to the southwest. The first screaming rounds striking Gist's men were devastating ones. One of them killed a member of Gist's staff, Lieutenant Joseph Clay Habersham. The exploding shell tore off both of his legs and mutilated his body. States Rights Gist was fortunate to escape the deadly artillery rounds, but it was a seemingly innocuous bullet wound in his hand that turned into his Achilles heel. The injury forced that proven–tough man from the field, and removed him from his command for six weeks.[23]

The success of Walker's division depended upon the achievement of Gist's brigade. Gist was replaced by Colonel James McCullough of the 16th South Carolina. The change of command from a confident and inspirational brigade commander to one who was brand new to that responsibility weakened the brigade's aggression against Fuller's flank. General Walker was in position to fill that void. With his faded sombrero topping off his rail-thin body, Walker was easy to recognize astride his iron gray horse. As he rode among the Carolinians and Georgians of Gist's brigade, Walker exhorted them forward. "One more charge and the day is won!" he bellowed. "Follow me!"

Follow they did. Walker led them out of the woods and into the clearing where even General Dodge could pick him out among the surging Southern soldiers. A fusillade of small arms fire thudded into the hides of the horses of the Confederate general and his staff. Walker's gray mare dropped underneath its rider. The general popped up immediately, but he could not escape a second swarm of Yankee lead. A bullet tore through his lungs and killed him while he was still on his feet. Walker's body pitched forward to the ground. "Bring off the general!" shouted his men; Carolinians responded by bearing Walker's lifeless body to the rear.[24]

Walker's death killed the momentum of his division. By 1:15 P.M., the most severe threat to Dodge's corps had been successfully and completely repulsed. Gist's brigade was essentially through for the day. Its casualty totals were never tabulated, but in all likelihood the brigade was reduced by at least 200 dead, wounded, and captured soldiers. Fuller's defense proved costly, 280 killed, wounded, or missing Union soldiers—eight times the casualties suffered by Rice's brigade an hour earlier.[25]

Brigadier General Hugh W. Mercer was immediately informed of Walker's death and took over command of his division. The new division commander was the namesake grandson of one of George Washington's generals, killed in the Battle of Princeton during the Revolutionary War. Mercer was fifty-five years old, but his physique was so broken down as to make him appear and act like a man at least ten years older. (Indeed, Mercer would survive the battle only to be relegated to lighter duties in Savannah a few days later.) As decrepit as he was, Mercer was the only officer remaining in the entire division with the rank of general but also one who could not come close to the experience, confidence, and aggressiveness of General Walker.[26]

Mercer had but one fresh brigade to commit into the fight—his own. Those Georgians had tarried in the woods while George Smith's brigade was repulsed in front of them and Gist's men were manhandled northwest of their position. The reserve position proved a dangerous one as the constant Union cannonading killed and wounded several Georgians there. Colonel Charles H. Olmstead of the 1st Georgia Infantry was victimized by a Union shell that exploded in the woods close to Mercer's brigade, spewing shrapnel everywhere. One of the iron chunks smashed against Olmstead's head and unhorsed him. Suffering from a concussion, he was out of the fight. Olmstead's injury occurred just as General Mercer ascended to division command and it was significant because he was the senior ranking colonel of the brigade. That left Colonel William Barkuloo of the 57th Georgia infantry as the next ranking officer still on two legs.[27]

General Mercer notified Colonel Barkuloo that he was the new brigade commander and ordered him to send the Georgians forward. Barkuloo's men advanced over the ground where the Georgians of Colonel George A. Smith's brigade had attempted an attack a half an hour before. That brought them out at the creek valley 500 yards in front of Mersy's brigade. Barkuloo looked across the field and up the ridge where Fuller's men on the left and Sweeny's men on the front and right, supported by Laird's battery, convinced him not to martyr his men there. A company officer agreed with Barkuloo's conclusion by stating "that it was madness to advance our little brigade." Losing 15 men to artillery fire, Barkuloo tucked his command back into the trees and eventually returned to his reserve position. The effectiveness of the Union artillery must have been the deciding factor. The two XVI Corps batteries fired 1,119 rounds of ammunition—perhaps three-quarters of those rounds were expended between noon and 1:15 P.M., an average of fifteen shots per minute among the 12 guns of those two batteries.[28]

Walker's division was out of the fight in less than an hour from the first contact with the XVI Corps. Like Bate's men who attacked before them, the assaults by Walker's men were disjointed and unsupported, allowing seven southward-facing Union infantry regiments and one battery to beat them back. The lost opportunity was not lost on the soldiers who survived the offensive. "Walker's division failed to carry the Yankee works on account of *bad generalship,*" wailed Robert G. Mitchell of the 29th Georgia. The problem had less to do with bad generalship than with too few generals in the division. With the death of Walker and the wounding of Gist, General Mercer was the only officer left in the division to hold the rank. All three brigades were led by colonels who ascended to command between 12:30 and 1:00 P.M., serving under a new division commander whose talent was as limited as his experience at that level of command.[29]

The repulse of two divisions of Hardee's corps by the Union XVI corpsmen serving under General Dodge did not end the rearward threat to the Army of the Tennessee. Two miles northeast of Bate's repulsed line stood Decatur, the sleepy Georgia town that had been aroused by the entry in and out of its borders by McPherson's army two days earlier. Since then, Decatur served as a wagon park for the supply train of the Army of the Tennessee. Approaching the town from the south were two divisions of 3,000 cavalry under the command of Major General Joseph

MAJOR GENERAL JOSEPH "FIGHTING JOE" WHEELER, C.S.A.

Wheeler commanded two cavalry divisions in the Battle of Atlanta, and his men fought for two days dismounted as infantry. One of the youngest corps commanders in the Confederate army, Wheeler later served in the U.S. Army in the Spanish-American War and for that service is only one of two Confederate generals buried in Arlington National Cemetery (the other is Brigadier General Marcus Joseph Wright). *(Courtesy of the Library of Congress)*

Wheeler. Hood's adjusted plan called for Wheeler to strike Decatur from east to west, disrupting the supply line and wreaking havoc directly behind McPherson's army. Wheeler understood that Decatur was not only the true "left" of General Sherman's entire three-army district, it was the point where the utter disruption of the district was intended to begin.

Wheeler reconnoitered Decatur at noon, just at the start of Bate's attack upon Sweeny 2 miles down the Fayetteville Road. "General Hardee supposed the place to be occupied by cavalry," reported Wheeler, "but . . . I found that a division of infantry, strongly intrenched, occupied the town." Wheeler was mistaken. He did not see a division; he instead had been observing Colonel John W. Sprague's brigade, three regiments buttressed by 6 cannons, which had replaced a cavalry guard the day before and had been charged with the responsibility of guarding nearly 1,600 wagons and the four- and six-horse teams that pulled them. Detached from Fuller's 4th Division (XVI Corps) to protect the supply train from exactly what Wheeler was planning to do to it, Sprague deployed the cannons on hills surrounding the Georgia Railroad that cut diagonally below the town and had his infantry placed across the roads leading into Decatur from the south. Colonel Sprague, an Ohioan in his midforties whose full, graying beard and piercing eyes made him look a little like the late rabid abolitionist John Brown, had spent half of the first year of the war in rebel prisons, but the incarceration failed to soften him. He remained as pugnacious as he was ambitious. Recommending his promotion, a superior characterized Sprague with three words that spelled trouble for Wheeler, "He will fight."[30]

So would Wheeler, who was obviously in a better position to do so at Decatur than he had been the previous two days at Bald Hill. Wheeler rode back to his cavalry and ordered them to dismount. Placing his men in lines of battle Wheeler sent them toward the town as they crept along each side of the Fayetteville Road. As they inched within a mile of Decatur, Sprague's men spotted them. Wheeler had artillery with him and the cannons were unlimbered in the woods and opened upon the 63rd Ohio infantry and several companies of the 25th Wisconsin Infantry advancing southward toward that flank. Within ten minutes the Union soldiers fell back across the railroad, followed by the only other regiment on the field, the 35th New Jersey. The time passed 1:00 P.M.[31]

Colonel Milton Montgomery of the 25th Wisconsin took a bullet in the arm that broke his wrist and weakened him enough to fall captive to Wheeler's Rebels. Lieutenant Colonel Jeremiah Rusk took command of the 25th and nearly suffered a worse fate in front of his Wisconsin regiment. As the companies of the 25th Wisconsin began to fall back to the courthouse square upon Sprague's orders, Rusk's horse carried him too far ahead of his men and it meandered toward Wheeler's attackers. A Confederate grabbed the bridle while another got hold of Rusk's sword. Rusk drew a revolver with his free hand and fired into the body of the man holding his horse. Relinquishing his sword to the other Southerner, Rusk wheeled around and galloped northward back toward the center of town, but his horse was shot dead beneath him and the animal collapsed and pinned Rusk's leg. Twenty Wisconsin men immediately rushed forward to save their lieutenant colonel, freeing Rusk from his dead mount and escorting him rearward.[32]

Colonel Sprague rallied his men at the town square as Union wagons had already begun to roll northward to safety toward Roswell. Wheeler scooped up more than 100 prisoners at the edge of town and attempted to dislodge Sprague's defense with a series of reckless charges. Artillery and infantry rounds stopped the cavalry in their tracks and sent them reeling back to the cover of the woods. Casualties mounted within Wheeler's ranks; some of them were absolutely gruesome. D. F. Fields of the 11th Mississippi would forever be haunted by the memory of one of his men who "had the front part of his skull shot off, but it did not break the membrane around the brain." Fields and a companion carefully carried the victim behind the lines and set him down behind a huge stump. "I had to hold his hands to keep him from tearing out his brains," remembered Fields. "It was a sickening sight."[33]

Wheeler anticipated a tougher fight for Decatur because he was facing infantry instead of enemy cavalry, which he expected to be guarding the wagons. Yet, as the battle waged for over half an hour even he must have been surprised at the viciousness of that protracted encounter. Sprague held his men firmly at Decatur's town square as Wheeler continued to mount pressure upon his front and flanks. One of Sprague's three regiments ran out of ammunition and two of his 6 cannons had to shift to meet the flank threat. Sprague gained assistance from men that were left behind by the previous occupants of Decatur, including musicians and a few hundred cavalrymen either sick or without mounts. Some of them fell in with Sprague's brigade and were armed with Spencer repeating carbines, a valuable cavalry weapon that fascinated the hard-pressed foot soldiers. They also received unexpected aid from two regiments dropping down to Decatur from Roswell who reached the battlefield in time to keep Wheeler from puncturing Sprague's defense.

They withstood long enough to safely haul down the Stars and Stripes from the Decatur courthouse. Satisfied that the wagons had a big enough head start not to be overtaken by Wheeler's attackers, Sprague withdrew northward from Decatur and set up a tough defense one mile from the scene at the junction of two roads. Wheeler's men then owned the town, along with the hospital stores, tons of equipment, and scores of Union prisoners, but only six wagons. Sprague reported 242 officers and men killed, wounded, or missing—over a quarter of his engaged force. Wheeler's losses in that encounter were never officially tallied, but considering the aggressive nature of his assault, an estimation of 300–400 casualties in his two divisions is realistic. Sprague's stubborn defense and the salvation of over 1,500 wagons did not go unnoticed. A week later Sprague earned a brigadier generalship and nearly thirty years after that he was awarded the Congressional Medal of Honor "for Distinguished gallantry at the Battle of Decatur, Ga., July 22, 1864."[34]

For the moment, at 1:30 P.M. on Friday, July 22, Wheeler had command of the region. He was in a tremendous position to form more than 2,000 available cavalrymen and coordinate an assault westward, down the line of the Georgia Railroad toward the back of the XV Corps of the Army of the Tennessee. The temptation to pursue Sprague and the wagons, however, was too much for Wheeler. He ordered his command to head northward, not westward, and in doing so, he disrupted the spirit of Hood's initial plan. Before his divisions could act upon Wheeler's wishes three of Hardee's staff officers galloped into Decatur in rapid succession and delivered Hardee's urgent plea to reinforce his attack south of Wheeler's position. Wheeler complied. "The pursuit [northward] was stopped and all my available troops moved at a gallop toward General Hardee's position."[35]

It was a unfortunate decision by General Hardee, perhaps borne out of some desperation and realization that he was unable to fulfill Hood's intention on that portion of the field. Between 1:15 and 1:30 P.M. opposing fire slackened across that portion of the battlefield. A tremendous opportunity for Hood's army had just been squelched by four brigades and four batteries from Dodge's corps. The five brigades of Bate's and Walker's division attacked haphazardly, because they were understrength from overnight straggling and in need of quality leadership at the brigade and division level to coordinate their assaults. The experience, talent, and tenacity of the Southern foot soldier were wasted in that field, neutralized by Federal defenders who were more ably led by their brigadiers and division commanders. Much of the same troubles existed for Wheeler at Decatur. The result was a stalemate in the rear of the Army of the Tennessee, which equated to a victory here for Dodge and his half-sized corps. Fourteen thousand Americans, about equally distributed between North and South, had contested for possession of the field. The cost for Dodge's men was close to 700 men killed, wounded, or captured. Wheeler's, Bate's, and Walker's losses in the first seventy minutes of that battle cannot be accurately tallied, but can be safely estimated between 1,100 and 1,400—almost twice that of the defenders. The butcher's bill for that battle reached 2,000 in less than ninety minutes—an average of 25 soldiers killed, wounded, and captured every minute since noon.[36]

It was just the beginning. The abandonment of Decatur, such an integral part of Hood's intentions, illustrated how the Battle of Atlanta had formed a life of its own. As General McPherson watched the repulse of States Rights Gist's brigade he could breathe a sigh of relief that the Confederates had failed at caving in his thin blue line behind the main body of his army, but the relief was short lived. It was superseded by a growing concern over the inviting gap between his position and Blair's XVII Corps troops half a mile west of them. His desire to fill that gap—and his insistence to put his own handprint on the plan—was destined to change the complexion of the battle.

6

❧

SACRIFICE

It was 12:45 P.M. when General McPherson first took action to fill the wooded gap between the XVI and XVII corps. From a knoll behind General Fuller's division, McPherson watched Morrill's brigade effectively counterpunch Gist's brigade and—according to General Fuller—leave the southeast corner of the contested field "well carpeted with butternut." That opened the wagon road that ran through the woods and linked the XVI Corps with the XVII Corps. McPherson sent his inspector general, Lieutenant Colonel William E. Strong, on a mission to check with General Frank Blair about the condition of his XVII Corps, and to notify Brigadier General Giles Smith to hold his vulnerable position. McPherson wished both commanders to know that he would plug the gap. Strong galloped off following a road that carried him to each of the commanders. From Giles Smith, Strong learned that the Rebels were apparently feeling for an opening between the XVI and XVII corps to exploit.[1]

Giles A. Smith had been in charge of the 4th Division of the XVII Corps for a day and a half. Smith was about to receive the greatest test of his leadership under fire. His division had dug in south of Bald Hill, with one brigade facing southward to counter an attack against the flank that Smith deemed inevitable. Smith was under no false pretenses; if he was correct on where the Rebels would assault, his division would receive the brunt of that attack. His experience also told him that the number of dead and wounded he would incur could be abominable.

At noon, right when Dodge's three brigades came under attack half a mile behind him, Giles Smith was at the southern end of his line, a position manned by Colonel William Hall's brigade, infantry consisting entirely of Iowans. Inspecting the position taken up by the four Iowa regiments, buttressed by 6 Napoleons of Battery F, 2nd U.S. Light Artillery, Smith knew the position was solid, but not strong enough; yet there was little else he could do. Giles Smith visited the regimental commander and paid special attention to the pivot of the brigade—the 16th Iowa Infantry. Smith held a brief discussion with the 16th's commander, Lieutenant Colonel Addison H. Sanders, who remembered Smith's verbal orders to "have my regiment ready to fall in at a minute's notice." The general stressed that those works must be held, for the safety of the division depended on how long the Iowans could defend their position. Sanders believed that Smith was essentially telling him that his regiment might need to be sacrificed for the survival of that sector of the line.[2]

Chain of command, for all practical purposes, was ignored. That realization did not set well with Colonel William Hall, the Iowa brigade commander, who appeared to be rendered irrelevant by his day-old superior officer. A small, irritable, and nervous man whose long, black hair and big, black eyes failed to detract from his strikingly sallow complexion, Colonel Hall was not well liked by the rank and file of his command—they still called themselves "Crocker's Iowa Brigade" after the previous commander, Colonel Marcellus M. Crocker, despite the fact that Crocker had been reassigned over a year before and Hall had commanded them for most of 1863 and the entire Atlanta campaign to date. Notwithstanding the absence of a bond to their commander, the Iowans never questioned Hall's bravery, for despite how sickly he always looked, he never shirked his duty. "If danger was at hand, he never was the second man present," insisted another Iowa officer.[3]

Indeed, danger was at hand—all attributed to the precarious position of the brigade. Sanders's 16th Iowa Regiment was down one-fifth of its strength after a detachment of 83 men left on fatigue duty, leaving 342 officers and men stretching from the Flat Shoals Road on its right to a diverging road on its left. One 2-gun section of the 2nd Illinois Light Artillery, Battery F, protected its right flank where the 11th Iowa extended in an arc. Directly behind the 16th was another regiment, the 13th Iowa, and the final regiment of the brigade, the 15th Iowa, entrenched on the left of the

16th but 30 yards behind it. Altogether, Hall's Iowa brigade approached 1,500 soldiers rank and file. By its extended position the 16th Iowa was the most vulnerable of all the regiments in the brigade.[4]

Adding to the vulnerability was the gap between Hall's left (represented by the left flank of the 15th Iowa) and the 27th Ohio of Morrill's brigade of Fuller's division. The gap was 1,000 yards of rugged wooded terrain, an ideal location for advancing Confederate troops to invade to escape both infantry and artillery fire. Gist's brigade, although unable to exploit the initial success it gained against the 64th Illinois, had still locked Fuller in place and prevented him from stretching out his already thin line to shorten the gap. That made the 16th Iowa vulnerable to a frontal assault against it, and the 15th Iowa susceptible to a flank attack upon its left.

Staff officer Lieutenant Colonel Strong assured General Giles Smith that General McPherson would address the need to fill the gap. Strong galloped off to return to General McPherson at approximately 1:00 P.M. No sooner had McPherson's staff officer disappeared in the woods east of the Iowans than the head of Patrick Cleburne's three brigades of 3,500 men had worked themselves free from the tangled underbrush and charged headlong into the left flank of the Army of the Tennessee. Brigadier General Daniel C. Govan's Arkansas brigade exited the woods and marched in double line of battle. Govan's available force consisted of what used to be ten regiments, all low in numbers and consolidated into five units, guiding along each side of the Flat Shoals Road (another regiment, the 3rd Confederate Infantry, was not with the brigade for that assault). Govan's brigade was a testament to the hard fighting the Army of Tennessee had endured throughout the war. Not one of the two-regiment consolidations exceeded 300 men and one of them, the 2nd/24th Arkansas, numbered less than 200 men. In all, 1,200 Confederates directly challenged a more numerous Iowa brigade.[5]

The Confederate force was supposed to have twice as many attackers. Brigadier General James A. Smith had aligned his Texas brigade to the right of Govan's men deep in the woods near Cobb's Mill and that was how they initiated their advance. Once Govan engaged the Iowa skirmishers, his attack separated from Smith's Texans who could not hold the line due to intervening bushes and marshes. Govan did benefit from artillery support. Notwithstanding the diminished infantry force, additional firepower buttressed Govan's advance. An artillery battalion trailed the Arkansas regiments, three batteries of 12 cannons commanded by Captain Thomas J. Key. Unfortunately for the artillerists, the woods they traveled through appeared to offer no open high ground to unlimber their cannons.[6]

Military doctrine dictates that an attacking force cannot dislodge an entrenched opponent with artillery support in a head-on assault unless the attackers can mass more than three times as many soldiers as the defenders, a ratio of superiority rarely appreciated or employed by an attacking force on a Civil War battlefield. General Govan did not enjoy the numbers advantage to succeed. Making matters worse was the character of the nonhuman defenses he had to conquer. Each of the Iowa regiments had encased itself in substantial rifle pits. Georgia soil was excavated and piled and packed in front with logs and branches added to the earthwork to better conceal the Northerners. In front of each regiment was a cleared space covering 50 yards, cleared that is except for contraptions of felled trees, sharpened oak branches, and underbrush—called abatises—designed to thwart the progress of the attackers. Rather than aligning the four Union regiments in a straight defense, the brigade had a scattered alignment with no two units exactly in line with each other. That increased the killing potential of the marksmen behind those rifle pits. Indeed, Govan's men were destined to enter a living hell.

At the same time Govan's Arkansas brigade initiated its assault against the left flank of Blair's XVII Corps, General McPherson personally acted to protect the eastern flank and rear of that corps. Lieutenant Colonel Strong returned to McPherson and both men rode onto the same path that led from the XVI to the XVII Corps positions. They did not hear any appreciable skirmish fire ahead of them, and could not have known that their entry into the gap would coincide with Cleburne's attack against the southern flank of Blair's troops, but they had already deemed the attack against that position to be inevitable. Yet here they were, the commanding general of the Army of the Tennessee, his lone staff officer, and a few orderlies heading into a wooded gap without protection.

General McPherson had ridden that road earlier in the morning; it was not unfamiliar to him. Accompanied by Lieutenant Colonel Strong, McPherson reached about halfway between the flanks of those two corps. McPherson checked his horse and left the road, carefully scouting the ground over to the south all the way to a distant ridge. That, McPherson maintained, was the ideal place to post reinforcements. Returning to the road, McPherson ordered Strong northward to General Logan with an order to send down Colonel Hugo Wangelin's Missouri brigade from its reserve position in the rear of the XV Corps to occupy that position in the gap. Strong departed McPherson's side before 1:30 P.M., leaving the Union army commander in the road.[7]

Strong galloped away from an erupting maelstrom, one that exploded upon the XVII Corps and, ultimately, General McPherson. Govan's assault against Colonel Hall took several minutes to unfold. The first order of duty for the Arkansans was to brush back the Iowa skirmish line challenging them. The pickets fell back to their rifle pits after firing a couple of rounds, but Lieutenant Colonel Sanders of the 16th Iowa was not satisfied with the rapid return of companies B and G of his regiment. He sent them back out, ostensibly to buy more time for his regiment to prepare for the inevitable attack. According to an Iowan in the rifle pit, "they did not go 10 rods [55 yards] until they came back on the run and the balls commenced to whistle over us." Another remarked, "On came the enemy with volleys of musketry and demonic yells." Sergeant Amos Sniff of the 16th Iowa characterized Govan's rush toward them as "an avalanche." Colonel Benjamin Potts, commanding the 1st Brigade just north of Hall's Iowans, noted that the assault commenced "about 1.20 P.M."[8]

Lieutenant Walter H. Powell of the 2nd Illinois Light Artillery, Battery F, was in charge of the 2 Napoleons between the 11th and 16th Iowa rifle pits and he immediately began pummeling the charging Razorbacks with twelve-pound rounds at a distance of 200 yards, but Lieutenant Colonel Sanders convinced him to stop; he was so confident in his entrenched position that he viewed the situation as an opportunity to trap the Confederates and annihilate them. He ordered his regiment to withhold their fire until he delivered the order. Reminiscent of Bunker Hill during the American Revolution ("Don't fire until you see the whites of their eyes"), Sanders allowed Govan's men to enter into the cleared space in front of the rifle pits and there—just 50 yards from the barrels of his regiment—he commanded the rear line to aim low and fire, immediately followed by the front rank, and then for both lines to fire at will. "The result of our fire was terrible," reported Sanders, "the enemy's line seemed to crumble to the earth, for even those not killed or wounded fell to the ground for protection."[9]

The 2nd/24th Arkansas was the recipient of Sander's wrath. Yankee lead thudded into them without mercy, killing a dozen men outright and wounding four score and more. Within fifteen minutes half of that unit was down and less than 100 men remained, all hugging the ground for dear life among their dead and wounded comrades. One hundred yards west of them, across the Flat Shoals Road, the 1st/15th Arkansas fared little better. Facing off against the 11th Iowa, those Razorbacks had a seemingly impossible task against 2 cannons and a regiment larger than theirs. As bullets and shell fragments shredded their ranks, they countered with volleys of their own, hitting the 11th Iowa with a cross fire as they inched toward the rifle pits on an angle. Colonel Hall attempted to rectify that with more manpower. He ordered up two companies of the 13th Iowa to the left of the 11th, nearly placing them in the roadbed. At the same time two additional companies of the same reserve regiment were sent forward 100 yards to support the 16th Iowa.

Before the reinforcements reached Hall's men, Arkansas troops had penetrated the works. Private William Bevins of Company G, 1st Arkansas, would never forget the mad rush four of his company mates made against the 11th Iowa:

It was death anyway, so they ran forward firing on the troops with terrible accuracy. One man had a bead on Thomas when Murphy shot the fellow. One hinged for Murphy when Thomas bayoneted him. So they had it—hand to hand. Poor Hensley was killed, Murphy terribly wounded, Baird wounded, but Thomas would not surrender. He bayoneted them until they took his gun, then he kicked and bit until they finally killed him there. Four men had killed 25 Yankees, but only one of the four lived to tell the tale. To question the morale of such men is farcical.[10]

Those four Razorbacks were hardly alone in their assault against the Union breastworks. Nearly half of Govan's brigade surged against the 11th Iowa and the 16th Iowa. That left the right flank of his attacking line battling the 15th Iowa. Here Govan's men were unmolested by Union artillery and they outnumbered the Federals, but not by enough to overrun their works by a bull rush. The abatises between the opposing lines here were so thick and numerous that Govan's adjutant called them "almost impassable."[11]

Colonel John E. Murray of the 5th Arkansas got his men past that creative curtain. Murray took overall charge of his own consolidated unit, the 5th/13th Arkansas and the right wing of Govan's attack (including the 8th/19th and 6th/7th Arkansas). Murray had been the most impressive subordinate to General Govan. Dubbed the "Boy Colonel" for his promotion to lieutenant colonel at the age of eighteen in 1861, Murray was still a youthful twenty-one years old at the Battle of Atlanta, but was then a full colonel who had commanded Govan's brigade in brief stints during the previous winter. A brigadier general's commission seemed inevitable, which would make Murray the youngest one in the Confederate army.

Colonel Murray conquered the abatises but his regiment faced the point-blank fire of the 15th Iowa directly ahead of them and the enfilading musketry of the 16th Iowa to their left. The two-sided assault stopped the Razorbacks in their tracks. In a feat of inspiration, Murray rallied his men by grabbing the flag of his regiment and charged with the 5th/13th Arkansas to the earthworks of the 15th Iowa. Mounting the parapets, Arkansas and Iowa soldiers engaged in a brief, hand-to-hand fight. Murray dropped with a mortal wound. One hundred Arkansans joined him on the casualty list as the Iowans desperately clung to their position.[12]

Notwithstanding the repulse of Confederates in front, nothing protected the flank of the 15th Iowa, allowing Govan's right-hand regiments, the 6th/7th Arkansas and the 8th/19th Arkansas, to pass by the Union left, covered by woods and advancing through a protective ravine, while a battalion of the 5th/13th Arkansas crept closer and closer to the front of the Iowa entrenchment. Govan reined in the right-hand units, ordering them to turn to the left to aid his left-flank force in the entrenchments.

An unexpected prize awaited the flanking Arkansas units. Crossing an east-west wagon road that ran through the woods here, the Razorbacks shocked the two lieutenants leading the 6 cannons of Battery F, 2nd U.S. Artillery, from their original position at the XVII Corps entrenchment line to the endangered XVI Corps position half a mile to the west. The battery was a XVI Corps unit, recalled to assist the other two batteries there. Lieutenant Albert M. Murray made the unfortunate mistake of taking that narrow road when another wagon road, a few hundred yards north of them, would have assured a safe arrival to General Grenville Dodge. Before the guns could be unlimbered to contest the Arkansas infantry at point-blank range, Murray and his entire battery were swept up and escorted to the rear as prisoners of war.[13]

It was a dire situation for Colonel Hall, who attempted to reinforce the left flank of the 15th Iowa by peeling off more companies of the 13th Iowa and sending them to their aid. Giles Smith ordered Colonel Potts to support Hall's left flank with regiments from his brigade. Potts chose a battalion of the 3rd Iowa Infantry and two companies of the 53rd Illinois to hustle northwestward and buttress the left of the 15th Iowa. He also sent a portion of 53rd Indiana eastward to do the same.[14]

It was too late. The Razorbacks were already working their way around the flank before succor arrived. They loosed several heated volleys upon Potts's reinforcements, killing and wounding several, including Captain Pleasant T. Mathes, the 3rd Iowa commander, whose body was left on the field. Those not shot up in the two reinforcing regiments returned to the safety of the XVII Corps works near Bald Hill. Overwhelmed by Arkansas troops in front and flank, Colonel William W. Belknap, commander of the 15th Iowa, ordered his men to abandon their rifle pits and fall back to a new line several hundred yards northwest of them. That action necessitated the withdrawal of the 13th Iowa, who had dispersed most of its companies as skirmishers and reinforcements and had no remaining strength in its entrenchments.[15]

Insurmountable pressure forced back the 15th and 13th Iowa regiments, leaving the 11th and 16th Iowa and the 2 cannons in the road to fend off Govan's surging and swirling hurricane of troops. Giles Smith had already prepared a fall-back position and ordered Colonel Hall to order the remaining regiments to extricate from their works and head to that new line. The 11th Iowa needed not be told twice. Threatened by a cross fire against its arc formation and worried about both flanks being enveloped, the 11th's commander, Lieutenant Colonel John C. Abercrombie, ordered his men out by the right flank, abandoning their position and heading westward. Some stayed inside, resigned to their fate; others were shot down and fell back into the works. Most of the 11th Iowa, however, successfully escaped, jumping over the line of entrenchments 300 yards off to their right. Safely behind the earthworks, one of the escapees, noted, "From this position we could see the rebel troops closing around the 16th Iowa."[16]

Indeed, the 16th Iowa was the lone Union force remaining in that sector, and they had stayed too long. Lieutenant Colonel Sanders insisted that the trapped 2nd/24th Arkansas thirty paces in front of his works had raised the white flag to surrender. Sanders halted his fire and allowed

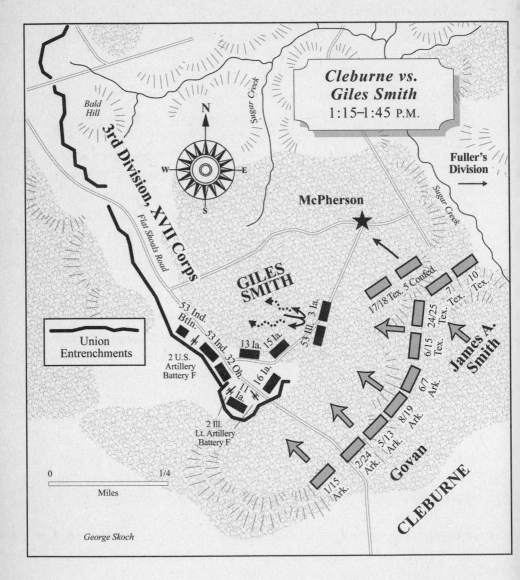

Cleburne vs. Giles Smith
1:15–1:45 P.M.

Bald
Hill

Sugar Creek

3rd Division, XVII Corps

Flat Shoals Road

N

W   E

S

Fuller's
Division

Sugar Creek

McPherson

GILES
SMITH

17/18 Tex. 5 Confed.

7 Tex.

10 Tex.

24/25 Tex.

6/15 Tex.

James A. Smith

53 Ind.
Btln.

53 Ind. 32 Oh.

13 Ia.

15 Ia.

53 Ill. 3 Ia.

6/7 Ark.

Union Entrenchments

2 U.S.
Artillery
Battery F

11 Ia.

16 Ia.

8/19 Ark.

6/7 Ark.

2 Ill.
Lt. Artillery
Battery F

5/13 Ark.

Govan

2/24 Ark.

0   1/4

Miles

1/15
Ark.

CLEBURNE

George Skoch

the Arkansas troops to enter his works. If true, that preoccupation with over 100 captures diverted the Iowans' attention from the remaining regiments of Govan's brigade who had entered the abandoned works of the 15th Iowa on their left flank and then the 13th Iowa 100 yards behind (north of) them. Then General Govan called on Sanders to surrender his regiment. Only 25 of Sanders's Confederate captures had been escorted rearward; the remainder posed an additional problem for him—they held on to their weapons. Bolstered by the presence of their sister regiments in the Iowa works around them those "captures" turned the tables on Sanders. With guns raised, they insisted that *he* surrender.

Sanders refused. From the east side of his works, Sanders bolted westward to encourage his command to escape to the right. An Arkansas officer hurriedly borrowed a pistol from a comrade and fired at the fleeing Union commander. The bullet entered Sanders's thigh, but the flesh wound did not impede him. In any case, the presence of the 1st/15th Arkansas in the works of the 11th Iowa convinced him that he was then completely surrounded. Unable to cut his way out, Sanders quickly collected his command in the works. Looking to the north they observed Govan's men prepared to charge upon them with fixed bayonets. It was a hopeless position. Rather than endure the inevitable slaughter of his men, Sanders surrendered his soldiers—all 240 of them in the works. The two companies of 13th Iowa soldiers assisting him were also forced to surrender.

The Union defense remaining in that sector was the 2 cannons of the 2nd Illinois Light Artillery manned by Lieutenant Walter H. Powell. Surrounded on both sides by Razorbacks in the Iowa rifle pits, Powell could only enable his caissons to escape. He surrendered himself, his 2 Napoleons, and approximately thirty artillerists to the Confederates. Despite the outcome, Powell's superior officer, Major John T. Cheney, praised the performance of that section of the battery, lauding them for "acting as artillery always should do." (Powell would survive his imprisonment to join his cousin, John Wesley Powell, on a famous exploration of the Grand Canyon five years later.)[17]

Less than half an hour from their initial advance, Govan had conquered the longest odds to sweep away Hall's entire Iowa brigade, killing, wounding, and capturing more than 400 blue-clad soldiers and 8 cannons. The contrast between his brigade's accomplishment with the ultimate failure of the six Confederate brigades comprising Walker's and

Bate's commands was striking. He then owned 300 yards of the Union left flank, but the cost was severe. He lamented the loss of over 300 killed and wounded men in twenty minutes of work, including a high proportion of company and regimental officers. None of those was more promising than Govan's "boy colonel," John E. Murray of the 5th Arkansas, who was cut down in front of the 15th Iowa earthworks. "His loss is irreparable," grieved Govan, "and has cast a gloom over the whole command, where he was universally beloved." As his brigade escorted prisoners and tended to their casualties while manning their hard-fought gains, the rearward brigades of Cleburne's division were upon the field and filling in the gap between the Union XVI and XVII Corps.[18]

Even before Hall's survivors scampered across the XVII Corps earthworks west of the Flat Shoals Road, General James A. Smith's Texas brigade entered the southern end of the gap between the XVII and XVI Corps. The Texans came in on the right of Govan, part of assisting the Arkansans in front of the 16th Iowa Infantry. Like the Arkansas brigade, the Texans were consolidated into two-regiment pairings. Most of those consolidations still numbered fewer than 200 soldiers, with one only half that size. Smith's men likely guided themselves along Govan's right as they moved to exploit the fact that no Federal troops stood in their path. The first troops from that brigade entered the gap between the XVI and XVII Corps at 1:30 P.M.[19]

General McPherson found himself at the worst possible place and at the worst possible time. He must have heard Govan's assault upon Hall within a few minutes after Lieutenant Colonel Strong's departure to escort Wangelin's brigade into the gap. McPherson trotted on the road toward the line of the XVII Corps, accompanied only by an orderly. Within seconds, Colonel Robert K. Scott, a brigade commander in Mortimer Leggett's division of the XVII Corps, appeared on the same road within yards of McPherson (Scott was attempting to return to Bald Hill from the guard detail he had posted at the corps hospital train). Also on that road was Lieutenant William H. Sherfy, a XV Corps signalman who could see Cleburne's Confederates swarming into the wooded gap. He rode ahead of at least three other signal officers to warn McPherson as he watched the general enter the danger zone. McPherson shrugged off Sherfy's warning and continued westward on the byroad.[20]

One hundred yards farther down that road McPherson found out that he was trapped. A small body of Confederates had penetrated northward all the way to the edge of the wagon road. These Southerners were mostly Tennesseans serving as a battalion of the 5th Confederate Regiment, commanded by Captain Richard Beard. The unit had recently joined the Texas brigade after transferring from a broken, hard-luck brigade, and then found themselves in a most advantageous position as McPherson reined up in front of them. "He was certainly surprised to suddenly find himself face-to-face with the Rebel line," wrote Captain Beard of McPherson's reaction, not yet knowing the general's identity but discerning that he was at least a corps commander. Less than 10 yards from the Confederates, McPherson stopped as Captain Beard raised his sword as a sign to surrender. Several other members of the company ordered McPherson and his trailing cortege to halt. McPherson refused Beard's very clear signal. Instead, he raised his hat in a polite gesture, wheeled his horse, and attempted to head northeastward off the road and through the woods to safety.

Captain Beard was not going to let him get away. He had a sure-shot corporal at his side, a Mississippian named Robert Coleman whom Beard ordered to fire upon the general. Coleman dutifully complied and aimed at McPherson just as the general bent over the neck of his galloping horse to minimize his exposure. It didn't work. Southern lead struck McPherson through the right side of his back and—because of his bent position—it penetrated diagonally upward through his torso and exited his left breast. The bullet unhorsed McPherson 20 yards north of the wagon road as the rest of the Confederates in Beard's command loosed a volley at the other Union soldiers near him, trying to scatter away from him. Their shots struck more horses than men. Three bullets struck McPherson's beautiful black horse; it limped away and escaped. Colonel Scott's horse was shot out from under him and incapacitated the colonel as he slammed to the ground. McPherson's orderly and two signal officers were run into trees by their spooked mounts, including Lieutenant Sherfy—the man who had warned McPherson minutes earlier to no avail. Dazed and injured, but able to walk, the signalman returned to his feet and wobbled into the woods. (His pocket watch was permanently damaged, stopping perhaps twenty minutes later at 2:02 P.M.)[21]

Captain Beard walked up to the fallen general, believing him killed instantly as he lay motionless with his knees and face pressed into the road

STEREOPTICON SLIDE (AN EARLY FORM OF 3-D) OF THE PLACE
WHERE GENERAL MCPHERSON FELL.

The small white square of paper on the thin tree in the background denotes the spot where McPherson was struck. A monument stands on that spot today, surrounded by houses and streets instead of woods. The wagon wheel placed across the simple byroad is close to the spot from where the Confederate soldier who shot McPherson aimed and fired eastward at the fleeing army commander. The woods surrounding the road filled in nearly the entire half-mile gap between the Union XVI and XVII corps. *(Courtesy of the Library of Congress)*

dust. The Confederates still did not know exactly who he was. Beard then approached the fallen Colonel Scott nearby and asked him who the fallen general was. "Sir, it is General McPherson," responded Colonel Scott with eyes swimming in tears. "You have killed the best man in our army."[22]

McPherson, in fact, was not dead, but death in minutes was inevitable. McPherson's orderly had been knocked off his horse when the young man's head struck an overhanging limb. He had fallen hard, right next to his general, knocked senseless for a moment or two. When he came to, he could see McPherson lying on his right side, his hand lifted up to the hole in his chest, "while the blood flowed in streams between his fingers." The dying commander shifted onto his back as the orderly was jerked away before he could tend to his general. Members of the 5th Confederate helped themselves to some of McPherson's personal effects—including his hat, field glasses, a dispatch book, and his sword belt (McPherson did not have his sword with him that afternoon). They took his watch, but left the diamond ring glistening from his pinky finger and they also overlooked a money-filled wallet.

Captain Beard ordered his men off to continue their pursuit westward, taking Colonel Scott and the orderly with them, but McPherson was alone for only a few minutes. Private George Reynolds of the 15th Iowa of Hall's overrun brigade was making his way back to the corps hospital to tend to his bullet-shattered arm when he stumbled upon McPherson lying on his back in the thick underbrush. Not knowing how fortunate he was to be passing through an interval with no Rebels in the woods near him, Reynolds folded a blanket to prop McPherson's head and moistened the general's lips and forehead with his canteen water. Reynolds alone was there when McPherson died. Unfortunately he could not prevent another Union soldier, an unnamed vagabond, from rifling the dead commander's coat and stealing the money that was overlooked by Beard's Confederates.[23]

At the same time Private Reynolds witnessed McPherson take his last breath, the gap was invaded by Union soldiers charging from the east. That was the second thrust parried by General Fuller, commander of the 4th Division, XVI Corps, who determined to kill the new threat to Dodge's right flank. His infantry, represented by Morrill's brigade, had been facing westward toward the woods since attacked there less than an hour earlier by Gist's brigade, which had apparently pulled back after the death of General Walker and the wounding of General Gist, but James A. Smith's Texans posed a new threat, for they then covered the wagon road connecting the XVI and XVII Corps. More than that, by seeping northward into the woods, Smith's Confederate brigade then enveloped Dodge's flank again.

Fuller sent an aide eastward across the ravine cut by Sugar Creek to order Laird's battery to fire over their heads into the woods. Under that canopy of artillery rounds, Fuller ordered the 64th Illinois on a solitary mission—to enter the woods and open a flank fire on the rebel line. Ostensibly, Fuller's goal was to send one regiment on the flank while the others, particularly the 18th Missouri, opened up on the Confederates of Smith's brigade from the front. According to General Fuller, "Lieut. Laird soon began to drop shells beautifully into the edge of the forest." Then the cannons ceased and the infantry charged into the woods.[24]

As the 18th Missouri penetrated in front, the 64th Illinois assailed the woods from the northeast, driving over 500 yards and capturing at least 40 Confederates, including a couple of men from the 5th Confederate Infantry who had some of General McPherson's belongings in their possession. The Illinois men advanced as far as McPherson's body, allowing an ambulance to swiftly rush in and remove it from the woods to carry northward to Sherman's headquarters, but they could not hold their new advanced line. Lieutenant Colonel Michael W. Manning, commander of the 64th, deemed his position untenable. "About this time," he reported, "the enemy was in my front, flanks, and rear, pouring upon the regiment a deadly and galling fire." The 64th Illinois was 350 strong when they rushed into the woods; but in less than ten minutes they were down 83 men, including half of their officers. Colonel Morrill, the 1st Brigade commander (4th Division) and former head of the regiment, had personally led his former command into the woods before he was forced off the field with his second wound of the afternoon. Down 1 out of every 4 men who had charged into the gap, the Illinois men retreated pell-mell beyond their original line and tried to reform in a wood lot a quarter of a mile to the rear.[25]

James A. Smith's men were unable to take advantage of the new gap in Fuller's line. Laird's 6-gun battery rolled an iron surf over the Texans and Tennesseans before they could possibly renew an assault upon Fuller's weakened line. Then aided by Captain Andrew Hickenlooper, the chief of artillery for the Army of the Tennessee, Laird's battery continued its dominance over the Southern infantry. As Fuller's men flattened themselves on the field, the Ohio battery lofted shells over them, exploding into the woods housing Cleburne's men and raining terror upon them. "And here let me say," stressed General Fuller in his official report of the action, "this Ohio battery . . . did more toward defeating the enemy than is often accomplished by six guns."[26]

Dodge did not know the fact that the threat against his thin blue line would be the last serious one posed by Hood's army on July 22. Elements of four Confederate divisions had attacked or tested his position and his men had held firm, primarily from the support of artillery, but Dodge did know that the head of the army was dead and the weight of Cleburne's division—a force that had proved one of the most devastating in 1864—was aiming in a different direction.

7

TWO-SIDED FIGHT

John Bell Hood shifted to his third location in twelve hours during the early afternoon of the Battle of Atlanta. After briefly fielding dispatches in the park across from the Atlanta Hotel just north of the great depot in the center of the city, Hood and his staff rode out eastward toward the fairgrounds. On a hill near the City Burial Place stood the elegant estate of Lucius J. Gartrell, a former Georgia colonel and a member of the Confederate Congress. There, one mile from General Hardee's assault, General Hood settled into his new headquarters and listened to the continuous rumble of battle.[1]

The attack began several hours later than planned, which allowed McPherson to reposition troops of the XVI Corps to protect against the rearward assault that had surprised the attackers of Bate's and Walker's division perhaps more than the defenders in the three brigades under Sweeny and Fuller. The delay was less the fault of the commanders conducting the flank movement than it was of the abominable terrain that sapped time and manpower from Hardee's corps, but that was unacceptable to Hood, and Hardee was the obvious culprit for the delay.

As the second hour of the afternoon and of the battle neared its close Hood was unaware of two factors that worked in his favor. He had not been informed of General McPherson's death, which had decapitated the enemy army—at least temporarily. He was also unaware that adjustments in the flanking column had somehow allowed for simultaneous assaults against the Union defense from nearly opposite directions: the southwest and the east. Better yet for the Confederates was that the movements for those attacks were commencing simultaneously from the woods south of the Union position. The recipient of those attacks would be the XVII Corps of McPherson's army, the same corps that had lost several hundred men attacking Bald Hill the day before and the same corps that had one of its brigades routed from its trenches at 1:30 P.M. with the loss of hundreds more killed and wounded, and two batteries and an entire regiment—the 16th Iowa—captured. General Blair's corps was down nearly 1,200 men in less than thirty hours, and he had no idea that the blows that would strike him over the next six hours would double those losses.[2]

General Hardee's readjustment of General George Maney's Tennessee division set the stage for those multidirectional attacks. Hardee decided to shift Maney's four brigades, originally designed to attack in line with General Cleburne, from the right and rear of Cleburne to his left. The repositioning had been costly, for it separated one brigade (Lowrey's) in Cleburne's division from the other two and guaranteed a delayed assault by it, but it also gave Cleburne strong support on his left as well as presenting a new front from which to harass the Union army.

Attrition over the course of the campaign had forced a consolidation of twelve of Maney's smallest regiments into six larger ones. Eleven other regiments retained their original identity, but were likely much smaller than the consolidated units. The four brigades made Maney's the largest Confederate division of Hardee's corps, a force nearing 4,000 officers and men.[3] The regiments were led by veterans, but General Maney himself was new to his command. Ascending from supervision of one brigade to four due to the promotion of General Benjamin F. Cheatham to command Hood's old corps, Maney's constant change of direction by Hardee's early morning realignment was difficult for a general used to handling a force a quarter of the size he was leading on July 22. He had previous battle experience with those men two days earlier at Peachtree Creek where his division had crossed Tanyard Branch near the center of the Confederate line, yet "escaped" with 277 killed and wounded men, about a tenth of Hood's total losses even though they represented a quarter of the Confederate brigades on the battlefield that day. Two of those brigades took 90 percent of Maney's losses that day, suggesting the other two were generally held in reserve.

Still, the frontline brigades had proven tentative that day, deciding the cost was too heavy in human lives to rush headlong against the enemy line.

Those casualty figures at Peachtree Creek could lead to suspicion about the lack of aggressiveness by Maney on the tactical offensive. Killed and wounded men are a crude gauge of the fighting nature of troops since many factors contribute to battlefield casualties. Given that his men had advanced on low marshy ground, unprotected, as they worked their way toward the Union center that day, the loss of barely 5 percent of his at-tacking force (about 15 percent in the two heaviest-engaged brigades) is nearly impossible to conceive. Hardee's success against the XVII Corps on Friday, July 22, would require a more spirited assault by the Tennes-seans east of Atlanta than they exhibited two days earlier north of the city. Working against them were the stark and solid memories of six battles over the previous thirty months where they had rushed into maelstroms of certain death. The Tennesseans had to fight those awful memories as well as human nature in order to do it one more time that Friday afternoon.[4]

General Maney's division essentially aligned in an arc south of the Union line, concave to the north. One brigade, commanded by Brigadier General Otho French Strahl, worked into position southwest of Giles Smith's line of the XVII Corps. To their right (east) aligned the pivot of the division, Colonel Michael Magevney's brigade, two of its regiments set to swing northeastward against the Federal fortifications, and the re-mainder of the brigade positioned to do likewise from the right side. Col-onel Francis M. Walker's brigade and Colonel John C. Carter's brigade continued shifting behind them.

No one ever indicated whether all brigades of Maney's division had been ordered to attack at the same time. If that was the intention, Strahl's brigade on the left violated the plan. Ohio born and bred, General Strahl had been practicing law in Tennessee at the outbreak of the war and had led a regiment in the brigade in 1862. A series of promotions followed, leading him to command his brigade for a year. His brigade was in the back line at Peachtree Creek and had been spared the casualties that marred two other brigades of the division. Strahl's Tennesseans were in position and moved off at 1:45 P.M., just after General Govan's successful rout of Hall's Iowans from their trenches. Advancing in three lines of battle, Strahl led 1,000 Tennesseans in their first assault since the Battle of Chickamauga ten months earlier (a battle where Strahl had been cited for gallantry).[5]

The tormented division of Giles Smith would be the recipients of Maney's initial attacks. The Iowans of Hall's brigade, along with the small force comprising Potts's brigade, had just reformed on the west side of the breastworks across the Flat Shoals Road and were facing eastward toward Govan's Arkansans. "Skirmishers were immediately ordered out," reported General Giles Smith, "who discovered the enemy not far back, but apparently in no condition to renew the attack." The relief was short-lived; Strahl's Tennesseans were discovered advancing toward them—from behind. With an enemy then on two fronts and already having absorbed close to 1,000 casualties in the past two days—with only seven regiments—Smith's 4th Division faced their greatest threat at that moment.

The capitulation of the 16th Iowa half an hour before further reduced Smith's division to six regiments and two companies of another, a force reduced to 1,800 officers and men. Rather than gamble on which side of the earthworks to align his men, Giles Smith essentially abandoned that position. He aligned his men perpendicular to the earthworks in two lines, 75 yards apart. The southernmost line consisted of two regiments of Hall's brigade, the 11th and 15th Iowa; behind them stood Potts's men. Both lines anchored their left flanks upon the earthworks, leaving one Iowa regiment, the 13th, facing eastward against Govan's brigade. Giles Smith had decided that Strahl's brigade was his greatest threat as he aligned in a cornfield to meet it.[6]

Strahl struck Smith close to 2:00 P.M., enveloping the right flank of the 15th Iowa and driving the other Iowans in the frontline away within five minutes. That left Potts alone to face off against the Tennesseans with an equal force of about 1,000 men in an open field without cover of any kind between the opposing forces. Potts's westernmost regiment, the 32nd Ohio, anchored the right flank of the brigade, bending the makeshift Union line from south to southwest to better confront the Tennesseans. Notwithstanding the immediate success against the frontline regiments of Iowans, Strahl could not drive Potts's brigade away from the field. The Ohioans in particular proved to be pesky soldiers; a sound and solid embodiment of the Buckeye stalwartness was its "Fighting Chaplain," Russell B. Bennett. Cautioning the regiment to "lie low" in the cornfield, Chaplain Bennett disregarded his own admonition and stood erect, firing the rifle of a nearby prone private at the approaching Tennesseans. The prone soldier reloaded the gun and handed it back up to the preacher who would aim and fire again. Bennett somehow escaped with his life, but the unfortunate soldier in charge of his weapon was struck by a bullet while lying in the field and was killed. "I cannot forget the brave conduct of Chaplain R. B. Bennett," noted Colonel Potts in his official report of his brigade's participation in the battle.[7]

General Strahl withstood mounting casualties in his brigade as he ordered three unsuccessful assaults against the 32nd Ohio and the other regiments of Potts's brigade supporting them. According to a lieutenant in the 5th Tennessee, the volleys fired by Potts's brigade appeared "too destructive." That certainly proved the case for General Strahl who was wounded so severely as to not be able to lead his men. The only colonel in the brigade, John A. Wilson of the 24th Tennessee, was also out of the contest with a severe injury. That left Lieutenant Colonel James D. Tillman of the 41st Tennessee as the next ranking officer and he immediately ascended to brigade command. It was especially unfortunate for his regiment, for its commander, Major T. G. Miller, took a bullet in his leg (it required amputation) and had to turn the command over to a captain. Lieutenant Colonel Tillman proved a far cry from the experienced General Strahl. Not wishing to wage a protracted fight in the cornfield, Tillman withdrew Strahl's brigade from the contest and headed back to the woods from where they initiated their attack.[8]

It is unlikely that General Maney was on the far left of his division at that time, for General Strahl was the only subordinate with the appropriate brigadier's rank (the other three brigade commanders were colonels). Maney would have placed a greater emphasis on the center or right-side brigades, a sound command decision, but an unfortunate circumstance for the Confederates. Had General Maney been present to superintend Lieutenant Colonel Tillman in his new command, it is unlikely the Southerners would have left the field as early as they did.

The sudden disappearance of Tennesseans from the Atlanta side of the breastworks allowed General Giles Smith to realign his forces for a fourth time in forty-five minutes. Potts's brigade remained in place perpendicular to the line of XVII Corps earthworks, while Colonel Hall attempted to re-form his Iowans to repulse an attack closer to the

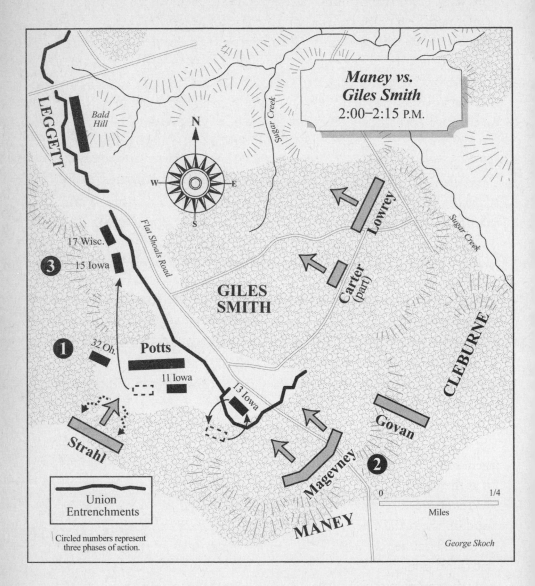

*Maney vs.
Giles Smith*
2:00–2:15 P.M.

LEGGETT

Bald
Hill

Sugar Creek

Sugar Creek

N

W — E

S

Lowrey

17 Wisc.

15 Iowa

Flat Shoals Road

GILES
SMITH

Carter
(part)

CLEBURNE

32 Oh.

Potts

11 Iowa

13 Iowa

Govan

Strahl

Magevney

MANEY

Union
Entrenchments

0   1/4

Miles

Circled numbers represent
three phases of action.

George Skoch

southwestern earthworks. That offensive was conducted by Colonel Michael Magevney's Tennessee brigade, striking the XVII Corps flank from the south, over much of the same ground that General Govan's Arkansans had cleared twenty minutes before. Govan's men were re-forming in a safer region off to the east, clearing the way for Magevney's men to continue to roll up the Iowans from their new position. Traversing the original works held by Hall's men at noon that day, the 12th/47th and the 13th/154th Tennessee angled in from the east while the 11th and 29th Tennessee closed in from the west, pushing the Union flank northward as the flanks of Magevney's brigade closed in on the center.

"The enemy Commenced retreating up thier [sic] works as soon as we Charged them," crowed Captain Alfred Fielder of the 12th Tennessee, "and we having an enfilading fire upon them and they being in great Confusion & huddling together we mowed them down with awful havoc." The Iowans were caught in a vise, desperately trying to escape the trap by jumping from one side of the works to the other to combat each side of Southerners harassing them. Colonel John Shane of the 13th Iowa admitted the disorderly state of his regiment "owing to the numerous detachments, independent commands, and stragglers which at that time thronged the road." The Iowans re-formed just in time, reported Shane, "as the enemy were then within rifle-range and approaching our position from two directions in heavy force." The 13th Iowa and its neighboring regiments of Hall's brigade delivered ragged volleys at the Tennesseans by a tactic the Southerners had never seen before in a Civil War battle. "They would Jump first on one side of the works and then on the other," noted a Tennessee soldier, "but we being on both sides and pouring upon them such a galling fire they continued steadily to give way firing back at us as they went."[9]

Tennesseans pursued the hop-scotching Iowans as they pushed northward up the XVII Corps breastworks, some of the Southerners picking up loaded Yankee rifles left in the ditches. Magevney's attack petered out due to his brigade's loss of cohesion and the concentration of Hall's brigade to repel them. The fighting for the 13th Iowa was not through for the day, but at 2:00 P.M. that Friday, they were perhaps the hardest luck regiment remaining on the field. Their casualties told the entire story. The unit had tallied 400 officers and men the previous morning but had been reduced to 150 soldiers since then due to casualties and captures.

With no time to lick their wounds, the regiments of Hall's brigade prepared to meet a renewed threat from the east. An inkling of that threat
had already passed the position at the time that Strahl launched his attack from the southwest and Magevney's brigade from the south. That
threat emanated from some of the same troops who were forced from
Bald Hill the day before. Soon they would attempt to reclaim that position from the same direction Blair's Union troops drove from on July 21.[10]

Brigadier General James A. Smith's brigade of Texans and Tennesseans had completely disrupted the Union command by killing the head of
the Army of the Tennessee, General McPherson. Then they had an equal
opportunity to deliver a devastating wound to the body of that army.
Part of the Texas brigade had meandered and malingered in the wooded
gap between the Union XVI and XVII Corps. That was particularly true
for members of the Tennessee regiment in that brigade, the 5th Confederate, while scattered companies of Texans either helped Govan's Arkansans or attempted to take another run at Fuller's division. Still, General
James A. Smith had most of his men in order—at least 1,000 soldiers
under arms—as he pushed forward, northward through the gap and into
a region that threatened the Union rear.[11]

"Occasionally, there is a terrible shooting to our right or left, and sometimes nearly behind us," noted one of the Texans, "but the woods are so
thick that we can't see but a short distance." The Texans thrust northward with a slight angle to the northwest. They advanced nearly parallel
with the line of the XVII Corps earthworks 1,000 yards west of them.
Unimpeded by enemy troops, the Texans raced forward with "ungovernable enthusiasm," as described by their commander. Yet General James A.
Smith stressed the "ungovernable" aspect in his report, for he lamented
that his brigade line stretched too far across, which materially weakened
it; still he raved about the "great spirit and vigor" of the Texans as they
tumbled out of the woods at a point within a mile of the Georgia Railroad. Those Confederates, under the cover of the woods, had managed to
position themselves north of the entire XVI Corps line to their right and
the XVII Corps line to their left. A member of Blair's corps recalled "a
long line of rebels" passing through the woods east of their position, "as
though we were beneath their notice." The Union soldiers poured a volley into the left flank of the Texans—men they could not see—that had
little effect on their northward foray.[12]

Unfortunately for the Confederates, they had approached the only unengaged corps of the Army of the Tennessee—Major General John A. Logan's XV Corps. Logan's southernmost division, the 4th, commanded by Brigadier General William Harrow, had extended from the XVII Corps line by bending due northward from a point above the Bald Hill. Harrow was a unique character for that Union army, a transplant from the Army of the Potomac who had enjoyed victory on the fields of Gettysburg the previous July. A tough disciplinarian, Harrow had attracted the wrath of his subordinates and soldiers, but his sound soldier experience and instincts in the early afternoon of July 22 saved his division from a disaster. Having heard the attack upon the flanks of XVI and XVII corps during the noon hour and watching Union stragglers, caissons, and wagons pour from the trees behind his left flank, Harrow applied some preventative medicine to his division. "I at once attempted to anticipate any action of the enemy, by directing Colonel Charles C. Walcutt to face to the rear, and swing his command around so as to face toward our left flank."[13]

Harrow chose Walcutt's brigade because it was the most successful and experienced brigade of his division in that campaign, a perception that placed Colonel Walcutt on a clear path to become the youngest general in the army at the age of twenty-six. Walcutt pulled his troops out of the division line as the bookend brigades extended their flanks to fill the new vacancy. Walcutt led his regiments into a cornfield 400 yards behind (east of) the main army line. Facing his men southward toward the tree line, Walcutt had barely put the units in line when the Texas skirmishers made their appearance by exiting the woods in front of him.

The Texas brigade closed in on their skirmishers and stopped in its tracks upon the unexpected appearance of nearly 1,000 blue-clad soldiers blocking its path merely 150 yards away. General James A. Smith needed support and he needed it immediately. "Finding that my brigade was far in advance of the troops on my right and left, and that the position was insecure, I dispatched an officer to communicate the same to the major-general commanding [Cleburne], with the requests that re-enforcements be sent forward," Smith explained. As the time neared 2:00 P.M. General Cleburne determined it was unrealistic to send Smith timely assistance.[14]

Walcutt's men refused General James A. Smith the time necessary for reinforcements. According to one of the Texans, "The Yanks had discovered

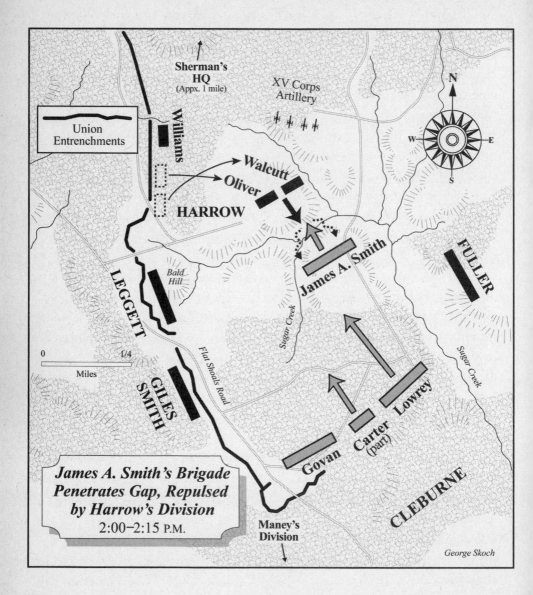

Union
Entrenchments

Sherman's
HQ
(Appx. 1 mile)

Williams

XV Corps
Artillery

N
W   E
S

Walcutt
Oliver

HARROW

Bald
Hill

LEGGETT

James A. Smith

FULLER

Sugar Creek

0   1/4
Miles

GILES SMITH

Flat Shoals Road

Sugar Creek

Govan   Carter   Lowrey
        (part)

CLEBURNE

*James A. Smith's Brigade
Penetrates Gap, Repulsed
by Harrow's Division*
2:00–2:15 P.M.

Maney's
Division

George Skoch

there was only a skirmish line of us; they began to get over their scare and get together again, and began to shoot at us." Walcutt's brigade peppered Smith's Texans with several volleys that were not returned with nearly the same intensity. General Harrow, overseeing the action, called it "short and decisive." Perhaps so, but it was not by a simple counterpunch. Walcutt's brigade received timely assistance to add power to that punch. Major Thomas Maurice, the chief of artillery of the XV Corps, placed 2 cannons in position to support Walcutt's infantry. The guns swept a ravine holding prone Confederates, tormenting whom it could not kill. Major Maurice then moved 10 more guns in support of the battery section already in place. In all, he repositioned three batteries from their original line, where they had generally faced toward Atlanta, to points covering the region of woods and fields between the XVI and XVII Corps. The redeployment guaranteed no further advancement by the Texans as well as no surprises from behind, but it considerably weakened the support required by the remaining divisions of the XV Corps facing westward.[15]

Walcutt's infantry and Maurice's artillery successfully pinned the Texas brigade in the fields fronting the woods from which they emerged. General Harrow delivered the coup de grâce with the timely insertion of infantry from Colonel John M. Oliver's brigade. Oliver sent out two regiments to extend the right flank of Walcutt's infantry line. That they did, lying prone in the open field and trading fire with Smith's Confederates. Oliver broke the stalemate by sending out one more regiment—the 15th Michigan—to charge from northwest to southeast beyond the right flank of Harrow's improvised line.

The order turned out to be one of the timeliest of the battle. General James A. Smith had already concluded that he could not break the stalemate and that it would be suicide to continue to wait for Cleburne's reinforcements—if they were to come at all. He had already lost over 100 in killed and wounded in that field. The cross fire by Oliver's regiments was the deciding factor. Smith ordered his Texans and Tennesseans back into the protection of the woods. As he pulled back his men from right to left, he took a bullet or shrapnel from the Yankees and was forced to leave the field. Lieutenant Colonel Robert B. Young of the 10th Texas took over. Unfortunately for the Confederates, four companies of the 15th Michigan charged during the command change and the left side of the Confederate line apparently did not receive Smith's order. The result was a catastrophe for that proud brigade. The consolidated 17th/18th Texas and a portion of the 5th Confederate were stuck out in front; those men were at least 100 yards in advance of the rest of the Texans retreating from their right and had no support on their left.

The battalion of the 15th Michigan rushed forward "on a dead run" and crashed into that exposed force. The gunfight between them was so close that one of the Texans described it as "almost a hand-to-hand encounter." With a portion of Oliver's brigade on their flank and rear, the ranking Confederate officer—Major Richard J. Person of the 5th Confederate Infantry—put an end to the inevitable and ordered his officers and men to surrender. Union Private Charles F. Sancraite seized the standards of the 5th Confederate. Along with that prize Sancraite would win the Congressional Medal of Honor.[16]

Three companies of the 99th Indiana west of the 15th Michigan also enjoyed a capture for Oliver's brigade. As they ascended a small knoll they could see a Confederate flag 40 yards ahead of them, but the crest of the hill shielded each side from seeing the troops of the other. Captain William V. Powell of Company I was in charge of the Hoosier detachment and he took advantage of his unseen position by ordering his men to lie prone and fire a volley as close to ground level as possible. The tactic worked; bullets struck few Southerners, but the volley confused the little major commanding enough to lure him to the hill crest. Captain Powell and his men jumped to their feet and pounced on their prey without firing another shot. They captured more than 100 Texans and the cherished flag of the 17th/18th Texas (the same hard-luck regiment that lost most of a company to one artillery round a day earlier at Bald Hill).

A grudge prevented the Indiana men from being recognized for their exploit. Before he wrote his official report of the battle, Colonel John Oliver had passed around a petition to regimental officers in his brigade in an effort to obtain an impressive list of signatures to seal his bid for promotion to brigadier general. The colonel and lieutenant colonel of the 99th Indiana refused to sign it. Oliver stayed a colonel and may have enacted his revenge on the Indiana men. The official report he submitted omitted any mention of the Hoosier capture; instead Colonel Oliver credited the 15th Michigan—his former and favorite regiment—with the capture of the flags of the Texans and the 5th Confederate Infantry and all the 182 officers and men from those two regiments who surrendered to his brigade.[17]

The Texas brigade lost in excess of 250 men killed, wounded, and captured in the fight against the XV Corps—close to a quarter of the engaged force. The new ranking brigade officer was a lieutenant colonel while company officers were forced to lead each of the regiments as they dropped back into the woods; most of the force was too wounded and disorganized to be a factor for several hours. Harrow's coup was accomplished by two brigades with tremendous artillery support. It not only saved the XV Corps from an unpleasant surprise from behind, it removed a quarter of Cleburne's punch and did so with few recorded casualties.

Nevertheless, the XV Corps was then oriented on two fronts, facing east and south with a nearly equal split of artillery. At the conclusion of that rearward action, the corps lost its commander—not by attrition, but by promotion. The Army of the Tennessee staff officers assured General Sherman by 2:00 P.M. that McPherson was dead. Consequently, Sherman sent verbal orders to be delivered to Major General John A. Logan that, as the ranking corps commander of the army, he was then in charge. Logan turned over his corps to his ranking subordinate, Major General Morgan L. Smith. The loss of an army commander ultimately forced five officers into new and elevated roles: army, corps, division, brigade, and regiment. The new commands and change of position of the XV Corps would increase their vulnerability to a concentrated assault. None of that mattered at that moment to General Logan, who took the news of his commander's death and turned it into a rally cry. "McPherson and Revenge," Logan bellowed in his stentorian voice, trained for a decade to carry to thousands at political events. He also took his former experience as a jockey (racing for his father during his teenaged years) as he galloped at breakneck speed down the line of the XV Corps and veering eastward across the defense of the XVI, yelling out McPherson's name to avenge.[18]

General Cleburne must have sensed the opportunity for victory escaping him. His division had begun their action so well about forty-five minutes earlier. Govan had overtaken the works originally created and held by Hall's Iowans, but a combination of casualties, exhaustion, and confusion had prevented the Arkansas troops from routing Giles Smith's division from their second defense line. The Texas brigade under General

James A. Smith had not only slipped through the gap between the XVI and XVII Corps, a portion of the brigade carried the battle all the way up to the rearward position of the XV Corps, holding the upper midsection of the Army of the Tennessee. Still, part of James A. Smith's brigade stayed with Govan on the left and another part had aligned with Mercer's division and had taken a stab at Fuller's men on the right—both of those attacks had been stymied. The bulk of James A. Smith's command had been equally thwarted by Harrow's Union division in the ravine one mile north of the flanks.

Unlike General Bate and General Walker, Cleburne was able to deploy a battery to soften the position he intended to assault. Captain Thomas J. Key had ascended to command of Hotchkiss's Battalion the day before, taking over for the wounded namesake commander. After being forced back from attempting to turn the captured Illinois guns upon their own troops, Key brought up sections of the batteries of Hotchkiss's Battalion through the woods north of Govan's position and spliced in guns from Captain William B. Turner's Mississippi Battery. He succeeded in disrupting the developing Union defense with several rounds of canister, cutting off 400 Iowans from their new position. (They escaped as soon as Key stopped firing.)

Cleburne stood well behind Govan's brigade where he and General Hardee monitored the progress of his division's offensive. Here, the general would have received Govan's request for reinforcements and he would have fielded J. A. Smith's request as well. Captain Key found him there; proud of his brief artillery barrage, Key haughtily announced, "Generals to the front"—a remark Key noted caused Cleburne to smile. Savvy and experienced with a cool head in the midst of the crash and commotion of battle, Cleburne appears to have recognized the gap that then existed between his two committed brigades, an opening that must be exploited by his third and final brigade. He ordered Lowrey's brigade to break the stalemate in the Union rear.[19]

The Battle of Atlanta had just completed its second hour when the entry of Patrick Cleburne's third and final brigade magnified the character and intensity of the contest. Brigadier General Mark P. Lowrey—a former Baptist minister in Mississippi—entered the fray leading six regiments and a battalion of Alabamans and Mississippians. Lowrey's brigade had fought in each of the past two days at Peachtree Creek and against Bald Hill; his ranks were thinned by ninety losses in the process. The remaining brigade was experienced but tired for they had spent a second sleepless night near Atlanta.[20]

Like the other two brigadiers in Cleburne's division, Lowrey had commanded a brigade throughout that active campaign and had led them well, but the woods south of the attack line proved to be the great neutralizer for him as he was frustrated in attempting to keep a 500-yard interval behind J. A. Smith's brigade before Smith's entered the contest. The constant shifting of the lead brigades as well as the limited view irritated Lowrey to the core. Making matters worse was the mass confusion in one of General Maney's Tennessee brigades behind him. Maney's men broke their instructions to stay 300 yards behind Lowrey and instead they marched through his ranks, costing Lowrey considerable time to reestablish his marching formation. Ordered by General Hardee to move by the left flank to support Govan's attack, General Cleburne rescinded that order just as Lowrey had his brigade in motion toward that direction. Lowrey's final instructions were "to move rapidly to the front and charge the works." Cleburne added that "no time must be lost."[21]

Lowrey had little support from his right for his brigade's assault, but the left flank added Tennesseans from Colonel John C. Carter's brigade of Maney's division. With the added troops, Lowrey's force would mount a formidable assault if he could concentrate his men on a weak or unsuspecting portion of the Union line. Govan's men had overtaken the works of Hall's Iowans on Lowrey's left, but they had not yet been able to reform and apply pressure to the new line of Giles Smith's two brigades then facing eastward and expecting the Arkansans to renew the assault. Lowrey's men passed General James A. Smith's brigade on its right; "which had been repulsed and was reforming" noted Lowrey, an obvious reference to the bloody nose the Texans received by the punch of the XV Corps. At least three of Smith's regiments, the 6th, 10th, and 15th Texas, had reorganized and then supported Lowrey's right, adding a few hundred more soldiers to Lowrey's attack. Other parts of the Texas brigade were sent out as detachments in the woods. Captain Samuel Foster, heading one of those detachments, bore witness to a surreal aspect of combat:

> We started back through the wood, but had not gone more than fifty
> yards before a Yank appeared before us. I ordered him to throw his gun

down. Instead of doing so he cocked his gun, and aimed at me not more than 20 feet away, and in an instant would have fired, but one of my men (Jake Eastman) was too quick for him and shot him down, the ball passing in the lower part of his bowels and out at the small of his back, which dropped him in his tracks. Eastman then went up to the Yank, gave him some water and they made friends, the Yank forgiving him saying, that he had done wrong, in not throwing his gun down when I told him to.[22]

General Cleburne's new wave of assaults—consisting of Lowrey's brigade and a small portion of Smith's brigade and assisted by Tennessee regiments from Carter's brigade in Maney's division—angled westward in the woods close to 2,000 strong. It was thus far the largest assaulting force of the day and they were destined to strike the Union line south of the new XV Corps position and north of Hall's original breastworks.[23]

The Confederates advanced unimpeded through the wooded gap despite Union efforts to close that open door. Minutes before the catastrophe that befell General McPherson, he had ordered a reserve brigade of the XV Corps to hustle down and fill the gap. The brigade was the Missouri men under Colonel Hugo Wangelin. With nearly 1,000 soldiers in his six regiments, Wangelin received his orders close to 2:00 P.M. and headed southward from a reserve point near the railroad. He traversed the ground originally occupied by the right flank of the Texans when they had been thrown back from their attempt to strike the rear of the corps, and their line of march was well east of Lowrey's advance from the opposite direction. Once he reached the gap, Wangelin ordered his regiments to construct breastworks and they spent the next three hours doing just that, not realizing the two close calls they had experienced during their march to fill the gap. General Blair was not pleased at the lack of succor provided to his XVII Corps, complaining that Wangelin's brigade "was so very small . . . that it did not near fill the gap, and the enemy had already, before this brigade had time to assume its position, passed through the interval and attacked the Seventeenth Corps directly in the rear."[24]

Lowrey's men struck the northern sector of the XVII Corps nearly one hour after Govan's Arkansans had initiated Cleburne's attack upon

MAJOR GENERAL PATRICK RONAYNE CLEBURNE, C.S.A.
Hood's most experienced and talented division commander, Cleburne zealously hurled his three brigades against the Union rear throughout the afternoon of July 22, and he followed up with a spirited evening assault. He survived the battle and the Georgia campaign but was killed four months later in Tennessee at the Battle of Franklin. (*Courtesy of MOLLUS-Massachusetts, USAMHI, Carlisle Barracks, Pa.*)

the southern flank of Blair's corps. It certainly wasn't planned that way, and the long interval between the Confederate brigade offensives should have provided ample warning to the Union troops manning the trenches on and surrounding Bald Hill. Those were the two brigades of Mortimer Leggett's division, the same troops that had seized the hill from Cleburne's men the day before. Ironically, those two divisions were facing off in consecutive days but in opposite directions.

General Leggett was not oblivious to what had transpired behind his lines over the past two hours. His division consisted of three brigades, although one of them was only a regiment, and a battalion (about half of a regiment). In all, Leggett had nine infantry regiments from Illinois, Wisconsin, and Ohio—the heart of the Old Northwest Territory—manning earthworks that stretched 600 yards up and over Bald Hill. His men had faced westward throughout the morning, but ever since Hall's brigade was overrun south of him, Leggett realized that he was potentially threatened in three directions: front, flank, and rear. Minutes earlier they had heard the fighting of the Texas brigade against Walcutt's division of the XV Corps northeast of where they stood. Believing they were about to be challenged by the Rebels, an Ohio infantryman confessed, "We felt the situation was awful."[25]

The feeling was justified. Around 2:15 P.M. Cleburne's men announced their approach from the southeast to Bald Hill with "demoniac yells," as Leggett described it. It was the same time that Strahl's brigade was in the final throes of engaging Potts's brigade 400 yards southwest of the knoll and also marked the time that the Texans threatened the hill from the woods directly east of it. Bullets flying from all three directions unnerved the Union defenders. Colonel Bryant of the 12th Wisconsin bellowed, "Get into the works, boys! Get into the works!" When asked which side of the earthen embankment they should occupy, the overexcited commander declared, "I don't care which side, but, *Get into the works!* And do it quick!"[26]

Bryant's superior officer, Brigadier General Manning Force, proved to be a cooler commander during the Confederate convergence upon his exposed brigade—but it must have appeared to one frightened subordinate that Force had committed to a defeatist response to an enemy threat. Force ordered the young officer to get him a flag. Several minutes later when the flag had not been produced, Force sought out the subordinate and discovered him trying to procure white cloth for a surrender flag—a term lacking from Force's vocabulary. Normally devoid of emotion, Force was livid at the misinterpretation of his intent and dressed the young man down. "*Damn* you, sir!" cursed the general, "I don't want a flag of *truce*; I want the American flag!"[27]

General Leggett shared the mindset of General Force. Deciding that the Confederates coming from the eastern directions posed a more imminent threat than did the Tennesseans losing their contest to Potts's brigade, Leggett quickly ordered his regiments to jump over to the western side of their earthworks and turn toward the woods, "their faces to the east and their backs toward Atlanta." The Confederates advanced under cover of the woods and poured into a field less than 100 yards from Leggett's line. Leggett's regiments were aided by one regiment from Hall's routed brigade, the 15th Iowa infantry commanded by Colonel William Belknap, who then anchored the right of Leggett's eastward-facing line. Belknap's men were about to engage in their third fight and third direction in one hour. Fewer than 300 Iowans remained in Belknap's regiment, but the addition of the Iowa regiment brought Leggett's defense to ten regiments—nearly 3,000 infantrymen.[28]

The Confederates rushed toward the Union earthworks, determined to claim the trenches for themselves. Yankee lead tore into Rebel bodies, snapping bones, severing blood vessels, and piercing vital organs. "Their first line was wiped out," declared one of Leggett's men, "but by the time we had sprung to our feet and reloaded, another line had come up." Characteristic of Cleburne's entire division, Lowrey's brigade kept up their assault. They did say "die," but they never said "quit." A living and breathing symbol of the incredible toughness of that brigade was Joel C. Archer of the 16th Alabama. His skull had been fractured in the battle of Chickamauga several months earlier, yet he continued through the subsequent Georgia campaign carrying a piece of his skull as a souvenir.[29]

Leggett's troops required about half a minute to reload but the Alabamans, Mississippians, Texans, and Tennesseans were upon them before they could level their rifles for a second volley. The left of the Confederate attack line careened into the works protecting the 17th Wisconsin and the 15th Iowa Infantry. One of the Iowans noted, "On came the enemy with volleys of musketry and demonic yells." Leading the assault against the Union position was the 45th Alabama of Lowrey's brigade, commanded by Colonel Harris D. Lampley, and the 38th Tennessee of Carter's brigade, led by Lieutenant Colonel Andrew D. Gwynne. Their troops pulsed toward the Iowans and Wisconsin men. Colonel Lampley was particularly conspicuous as he exhorted his Alabamans forward by waving his light felt hat.

Ordered not to shoot until each had marked a specific Confederate, the bluecoats silently waited. They loosed their aimed volley with little time and distance to spare. A Wisconsin soldier described that part of the battlefield as "red hot," but there were no casualties recorded on the

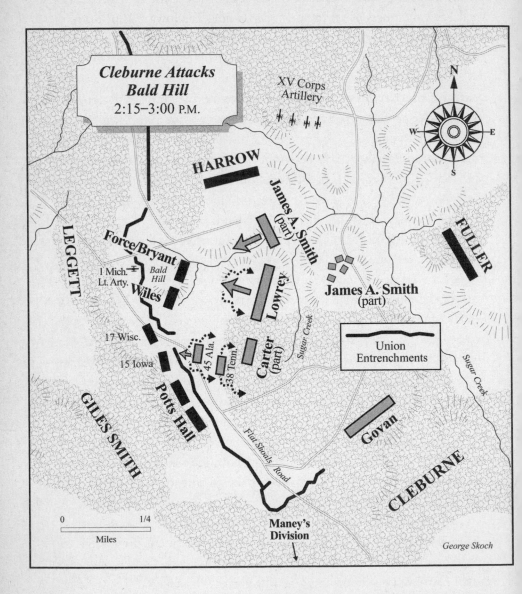

Cleburne Attacks Bald Hill
2:15–3:00 P.M.

N
W E
S

XV Corps Artillery

HARROW

James A. Smith (part)

FULLER

Force/Bryant

1 Mich. Lt. Arty.

Bald Hill

LEGGETT

Wiles

Lowrey

James A. Smith (part)

Sugar Creek

Sugar Creek

17 Wisc.

15 Iowa

45 Ala.

38 Tenn.

Carter (part)

Union Entrenchments

Potts Hall

GILES SMITH

Govan

Flat Shoals Road

CLEBURNE

0   1/4
Miles

Maney's Division

George Skoch

Union side. Scores of Confederates—mostly Alabamans—in that sector were cut down at point-blank range before they reached the earthworks, including three color bearers shot down in rapid succession. Somehow Colonel Lampley reached the eastern base of the Union embankment with a few members of his regiment at his side. The Iowans kept firing at them but had to hold their weapons in outstretched hands at nearly right angles to their bodies in order to fire at their enemy below. Colonel Belknap yelled down for Lampley to surrender, but the request was refused. As Belknap mounted the parapet he could see how irate Lampley was as he turned eastward and cursed his nonexistent command as cowards. Escaping enemy bullets that whizzed by his face and through his beard, Belknap seized the opportunity to capture Lampley while his attention was diverted. The burly Iowan reached down and clenched his hands upon Lampley's coat collar, and—with the help of a nearby corporal—hoisted Lampley up and over the breastwork as a prisoner of war. Belknap berated his opponent for denigrating his troops. "Look at your men!" he pointed out to Lampley as they scanned the carnage, "They are all dead! What are you cursing them for?"[30]

Major George C. Freeman of the same regiment was also captured as was Lieutenant Colonel Gwynne of the 38th Tennessee. Dozens of Alabamans and Tennesseans and their prized flags suffered the same fate. They were the fortunate ones; just as many of their comrades lay dead on the field; even more suffered battle wounds. One of those injured leaned against the east side of the breastwork, afraid to return to his command and refusing to surrender to the Wisconsin men on the other side of the works. Edward Riley, a private in Company F of the 17th Wisconsin, made the final decision for the vacillating Confederate. Riley borrowed a rope from the regimental cook, lassoed the wounded man, and hauled him in.[31]

Cleburne's assault was more menacing north of that sector, the region surrounding and including Bald Hill. Leggett's two-brigade defense would be sorely tested over the next two hours by nearly 2,000 Confederates of Carter's, Lowrey's, and James A. Smith's brigades. The Tennesseans of Colonel John C. Carter's brigade had apparently intermingled with Lowrey's command, explaining how the 38th Tennessee suffered side by side with the 45th Alabama. To counter, Leggett had the services of nine regiments from Ohio, Illinois, and Wisconsin. They still had skirmishers fanned out westward, between the earthworks and Atlanta. Those skirmishers then protected the backs of their brigade against what could be a devastating assault from the opposite direction. Fortunately for Leggett's division, that since the repulse of Strahl's Tennessee brigade by Giles Smith's men fifteen minutes earlier, no new Confederate assaults had been generated from the west side of the Union-occupied works.

Still, Leggett and his men felt no relief over that fact, for that threat would remain with them for the remainder of the day. Never before had those veterans had to look over their shoulders while battling in the opposite direction, and never before was the battle in which they were engaged as intense and deadly as the fight for Bald Hill on July 22, 1864. Here, 4,000 soldiers Blue and Gray waged war for the possession of the prominent knob and the ground surrounding it. Should Cleburne's men steal the hill away from Leggett, the new toehold would not only signify the loss of half of the Union defensive line, but also serve as the fulcrum from which to plant batteries and roll up the remainder of the Army of the Tennessee—including the isolated XVI Corps east of the hill and the XV Corps north of it. That accomplished, a Confederate-controlled battlefield thus threatened the Army of the Ohio and the Army of the Cumberland at the same time. Both sides realized the importance of that hill the day before and shed buckets of blood to own it. More blanched bodies were destined to be sacrificed the second go around.

Leggett's single greatest advantage to hold the position was the skill and experience of his prized brigadier, Manning Force—the pale and impassive general who took the hill from Hood early on July 21. Leggett counted on Force to govern a stalwart defense under pressure not witnessed in previous campaigns in Missouri, Mississippi, and Tennessee. Based on the flag incident at the opening fire upon Bald Hill (when Force berated a subordinate for considering surrender), all indications were that General Force was ready to battle. He sent his adjutant, Captain James B. Walker, to the rear to deliver an order, but the officer had only gone about 20 yards when he dropped to the ground with a gunshot wound to the thigh. General Force immediately rushed to Walker's side and attempted to help him up when he was also struck by enemy lead. The bullet passed sideways through Force's mouth, entering just below the eye through the left cheek and exiting at the same point through the right, carrying away a portion of his upper jaw in the process of its de-

BRIGADIER GENERAL MANNING FERGUSON FORCE, U.S.A.

Leggett's most reliable brigade commander, Force was wounded in the face defending Leggett's Hill on July 22, 1864. He recovered from the grievous wound and was awarded the Congressional Medal of Honor in 1892 for his performance in the battle. *(Courtesy of MOLLUS-Massachusetts, USAMHI, Carlisle Barracks, Pa.)*

structive path. Writhing in pain, General Force was quickly tended to. He would survive, surprisingly without any loss of speech or sight, but he was out of the fight.[32]

Under those dire circumstances, the excitable Colonel Bryant inherited Force's brigade and immediately assumed command. The other brigade of Leggett's division was also robbed of its commander: Colonel Robert Scott had been captured near where General McPherson was killed, leaving his brigade headless during the opening assaults. Lieutenant Colonel Greenberry F. Wiles, the ranking officer of the 78th Ohio Infantry, eventually led the brigade that day after it was determined that the missing Colonel Scott was indeed captured. Wiles had his regiment and the 20th Ohio Infantry immediately under his control and welcomed the third regiment, the 68th Ohio, which had returned from detached service just as the brigade reversed its formation to face Cleburne's storm.

Also reversed and ready to assist the Union infantry were two batteries of artillery from the XVII Corps. Ensconced on Bald Hill were four howitzers of Battery D, 1st Illinois Light Artillery—guns created to fire twenty-four-pound rounds of death. Edgar H. Cooper, known as "the boy captain," commanded those artillery pieces. One hundred yards south of the hill, on a less prominent elevation, stood Captain Marcus D. Elliott of Battery H, 1st Michigan Light Artillery. That was the "Black Horse Battery," identified by the jet-black horses that pulled the black steel guns. Elliott had 4 of his 6 rifled Rodmans with him. One section of his battery and an Ohio battery were farther south on the XVII Corps line, the portion overrun by Govan's Arkansans an hour earlier. One of those 6 guns was captured and the rest were scattered in the confusion of the opening attack. Although only 8 of the original 14 guns remained in line, they were pointed toward the woods east of them and separated only by a twenty-acre field.[33]

Conspicuously absent from the Union defense on Bald Hill was General Blair, the corps commander, who was not seen on the contested mound during the afternoon of July 22. After visiting General Dodge at the XVI Corps position, Blair returned to his headquarters several hundred yards northeast of the height and communicated with General Leggett through signal officers. Blair's traditional style was unlike the other top commanders of the army, Generals McPherson, Logan, and Dodge, who prided themselves on their visibility to their men. Blair's behind-the-scenes leadership was opposite to the ostentatious displays of his peers at corps command; it also fostered rumors about where he was and what he was doing during the Battle of Atlanta. A Wisconsin soldier in the XVII Corps revealed, "It was a common remark that we never saw General Blair when the bullets were flying." Soon after the battle, unsupported accusations circulated in Washington about Blair's conduct on the battlefield. Senator Henry Wilson sent that rumor to the Executive Mansion, writing Abraham Lincoln about how "the drunkenness and incapacity of Frank Blair" hampered the army during the battle, going on to make the preposterous claim that "McPheirson [sic] lost his life on account of [Blair's] blundering." Blair had no idea that his muted inspirational abilities and willingness to delegate authority to Walter Gresham, Giles Smith, and Mortimer Leggett would severely wound his reputation. "The fact that the Third and Fourth Divisions of the Seventeenth Corps had such gallant and popular commanders as Generals Leggett and Gresham, compensated largely for the lack of confidence in the corps commander," surmised a soldier in Blair's ranks.[34]

Cleburne's assault easily diverted the Bald Hill defenders from seeking out the presence of their corps commander. Hand-to-hand combat was a relative rarity on Civil War battlefields; opposing lines were slaughtered by rifled weapons hundreds of yards from that type of contact. On July 22 the wooded camouflage concealed Cleburne's attackers until hand-to-hand contact became eventually inevitable. "We were in an open field . . . lying flat on the ground, when the Johnnies came up with their accustomed yell," declared W. S. Ayres of the 78th Ohio. "Their first line was wiped out, but by the time we had sprung to our feet and reload another line had come up. We waited until they got within twenty yards of us before we opened fire; and when we did, such slaughter I never saw before or since." According to a Wisconsin soldier, "we let them have it right in the bread-baskets." The Union men wiped out the first line of Confederate attackers, including a third of the 32nd Mississippi, which succumbed to a hailstorm of leaden bullets and artillery iron. The Confederate second line fared little better as it was cut down by another unified volley. "It seemed as if no man of all the host who were attacking us could escape alive," declared an artillerist about the Southern attackers, "and yet, still yelling, they persisted in their desperate undertaking."[35]

The Yankee infantry and artillery did not have twenty to thirty seconds to reload for a third fusillade, for Lowrey's third line reached the eastern side of the earthworks and found additional protection from a line of trenches dug on their side of the earthen walls (that was the intended Union side earlier in the afternoon). The western side provided only meager protection for Leggett's men. Taking advantage of the moat, the Confederates crawled undetected along the trench line and within 10 yards of their enemy. Lieutenant E. E. Nutt of the 20th Ohio later surmised, "Many of them were directly opposite us, keeping down to load, then they would rise and fire in our faces, and receive a charge in exchange." But those point-blank exchanges were brief ones. The opposing forces were so close that they considered it a waste of time to do the requisite multiple steps to load and fire a rifle when the opponent was less than 20 feet away.

At that point the soldiers' romanticized vision of exchanging infantry volleys while standing in well-dressed lines gave way to a rudimentary gang fight. "We fixed bayonets," recounted an Ohioan, "and then and there we had it with clubbed muskets, fisticuffs, and wrestling." Swarms of soldiers attempted to pull their opponents across the breastworks, much like Colonel Belknap had done with Colonel Lampley. Appearing as angry as they were desperate, the Mississippians, Alabamans, and Texans mobbed the blue-coated defenders of Bald Hill. The brawl intensified around the color bearers of the opposing regiments. Two of the flag-carrying members of the 32nd Mississippi were cut down seconds from each other; 2 men of the 5th Mississippi met the same fate carrying the colors of their regiment. Another Confederate flag bearer rushed up to the Union earthworks and stuck his regiment's colors into the ground as a beacon to rally his regiment around it. As the Southerners coalesced around that planted flag, Captain John Orr of the 20th Ohio led a few men from his company over the wall, cutting down several Rebels with his sword and annihilating the enemy's attempt to get a foothold on the hill. Within minutes the Rebels in front of the Ohioans receded back to the base of the hill while Captain Orr escorted about fifty of them as prisoners of war. Neither Orr nor his sword were done for the day.[36]

Undoubtedly the most conspicuous flag bearer on the field was Henry McDonald of the 30th Illinois, a big burly man whose size alone attracted enemy guns and fists. The giant held the flag of his regiment in his left hand and on his right side he wielded a carbine, a short-barreled cavalry rifle that was captured close to the same spot the previous day. One of Lowrey's men seized McDonald's left arm to capture his flag but was oblivious to the weapon the Yankee held to keep possession of it. The Rebel was destroyed by a gunshot traveling the shortest distance to its mark that day.[37]

The opposing infantry totaled nearly 2,000 men per side on and surrounding Bald Hill. That placed Leggett's men at a substantial advantage over Cleburne, but no one told the Confederates that the odds were stacked against them. Gunpowder smoke from rifles and cannons formed a sulfurous fog that enveloped the participants and cut their view so severely that an infantryman complained that "we could not distinguish friend from foe five feet off." One of the Illinois artillerists claimed, "Only as the breath of a passing breeze blew the smoke away could the movements of the enemy be discerned clearly; but his unearthly yell could be heard above the sound of muskets and cannon." The smoke enabled some soldiers to liberate captured comrades and others to club or bayonet their enemy once they were sure they were striking someone who hailed from the other side of the Mason Dixon line.[38]

Confusion reigned on Bald Hill at 3:00 P.M. when artillery rounds rained over the contestants. The Union defenders quickly discerned that the menacing rounds emanated from the direction of Atlanta. That confirmed their worst fear—attack from two directions. An Illinois soldier vividly recalled that "the two lines were so close together the cannon balls went into the Confederate lines, killing their own men. They would dodge from these balls and the boys would holler at them not to dodge, that it was their own guns."

Lowrey's men really weren't dodging at that point, however, they had begun to give up the fight, for the casualties had swayed the momentum considerably. Colonel John C. Wilkinson of the 8th Mississippi was killed near the works along with eight other commissioned officers of the brigade. At least three dozen other officers in the brigade were wounded and ten were missing. Those losses would normally paralyze an attacking force, but the gang-style fighting at the trench line ironically overshadowed the dearth of leadership. The mounting casualties in the ranks were even more telling. Too many Confederates were cut down to sustain the fight. In less than an hour, Lowrey lost more than 500 gun-toting soldiers—over 40 percent of his engaged command. Union casualties were significant but proportionately less, perhaps half of the Southerners in that sector of the battlefield.[39]

General Lowrey witnessed their efforts in what was growing more apparent as a forlorn hope. "I never saw a greater display of gallantry," he stated with pride, but with the collapse of his left flank and the tenacious defense of Leggett's men on and surrounding the treeless knoll, Lowrey realized he could not capture and hold the ground without more men entering the fray. As the time passed 3:00 P.M., Lowrey's attack, including his flank supports from the Texans on his right and Tennesseans on his left, dipped below 1,500 officers and men. He was then appreciably outnumbered by at least 400 Union soldiers and 8 perilous artillery pieces. Rubbing salt in the Confederates' wound was the fact that they attacked with no artillery support behind them—their guns could not deploy in the woods—and were forced to absorb friendly-fire casualties from Confederate batteries firing from the west. Minutes after 3:00 P.M. Lowrey sent orders for his mauled brigade to disengage, cross back over the creek, and return to the shelter of the woods east of Bald Hill.

Lowrey had no idea at that time that over 3,000 Confederate troops stood within supporting distance of his brigade in and near the wooded gap separating the two Union corps. At least 500 Texans mingled behind Lowrey's right with no inclination to help the 200 or so members of the engaged portion of their brigade after the loss of their commander and the luckless bout with Harrow's division of the XV Corps just an hour before. The same could be said for the 700 members of Govan's brigade off to Lowrey's left. Those Arkansans were spent after the grand success they achieved ninety minutes earlier. Together, the Arkansans and Texans had apparently spilled too much blood and dripped too much sweat to be expected to effectively attack again so soon.

More puzzling was the absence of support of the Tennesseans from Carter's brigade of Maney's division. With the exception of the 38th Tennessee, which engaged side by side with the 45th Alabama on Lowrey's left, the regiments of that brigade provided minimal reinforcements for Lowrey. (Captain Key, the artillery commander, complained that he urged that brigade to charge "but it was impossible to get them forward.")[40] Farther back was Walker's brigade of Tennesseans, up to 1,500 soldiers marching to and fro but not entering the fray. Had either of those two Tennessee brigades been fully committed to the attack, Lowrey's assault would have approached 3,500 men, a force 70 percent larger than what was actually deployed. Those brigades fought in different divisions and it would take considerable time for General Maney, General Cleburne, and General Hardee to organize them for another assault upon Bald Hill.

Unlike the horrors suffered by the Orphan Brigade during their retreat from the XVI Corps, Lowrey's regiments were able to return to cross the open twenty-acre field and return to the woods with relative ease. The Confederate cannon fire from the Atlanta side of Bald Hill made that possible, for it commanded the universal attention of Leggett's division. It also provided an opening for wounded Confederates to escape capture. A. G. Anderson of the 7th Texas of General James A. Smith's brigade was shot in the shoulder in front of the breastworks on Bald Hill just when the retreat was ordered. "I crawled as fast as I could, but began to get blind from the loss of blood," he recalled. He reached the edge of the woods and plunged into a pond—right near his wounded brigadier, General J. A. Smith. It was a fortuitous moment for Anderson, who was hoisted upon Smith's horse and carried rearward to a field hospital.[41]

Rather than harass Cleburne's retreating soldiers, Leggett's brigades and batteries reacted to the western threat by reversing their front. For the third time in an hour, they crossed over their works to face westward in the direction of Atlanta. More specifically, the 4 Napoleons of Captain Ruel W. Anderson's Georgia Battery had been launching its twelve-pound rounds from the smoothbore barrels of its bronze cannons 400 yards from Leggett's batteries. The Union guns responded swiftly and effectively. According to Captain Elliott of the Black Horse Artillery "it took only about fifteen minutes to clear them out." Perhaps so, but surrounding and supporting the Georgia guns was an entire division of Georgia militia, twelve regiments organized into four brigades and commanded by Major General Gustavus W. Smith.

General G. W. Smith took his orders directly from General Hood, but on that afternoon he decided to advance without waiting for orders from Hood or either of the corps commanders. G. W. Smith reported his belief that Anderson's guns had silenced Leggett's batteries in ten minutes. Regardless of who neutralized who, the fact was the artillery had ceased and G. W. Smith advanced close enough to see Leggett's men on and around Bald Hill who showed themselves by lifting their heads above the breastworks. Smith could see how eager his men were to attack the hill, but he also knew how raw those troops were and had been in enough battles over the past three years to appreciate the strong position.[42]

Between 3:00 and 3:15 P.M. on July 22 marked the first point in three hours where there was a distinct lull that had overtaken the battlefield. At the cost of 3,000 Confederate casualties, General Hardee's attack, after a fruitless start on the left rear of the Union army, had pushed in the Federal left, captured 9 cannons, beheaded the enemy army, and captured, killed, and wounded over 2,000 Yankees, still, the core of the Union left had held firm. Five thousand American soldiers were out of the contest in three hours—an average of a Yankee or Rebel casualty every other second of the fight.

No one believed the three-hour battle was over; but at the same time, no one ever revealed their belief in the sobering fact that the halfway point of that contest had yet to be reached.

8

BLOODY DIVERSION

s General Cleburne's assault of Bald Hill waned to near silence, the
ambulance wagon bearing the body of General McPherson rolled 2
miles north of Bald Hill to General Sherman's headquarters at the
Howard house, the home of Augustus Hurt. Sherman ordered the escorts
to carry the body inside as aides yanked a door free from its hinges and set
it down to serve as a temporary bier for the dead general. "He was dressed
just as he left me," noted Sherman, who studied the path of the fatal bullet
with the help of an army doctor. Sherman was crushed by the death of his
protégé, but he took no time to reflect upon what could have been. Logan
had commanded the army for about an hour and by the dissipating
battle sounds south of him, Sherman must have been relieved that Hood's
three-hour offensive had failed to turn the flank of the Army of the Tennessee. Still, as 3:00 P.M. came and went, Sherman's experience—and the
warnings of Hood's tenacity that were previously supplied by Schofield
and McPherson—would have told him that the battle was not yet over.[1]

At his headquarters near the city cemetery a mile east of Atlanta,
General Hood had stewed for hours over the lack of progress of Hardee's
corps against the Union left. Notwithstanding his decision to change
Hardee's intended march to Decatur and shorten it to an attack upon the
rear of the southern flank of the enemy, Hood never appeared comfortable with that very necessary adjustment. He had spent an entire restless
morning listening for the sound of battle that was supposed to commence at daybreak.

The long anticipated rolling sound of battle hit Hood's ears close to noon. He listened to the attacks from south to north against the XVII Corps and soon learned that Maney's division was not in the rear of an unsuspecting opponent as his plan suggested, but apparently attacking the entrenched flank. (He either personally observed or received an aide's report of Strahl's brigade pressing northeastward toward Bald Hill.) Hood was disgusted at that discovery, for in his eyes it completely up-ended his battle plan to throw Sherman into chaos and send him reeling toward Peachtree Creek. Still, Hood had no way of knowing at that time that the XVI Corps posed an incredible roadblock in the rear or that Cleburne's division had actually struck the enemy from the rear as he had intended it to. The fact that a portion of Maney's division was attacking northeastward actually increased the chaos and stress upon the Union left flank, another point that Hood had yet to appreciate.

So, at 3:00 P.M. Hood had to accept the stark reality that McPherson's army (he had yet to learn of that general's demise) had been struck hard but had refused to leave the field. Making matters worse was the inevitability that Union reinforcements would head toward the contested flank to buttress the Yankee defense. That not only guaranteed more casualties in Hardee's corps, it could separate Hardee from the rest of Hood's army, and it also risked the continuation of apparent Union plans to extend southward from the eastern locale and take over the Macon Railroad, the iron lifeline running into Atlanta from the south. Hood never admitted that his grandest of wishes—the roll-up and retreat of all Union forces threatening Atlanta—had all but completely disintegrated. Nevertheless, Hood still hoped for the destruction of the Army of the Tennessee. It was still possible, but a new plan had to be devised.

Hood issued orders to be delivered to General Cheatham, commander of Hood's old corps, orders that stopped Cheatham from "take up the movement" and fueling a rout that was supposed to be created by Hardee and Wheeler. There was no rout to fuel. Instead, Hood then saw Cheatham's corps as a diversionary force to hold the XV Corps in place to prevent them, and perhaps Schofield's Army of the Ohio north of them, from reinforcing the XVII Corps on the Union left. Hood ordered Cheatham to move forward with his corps, and attack the position in his front.[2]

Benjamin Franklin Cheatham was not a brilliant general, but his history as a division commander in the Army of Tennessee was virtually unparalleled. Although not a West Pointer, he earned command of Hood's corps not only because he was the senior division commander in the Army of Tennessee, but also because he was the most experienced one, even more so than General Cleburne. Cheatham's reputation as a hard fighter was nearly matched by rumors that he was just as hard a drinker, although he appears to have abstained from the habit during the course of battles. Nashville born and raised, that forty-three-year-old former farmer and Mexican War veteran was synonymous with Tennessee and was the idol of his all-Tennessee division throughout 1862, 1863, and the Atlanta campaign of 1864. The only oddity of elevating Cheatham to lead a corps three days before the battle of Atlanta was that only one Tennessee brigade existed in the three divisions he took over.

By the midafternoon of Friday, Cheatham had the freshest and largest Confederate corps at Atlanta. Fourteen thousand officers and men occupied his twelve brigades—troops not engaged two days earlier at Peachtree Creek, not fatigued by an overnight march, and not consumed as casualties in a monstrous battle entering its fourth hour. Hood apparently liked them where they were. They were in position to fuel a rout expected by the surge of Hardee's and Wheeler's men against the flank and rear of the Army of the Tennessee, but at the same time they were available at a moment's notice to shift westward and link up with the right flank of General Alexander P. Stewart's corps and thus double the defensive manpower in Atlanta's northern environs should General Thomas threaten that sector with his Army of the Cumberland. Hood had attacked Thomas's army with two corps two days earlier; he must have believed he could defend with two corps should the reverse occur.

Should Cheatham's entire corps attack if the intention was to create a diversion? Perhaps Hood left that to Cheatham's discretion. With less than five hours of daylight remaining on July 22, Hood must have been less concerned about Thomas attacking Stewart's corps that day. Yet that possibility still existed. Most important was the outcome of the battle east of Atlanta. Hood might not achieve the rout he had planned for, but the successes reported to him would have convinced him that he was on the verge of a victory nonetheless.

The most puzzling aspect of Hood's generalship was keeping Cheatham's corps out of the primary action for two consecutive battles, particularly since those were the men that Hood had led for four months. Hood later attributed the decision to Cheatham's inexperience as a corps commander, but given Cheatham's experience and solid reputation as a division chief, there appears to be a more satisfying reason for holding his former corps from action that long. That corps had not succeeded in offensive action two distinct times during the campaign when Hood had led them. At Resaca on May 14–15 and six weeks later at the Battle of Kolb's Farm, the corps had failed to carry an enemy line when it attacked under Hood's leadership. Their failure rested with Hood, whose reputation for punishing attacks had been gained with a brigade, a division, and a corps (the latter at Chickamauga), consisting of troops he had led from the Army of Northern Virginia—Lee's army. Hood's success as a corps commander during the Atlanta campaign had only been achieved on the defensive, most notably at the Battle of New Hope Church on May 25. Perhaps Hood's lack of faith in the ability of the divisions and brigades of that corps to attack and carry a position convinced him to use Cheatham in a more passive role, first to "take up the movement," and then to "create a diversion."[3]

Cheatham received his orders and issued directives for each of his divisions. Cheatham was not hampered by the clamp that a diversionary attack would normally place on the assaulting force. Cheatham planned to engage all of his divisions and nearly every brigade of each division. Cheatham was going to treat his mission as a full-scale assault to destroy the opponent in front of him, not as a diversionary attack with the primary goal to hold them in place. To maximize the killing potential of the attack, Cheatham prepared an *en echelon* assault from south to north, each division advancing fifteen minutes after the one to its right. As it turns out, that tactic would have been the preferred one if Cheatham was following Hood's initial plan to push the Union army northward as it was routed by Hardee's rear and flank strike.

Cheatham's southernmost division would battle first. That force was the four brigades of Tennesseans, Georgians, Alabamans, North Carolinians, and Virginians commanded by Major General Carter L. Stevenson. They were the only one of Cheatham's three divisions deployed and prepared to advance and attack at 3:30 P.M. Stevenson had 4,500 Confederates at his disposal. His division occupied ground near the midpoint between Atlanta and the Union works. Facing east with his right flank in line with Bald Hill and his left extending across a front to face off against the right of General William Harrow's division of the XV Corps, Stevenson appears to have begun his advance with two brigades in the frontlines and the other two in reserve behind them. At 3:30 P.M. he began to engage the bluecoats in rifle fire.

The first recipients of Stevenson's bullets were the most harried soldiers on the field. Manning Force's brigade had been led by Colonel Bryant of the 12th Wisconsin after General Force was escorted northward with the ugly facial wound received earlier that afternoon. Bryant's brigade should have been warned about a western threat to their position twenty minutes earlier when the Black Horse Battery 100 yards down the line had engaged and silenced the Georgia battery commanded by Captain Anderson. The Buckeyes and Badgers on and north of Bald Hill would relish in postwar claims of reversing directions several times during the battle to fend off simultaneous attacks from the east and west. A member of the 20th Ohio likened the position-changing infantry to "a long line of these toy monkeys you see which jump over the end of a stick." Jump over the other side of the works they certainly did, but at that point in the battle it was completed after an eerie lull lasting nearly twenty minutes and at a time when Cleburne was no longer posing a serious threat from the woods draping east and southeast of Bald Hill.[4]

The threat to the Union position then emanated west of Bald Hill in the form of Brigadier General Alexander W. Reynolds's brigade of four regiments (two from Virginia and two from North Carolina), the only brigade carrying regiments from those two states in Hood's entire army. That appeared to be the only distinction those men would carry that day. Reynolds's men, about 1,200 strong, halfheartedly fought Bryant's defenders, giving up the contest after taking fewer than thirty members killed or wounded. Surprisingly, the brigade abandoned more men behind as healthy prisoners in Union hands than those who had suffered battle wounds in that short-lived bout.[5]

Support for the Confederates stood in position to the right and rear of Reynolds's brigade. That was the Georgia militia, four brigades commanded by Major General Gustavus W. Smith. The militia had been called out a few weeks earlier by Governor Joseph Brown—earning them the nickname "Joe Brown's Pets." G. W. Smith claimed a force of "2,000 muskets" (about 2,200 officers and men). Protecting Anderson's Battery in its 3:00 P.M. exchange with the Union guns south of Bald Hill, Smith's militia was antsy to attack the Yankees 400 yards east of them. G. W. Smith—who was under orders from General Hood directly—considered what his eager men wanted, especially with the protection of Stevenson's division guiding him on his left (northern) flank. Reynolds's retreat, followed by Stevenson's shift farther northward, left the Georgians in a dangerous spot without protection on either flank. "I considered it useless to make an isolated attack," Smith wisely concluded, as he continued to hold his position on fairly open ground. Over the next two hours he would lose 50 militiamen as casualties in that exposed position, neither charging nor retreating the entire time.[6]

The hasty abandonment by Reynolds's brigade and the stagnant position of Smith's militia removed any threat to the XVII Corps from the west for the rest of the afternoon (although those soldiers did not know that at the time). Stevenson's division was still in the fight; however, his left flank represented his new battle front. The second brigade of attackers, Brigadier General Alfred Cumming's five Georgia regiments, surged forward nearly simultaneously with Reynolds's brigade. Those Southerners struck north of Bald Hill against a line of breastworks defended by Harrow's division of the XV Corps. General Harrow described the assault as "vigorous," but it wasn't nearly enough. Twelve hundred Confederates attempted to take the earthworks supposed to be manned by Walcutt's and Oliver's brigades, but Walcutt's men were not there; they were still in the rear of the line oriented southward. Only three regiments from Oliver's brigade covered a line of entrenchments designed for treble their numbers. The 70th Ohio met the approach head on, Major William Brown reporting "the firing was very heavy along the entire line." Another Ohioan witnessed one of the Georgia color bearers plant the flag just a few feet from the Union line, "but it required only one well-directed volley from our guns to move them back with greater speed than when they came forward." After absorbing 40 casualties in his ranks while inflicting very few as he probed the Union position, General Cumming retired his brigade from the contest.[7]

The Union position was weak; less than a handful of regiments oriented in the direction of Stevenson's attack (the rest of Harrow's division was in the rear facing southward into the wooded gap between the XVI and XVII Corps). The thin segment of the XV Corps line north of Bald

Hill was inviting a breech, but Stevenson's attacking formation prevented the Confederates from exploiting the weak Union position. He advanced with two brigades in front and two behind. The result appeared as a half-hearted assault. Had Stevenson thrown in a third brigade in to the left (north) to attack with the other two, the sheer size and numbers of ten regiments of 3,000 Confederates would have been unstoppable for the skeleton force manning the works in front of them—just five total regiments in Harrow's entire division faced in their direction with absolutely no artillery support. Instead, Stevenson's attack petered out and the division commander seemed content to hold his position rather than commit any more to that assault.[8]

Stevenson's stagnancy masked a weakness in the XV Corps defense and it was a big opportunity lost for General Hood. Stevenson proved true to form as a mediocre offensive tactician, for it was his third straight battle in which he was unable to meet the corps objective on the attack. Stevenson failed to take advantage of an exploitable Union position at Resaca on May 14 and at Kolb's farm on June 22. The inability to muscle through the XV Corps line north of Bald Hill on July 22 was his most egregious of the three, and a huge source of relief for General Harrow on the other side of the line. If Stevenson fielded a report of the action, it has never come to light. It can be said that he followed to the letter of the order an assault plan that was designed to create a diversion. Yet, none of the other division commanders in Cheatham's corps would be that passive.[9]

It was nearly 3:30 P.M. when the second division of Cheatham's corps initiated its march to enter the fight. Brigadier General John C. Brown held the helm of that division, and while he could claim that he was more experienced with his command than his corps commander, the sobering fact was that Brown had been in charge of those 5,000 men for twelve days—just one week longer than Cheatham had with his corps. Like Cheatham, Brown was not a "homegrown" product with that force. He transferred from brigade command in Stevenson's division after a severe eye injury took out the division's original commander, Major General Thomas C. Hindman. That transfer was an unusual move considering that Brown held the same rank as Arthur M. Manigault, who was compelled to maintain command of his brigade and take his orders from a fellow brigadier general who outranked him by eight months from the date of his commission, but one who knew next to nothing about the same troops Manigault had known since the division was formed.

Brown appeared to never attract bitterness or criticism from his new command and even Manigault probably preferred to answer to Brown rather than the irascible Hindman, whose departure Manigault maintained was ironic, for Hindman had been "anxious to get away, and everybody else equally so to get rid of him." General Brown also had a positive reputation across Hood's army as an experienced, fearless, and talented leader. He had gallantly led troops at Perryville and Chickamauga, two iconic battles where he sustained wounds. He was also cited for his bravery at Missionary Ridge and Dalton, two contests where the Army of Tennessee was forced to leave the field. Brown's promotion to major general appeared inevitable. He was imbued since his teenaged years with the prime ingredient necessary for success on the battlefield. As a seventeen-year-old back in 1844, Brown was in the audience when former President Andrew Jackson spoke of successful land acquisition in the Southwest and beckoned likewise for expansion of the country northwestward by declaring, "Now for Oregon and Fifty-four-forty!" Upon hearing "Old Hickory" refer to the latitude making the news that year, Brown yelled back to Jackson, "Or fight!" The two-word rejoinder completed a popular slogan that year; it also highlighted young Brown's mantra that he maintained thirty years later.[10]

Unlike his former superior, General Stevenson on his right, Brown intended to commit his entire division to the fight. He ordered them out of the trenches and sent them eastward shortly before 3:30 P.M. The Georgia Railroad split the advance down the center and served as a guide for the flanking regiments of Brown's four brigades. Manigault's brigade of Alabamans and South Carolinians was north of the railroad, while Colonel John C. Coltart's Alabama brigade was south of it. The two forces moved out in unison with each flank guiding twenty paces from the railroad. Colonel Samuel Benton's brigade of Mississippi solders advanced behind Coltart's men, and Colonel Jacob H. Sharp's Mississippi regiments paced themselves behind Manigault. One mile separated the two jagged lines of earthworks between the two main bodies of troops.[11]

Opposing the advance of Brown's division were two lines of human obstacles. A skirmish line of Illinois and Ohio troops confronted the Confederates 500 yards into their advance. Manigault's and Coltart's men swept them away seemingly in seconds, but 400 yards later a more significant blocking force, two regiments of infantry and a section of Illinois artillery, ensconced themselves behind a rudimentary earthen line on a rise of ground. The 2 cannons had been particularly troublesome for Manigault's men; one South Carolina officer complained that they "gave us a lively shelling" even before the movement commenced. Cheatham, in overall command of the corps, responded with his own batteries, which rolled in behind the advancing lines of infantry, firing over their heads toward the Union pickets and beyond.

Colonel Wells S. Jones of the 53rd Ohio commanded the two lines of Union skirmishers, a responsibility Jones found out he was overqualified for because a half an hour earlier he received word that he had inherited the 2nd Brigade of the 2nd Division of the XV Corps to which his regiment belonged. Jones had placed his second line of troops on the elevation late in the morning to support the skirmish line, which had disintegrated in front of him. As an awesome enemy force marched directly toward him, Jones ordered off the artillery and it rolled swiftly to the rear, pulled by galloping horses. The Union infantry line was uprooted from the primitive works and followed the cannons eastward, but Jones apparently had kept them there too long as Manigault claimed to have captured scores of surrounded soldiers. Regardless, Jones quickly returned his men to the main XV Corps line where he could assume command of his entire brigade for the first time.[12]

When he reached his new command half a mile farther at 3:30 P.M. Jones quickly formed them for the inevitable assault, one that all the XV Corps troops on both sides of the rail line could see. The two leading Confederate brigades of Brown's division happened to be heading toward a stripped and relatively isolated infantry line. The strength was north of the railroad where Jones had six regiments positioned to meet the threat. They covered the works directly west of the redbrick dwelling of George M. Troup Hurt, a Georgia soldier and cotton plantation owner of Columbus, Georgia. Hurt had not yet finished that two-story structure that he had intended to use as a summer home, ostensibly locating it to be within hailing distance of his brother, whose mansion on the hill half a mile north of that house was currently used as General Sherman's headquarters. The brick house faced south where the Georgia Railroad ran 250 yards in front of it. About 50 yards west of there the railroad and road to Decatur ran through a distinctive cut, one accentuated to 15 feet deep and 20 feet across by the construction of the earthworks. The railroad and road separated on each side of the cut, running perpendicular to the earthworks.[13]

Swampy ground isolated Jones's brigade from their northernmost support—the 1st Division of the XV Corps commanded by Brigadier General Charles R. Woods. After he sent off Colonel Hugo Wangelin's brigade to help fill in the gap between the XVI and XVII Corps, Woods's remaining two brigades numbered 2,000 infantry officers and men in seven regiments, a force slightly larger than the number of soldiers in Jones's six regiments. Between the left of Woods's position and the right of Jones's brigade was a swampy creek valley 250 yards across. No troops manned that area due to the constrictive nature of the marshy ravine. That meant that Jones's brigade would operate without reserves and without infantry support on its vulnerable flank.[14]

The weakest part of the Union infantry defense, however, was the entire stretch of works from the railroad cut southward for over half a mile. Only three regiments of one brigade remained to man that region with infantry. Ninety minutes earlier, half of that brigade and its commander, Colonel James S. Martin, had been sent southward to reinforce General Harrow's repulse of General James A. Smith's brigade of Texans from Cleburne's division. They had not returned by 3:30 P.M., leaving Lieutenant Colonel Samuel R. Mott in charge of that paltry force of less than 1,000 men to stretch over 1,000 yards of ground. It meant no reserve line for the entire 2nd Division, the force of 2,500 men that stood directly in the way of a division that had around 5,000 men approaching them.

Unknown to General Brown was that his assaulting division held a nearly two-to-one advantage in infantry strength and the opportunity to exploit an isolated force without reserves. The other advantage unknown to General Brown was how raw the key leaders of the opposing division were. The new Union division commander (Brigadier General Joseph A. J. Lightburn), both brigade commanders (Wells Jones and Samuel Mott) and one quarter of the infantry commanders had just been promoted to those positions over the past hour and a half. The most important advantage for General Brown was also something that he could not yet appreciate—half of the Union artillery that buttressed the Union

A PHOTOGRAPH OF THE CONFEDERATE EARTHWORKS
AT THE GEORGIA RAILROAD.

From this position, General Hood's diversionary assault was launched with two divisions of Major General Benjamin Franklin Cheatham's Corps in the mid-afternoon of July 22. The tremendous action waged one mile east of this position (to the left of the picture) inspired the famous cyclorama of the battlefield. *(Courtesy of MOLLUS-Massachusetts, USAMHI, Carlisle Barracks, Pa.)*

position around the railroad at 2:00 P.M. was no longer opposing him at 3:30 P.M. Two entire batteries that had flanked the southernmost region of Lightburn's division had been sent to the rear and southward to support General Harrow. In addition, two howitzers from the 1st Division a half mile north of the Troup Hurt house were sent on the same mission. None of those artillery pieces had returned to the positions they held earlier in the afternoon.[15]

What remained to repel the initiation of Cheatham's attack were 10 cannons from two Illinois batteries surrounding Jones's brigade and no cannons for nearly one mile southward from the railroad bed. Battery A of the 1st Illinois Light Artillery had 6 cannons positioned at the railroad and slightly north and south of it, and 4 cannons from Battery H of the 1st Illinois Light Artillery (De Gress's Battery) occupied a position just north of the Troup Hurt house. Had General Hood ordered Cheatham's divisions out to attack simultaneously with Hardee's corps between noon and 1:00 P.M., Brown's division would have been facing off against 10 more cannons and 1,500 more men than the force that then opposed him, a detached force that had yet to contribute in the new direction they were sent. So, by happenstance, Hood's battle plan was providing a greater mismatch in his favor than he could have imagined.[16]

The half mile of terrain between the Union earthworks at the Troup Hurt house and the leading brigades of General Brown's assaulting division was more open south of the railroad than north of it. Three homes stood across the works from the XV Corps position and down the road to Decatur. The southernmost home was owned by a planter named James Brown; slightly east of his house was another frame-constructed home on high ground, owned by a family surnamed Russaw. The northernmost home of the three stood closest to the Union works, just north of the road to Decatur and merely 150 yards southwest of the Troup Hurt house. To the soldiers that two-story dwelling was simply the "white house."[17]

Manigault's brigade enjoyed some protection from a belt of woods that covered them over the final quarter mile to the breastworks. The trees shielded them from the shelling of Union cannons and the carefully aimed fire from XV Corps sharpshooters. Manigault's men took the brunt of the Union shelling about 100 yards from the opposing line. Forced to halt to wait for Coltart's brigade to align with them south of the railroad, Manigault's brigade was subjected to artillery fire from at least 8 cannons aligned on each side of the Troup Hurt house. Two Carolina regiments closest to the railroad had marched in more open terrain and seemed to suffer the most from the courage-robbing fire. Colonel James F. Pressley sent members of the 10th and 19th South Carolina into the white house just west of the XV Corps earthen line. Those Carolinians entered the frame building, raced up the stairs, aligned on the second-floor piazza, and pointed their rifles from upper-story windows. Those new sharpshooters began to pick off blue-clad soldiers by firing down upon them from a point less than 200 yards away while monitoring the strength of their opponent's position.[18]

As the time passed 4:00 P.M. the only significant action transpiring across the eastern Atlanta battlefield was Cheatham's frontline pressing upon General Lightburn's division. Coltart's brigade descended upon the remaining three regiments of Martin's brigade south of the Georgia Railroad while Manigault's men emerged from the woods in front of Jones's brigade. It was an awesome spectacle for those XV Corps soldiers, despite the fact that most of them had seen it so many times before, from Shiloh to Chattanooga, and more recently from Resaca to Kennesaw Mountain. Here, east of Atlanta, the sight and sounds of line after line of Confederate soldiers emerging from the trees was spectacular to behold. "How beautiful! How regular!" recalled Lieutenant George Bailey, a Missouri officer on General Morgan L. Smith's staff, who admitted that at that moment existed "a conflict between fear and admiration." General Manigault revealed equal admiration from the Southern perspective. Gazing upon the blue-clad lines with their flags fluttering in the breeze, Manigault recalled, "I saw and noticed all this only for a moment, and thought it looked very pretty."[19]

Fear remained in some, but admiration gave way to resolve in the ranks of Blue and Gray. Manigault's advance was slowed by fire from front and flank, as (XV Corps) 1st Division artillery a half mile north of the point of attack sent screaming iron into the Southern ranks while Captain De Gress had his 4-gun battery working with skill and rapidity from their position just north of the Troup Hurt house. De Gress had been firing both solid shot and exploding shells at distant Southern batteries of Cheatham's corps for nearly two hours before the two front brigades of Brown's division emerged in their front and left. De Gress was then permitted to fire canister once General Morgan L. Smith (the new XV Corps commander) had been assured that all of his skirmishers had returned to the works. That particular round was the deadliest to fire at ranges up to 500 yards. When the cylinder casing blew apart as the round left the muzzle of the cannon, a huge shotgun effect resulted by the creation of a vertical iron hail pelting anything in their paths. The round was deadly enough when spewed by cannons capable of ten or twelve-pound rounds, but De Gress's twenty-pounder Parrotts were nearly twice as destructive. Forty-eight balls rained mayhem with each canister belched forth by each of the 4 guns. Two ten-pounder Parrotts from Battery A of the 1st Illinois Light Artillery stood on the other side of the brick house and lent their support to De Gress's men, also firing canister from a deadly range.[20]

Manigault's men were cut down or tormented by the fusillade of 500 of those balls every minute, mixed in with thousands of conical leaden bullets fired from the rifle barrels of Union infantry. The entire brigade was staggered by the devastating fire and blinded by the thick smoke that quickly enveloped the region. With no woods to protect him, Manigault saw the cohesion of his brigade disintegrate, replaced by huge gaps in his lines and a nearly frozen advance. Carolinians near the white house hid behind it for cover, but others without protection broke ranks and scampered for the safety of the rear. In doing so, they upset the ranks of the Mississippians of Sharp's brigade, who were marching behind Manigault to support him. Lieutenant Robert Gill of the 41st Mississippi was so disgusted with the display of his fellow Confederates that he called on his company "to shoot the cowardly scoundrels." General Manigault was forced to admit at that moment "things looked ugly."[21]

Things looked no better initially for the Confederates advancing on Manigault's right, south of the railroad. Coltart's men had lost their alignment and instead of keeping twenty paces from the railroad, a gap of nearly 200 yards had widened between the flanks of the frontline brigades. That not only exposed Manigault's right flank to concentrate Union attention on him, it also shifted Coltart's attack line farther to the south. That initially had forced the entire frontline of Brown's division to halt for several minutes until General Brown rectified the problem by ordering the Mississippi brigade of Colonel Samuel Benton to move forward and replace the Alabamans in the frontline. One of Coltart's Alabama regiments marched with the consolidated Mississippi regiments, boosting the frontline assault in that sector to 1,000 officers and men.[22]

Only two Northern regiments remained from Martin's brigade to oppose the attackers, the 57th Ohio near the railroad, and the 55th Illinois off the left flank of the Buckeyes. Six cannons from Battery A, 1st Illinois Light Artillery also were positioned to repel the assault. The defense watched the Alabamans' approach, "with the usual ear-piercing yell." According to one of the Illinois men, "We held our fire until the rebs were within 60 yards of us, when we gave them a volley of musketry and artillery which staggered them considerably." A few more volleys from the Illinoisans froze up Benton's men, while sending hundreds reeling and fleeing, much like Manigault's men north of that position. Those remaining hugged the ground a mere 50 yards from the works. The Mississippians

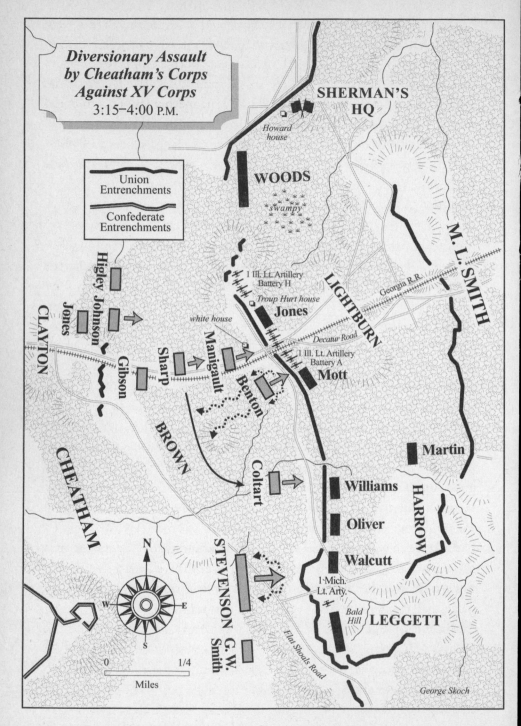

Diversionary Assault
by Cheatham's Corps
Against XV Corps
3:15–4:00 P.M.

SHERMAN'S
HQ

Howard
house

WOODS

swampy

Union
Entrenchments

Confederate
Entrenchments

Higley Johnson

Jones

CLAYTON

Gibson

Sharp

Manigault

white house

I Ill. Lt. Artillery
Battery H

Troup Hurt house

Jones

LIGHTBURN

Georgia R.R.

M. L. SMITH

Decatur Road

I Ill. Lt. Artillery
Battery A

Mott

Benton

BROWN

Coltart

Martin

Williams

Oliver

HARROW

Walcutt

CHEATHAM

STEVENSON

G. W. Smith

N

W   E

S

0   1/4

Miles

1·Mich.
Lt. Arty.

Bald
Hill

LEGGETT

Flat Shoals Road

George Skoch

were further demoralized when their commander, Colonel Benton, went down with two wounds, a bullet through the foot and a shell fragment in his upper chest (the foot required amputation; both wounds would prove fatal six days after the battle). Colonel William F. Brantley took over the brigade at the worst possible time to learn the mechanics of a command several times larger than his expertise and experience. Brantley sent orders for his prone men in front of the works and behind trees and stumps to extricate themselves and withdraw to a safe position a quarter of a mile to the rear.[23]

The repulse of Brantley's brigade infused their enemies with confidence. A member of the 55th Illinois claimed they were "proudly exultant, and intoxicated with the wine of victory—a victory with almost no loss." But it was much too early to celebrate. Coltart's Alabamans—including 50 men of the 39th Alabama who pried themselves from the Mississippians—had already begun to shift another 300 yards to the right at the same time the Mississippians were advancing straight on. That redeployment placed the new front of the Alabamans nearly one-third of a mile south of the railroad. Here they advanced with no artillery opposing them and only two isolated regiments of Colonel Reuben Williams's brigade from William Harrow's division in the earthworks with no reserves in the Union rear.[24]

At 4:15 P.M. Colonel Coltart launched the assault with his Alabama brigade from his new position, not knowing that he was blessed with the good fortune of opposing the weakest part of the Union line south of the Georgia Railroad. Even as his troops closed the quarter-mile gap between the opposing lines, a rejuvenated assault at and north of the railroad bed had begun to turn the tide of the contest. Manigault had met with a shower of lead and iron from Colonel Wells S. Jones's brigade and 6 cannons from two Illinois batteries, aided by additional Union artillery pieces half a mile north of the Troup Hurt house. Stalled in his tracks, Manigault's predicament ended with the arrival of Colonel Jacob H. Sharp's Mississippi brigade. Next to General Manigault, Sharp was the most experienced of Brown's four brigade commanders, although he had held the helm of the brigade for only ten weeks prior to the battle. Sharp had kept his Mississippians 100 yards behind Manigault's men and had even sent messages to the frontline troops to offer assistance during the first minutes of action. The offers were refused, but became necessary.

As it turned out, merely the presence of Sharp's regiments sparked a resurgence in Manigault's brigade. "The men saw them, and gathered confidence," insisted Manigault. The Alabamans and Carolinians were then determined to complete their mission. Surging forward between deadly discharges from Union artillery aimed in their direction, the frontline Confederates stormed the breastworks. The 10th South Carolina Regiment near the right of Manigault's line, considerably weaker in numbers from rearward bound soldiers in their ranks, charged along the north side of the railroad until they reached the cut running through the fortifications. The second attempt proved easier as thick battle smoke and a ravine screened their approach to the Union line. Colonel James F. Pressley led the 10th Regiment forward, some rushing through the cut while others scaled the low works between the cut and the wagon road 20 yards north of it. Several Gamecocks fell dead and wounded, including Pressley, who was shot through the shoulder on top of the works and was borne from the field, but he had done his job well, for his men reached a portion of the line poorly defended by XV Corps infantry. The infantry near the position melted away, leaving an open path to the first cherished prize for the Southerners—the cannons of Battery A, 1st Illinois Light Artillery.[25]

Battery A was a Chicago artillery regiment, formerly known as the Dearborne Artillery Militia Company. On July 22 it was actually a consolidated unit, formed from the remnant of Battery A and B with the expiration of service of the 1861 recruits only days before the battle. One section stood between the railroad and the road to Decatur; another section occupied ground south of the railroad and a third section stood north of the dirt road. Even before the Rebels broke through the works, a series of mishaps portended doom when two artillerists in the battery had their forearms blown off because the guns each manned discharged prematurely.[26]

The South Carolina infantry prepared to inflict a great deal more pain on the battery, swarming upon it before the next rounds of double canister could be rammed down the barrels. Lieutenant Samuel S. Smyth commanded the battery and stood next to the northernmost section. Major John R. Hotaling, a XV Corps staff officer and one of six brothers fighting for the Union, had also ridden up to the battery to oversee that position. "I stood by the right section, talking to Lieut. [Samuel] Smyth, and thought we had repulsed the massed assault," admitted Hotaling. "We had, but it was only the first line; the powder smoke was so dense and I was stooping to look under the cloud when the second line of [Confederates] poured over our works and through the cut, gaining our rear."[27]

The Southerners lit upon the battery so swiftly that few escaped unscathed. The Carolina troops shot man and horse alike in an effort to prevent the guns from being rolled to safety. Ten artillerists were killed, several wounded, and twenty-one others forced to surrender, including the battery commander, Lieutenant Smyth; fifty-six battery horses were also killed or wounded. All 6 cannons fell into the hands of the 10th South Carolina. One of the artillerists "played possum" by feigning death the moment Lieutenant Theodore Raub was struck down at his side. He was able to continue the ruse even after the Gamecocks flocked over the captured cannons, kicking him and stomping on him in the process.[28]

The 24th Alabama charged in on the heels of the victorious Carolinians. Captain Starke H. Oliver passed the captured guns of Battery A and came upon Lieutenant Raub leaning against a tree, staring in stunned silence with his sword in his right hand while his left arm draped over his stomach, just a few feet behind the guns. Oliver ordered Raub to surrender and head toward the Confederate rear west of them but the Illinoisan insisted that he was too wounded to walk. At that moment Oliver could see that Raub had been holding his arm over his slit abdomen to prevent his protruding bowels from dropping out from the long, deep, and obviously mortal cut. With the help of another Confederate soldier, Oliver carried the dying officer to a ditch behind the earthworks where they gently placed him. Lieutenant Raub died within an hour in that secluded spot.[29]

Major Hotaling escaped the maelstrom. He had survived close calls in the past, bearing a reminder of that across his face in the form of a sabre scar received during the Mexican War. Disregarding repeated calls to surrender, Hotaling discovered a ravine east of the battery near where the caissons stood. There he stayed, rallying soldiers from different commands to coalesce around him. He was essentially using the ravine as a recruiting station to form a new hodgepodge regiment, one that would counterstrike as soon as Hotaling was satisfied he had enough men to make a difference.[30]

The successful exploits of the 10th South Carolina opened the door for the 19th South Carolina behind it and the Alabamans north of them. All had rushed forward through the cut or over the works. That proved all too much for the 47th Ohio Infantry of Jones's brigade, one of only three regiments north of the railroad cut positioned to protect Battery A off its left flank and De Gress's cannons off its right flank. Low-hanging battle smoke concealed what had quickly become an overwhelming presence of the Confederates deploying from the cut they then owned. Herculean efforts by Lieutenant Colonel John Wallace of the 47th Ohio to form a new line on each side of the flags of the regiment could not stem the gray tide. As Private William Bakhaus revealed, "Lt. Col. Wallace ordered us to rally around him, but in this instance I must admit that I did not obey orders, but commanded myself to rally to the rear, and did so in double quick time." Too many Ohioans followed Bakhaus's cue, leaving Wallace and members of the color guard essentially alone to be captured in short order. New 2nd Division commander Brig. Gen. Joseph Lightburn rode to the rear to prepare a secondary defensive line while his new brigadier, Colonel Wells Jones, moved to the right to try to get a battle line formed from the remainder of his troops just north of the Troup Hurt house.[31]

Captain De Gress and his subordinates, manning the 4 twenty-pounder Parrotts, stood north of the brick house with portions of two other Ohio regiments surrounding the house in front of them and immediately to their left. Those regiments—the 30th and 37th Ohio—buckled under the overwhelming presence of Manigault's men in front of the breastworks and then flanking them from the left (south) where the Carolina men had penetrated the railroad. Confederate numbers here doubled at that time when Sharp's Mississippians entered the fray on the heels of Manigault's brigade. With more than 2,500 Confederates at or inside the XV Corps works, the outcome around the Troup Hurt house appeared decided. Unable to form a resisting line of regiments of his brigade north of the railroad, Colonel Jones ran to Captain De Gress and urged him to retire from the field and save his guns.[32]

It was way too late for that. De Gress managed to turn his left 2 guns toward the left (south). Loading one with canister, De Gress fired it himself at Confederates closing within 20 yards of him. He ordered the guns spiked to prevent them from being fired upon his own troops after their

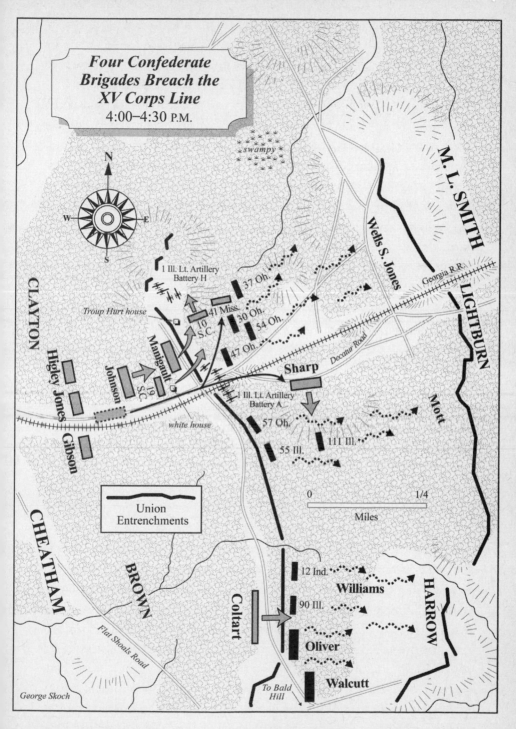

Four Confederate Brigades Breach the XV Corps Line
4:00–4:30 P.M.

N
W E
S

swampy

M. L. SMITH

Wells S. Jones

Georgia R.R.

LIGHTBURN

1 Ill. Lt. Artillery Battery H

Troup Hurt house

37 Oh.

41 Miss.

30 Oh.

54 Oh.

10 S.C.

47 Oh.

CLAYTON

Manigault

Johnson

19 S.C.

Decatur Road

Sharp

Mott

Higley

Jones

1 Ill. Lt. Artillery Battery A

white house

57 Oh.

Gibson

55 Ill.

111 Ill.

Union Entrenchments

0   1/4

Miles

CHEATHAM

BROWN

Coltart

12 Ind.

90 Ill.

Williams

HARROW

Oliver

Flat Shoals Road

Walcutt

To Bald Hill

George Skoch

inevitable capture. De Gress was forced to abandon his artillery pieces and escaped with the few artillerists willing to protect them. Although De Gress escaped, 9 of his men could not get out in time. A mixture of Manigault's men and Mississippians from Sharp's brigade lit upon the battery and captured all 4 cannons. Those guns plus Battery A of the 1st Illinois Light Artillery made 10 in all for the Southern breach into the XV Corps lines.

The two penetrating Southern brigades threatened the entire XV Corps position. Immediately affected were the three regiments of Martin's brigade south of the railroad. After successfully repulsing Benton's Mississippi brigade in their front, the Illinois and Ohio regiments lost sight of the Confederate penetration along the Georgia Railroad to their right. Officers barked out orders to oblique to the right to face the new danger north of them. "It was too late," admitted one of the foot soldiers in the line, observing the entire region north of the railway "swarming with Confederate soldiers, the battery captured, and hundreds of the enemy coming up in serried ranks from out the railroad cut behind our right companies." Like a chain of falling dominoes the regiments south of the line dropped back into the woods and eventually to their original line of works half a mile east of the attacked line. Twenty minutes after the first exchange of infantry fire, Lightburn's entire division was gone. Perhaps as many as 1,800 infantry soldiers had evaded the casualty list and had fallen back to the interior line of works. But nearly a third of their comrades would not be joining them. Close to 700 officers and men had been killed, wounded, or captured; all of Lightburn's cannons were then in the possession of Cheatham's corps.[33]

The absolute disappearance of a Union division in the center of a corps line with its replacement by two butternut brigades began to unravel the rest of the XV Corps. William Harrow's division south of Lightburn's position suffered the soonest. Regiments from two brigades of Harrow's force had already been active two hours earlier when they put an end to the northward penetration of Cleburne's attack. Harrow was also forced to contest the weak eastward thrust of Stevenson's division during the three o'clock hour. At 4:00 P.M., Harrow's northernmost brigade, commanded by Colonel Reuben Williams, parried another eastward Confederate assault, that one by Coltart's Alabama brigade, which had stabbed directly at his position just as the attack by Benton's Mississippians had begun to wane off to his right. Ironically, Alabamans faced off against each other, for Colonel Williams had recruited Union-loving Alabamans into the ranks of the 12th Indiana Infantry (his former regiment) when the XV Corps was encamped near Scottsboro, Alabama, the previous winter and early spring. Included in the Indiana ranks was an Alabama soldier firing at Coltart's men while one of his family's slaves sat next to him biting off the tops of the paper cartridges and handing up the gunpowder and bullet wrapped in paper to him. "It was not often, surely," noted Williams, "that a Southern-born man fought on the Union side during the 'War for the Union' with his own slave to assist him."[34]

Colonel Williams and his men were doubly pleased and relieved at the success of their stand, for the brigade was down to two regiments, the 90th Illinois and Williams's own 12th Indiana to its right (one regiment was detached in Marietta and another, the 26th Illinois, had been sent southward to reinforce Colonel Walcutt's position). Although they covered nearly 500 yards of works with only 600 men and no reserve, the volleys from the Yankees broke Coltart's brigade twice, each repulse sparking more confidence in the defenders. Williams recalled how ecstatic he and his command felt at that moment, "None of the troops or myself even thought of disaster, and 'the boys' were already making jests out of the various matters witnessed by them during the fight and repulse, when all at once came a volley from perhaps a thousand men fired straight into the backs of both of my regiments, at fairly close range."[35]

Perhaps Williams exaggerated the strength of the blow to the back of his brigade, but not by much. Indeed, several hundred members of Sharp's Mississippi brigade had penetrated deep into the Union fortifications and veered to the right, facing south, while Manigault's brigade with the 41st Mississippi of Sharp's brigade (and perhaps another Mississippi regiment) had forced their way northward from the railroad. Colonel Williams was shocked at the sudden turn of events that then jeopardized his two regiments. He ordered his command rearward to re-form behind an old stone building a quarter of a mile directly behind his line. He did that without approval from his division commander, General Harrow, who was nowhere near the harassed portion of his line, and apparently without warning the next brigade to his left, commanded by Colonel John Oliver. Also surprised on his right and rear, Oliver ordered his three regiments in the works to fall back as well. Then with uncontested works in front of them, the Alabama troops in Coltart's brigade moved eastward again and occupied them with minimal loss.[36]

That left Walcutt's brigade from Harrow's division as the only XV Corps troops south of the railroad and north of Bald Hill. Positioned to cover the wooded gap and to protect Leggett's position at Bald Hill, Walcutt's soldiers would easily become a major attraction for Confederate fire from north of them. General Harrow recognized that and sent an order for Colonel Walcutt to fall back with the brigades of Williams and Oliver. The order would preserve his division and reinforce a strong second line, but Harrow's order jeopardized Leggett's defense of Bald Hill. Once Walcutt received the order and abandoned his line, Leggett would most certainly be surrounded on the north, east, and west by enemy soldiers. By saving Walcutt, Harrow's order risked killing off Leggett. If Bald Hill fell to Hood, the entire position of the XVI and XVII Corps would be untenable and the battle would most certainly end in Confederate victory. Atop Bald Hill, General Leggett recognized the importance of Walcutt's position more than anyone. Without possibly knowing that an order was on its way to Walcutt to fall back, Leggett galloped northward to meet with Walcutt and to apprise him as to how vital the flank protection was to the defense of Bald Hill.[37]

At 4:30 P.M., as the Union defenders from the XV Corps fled back to half a mile eastward of their original line of works they had constructed on July 20, the Confederates established a tenuous toehold in the new section of real estate they acquired. Confederate reinforcements began to arrive in the form of corps commander Benjamin Cheatham's remaining division, led by Major General Henry D. Clayton, whose four brigades were advancing directly behind General Brown's engaged brigades and north of them. Opposing those approaching 4,500 fresh Confederates were about half as many Federal soldiers from two of the three remaining infantry brigades of the XV Corps on the field, the two brigades of the 1st Division several hundred yards north of the Troup Hurt house. Walcutt's brigade of Harrow's division was also in its position, but they were mostly oriented southward to aid the XV Corps. Between those two Union positions was three quarters of a mile of earthworks then owned by Brown's division of Cheatham's corps. That fact was not realized by General Hood because it had yet to be reported to him. Nor did General Hood realize that a rejuvenation of Hardee's corps was about to commence at the southern end of the battlefield. Major General Cleburne and Brigadier General Maney were in the process of massing troops for a grand assault against the weakened XVII Corps position.

Only 18,000 Union soldiers remained on the line as an organized body to face off against Confederate attacks. Two brigades (2,000 soldiers) of the XV Corps anchored the right of the Army of the Tennessee and were separated by nearly a mile from the remainder of the army by a line of earthworks possessed by Cheatham's Confederate corps. The rest of the organized XV Corps stood just north of Bald Hill, represented by Walcutt's brigade, Wangelin's brigade, and the reserves of two other brigades, a total of 4,000 men. These men buttressed the right flank of what remained of the XVII Corps on Bald Hill and angled southeast of that position. The two divisions of Blair's XVII Corps, still commanded by Giles Smith and Mortimer Leggett, were considerably weakened by two hours of assaults, which bled their strength down to 7,000 officers and men by 4:30 P.M. The inevitability of another grand assault coming from the south within the next hour did not help their morale.

Grenville Dodge's XVI Corps, half a mile east of Bald Hill, had suffered more than 500 casualties in the first two hours of the battle. With Sprague's brigade still licking its wounds at Decatur, Dodge remained in position with 4,000 soldiers in three brigades from Sweeny's and Fuller's divisions. All of the Union batteries supporting those three corps had been hard tested throughout the afternoon. Four batteries—19 cannons—had fallen into Confederate hands, leaving 1,000 artillerists to man the 77 cannons of the army still in position on Friday afternoon.

General Hood was at a tremendous advantage to modify a plan that could achieve the same result that he forecasted twenty-four hours earlier: the complete rout of the Army of the Tennessee with a possibility still alive for the subsequent removal of Sherman's entire district from the Atlanta side of the Chattahoochie River. The two attacking corps of his army were still intact. General Hardee's corps had suffered nearly 3,000 losses at that stage of the battle, but his stragglers were entering the ranks and reassembling for another attempt at the XVII Corps position. Two of his divisions were ineffective, but Cleburne and Maney still had fight left in their divisions. General Cheatham's corps had suffered much less than Hardee by 4:30 P.M., with almost 13,000 men available in the ranks. The two Confederate corps numbered close to 22,000 officers and men, certainly strong enough to exploit weakness at the Union left flank and to widen the breach of the right flank.

Hood still had the services of his uncommitted corps under General Alexander P. Stewart, a force of 12,000 that stood just north of Atlanta, an hour's march from the contested field. Hood had been wary of an attack by General Thomas and the Army of the Cumberland throughout the day, but with four hours of daylight remaining (the sun set at 7:49 P.M., with less than an hour of working light for an army after that), the possibility of an attack from the north waned with each passing minute. If General Hood committed 10,000 men from Stewart's corps against the Army of the Tennessee, he reasonably would have an army approaching 35,000 against an opponent numbering less than 20,000.

Hood never pulled that trigger. Stewart stayed in position north of Atlanta for the remainder of that Friday, perhaps for no other reason than the fact that Hood never appreciated the huge advantage he held at 4:30 P.M. "On the 22d we were ordered to be in readiness to attack the enemy . . . following the corps on our right [Cheatham's]," reported Stewart, "but for reasons unknown to me the battle did not become general." Still, even without the participation of Stewart's men, Hood's army had sufficient time, men, and momentum to accomplish what had not been realized to date in the Civil War—the complete destruction of a major field army. A XVI Corps soldier in the rear of all the swirling action still could appreciate the dire situation of his army. Noting the death of McPherson, the rout of the XV Corps, and the appearance of mass confusion in the supply and ammunition trains near him, the soldier took a moment to confess to his diary, "the day at this time looks gloomy for us."[38]

The Army of the Tennessee was on the verge of collapse and annihilation. The consequence of that potential Union disaster could ultimately affect the most important presidential election in United States history.

★ ★ ★ ★ ★ ★ ★ ★ ★ ★ ★ ★ ★ ★ ★ ★ ★ ★ ★

9

∿

A HUMAN HURRICANE ON HORSEBACK

For a body of troops that never reached even half the numbers of the famous Army of the Potomac, the Army of the Tennessee boasted skilled and successful commanders unmatched by any Union army during the then three-year course of the Civil War. First led by Ulysses S. Grant, succeeded by William Tecumseh Sherman, and most recently by the protégé of both, James McPherson, the army had to endure the death of its latest commander in the midst of a harrowing fight, a martyrdom experienced by a major army just once earlier in the war when the first commander of the Confederate Army of Tennessee, General Albert Sydney Johnson, bled to death at the Battle of Shiloh in 1862. That contributed to the eventual defeat of his army in that two-day battle. (Brigadier Nathaniel Lyon, in charge of a division-sized Union army, was the first commander killed in battle on August 10, 1861, at Wilson's Creek, Missouri.) In the first two and a half hours that followed General McPherson's death, his army had been bent but never broken by the seemingly relentless assaults of Cleburne's division. Nevertheless, at 4:30 P.M. on Friday, July 22, 1864, not only was the Army of the Tennessee broken, it was about to collapse under the weight of the penetrating assaults of Cheatham's corps against its right flank with a pending resurgence of Hardee's corps against the left.

No individual officer personified the Army of the Tennessee better than Major General John A. Logan, the fourth commander in the two-and-a-half-year history of the army and a man who had held the helm of the army for less than three hours. Logan was a homegrown product,

MAJOR GENERAL JOHN ALEXANDER LOGAN, U.S.A.

Logan was the senior corps commander who replaced the late General McPherson as the head of the Army of the Tennessee. Three years after the war he nationalized a regional grave-decorating tradition and called it Memorial Day, an annual tradition that is his legacy today. *(Courtesy of MOLLUS-Massachusetts, USAMHI, Carlisle Barracks, Pa.)*

entering the army before it was named for the river that coursed through the theater where the troops had gained their fame in 1862. Logan was General Grant's political general, helping Grant succeed on the battlefronts at Fort Donelson, Raymond, and Champion Hill, and on the home front with a stirring series of patriotic speeches delivered in Illinois between military campaigns in the summers of 1862 and 1863. U.S. Congressman Logan had entered the war as a colonel without a military education or previous battle experience; his regiment consisted of his Southern Illinois constituents. In any case, General Grant was so impressed with Logan's natural military instincts in the first months of action in 1861–1862, that he rammed through two successive promotions for Logan after President Lincoln had left the Democrat's name off his list of recommendations.

Major General Logan's star shone brilliantly throughout the Vicksburg campaign in 1863, so much so that he was rewarded with the prized command of the XV Corps at the end of the year. Logan led those troops in Georgia for eleven weeks, turning a corps that had a shaky record of accomplishment prior to the Atlanta campaign into one that broke a Union stalemate at Resaca, won a resounding victory on the Union right flank at Dallas, Georgia, and gamely assaulted the seemingly impenetrable Confederate defense at Kennesaw Mountain, all the while representing the fighting portion of the Army of the Tennessee for the first two months of the Atlanta campaign. Members of the XVI Corps were understandably irked at dropping out of newspapers because of the accomplishments of Logan and his corps, one of them railing that those newsmen had far too much "Logan on the brain."[1]

Those sniping comments, however, were rare and easily superseded by statements of awe and admiration, particularly in regard to Logan's unique gift of inspiration. After observing Logan in action, an Iowan in the XVI Corps insisted, "I am satisfied that the biggest coward in the world would stand on his head on top of the breastworks if Logan was present and told him to do so."[2] A member of the 31st Missouri hailed Logan with a glowing tribute in an 1864 letter to his wife:

I wish you could see him, riding along the lines on the eve of a battle . . . with his hat in his hand—his large dark eyes flashing like a glance of an eagle, his swarthy complexion relieved by his huge mustache, and his long, glossy, black hair falling, in tangled masses, about his neck—he is a picture for an artist's pencil. Brave as a lion—heedless in personal danger—full of a patriot's enthusiasm and fire; no wonder that his soldiers love and venerate the man!![3]

Indeed they did. General Mortimer Leggett admitted that Generals Grant and Sherman received the utmost confidence and respect when they rode down the lines while in charge of that army. "But when General Logan rode down the line," continued Leggett, "every voice was heard [in] a shout. He seemed to have a power to awaken all the enthusiasm that was in the troops, to the extent that no other officer in the army seemed to possess. He would stir up their blood in battle. The manner in which he sat his horse, the manner in which he would hold his hat . . .

seemed to have the power to call out of the men every particle of fight that was in them."[4]

No more important time existed for Logan to call out every particle of fight than in the late afternoon of July 22. At the start of it, ironically, Logan perhaps felt at ease. At the time Brown's division struck Lightburn's Union position at 4:15 P.M., Logan was with General Dodge, overseeing the near-completion of the U-shaped army line with the placement of three brigades of Schofield's Army of the Ohio to the left of the XVI Corps to extend Dodge's flank and cover the road to Decatur, facing eastward toward the town that Wheeler's cavalry had assaulted. Those very large XXIII Corps brigades of Schofield's Army of the Ohio added 7,000 troops to the Army of the Tennessee line, but aside from deployment on the field, none of those troops would need to be engaged in battle that day. On Dodge's right, the deployment of Colonel Hugo Wangelin's brigade and the three regiments of Colonel James S. Martin's brigade provided adequate filler for the gap that had existed between the XVI and XVII Corps for over three hours. Dodge had pulled his three brigades of the XVI Corps northward and re-formed them in a stronger position and to ease the connection with the XVII Corps near Bald Hill on his right. General Blair had also readjusted his line by bending back his left flank to complete the connection by flattening and squaring off the *U* shape in the Federal line. No heavy Confederate activity threatened any part of that portion of the field between 4:00 P.M. and 4:30 P.M.[5]

At 4:15 P.M. Logan received Captain Horatio N. Wheeler, his assistant adjutant general, who galloped to him from the collapsing XV Corps line to inform his general of the catastrophe that developed on the Union right. Immediately, Logan sent H. N. Wheeler to Colonel Martin off to the east, where he had been positioned with the XXIII Corps detachment off Dodge's left flank. Martin was ordered to return to the rest of his brigade with his three regiments. Knowing that would not be sufficient, Logan then directed Dodge to relinquish one of his brigades to him, advising him to borrow troops from the XXIII Corps on his left if his position was threatened. Dodge immediately ordered out Mersy's brigade from his new line.[6]

Mersy's brigade, numbering close to 1,000 soldiers, and Martin's three detached regiments, 750 officers and men, hustled northwestward as they converged toward the contested XV Corps line. They would arrive separately and independently, and both brigades were farther away from Manigault's and Sharp's brigades than their support. Confederate Major General Henry D. Clayton's division prepared to enter the fight with four brigades extending for a mile from the Georgia Railroad northward. One of Clayton's brigades, Brigadier General Randall Gibson's Louisiana troops, was held in reserve, an unfortunate decision for the Confederates given that Gibson was the only general and the most experienced of all of Clayton's brigade commanders that day. Still, Clayton was prepared to commit over 3,000 soldiers to the fight.[7]

A distinct interval between the assaults of Brown's and Clayton's divisions existed at 4:30 P.M., the second moment of silence across the Atlanta battlefield in the past ninety minutes. All the while, Confederates within the Union works "processed" their spoils of war. South Carolinians pulled 2 cannons from the captured Battery A westward on the Decatur road back to Atlanta. Following behind the brass cannons were several hundred Union prisoners of war from the 2nd and 4th divisions of the XV Corps. The captives were destined to head deeper into Georgia where they would be interned at Andersonville prison. Lieutenant George W. Bailey, a staff aid to General Morgan L. Smith, was one of those Federals fortunate to escape death or injury, but not fortunate enough to escape capture by jubilant members of Cheatham's corps. Escorted from the yard of the Troup Hurt house to Atlanta, Bailey observed the macabre nature of a battle:

> . . . we passed on the road through our works toward Atlanta. The cries and moans of the wounded arose through the thick smoke. Some Federal dead lay stretched in and near our works, but in front [west] of them was an awful scene. The ground for over one hundred yards was thickly strewn with the rebel dead and wounded. Many cries arose for "water"; some were struggling to extricate themselves from mangled heaps of dead, and calling for aid; some were vainly striving to stop the flow of crimson tide gushing from ghastly wounds; many were fitfully gasping their last breath. But the great majority were grim and cold in the strong embrace of death, lying in almost every conceivable position;

some were riddled with rifleballs; some were torn with grape and canister shot, and at not infrequent intervals the bodies were literally heaped together. There were young and old countenances; some distorted, others calm. Stony eyes gazed meaninglessly at us as we picked our way; others stared wildly into space.[8]

Most of the Union prisoners were treated well in Confederate hands, although the captors enjoyed moments to intimidate their prey. One of the Yankees, much frightened about falling into the hands of the 41st Mississippi, sheepishly asked Sergeant J. E. Neighbors, "Are you going to kill all of us?" The Mississippian's response was harsh and ominous—but it may not have been serious. "That's our calculation," responded Neighbors. "We came out for that purpose." Another member of the regiment prided himself on how he acted toward his prisoners. "It is a source of much gratification to me to know that during my three years in the Southern army I never treated a Union soldier unkindly, either by word or act," he asserted. The same soldier also claimed to capture vehicles containing whisky near De Gress's battery. If true, that capture delighted the captors more than the human prisoners did.[9]

The XV Corps prisoners were likely diverted southward as General Clayton's men prepared to continue the attack. Clayton designed an *en echelon* assault; i.e., brigade-sized attacks from right to left, each successive brigade initiating its assault after the one on its right has made contact with the enemy. That method necessarily sacrificed the leading brigade to rifle fire from the front and flank, but while the enemy enfiladed the initial assaulters, they would be subjected to a surprise front attack from Clayton's next brigade while their attention was diverted. Clayton directed his brigadiers to advance with the sun to their backs and to prolong the left flank by entering the fight in that staggered fashion.[10]

The first of Clayton's brigades to enter the fight were the six Georgia regiments under the overall leadership of Colonel Abda Johnson, formerly the commander of the 40th Georgia Infantry. Most of the regiments in that brigade were led by a newly promoted commander. John M. Brown, a lieutenant colonel and the brother of the governor, commanded the 1st Georgia State Line within the brigade, replacing the original colonel wounded at Peachtree Creek two days earlier. Captain Lovick P. Thomas found himself in charge of the 42nd Georgia for an absurd reason.

Major William H. Hulsey had commanded that regiment since May, but had taken a nap that July 22 afternoon, sleep deprived from overnight duty. He left instructions to be aroused if his regiment was called into action, but the person charged with that simple task failed in his duty, leaving Hulsey in a deep sleep and Captain Thomas in charge of the entire regiment.[11]

The Georgians of Johnson's brigade slipped into the Federal works on the victorious heels of Manigault's and Sharp's brigades of Brown's division. The 42nd Georgia swarmed around the Troup Hurt house, recently secured by the two successful brigades of Brown's division. The 40th Georgia, farther south of the advance, encountered much more resistance. Sergeant B. J. McGinnis resorted to extraordinary means to fight off the Yankee threat to the Georgians. Without a loaded weapon in his possession, McGinnis watched in horror as one of the blue-clad soldiers bayoneted a Georgian near him. McGinnis picked up a spade in the freshly converted trenches and used it as his bayonet swinging it and spearing the man who wounded his comrade and another man next to him. An Alabaman in Coltart's brigade also used a spade to incapacitate an Indiana soldier in Harrow's division. One of McGinnis's "spade victims" was found with a thigh broken by a pistol shot and three distinct cuts on his face from the makeshift weapon.[12]

Three Confederate brigades hovered within the XV Corps works in the region of the Georgia Railroad at 4:30 P.M., a penetration of more than 2,500 Southern soldiers (another 700 or so entered the Union line 1,000 yards south of them, where Coltart's Alabamans came in at Reuben Williams's old position). Behind Johnson's Georgia brigade and off his left flank came the Alabama brigade commanded by Colonel Bushrod Jones, a command of roughly 900 officers and men, including the pickets posted in front. He was nearly a quarter of a mile behind the Georgians and by the time he closed the gap, Jones realized the difficulty of trying to force his brigade into the breach created by the Confederate brigades in front of him. He rode up to the white house sitting just to the west side of the works where he met General Manigault and Colonel Sharp. They pointed off Jones's left flank to show him the folly of attempting to advance straight on as they had done before him, for the 1st Division of the XV Corps was massing troops north of the penetration point and preparing a counterassault. Jones trotted to his left, faced his regiments obliquely from east to northeast, nearly at a right angle with Manigault's brigade. Manigault was quite impressed with how his new brigade commander handled his troops, commending Colonel Jones as "one of the coolest fellows I ever saw, handling his command with great ease and judgement." At the time Jones likely did not have equal admiration for General Manigault. As Jones prepared to meet the threat northeast of him he was surprised to see that Manigault and Colonel Sharp had pulled off the regiments of Jones's brigade closest to the railroad and sent them into the works without his knowledge or approval.[13]

Jones encountered more problems on his left, for the force opposing his advance was significant and menacing. General Sherman claimed in his memoirs that he insisted the Army of the Tennessee fight the battle alone without help from Thomas or Schofield, his actions indicate otherwise. Not only was a division from the XXIII Corps deployed to the left of the XVI Corps, Sherman ordered some of Schofield's batteries deployed near the Howard house, directing them to shell the woods west of the Troup Hurt house to prevent Confederate reinforcements from entering the breached earthworks. A brigade from the XXIII Corps was deployed in front of their batteries. As it turned out, the Army of the Ohio batteries and deployed infantry (including the division protecting Dodge) contributed little to the outcome, but the fact remains that nearly 10,000 troops outside of the Army of the Tennessee were immediately ready to take part in the Battle of Atlanta.[14]

Between the XXIII Corps and the Troup Hurt house stood the 1st Division of the XV Corps and the 6 cannons remaining from the same division (2-gun sections from three different batteries). Major Clemens Landgraeber commanded those batteries and took full advantage of his experience and the elevated, enfilading position on the same rise occupied by the house used as General Sherman's headquarters. Landgraeber pulled the cannons from their pits and reoriented them toward the Troup Hurt house 800 yards south of the hill they occupied. Those guns rent the air with canister balls and spherical case shot. The rounds wreaked havoc on both sides. One mile south of the batteries, Colonel Reuben Williams was already forced to contend with flank fire from the Mississippians at the railroad on his right; Landgraeber's cannons inadvertently magnified their predicament with "overshots" that landed uncomfortably close to those Union soldiers. Afterwards Williams reasoned, "The shelling of our own troops aided the enemy considerably, but it was one of those accidents that sometimes occur in the excitement, the thunder, the roar and the crash of battle, and which at times is difficult to avoid."[15]

Firing toward his own troops was not only inevitable for Landgraeber; it was absolutely necessary. Moreover, artillery fire began to stymie the Southern surge with relatively large brigades into the breach. Two of Clayton's brigades doubled the number of Confederates at the XV Corps line, but the enfilading Union fire kept most of those reinforcements from immediately entering the works and penetrating deeper into the Union rear. Those inside the Union line—Manigault's brigade, Sharp's brigade, and portions of Johnson's and Jones's brigades—had already lost much of their drive by accumulating prisoners and were virtually stopped by the cannon fire. "The artillery practice of the enemy was splendid," admitted Manigault, whose brigade attracted the rounds from Landgraeber's cannons. "Their shells tore through the lines or exploded in the faces of the men with unerring regularity." The 36th and 38th Alabama regiments from Jones's brigade ran a gauntlet as they traversed a field in front of the works on the left of Manigault's men. They made it, but were not able to penetrate deep into the works. Still, they were satisfied for the moment to have a wall of protection to block the menacing rounds of artillery coming from northeast of them.[16]

The ebb and flow of battle had characterized the entire nature of the fight of July 22, 1864, but at 4:45 P.M. an unprecedented storm overtook the field—General Logan had returned to the corps he led earlier in the day. He arrived with his staff in tow, greeted by chants of "Black Jack, Black Jack" as he passed elements of his former corps. Logan imbued inspiration. A captain was awestruck as he gazed upon his general "galloping down the ranks like a man of iron." An Ohio private was equally awed, as Logan, "with fire in his eyes, came dashing down the road." An Iowan observed with pride as Logan galloped past him, "his long black hair floating in the wind and his big black mustache bristling with defiance."[17]

Logan had no idea that while he was attempting to restore the line vacated by Lightburn's 2nd Division and two brigades of Harrow's 4th Division, General Harrow had sent retreat orders to the only remaining force between Bald Hill and Wood's 1st Division near Sherman's

COLONEL CHARLES CARROLL WALCUTT, U.S.A.

Walcutt oddly stood out in the battle for insubordination by refusing to pull his brigade back to a rearward line east of his position. His refusal to abandon his position preserved the Union defense of Leggett's Hill and served as a rallying point for the Federal resurgence. *(Courtesy of the Library of Congress)*

headquarters one and a half miles away. That was Walcutt's brigade, the southernmost body of troops of the corps, split into one line facing toward Atlanta and the other directed southward to provide a protective cover to Bald Hill. When Oliver's brigade had begun to peel away to join Reuben Williams's regiments, Walcutt remained with his northern flank severely threatened by Coltart's Alabamans. General Leggett rode up to Walcutt to confer with him about his position relative to the protection of Bald Hill. As the two talked, Harrow's aide galloped in with an order to pull his brigade back to a new corps line 800 yards east of the threatened position. Leggett protested against that order; he had a vested interest in Walcutt's position, for if Walcutt vacated his line, Leggett risked being completely surrounded on Bald Hill. "I said to him the order was a mistake," recalled Leggett of that moment with Walcutt, informing him that Logan and Blair had ordered him to hold Bald Hill "at any hazard and at whatever cost," an order that would risk the annihilation of his entire division if Walcutt's men would no longer protect his northern flank.

Walcutt assured Leggett that he would not abandon him. Leggett remembered the haughty pronouncement of that young and talented colonel, "Walc[u]tt responded promptly, that he could stay there as long as I could, and that he would take the responsibility of disobeying orders, and doing so." Convinced by Walcutt's pronouncement, Leggett returned to his hill. Walcutt turned several of his cannons to the most immediate threat, orienting them from south to northwest, right at the Alabamans occupying the works vacated by Colonels Oliver and Williams. As he softened the position with cannon fire, Walcutt's regiments took up positions to conduct a charge to drive away Coltart's Confederates.[18]

As Walcutt held his position and Logan rallied his corps, additional help arrived in the form of Colonel August Mersy's brigade, from Sweeny's division of the XVI Corps, the three regiments designated to be the shock troops of the battle. Twenty minutes after they peeled away from their XVI Corps brethren, Mersy's regiments hustled up a dusty back road to the Georgia Railroad, reaching a curve in the rail line, bordered by a plank fence about half a mile east of the Troup Hurt house at 4:45 P.M. Logan met them here, urging and inspiring them. Colonel Mersy aligned his troops, the 12th Illinois on the left, the 81st Ohio in the center, and the 66th Illinois on the right. As those troops attempted to change their alignment from a marching column only 4-men wide to an attacking column 500 yards across, Confederate troops a few hundred yards to their west opened fire in an attempt to disrupt the formation. The color bearer went down along with several members of his company. Another bullet thudded into the side of Billy, Colonel Mersy's horse. The animal reared in a death lurch, throwing Colonel Mersy and hurling itself across the board fence. With only the hind legs of the animal dangling over the side of the fence in sight of the brigade, Colonel Mersy was stunned by the blow from his fall and by a slight bullet wound in the leg, but appeared more hurt by the death of his horse. He turned over command to Colonel Robert N. Adams of the 81st Ohio. As Adams took over he heard Mersy moaning in his thick German accent, "Oh! My poor Billy, my poor Billy," aware that the colonel loved his horse "more than some men love their wives."[19]

Adams crossed his new brigade over the railroad tracks and ordered them forward at the double quick. "As the order was given," remembered Thomas Shelley of the 81st Ohio Volunteer Infantry, "the boys started with wild yells that would have given credit to a whole tribe of Comanche Indians." Rushing parallel with the railroad to their left, they negotiated through a belt of woods and exited with the contested works in panoramic view. Surprised to see that region in total possession of Confederate forces, Colonel Adams continued to press his men westward. "We rushed for the bright guns," recalled Private Shelley, training their faces and footsteps toward the 4 glistening Parrotts of De Gress's Battery.[20]

The Southern troops around the Troup Hurt house, the railroad, and the captured cannons were threatened before the XVI Corps brigade stumbled out of the woods east of them. The initial Union XV Corps resurgence against their position emerged from south of the railroad. General Logan, General Lightburn, and General Morgan L. Smith, along with their respective cadres of staff officers and regimental officers, successfully collected enough troops from the routed 2nd and 4th divisions of the XV Corps to initiate a counterattack.

General Harrow observed Walcutt hold his position above Bald Hill and he used that brigade as a beacon to rectify his routed brigade under Colonel Oliver. Harrow countermanded the retreat order given to the 70th Ohio. Anchoring from that regiment, and spurred on by its throaty cheers, the 48th Illinois of Oliver's brigade—the only other regiment in line at the time—re-formed and charged westward. Coltart's Alabama brigade, occupying the works abandoned by Colonel Reuben Williams's men, caught the brunt of the countersurge. With an unprotected right flank to blunt the assault of those two Union regiments southeast of them, the Alabamans were ordered to retreat. The cheering Federals, imbued with confidence, reclaimed their works but not without paying a price. Colonel Lucien Greathouse of the 48th Illinois was killed, and 40 members of his regiment went down dead or injured with him. About 20 members of the 70th Ohio likewise fell, but their achievement allowed Reuben Williams to return his two regiments to the line they were forced to abandon twenty minutes earlier, doing so, admitted the commander of the 12th Indiana, "with but little opposition."[21]

Indeed, the Confederate opposition for half a mile south of the railroad

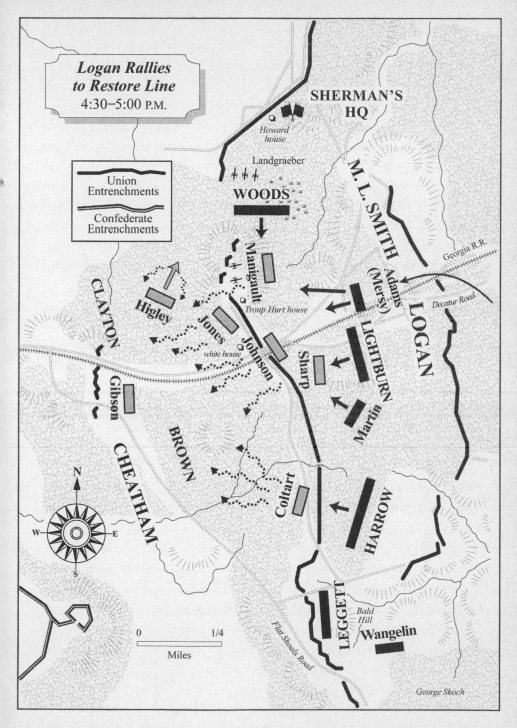

Logan Rallies to Restore Line
4:30–5:00 P.M.

SHERMAN'S HQ

Howard house

Landgraeber

WOODS

Union Entrenchments

Confederate Entrenchments

M. L. SMITH

Georgia R.R.

Adams (Mersy)

Decatur Road

Manigault

CLAYTON

Higley

Troup Hurt house

Jones

Johnson

LIGHTBURN

LOGAN

white house

Gibson

Sharp

Martin

BROWN

CHEATHAM

N
W   E
S

Coltart

HARROW

0   1/4
Miles

LEGGETT

Bald Hill

Wangelin

Flat Shoals Road

George Skoch

had disappeared, only materializing again in the Georgia militia opposite Bald Hill. That void was serendipitous for General Harrow, who had only four regiments of his entire division occupying the works with no artillery supporting them at the time. It also aided Colonel James S. Martin, who had half of his brigade supporting the western end of the XVI Corps line when he with his 750 soldiers was ordered to return to his noontime position. Martin's regiments caught no enfilading fire on their left as they traversed northwestward toward their original position.

Martin herded his men northward, parallel to the original line of works they awoke behind that morning. He came upon the remnant of his three detached regiments—the command of Lieutenant Colonel Mott—that had been routed by General Brown's division of Cheatham's corps half an hour earlier. Here Martin reunited his command. With his six regiments, and a few others positioned by General Morgan L. Smith (the new commander of the XV Corps) and General Lightburn (commanding Morgan Smith's former division), all moved forward.[22]

Additional inspiration bubbled over those soldiers, as attested by a member of the 55th Illinois. "Just as the regiment when at the rear was moving forward to this counter charge," he observed, "a well-known form came galloping furiously up the Decatur road on a coal-black charger streaked with foam, hatless, his long black hair flying, his eyes flashing with wrath—a human hurricane on horseback. It was 'Black Jack.'" General Logan was a dynamo: barking orders, sounding his battle cry, and throwing out words of encouragement to his former command. After sending Mersey's men off at the railroad, Logan had returned to the XV Corps urging everyone he could find to reclaim their lost real estate.[23]

Members of Logan's staff proved equal to his leadership. Major John R. Hotaling had continued to collect squads of soldiers while tucked away in the ravine within striking distance of Sharp's and Manigault's Confederates. Sensing the momentum changing in that sector and detecting the countercharge of Martin's brigade behind him, Hotaling and his hodgepodge regiment of 200 gun-toting men led Martin's charge toward the Confederate-held works. Those at the works and around the Troup Hurt house could detect that mass movement south of the Georgia Railroad easier and earlier than Adams's (Mersy's) brigade in the woods north of the railroad. Feeling the pressure on their right and also sensing troops from Wood's 1st Division of the XV Corps massing on the height north of them, General Brown and General Clayton both realized that the brigades of their respective divisions within the works were then vulnerable to cross fire. To prevent that, the two Southern generals quickly delivered orders for their men to fall back to the earthworks.[24]

Portions of three Confederate brigades were mingling around the Troup Hurt house and none was able to fire the spiked cannons of the captured guns of Battery H. Suffering from the lack of a unified command and without protection on their right and left, regimental commanders made two quick realizations: Adams's and Martin's men were converging upon them too fast and furiously for them to maintain their position and there was no time to bring off those captured cannons. Southern officers ordered all the battery horses shot, for slaying the animals would make it nearly impossible for the Yankees to roll them rearward should the Confederates be able to charge upon them again.

Martin's and Adams's brigades surged into the area overwhelmed by the sickening sound of screaming horses as they were slaughtered by Southern soldiers. The Federals pressed on and the Ohioans beelined to the prized battery. General Morgan L. Smith called it "as gallant a charge as I have seen during the war"—high praise, indeed, from a XV Corps commander about a brigade from another corps. Mason R. Blizzard of Company I, 81st Ohio, was the first soldier to reach the guns, getting there as Manigault's and Abda Johnson's men peeled away from them to fall back behind the earthworks. Close on the heels of the Ohioans rode the man who wanted those guns more than any other on the battlefield: Captain De Gress. "Going to the rear," explained De Gress, "I saw a brigade of the 16th A[rmy] C[orps] advancing and driving the enemy from our old Position and following them up I took possession of my Guns again."[25]

Mason R. Blizzard was the first man upon the battery, but the young Buckeye was joined by the rest of his Company I mates and the remainder of the charging regiment as well as Captain De Gress within seconds. De Gress enlisted the help of ten of the infantry and the sole member of Battery H with him to "unspike" the battery. A correctly spiked cannon could not be made operable in short order, but the makeshift method applied by De Gress in his hurry half an hour earlier then served in his favor. The impromptu gun crew loaded the first available gun and turned it westward toward the Southerners falling back toward safety. The 81st Ohio surprisingly proved a learned infantry regiment to work the artillery pieces. For the first two hours of the afternoon they watched Laird's and Blodgett's batteries in action, having carried ammunition to those batteries. Knowing that Laird had effectively fired double rounds, the Ohioans attempted to repeat the ingredients of that success. They loaded the gun with two twenty-pound shells. They pulled the lanyard, but the rammed shells exploded within the cannon, one that had a small defective crack in it from earlier in the campaign. That combination caused the cannon to explode with the shells, sending fifty- and hundred-pound pieces of brass and cast iron up and out 100 yards. "Not a man was hurt by the bursting of the Gun although they were standing thick around it," marveled De Gress. The other 3 guns that remained intact were soon working, because only single rounds were rammed down their barrels.[26]

Within seconds of the recapture of De Gress's guns, the 4 guns remaining from Battery A, Illinois Light Artillery were also seized by surging Union troops. The South Carolinians successfully removed two of the pieces but the other four were recaptured. Aiding in that recovery was the hodgepodge regiment formed by Major John R. Hotaling. Artillerist James W. Porter also lent a hand. Playing dead near the cannons while the Confederates were in charge of them, Porter popped up during their withdrawal, grabbed a rifle from a dead soldier, and fired away.[27]

Most of the organized Confederates had already pulled back behind the earthworks they created, but had belonged to the XV Corps that morning. General Brown was not satisfied at the position held by his division. Riding to and fro near the point of attack, he exhorted his regiments forward to reclaim their lost ground. "We charged with an awful yell," said Lieutenant Gill of the 41st Mississippi, who watched the bluecoats opposing his regiment flee for a second time in an hour. Picking up loaded but discarded guns, the Mississippian relished the sight that befell his eyes. "I never enjoyed a thing better in my life," he crowed in a letter to his wife the next day. "We had the pleasure of shooting at Yankees as they ran without being shot at much."[28]

A small pocket of Union soldiers ran rearwards, mostly from Adams's (Mersy's) brigade. The majority held their hard-fought and reclaimed position, aided by Landgraeber's batteries on the hill north of them. A new threat materialized on the left flank of the Confederates. General Charles Woods's division—down to two brigades of 2,000 men after the reassignment of Hugo Wangelin's brigade—had aligned to face the Confederate threat and awaited orders from General Morgan Smith to advance. Big and burly, Woods was an imposing figure at 6'3" in height and close to 250 pounds ("the most manly of men," claimed a contemporary), with the most unimposing nickname in the army—"Susan." According to Major General Oliver Otis Howard, a corps commander in the Army of the Cumberland, Woods earned the effeminate name at West Point, where the law of contraries was displayed in full bloom, "probably because of his ungirl-like qualities, except perhaps his modesty of deportment, for he was the largest, tallest, stoutest officer on the ground, showing at all times a nerve unconscious of danger."[29]

"Susan" Woods received verbal orders and advanced the two brigades of his division southward into the fray. His order came from General Morgan L. Smith, who received his orders from none other than General Sherman, who was overseeing the deployment of Schofield's batteries on the hill that housed his headquarters one-half mile north of De Gress's guns. Woods's seven regiments—all but two from Iowa—descended one hill, crossed the marshy ground in its creek valley, and ascended the contested height on which stood the Troup Hurt house and opposing forces on each side of it.[30]

Woods's 2nd Brigade, commanded by Colonel James A. Williamson, struck the flank and rear of Clayton's line at the earthworks, held tenuously by the 36th and 38th Alabama of Johnson's brigade and the three Alabama regiments of Higley's brigade. The three attacking Iowa regiments matched the numbers of the five Alabama regiments on the Confederate left flank, but their advantageous position, with Union guns supporting them, gave them the upper hand.

As Williamson's men struck the works, Colonel Milo Smith's brigade rushed in from the northeast, closing upon the Confederate position like a huge hinge. Driving all vestiges of Confederates away from the works, the Iowans, Missourians, and Ohioans swarmed around De Gress's battery, apparently abandoned by most of the 81st Ohio who had seized it earlier. The 1st Division soldiers claimed their capture, sparking a decades-long debate about who deserved the credit for possession of those contested cannons. Woods would insist in his official report and in his postbattle and postwar writings that his men recaptured De Gress's Battery, a claim that holds no water given the opposing accounts—including Captain De Gress's—that award the 81st Ohio and Adams's (Mersy's) brigade with that honor. At a cost of 77 men out of 2,000 engaged, Woods's division effectively mopped up that portion of the battlefield.[31]

No longer in dispute was the possession of the earthworks and the region earlier held by the XV Corps. It was back in Union hands, secured by 5:00 P.M. Both Confederate division commanders—Brown and Clayton—saw that their cause was lost. General Cheatham, whose presence throughout the hour-long fight has never been ascertained, had all but one brigade of his corps committed into the fight. For a diversionary assault, Cheatham's men certainly accomplished their mission but could stay no longer. He ordered his men back to their works.

For the 10th South Carolina, the order to withdrawal was painful to bear. "It did seem hard," lamented one of the Gamecocks. "We had built these breastworks, given them up to the enemy, re-taken them at a very heavy sacrifice and now we had to give them up again." The unsettling feeling that all of the sacrifice "had been for nothing" haunted them as they worked their way back to the safety of the works they had created a mile to the rear. The Carolinians and the rest of Cheatham's corps had inflicted more than 500 lethal and nonlethal wounds upon the XV Corps, captured 500 hundred others, and then owned 2 of their cannons, but the cost to the Confederates was horrifying. Close to 2,000 Southerners were killed, wounded, or captured in Cheatham's corps. Furthermore, the lines were back in the same appearance and position they held at the midmorning.[32]

Hood's corps-sized diversion had ended, partly because Hood sent it with a diversion in mind. Hood had always intended for Hardee's corps to carry the responsibility of rolling up the Union army, expecting that to be accomplished in the morning of July 22. Yet at 5:00 P.M. on Friday, with three hours of daylight remaining, another lull on the battlefield indicated that the battle of Atlanta was over.

It was an incorrect assumption, for General Pat Cleburne had one more act to perform before the curtain closed on that stage.

10

DESPERATION

The XV Corps—with more than a little help from the resurgent Adams's (Mersy's) brigade—successfully restored its original line by 5:00 P.M., a feat that was not even attempted by the Union army on the southern end of the line. General Hardee's three-hour assault against the XVI and XVII Corps had not swept those corps from the field, but it did force them to accept the loss of a large portion of their line. This was particularly true for General Giles Smith's division of Blair's XVII corps. Both of Giles Smith's brigades were rocked by Cleburne's attack and sent northward where they had intermingled with General Leggett's division for two hours. Nearly the entire extent of the XVII Corps line was gone; only its northern anchor on Bald Hill remained. Three quarters of a mile of Union earthworks were lost to the Confederates or sat in a tenuous position between Bald Hill and the Confederate line.

The remnant of the XVI Corps also was forced to adjust its position, pulling back northward to a position where its commander, General Grenville M. Dodge, could make the best use of the two brigades remaining in the Union rear. The new position, plus the arrival of Wangelin's brigade from Woods's division of the XV Corps between the two corps and the divisions of the XXIII Corps (Army of the Ohio) made the new Union line change from a fish hook appearance to three sides of a square, each three quarters of a mile long, with the Decatur road and the Georgia Railroad topping off that box. That determined Union defense was then designed to prevent any Confederate troops from entering the box and disintegrating its sides. With the successful repulse of Cheatham's Confederate corps in the west, the chief threat to the integrity of the defense would emanate from the south.[1]

General Blair was responsible for the lower left side of that box. Bald Hill protruded from the corner, a vision of carnage unseen in most previous battles of the Civil War. Blair's men had shed gallons of blood to retain possession of the hill and their commander was determined not to relinquish it. He tapped General Leggett to hold the hill with the handful of regiments comprising his 1st and 3rd brigades (Colonel George E. Bryant's and Colonel Adam G. Malloy's) facing westward, the 30th Illinois of Bryant's brigade serving as the corner regiment of the division, facing southward. Leggett shifted the three Ohio regiments of his 2nd Brigade (commanded by Lieutenant Colonel Greenberry F. Wiles) to extend eastward from the left flank of the 30th Illinois. In a cornfield at the base of the hill, Wiles positioned the 68th Ohio to the left (east) of the 30th Illinois, following farther eastward with the 78th Ohio and then the 20th Ohio. The remnants of Hall's Iowa brigade (Giles Smith's 3rd Brigade) completed the XVII Corps formation. The 11th Iowa took a position on Bald Hill, facing southeast. The 13th and 15th Iowa anchored the left flank of the southward-facing line, positioned off the left flank of the 20th Ohio. The regiments of Potts's 1st Brigade took the reserve position behind the Iowans and Ohioans.[2]

The six regiments in the frontline of the southward-facing portion of the corps prepared for the inevitable attack against their position. According to one of the soldiers, "Logs, rails or anything that could stop a Rebel bullet were hastily piled in line and every man with a tin plate and bayonet soon had a slight breastwork." Adding to the Union protection was artillery. The Black Horse Battery and the howitzers of Battery D, 1st Illinois Light Artillery, stayed on Bald Hill, prepared to sweep the field between the opposing lines.[3]

Additional focus on Bald Hill was directed at the protection on its crest. The prominent breastwork was originally constructed and held by Cleburne's men on July 20 and was constructed with a crescent moon shape oriented to the south and east. Since captured by Leggett's men, the additional walls were constructed to face west and southwest, all areas made thicker and higher than the original primitive structure. Thus, the works then looked like a fort with walls 8 feet high, "perpendicular on the outside and an inclined plane on the inside." Open only on the north, the horseshoe-shaped structure housed Buckeyes and Hawkeyes, primarily companies from the 11th Iowa Infantry. Surrounding the fort and facing away from it were the Union protectors, most from the Old Northwest Territory: Wisconsin men to the west and north (under Bryant), Illinoisans (Bryant's men), and Ohioans (Wiles's men), stationed southwest and south, and Iowans (under Hall) to the east, with artillerists from Illinois and Michigan reinforcing the entire knoll. "I claim no more for our regiment than that our position took us to the key to the hill," explained a member of Bryant's 12th Wisconsin, "but if it had not been for Hoosiers, Suckers, Hawkeyes, Buckeyes and Badgers, our stay there would have been short." The collective mission for the troops atop Bald Hill was never to lose possession of it.[4]

General Blair wished he had more men for his line, but he did not appear overly concerned about it. At 4:30 P.M. he had a dispatch sent directly to General Sherman. After notifying Sherman in writing that his two divisions had been "repulsing Hardee's corps with heavy loss," Blair made a most interesting request. "The enemy have become quiet," Blair revealed, "and if I had a fresh brigade I would recover all that I have lost and drive the enemy easily." General Blair did not expect to be attacked again, believing a handful of regiments was all the infusion he needed to recover the ground relinquished by Giles Smith. It is also apparent that by sending his request to General Sherman, General Blair did not know that Black Jack Logan was in charge of the army—evidence that Logan and Blair had not had a chance to communicate since the death of General McPherson.[5]

General Blair did not appreciate the foreboding sense within his ranks that the XVII Corps was about to be victimized by a huge attack commencing from the south, a Confederate assault larger and more devastating than the midafternoon attack they withstood three hours earlier. Shortly after the repulse of Lowrey's brigade at 3:00 P.M., General Cleburne had been rounding up all of his available troops for a grand assault. Ostensibly under Hardee's orders, Cleburne marked that mission with his signature. He rounded up fragments of his own spent brigades such as Lowrey's, Govan's, and James A. Smith's (then commanded by Lieutenant Colonel Robert B. Young), as well as lightly or uncommitted forces from other divisions in Hardee's corps to launch the largest coordinated attack of the day.

MAJOR GENERAL FRANCIS "FRANK" PRESTON BLAIR JR.
AND HIS XVII CORPS STAFF, U.S.A.

Frank Blair, the bearded commander seated in the center of the front row, was a political general and a member of a very prominent family. His corps arrived in Georgia in the middle of the Atlanta campaign. Blair's first big battle with the XVII Corps was Atlanta. He lost 2,500 men in two days of fighting, but his staunch defense against repeated attacks foiled Hood's grand plan. *(Courtesy of the Library of Congress)*

General Lowrey aided Cleburne in his efforts to round up troops for the grand assault. Hampered in that his own brigade was essentially inoperative—"cut to pieces," Lowrey later explained—Lowrey assumed the role of supporting the first line attack. He believed the opportunity for success came and went an hour or so earlier when he gained permission to attack with the Georgia brigade of Mercer's division, commanded by Colonel William Barkuloo after Mercer took over the division upon the death of General William H. T. Walker. According to Lieutenant

Hamilton Branch, "Lowrey then came galloping up to us and told us that we now had the yanks where we wanted them, and that now we would charge them and not leave one to tell the tale, and says he, I know that you are just the boys to do it." Perhaps they were, but their commander was not. Recently recovered from a severe illness, the July Atlanta heat consumed Colonel Barkuloo, who was forced to relinquish command to Lieutenant Colonel Morgan Rawls.[6]

As it turned out Lowrey's and Rawls's brigades would have to wait, for they literally bumped into Maney's division while trying to work their way through the woods to the flank, which delayed them considerably. Lowrey considered the true opportunity lost by the slowness of Maney's men, but as evening approached another opportunity arose and Lowrey was able to shift the brigades. Rawls's brigade shifted several hundred yards westward, from a point opposite the center of Dodge's XVI corps to one off the west flank of Blair's XVII Corps. Coalescing in that region were portions of every other division of Hardee's corps: two brigades from Maney's Tennessee division, Thomas Benton Smith's brigade of Georgians and Tennesseans from Bate's division, and Lowrey's and Govan's and a small portion of James A. Smith's brigade from Cleburne's force. Although representatives from seven brigades were forming there, the total number of soldiers prepared to participate topped off at 6,000 officers and men. Cleburne organized the attackers in two lines. The front consisted of Colonel Francis M. Walker's brigade on the left, Rawls's Georgians in the center, and Govan's men on the right.[7]

By far the largest and healthiest Confederate brigade on that mission was the Tennessee brigade of Colonel Francis M. Walker, a brigade that claimed an additional regiment—the 19th Tennessee—as a stipulation for Colonel Walker taking the helm of General Maney's former command. Colonel Walker was a sound replacement for General Maney. An experienced and gallant leader (and the nephew of Zachary Taylor), Walker commanded the only brigade in Hardee's corps not to take casualties up to that point on Friday; the Tennesseans had spent the entire afternoon marching and countermarching. Sam Watkins of the 1st Tennessee Infantry noted that their position was barely 200 yards from where they commenced their march the previous night, a revelation that bothered him nearly twenty years later. "It was a 'flank movement' you see," railed Watkins in 1882, "and had to be counted that way anyhow.

When one army makes a flank movement, it is courtesy on the part of the other army to recognize the flank movement, and to change his base."[8]

Frustration, though, was the only ailment suffered within the ranks of Colonel Walker's men. In fact, the long respite allowed stragglers to return to their respective regiments within his brigade. Colonel Walker's brigade was back to full strength, perhaps 1,500 officers and men. Rawls's brigade, having sustained only 15 casualties in front of the XVI Corps, likely carried 1,200 soldiers on the right of Colonel Walker. Cleburne probably roused up another 800–1,000 officers and men from the Arkansas (Govan) and Texas (Young) brigades of his division to represent the right flank of the Confederate attack line.[9]

At 6:00 P.M. Cleburne sent them all forward. Close to 3,500 frontline Confederates stormed the Union works; at least 2,000 more waited in a second wave of support behind them. The Tennesseans under Colonel Walker headed eastward, the Georgians under Rawls keeping pace in a northeastward path on their right, and Govan's Arkansans charging due north over some of the same ground Lowrey's brigade had captured three hours earlier. The Southerners reached the first set of earthworks, the old line once held by Giles Smith's division earlier that day. General Cleburne personally led the Tennesseans from Colonel Walker's brigade. With sword drawn, the general bellowed, "Follow me, boys." Follow they did, keeping but a few paces behind Cleburne, who was distinctively attired in a bobtail coat. Except for a Union skirmish line, the earthworks were undefended and easily claimed by the Confederates. Nevertheless, the main Union line looked ominous a quarter of a mile ahead of them on top of Bald Hill, and it stretched eastward for more than 1,000 yards.[10]

There were half as many defenders as there were attackers. Colonel Hugo Wangelin's XV Corps Missouri brigade of 900 officers and men bridged the left flank of Blair's XVII Corps with the right flank of Brigadier General John W. Fuller's brigade of Dodge's XVI corps. Those Missourians under Wangelin continued to escape any action by the sheer happenstance of their position. They would spend the rest of the battle witnessing a grand assault of Confederates against Blair's new and improved line. Wangelin's brigade was the only Union unit on the field not to be engaged. It registered a mere 5 casualties for its service on July 22. To their immediate right, the 13th and 15th Iowa also would view the action rather than participate in it, a circumstance of their deployed position that would benefit those decimated commands.[11]

Cleburne's point of attack was directed from opposite angles at the same regiments who had defended Bald Hill throughout the afternoon, however, the 11th Iowa was to get into the action as an additional deployed regiment on the knoll. For the second time in four hours, the Hawkeyes were struck by Govan's Razorbacks, advancing over the same path previously used by Lowrey's brigade. Ironically, the 11th Iowa was the only XVII Corps regiment that had grown in numbers during the afternoon with the return of three detached companies and an additional 100 men who had been on fatigue duty. Govan would have envied the Iowans' fortune, for his command suffered so much in their successful rout of Hall's brigade from their entrenched flank early that afternoon that it was a wonder that his brigade could take the offensive again just a few hours later. Attacking with no more than 900 men in the entire brigade (plus scores of Texans from Young's brigade on his right), Govan's brigade was weakened by the incredible number of regimental and company officers killed and wounded in his first attack of the day. With the loss of three quarters of his field officers and likely an equal proportion of company officers from the gallant action on the Union flank, most of Govan's companies and regiments entered the evening fight led by men alien to their new commands.[12]

That was a time for stellar leadership to be displayed from the lowest ranks. Captain William F. Bourne stood out as one to meet that challenge. Bourne grew up in Memphis and captained a company originally called "the Young Guard," which eventually became incorporated as Company B of the 3rd Confederate Infantry, a regiment of Arkansas, Mississippi, and Tennessee men led by a fellow captain throughout the Georgia campaign in 1864. The regiment was the only one in the brigade not consolidated with another, but it should have been because it carried a mere 70 men onto the battlefield. The 3rd Confederate missed the afternoon assault but came up in time to participate in the evening attack.[13]

Captain Bourne and the rest of Govan's men passed through the woods they had owned since the afternoon and swarmed into the open creek valley 300 yards south of Bald Hill. Govan made two quick and angst-filled discoveries that imperiled him much more than they had

Lowrey: First, the Union defenders had protected the east and south sides of the hill with earthworks covering their front and flank; and second, additional angling works then threatened the Confederate attackers with a menacing enfilading fire. Govan shifted his men slightly westward to face off directly against the 11th Iowa, more specifically at the southern side of the fort housing about 100 of them and led by Captain John Anderson of Company A. Captain Anderson was conspicuous while under fire here; a witness on the hill called him "a host in himself" as Anderson loaded guns for the privates, pointed out important developments to fellow officers, yelled out words of encouragement to all, and was even seen firing loaded rifles at the Arkansans.

As much as Union Captain Anderson was sound, Confederate Captain Bourne was awe inspiring. An Iowan in the fort was struck by Bourne's performance, although he obviously did not know his identity. "Just at this point a rebel officer was very conspicuous," gushed the Yankee; "he was always in the lead, cheering his men forward and urging them to go over the works, but the deadly fire of our rifles and their fast-thinning ranks outbalanced their leader's eloquence." The regiment melted away at the base of Bald Hill, leaving only dozens of those Confederates unscathed. Captain Bourne was not one of them. The Iowan remarked, "Several of us presented our regards to this officer, but no one saw him fall." Bourne was killed in front of his men, earning the respect of friend and foe alike.[14]

The efforts of Bourne and others in Govan's command enabled the brigade to grab a toehold at the hill by flattening themselves behind works they captured in front of the Iowans. They were unable to advance any closer, but they secured that position as the rest of Cleburne's attackers converged upon the hill from the southwest. Even behind the works Govan's losses mounted to obscene levels. As the evening waned, his brigade—formed from eleven regiments—looked more and more like one large regiment. Five hundred casualties for July 22 left Govan with less than 800 officers and men to fight the next day, but those men clung tenaciously to the ground they sacrificed far too much to acquire.[15]

Govan lost another valuable officer on southwest side of the battlefield where Cleburne and Maney had launched their attack with the Tennesseans and Georgians. Colonel George F. Baucum of the 8th Arkansas had been detached to skirmish for Cleburne, but he was wounded at the forefront of that assault. He survived, but scores of skirmishers perished in front of the Yankee guns. One of those dead was particularly conspicuous. Killed instantly by a bullet through his brain, the soldier remained in the position in which he took in his last breath, kneeling behind a stump with his rifle pointed toward Bald Hill.[16]

Notwithstanding the menacing advance of Govan's brigade from the south, Union artillery and infantry fire remained oriented to the southwest, toward the threat posed by the 2,000 men that moved in position behind their skirmishers. The defenders of Bald Hill fired upon the men from Colonel Walker's brigade and Rawls's brigade as they left the woods to converge upon the hill. Once they came into view, the killing intensified as the gunners rammed double rounds of canister down their muzzles. A member of the Black Horse Battery claimed that their performance against that assault was "our most deadly work." Three regiments on the west and southern side of the hill also blazed away at the attackers: the 30th Illinois, the 68th Ohio, and the 78th Ohio. Those regiments deployed outside the earthworks, draping the hillside across its southern and southwestern slope. Iowa and Wisconsin (Bryant's) troops covered the flanks as did the 20th Ohio down the eastern flank. They likely were unable to fire on the attackers, but were prepared to meet them if they reached the hill.[17]

The Tennesseans under Colonel Walker took severe casualties, which sent scores of men reeling back to the woods, but General Cleburne and General Maney rallied them and charged the works again. The Confederates rushed across the same cultivated fields where Potts's brigade had successfully fended off Strahl's regiments three hours earlier. The Union skirmish line witnessed the effects of artillery fire on the Tennessee men "which tore wide spaces in their ranks." Taking his first steps into the field, a soldier in the 9th Tennessee noted, "As I looked down the line, I could see men dropping by the scores." Struck twice by enemy lead, the soldier joined the casualty list of his regiment (a list with more than sixty names on it). Fortunately for him, he fell in a furrow between two ridges. That man-made ravine protected the wounded soldier and allowed him to remain in place for several hours as bullets and artillery rounds rent the air a few feet above him. "I remember that the crash of bullets against an old tree which stood near me was as continuous as the ringing of a bell," he recalled.[18]

More Union bullets and artillery rounds crashed into human bodies than into that tree, but the Union skirmish line, lying prone in the field between the two opposing lines, was harassed by musketry from both sides, which grew heavier and heavier. "The line of fire was picking our men out as they lay hugging the ground," complained Captain Gilbert Munson, General Leggett's picket officer, who was horrified to see so many killed and wounded in that helpless position. "Very many were shot in the head. Few tried to get back, even when wounded. They knew that to stand up while that sheet of lead was in the air was sure death. So they lay quiet and suffered."[19]

Neither the incessant metal hail nor the mounting casualties stopped Cleburne's charge. Colonel Walker's men forced Munson's skirmishers—at least those who dared lift their heads—back toward their original lines. Those Confederates were developing a double convergence against the Bald Hill defense. Not only were the regiments of Walker's brigade and Govan's brigade closing in upon the knoll from two directions, but the Georgians from Rawls's brigade added a new dimension by advancing more parallel with the Flat Shoals Road between those two brigades. Rawls led his troops northeastward toward the works created and held by General Leggett's division, peppered with lead and iron after every quick-step they took. They brushed away bluecoated skirmishers and traversed their light works and then struck the commanding earthworks lining the west side of the Flat Shoals Road where Rawls halted them. One of the Georgians considered that "the big mistake," for the Ohioans were merely shouting distance away from them. The Buckeyes did their talking with their guns, pummeling Rawls's men with a ferocious hail of bullets and locking them in position.

Most of the Georgians escaped an instant death or a painful wound by tucking themselves behind the Union works, but three huge gaps existed in that line of parapets, open points where Union batteries once stood. The Confederates crowding behind the works were unavoidably stuck on their side of the gaps, where Union infantry cut them down with relative ease. Locked in place and unable to charge into the Union line, dozens upon dozens of Southerners were killed and wounded, including Lieutenant Colonel Rawls who went down with a painful wound and had to be carried to the rear. Battle flags acted like magnets, attracting Union metal each time they were waved. The flag of the 54th Georgia (in Rawls's brigade) was perforated 115 times. The flagstaff was splintered by bullets, snapping in two places.[20]

As Lieutenant Colonel Rawls was escorted rearward, command of the Georgians then devolved upon Lieutenant Colonel Cincinnatus S. Guyton of the 57th Georgia. He became the *fourth* commander of that brigade in just five hours and took over his new duties under more trying circumstances than all of his predecessors. The Ohioans were less than 50 yards from his regiments at the works; Guyton's left flank had intermingled with the right flank of Colonel Walker's Tennessee brigade, throwing both into disorder, and, unable to hide his frustration, Guyton reported, "The brigade was in the utmost state of confusion as regarded its organization." Guyton was an aggressive commander who well understood that his command was most threatened while stagnant and not able to fight back. He ordered his men to advance, but the men could not respond. The officers, like those in Govan's brigade, had been thinned out by Northern bullets and artillery rounds and it was impossible for those not killed or wounded to organize their respective commands into attacking bodies while within point-blank range of their adversary. Guyton was forced to hold his men in place as the brigade absorbed 150 total casualties.[21]

Although Govan and Guyton were unable to breach Blair's XVII Corps' reconstructed line, they apparently were able to divert enough attention toward their threatening positions to allow Cleburne's intended line busters to assault the hill. Colonel Walker's Tennesseans absorbed as many as 100 casualties in the cultivated field west of Bald Hill, but enough of them were charging toward the embrasure on the knoll to carry their momentum onto its crest. Colonel Walker led his men on foot up the slope of the hill, waving his sword "in glittering circles above his head" to exhort his men forward. Hundreds of fellow Tennesseans followed him to the crest, but a ferocious volley pummeled them and halted the momentum. With his general's commission en route from Richmond, Francis Walker's promising career ended in that volley atop Bald Hill. Pierced by an enemy bullet Walker crumbled to one knee while his head dropped upon the other, seemingly freezing the dead colonel in prayer. "They were dropping here and there," remembered a Buckeye watching the approach from within the fort, "but on they came like cattle facing a storm, and in a few minutes they were masters of the situation outside."[22]

The Tennesseans were fighting the third battle for Bald Hill in thirty-three hours. The latest one appeared the most intense and ferocious of the three. The Tennessee regiments from Colonel Walker's brigade stormed the southwest and west side of Bald Hill, the region primarily defended by the 30th Illinois, 68th Ohio, and 78th Ohio, three regiments from two different brigades in Leggett's division who earlier had withstood Lowrey's assault under Cleburne with some hand-to-hand combat. History repeated itself in a matter of hours as Confederates clashed with Leggett's men atop the hill. A member of the 78th Ohio revealed, "We fixed bayonets and then and there we had it with clubbed muskets, fisticuffs, and wrestling." Yank and Reb punched, stabbed, and bludgeoned each other. Officers, who before that moment considered their dress swords "as mere playthings for the parade," used the ceremonial weapon to hack away at their opponent. At one point, a living body was used for tug-of-war, Confederates pulling at his feet to take him prisoner and Union soldiers yanking him from the other end to save him from capture. It was a melee once again for control of Bald Hill.[23]

Families were forever ripped apart and destroyed as a result of that fight. A prime example was seen with the Gochenour brothers of Company B, 78th Ohio. John and James fought side by side on the hill until James crumpled to the ground with a mortal wound. Distraught at the death of his brother in front of his eyes, John scaled and stood on a parapet; according to another in the regiment, he was "crazed with rage" as he sought revenge, but in a few minutes Rebel lead dropped him, too, and he died a bloody death next to the lifeless body of his brother.[24]

Flags and their bearers attracted the most attention; as gunpowder smoke hung and thickened at the top of the hill the colorful and lofted standards were some of the only visible beacons in that raging sea of battle. Confederate color bearers defiantly speared their flags into the battle-plowed ground on the crest of the hill—within 20 yards of their Union counterparts—and their men formed and rallied around those planted flags. Union flag bearers risked their lives to keep hold of their regimental colors, a repeat of their afternoon performance. Sergeant Russ Bethel of the 78th Ohio grappled with a Southerner determined to seize his flag. Two possession changes later, Bethel held the flag, but not before sustaining serious injuries to both of his legs and one arm. Another Confederate attempted to bayonet the burly sergeant and put an end to that contest;

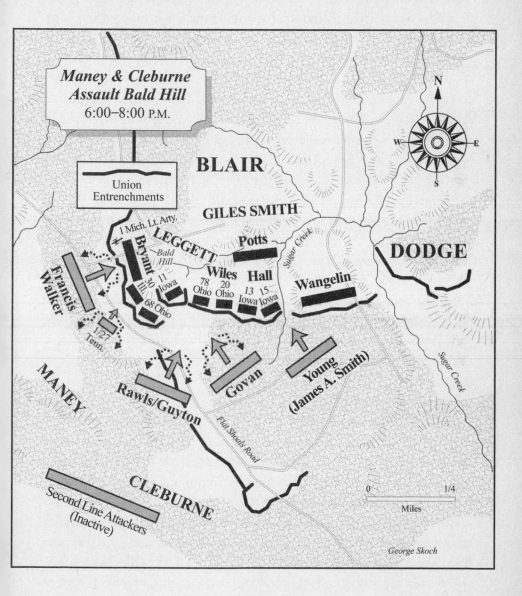

Maney & Cleburne
Assault Bald Hill
6:00–8:00 P.M.

Union
Entrenchments

BLAIR

GILES SMITH

1 Mich. Lt. Arty.

LEGGETT

Potts

Bryant

Bald
Hill

Wiles Hall

Francis
Walker

30
Ill.

11
Iowa

78
Ohio

20
Ohio

13
Iowa

15
Iowa

Wangelin

DODGE

68 Ohio

1/27
Tenn.

Rawls/Guyton

Govan

Young
(James A. Smith)

Sugar Creek

Sugar Creek

MANEY

Flat Shoals Road

CLEBURNE

Second Line Attackers
(Inactive)

0   1/4

Miles

N
W   E
S

George Skoch

just before he thrust his blade into Bethel he was cut down and nearly severed in two by Captain John Orr of the 78th Ohio who swung away at other Confederates rushing in and thus kept the flag in Bethel's possession. Also, the standard bearer of the 20th Ohio almost lost his flag to a Tennessee colonel, but members of the color guard intervened with their bayonets and it stayed in the hands of its regiment.[25]

For Henry McDonald, the big and bold color bearer of the 30th Illinois at the southwestern edge of the hill, the struggle for the flag ended far differently. Earlier that afternoon, McDonald retained his flag by shooting down one of Lowrey's men who had tried to grab it. As the sun dipped toward the hazy western horizon, members of the 27th Tennessee swarmed around McDonald as he stood on a breastwork, defiantly waving his flag. Sergeant Eli Detwiler of the 30th Illinois claimed that all cohesion was lost because "Our brigade was all mixed up and every man appeared to be fighting on his own hook and commanding himself." Every man fighting around McDonald's flag was on a mission to save it or seize it. Lives were sacrificed by both sides for that flag, but it was McDonald's death that finally ended the struggle. John C. Leird of the 27th Tennessee wrested it away and carried it with him back to the Confederate lines. "I must say there never was a braver soldier ever marched under stars and stripes," lamented McDonald's brother (also a 30th Illinois soldier), who grudgingly praised Private Leird over the incident, "We regretted very much to lose our flag, but honor the man who went into that 'death trap' to get it."[26]

Casualties mounted on the crest, the hillsides, and the base at an appalling rate. Colonel Walker's men did not discriminate between who or what they attacked. They made two attempts at the Union batteries on Bald Hill, but here they failed miserably. Captain Elliott, in charge of the Black Horse Battery, insisted, "Only a single man of the enemy reached us in two charges. His comrades were mowed down like grain." The futility of taking out those cannons likely diverted Colonel Walker's Tennesseans to focus their attack on the opposing infantry on the hillcrest.[27]

Action swirled and intensified around the U-shaped fort on the hill. According to Lieutenant Edmund Nutt of the 20th Ohio, the Tennesseans "tried to crowd in through the embrasures, and would load behind the earth embankments and fire in at the embrasures—a deadly fire as the fort was full of men." Most of those men were from the 11th Iowa, led by Captain Anderson, who had effectively repulsed Govan's brigade and then had to contend with that awesome threat. Here Anderson lost more than 100 men, but he kept calm control of his soldiers in the works. Lieutenant Nutt also led here; dozens of the fort's occupants were 20th Ohioans under his command. To stop the annihilation, sharpshooters were posted to pick off any Confederates "on the first appearance" in front of the earthen walls, while others loaded guns and handed them to the shooters. When the pressure against the fort waned, other sharpshooters climbed atop the earthworks, fired their weapons, and passed them back to be reloaded. That procedure was effective and efficient; a rolling, continuous discharge kept the fort in Union hands as gray- and butternut-clad bodies filled the passageways and other areas where a line of sight ended their lives. "The fort was held," concluded a relieved Lieutenant Nutt.[28]

That stage of the fight entered its third hour as the sun set ten minutes before 8:00 P.M. General Cleburne and General Maney had already fed in reinforcements, but they merely served as supports for the brigades of Govan, Guyton, and Walker. The Texas brigade, commanded that evening by Lieutenant Colonel Robert B. Young, extended Govan's right, but far to Govan's rear. With no brigades supporting east of them, the Texans could not advance against Blair's XVII Corps line. The assault could not be sustained and it began to ebb as organized Confederate commands pulled back behind the closest protection they could find and disorganized pockets of troops made themselves as inconspicuous as possible by flattening against the Georgia clay, fleeing to the woods from where they started, or crowding behind other works.[29]

Darkness failed to relieve the tension of a hard day's battle, as it had done in all the other battles of the campaign in northwest Georgia. Instead, the night intensified the harrowing experience suffered by both sides of that hard-fought contest on and surrounding Leggett's (Bald) Hill and Leggett's Fort (names universally applied to them by their defenders). The adjutant of the 11th Iowa respectfully observed, "Behind a small embankment about three feet high and seventy feet long, immediately in front of Leggett's Fort, a lot of brave rebels had collected.... All night long they kept firing at us, and we in turn at the flash of their guns." An Ohioan in the fort claimed, "Men went to sleep loading guns or waiting for them to be loaded, and snoring was a soothing refrain to musketry." The Confederates enjoyed no such refrains. "We remained all night in the work greatly exposed to the fire of sharpshooters. The position being raked by the enemy's artillery," complained a Georgia captain from Guyton's brigade in his journal. Here they would remain until the predawn hours of Saturday.[30]

Colonel Francis Walker topped the list of 53 Tennesseans killed and wounded in their failed attempt to seize Bald Hill. Based on the ratio of wounded and missing to killed in other engaged Confederate brigades that day (approximately 5 to 1), Walker's brigade must have suffered at least 250 casualties. They shed the most blood of any brigade of Confederate attackers, but Govan took nearly as many losses. Guyton's Georgians suffered over 150 in killed and wounded; thus, the cost to the Confederates exceeded 600 men in conducting that two-hour assault and withstanding the overnight retreat.[31]

Although ultimately unsuccessful, Cleburne and Maney inflicted an appreciable beating upon the Union defenders. Most of the 170 losses suffered by the 30th Illinois occurred in that evening assault; the 11th Iowa lost more than 100 men here; the 68th Ohio had 60 killed and wounded—every fourth man of that regiment was rendered hors de combat; the 78th and 20th Ohio suffered about 200 losses between them in those two hours. Adding in the small number of casualties from supporting units, Blair suffered 550 losses in the evening and night defense of Bald Hill, a result that brought his two-division corps losses to 1,800 for the entire Friday fight and 2,500 in a span of thirty-five hours.[32]

As the fire slackened after dark, General Logan, the commander of the Army of the Tennessee, rode across the positions held by all three of his corps, spoke with each of the corps commanders, and sent a brief report to General Sherman that night. He informed Sherman that he had reinforced Bald Hill with some fresh regiments, for he recognized that that spot was "the key-point to my whole position." Sherman relayed a synopsis of the day's actions to be telegraphed to Washington. "Fighting has been severe," reported Sherman, "and we have lost General McPherson, killed by shot through lungs while on a reconnaissance." Sherman closed with his belief (and hope) that the enemy would not be a threat to them in the morning, but his last line was both obvious and ominous at the same time, "Hood fights his graybacks desperately."[33]

Two miles west of Sherman's headquarters, General Hood sized up the day's outcome and wired the Confederate War Department of his conclusion. He gave Richmond the first news of McPherson's death, confirmed the death of General William Walker and the wounding of brigade commanders. The "fog of war" was still apparent in that early message as Hood overestimated the number of cannons and prisoners he captured. He stated that Wheeler won at Decatur and that his infantry routed the Army of the Tennessee from its works. "Our troops fought with great gallantry," effused Hood. That they did, but Hood failed to mention that Cheatham's corps was turned away from its penetration point and that the enemy still held that hill, thus commanded the landscape around it, a fact and realization that would prevent Hood from launching another assault upon it in the morning.[34]

The second struggle for Bald Hill on Friday lengthened the overall casualty list with a thousand additional names, a list teeming with nearly 10,000 names on it for the eight primary hours of fighting east of Atlanta and extending to Decatur. On average, a soldier fighting in that battle was stripped from the ranks every three seconds; 1 out of every 5 men who entered that fight would not answer the following morning's roll call. Soldiers from both sides had endured a most wicked day, one made almost unbearable by a combination of heat and carnage. It was a day more brutal than any other they had experienced in 1864, and for many, it was the most terrible day of their lives. For those who still cherished a romantic vision of the Civil War, the Battle of Atlanta defaced that image with a deep, crimson stain. "I can hardly write," managed one of the unscathed soldiers in a letter sent home three days later; "I was not hurt, but came so close to being killed that there was no fun in it."[35]

Morning's light would prove all too revealingly that there was no fun in anything that happened on July 22, 1864.

★ ★

11

❦

IMPACT

Saturday morning's light of July 23, 1864, was a sobering one for both punch-drunk "Tennessee" armies. The macabre was on display, hundreds of bodies strewn in grotesque forms. "I saw the worst shot man there that I ever saw," remembered a Tennessee soldier; "A cannon ball cut him entirely in two except a little strip of skin on each side." Three Confederate soldiers were found killed in a small plank house in front of the earthworks; an Alabaman claimed they "fell so near together that they could have been covered with a bed quilt." Thirteen Confederate bodies were discovered in a pile at a fence corner, not placed there by a burial detail but from a small company falling in one spot. A soldier in the 20th Ohio drew a sketch of a pile of bodies near the earthworks and labeled it: AFTER THE BATTLE OF ATLANTA—FORTY-FIVE DEAD IN ONE PLACE.[1]

Three vicious years of war had hardened the veterans to those post-battle scenes. Many took the opportunity to pull desired items from the clothes and haversacks of the stiffening bodies strewn around them. "Our men are getting boots hats &c watches knives &c off of the dead Yanks near us in the woods—lots of them," entered a Texan in his diary; "We cook and eat, talk and laugh with the enemy dead lying all about us as though they were so many logs."[2]

Posturing was prevalent, but distance artillery dueling was the only action witnessed on Saturday. "Shells are thrown freely and frequently into the city," wrote a newspaper correspondent from Atlanta at 10:00

A.M., "and I find it inconvenient to write a letter under their inspiration." Hugh Black, a Florida lieutenant in Bate's division, noted that Federal shells fell into the beleaguered city every day since July 20. It was all too much for him. "The morning after the fight I got as drunk as a badger and since that time I have not been called up to do any duty," Black revealed to his wife.[3]

At 10:00 A.M. flags of truce were hoisted, allowing burial details from both sides to remove the wounded and to bury their dead comrades. Shovels were sparse, forcing the burial crews to use their tin pans, plates, and bayonets as makeshift spades. Confederates were carried back to Cobb's Mill and Atlanta; Union men were treated in field hospitals east and north of the trench lines. The surgeons of both armies had worked without rest since July 21. The field hospitals on Saturday were an awful place to visit. Rough boards were placed parallel to each other to serve as makeshift operating tables where wounded men were placed to amputate their mangled limbs. An Iowan observed, "At the end of those tables, I saw piles of legs and arms two to three feet high."[4]

The battlefield remained as horrible a place for the soldiers—even without facing opposing fire. Bodies of humans and horses blackened and bloated in the heat of the sun. Stiff limbs protruded from all-too-shallow graves. Many of the wounded took an excruciatingly long time to receive treatment. A Mississippian complained, "I was shot through the head within twenty feet of their breastworks and never had a drop of water from 4 o'clock when I was shot till 6 o'clock next evening." Another Confederate soldier took twice as long to receive care after he was struck by a piece of a shell, primarily because he crawled into a boxcar on the Georgia Railroad and was not found for two days.[5]

The Army of the Tennessee survived but it nevertheless was significantly wounded. It was wrecked more than any other Western army of the Union since the Battle of Chickamauga. Of the 25,000 officers and men engaged against Hood's army on Friday, nearly 1 out of every 6 was not present for the morning roll call on Saturday. The official tally would take a few days and when it arrived the numbers were expected but still shocking. General Dodge's two divisions of infantry of the XVI Corps, who fought to protect the Union rear near Sugar Creek and at Decatur, paid dearly for their stubborn defense. Eight hundred of his 6,000 soldiers were killed, wounded, or captured, all but 33 coming from three brigades. Three batteries of the XVI Corps contributed 40 more men to the bloated list, most of those from the captured members of the U.S. Artillery, Battery F, who would have to adjust to their new life at Andersonville prison, 130 miles south of Atlanta. All 6 guns of the battery were captured.

The 15 percent casualty rate of the XVI Corps was higher than expected for a force on the defensive—although they were the only Union troops who fought without the aid of entrenchments—and reflected the back and forth action by Fuller's men; the two fronts were fought by the brigade of Mersy (and later Adams), and the stubborn defense by Sprague's men in their losing effort against Wheeler's dismounted cavalry at Decatur. Two wounded brigade commanders (Colonel Mersy and Colonel Morrill) were Dodge's most significant casualties in an undersized corps then reduced to the size of a division for the rest of the campaign.[6]

Yet General Dodge's corps suffered the least compared to every other Union and Confederate corps engaged on July 22. The XV Corps awoke with a new commander, General Morgan L. Smith, due to John Logan's ascension to command of the entire army, but they also awoke with 1,067 fewer men than the day before. Unlike Dodge's corps, half of the losses of the XV Corps were tallied as "missing," captured during the midafternoon assault by Cheatham's corps north of Bald Hill, an attack that reduced the XV Corps artillery power by 5 cannons, 4 captured and 1 disabled. The 1st Division, fighting from a position north of the Troup Hurt house, lost only 78 men that day of the 2,000 engaged. Thus, two divisions—9,000 men—were more than decimated. The XV Corps needed to adjust more than any other to new commanders. Not only was General Morgan L. Smith brand-new to corps command, so were two of his division commanders and three of their brigade commanders. All of that was due to General Giles Smith's transfer to commander of the 4th Division and Logan's ascension to army command. Notwithstanding the gritty and harrowing assault upon the XV Corps, it survived with a regimental commander—Colonel Lucien Greathouse of the 48th Illinois—as the corps' highest-ranking battle casualty of July 22.[7]

For the number of men engaged on July 22, General Blair's XVII Corps suffered the most of all the Union forces on the field, 1,800 officers and men killed, wounded, or captured. Not only did Blair's two divisions take more losses than the five divisions of the XV and XVI Corps combined, but Giles Smith's division took as many infantry losses (1,000) as the entire XV Corps—a result made more shocking by the fact that the division consisted of only nine regiments! Most of Blair's casualties were captured soldiers, including an entire regiment (the 16th Iowa). Like Dodge, Blair's whole XVII Corps consisted of four brigades, two of which had to adjust to new commanders with the loss of General Force (wounded) and Colonel Scott (captured) on July 22. The XVII Corps losses were exacerbated by the 800 casualties incurred in the evening of July 20 and morning of July 21, fighting the first of three separate battles for Bald Hill, a hill that retained the name of "Leggett's Hill" from that day forward. Blair was reduced to fewer than 7,000 soldiers on Saturday morning, a far cry from the 10,000 officers and men he carried into the campaign six weeks earlier.[8]

The Battle of Atlanta forever altered the Army of the Tennessee. For the first time in the campaign they would be operating without General McPherson at the helm. The news of McPherson's death hit everyone close to him hard. General Grant received the news at his Petersburg headquarters. Retiring to his tent, Grant wept. "The country has lost one of its best soldiers," the commander later stated, "and I have lost my best friend." Even General Hood, McPherson's West Point classmate, was stricken with "sincere sorrow." He graciously wrote a eulogizing statement from Atlanta.[9]

News of McPherson's death was telegraphed to the family of his fiancée, Emily Hoffman, in Baltimore the day after the Battle of Atlanta—the same day McPherson's body began its long trip to burial in his hometown of Clyde, Ohio. The message arrived near dusk while the Hoffmans were sitting in the unlit blue room. Emily's mother asked her daughter to read the unopened telegram aloud to the family from under a lantern in the hallway. Emily departed the blue room, quietly read the devastating news, and collapsed in a dead faint while clutching the telegram. She never let go of the grief, secluding herself in her room for several days and refusing to speak for several weeks. Even a touching, heartfelt letter from General Sherman failed to lift her from her depression. She would mourn McPherson's death for the rest of her life.[10]

McPherson's name topped an enormous list of Union battle casualties. The total battle losses of 3,722 for July 22 (and exceeding 4,500 since the evening of July 20) slimmed an already lean Army of the Tennesee to roughly 20,000 officers and men, with two more brigades remaining detached farther north in Georgia. The numerical strength of this army was at that time rivaled by a single corps (the XIV) of the Army of the Cumberland. The casualties inflicted upon the Army of the Tennessee at the Battle of Atlanta exceeded any loss in a single day of battle suffered by this army since it was named the Army of the Tennessee in October of 1862 (the army took greater losses on the first day of the two-day battle of Shiloh before it received this official name). The Union casualties of July 22 exceeded by more than two-fold any other day of the Atlanta campaign for Sherman's entire department. In the history of the Western-theater armies fighting for the Union, only Shiloh, Stones River, Perry ville, Chickamauga, and Chattanooga would post single-day losses exceeding the carnage incurred by the Army of the Tennessee east of Atlanta.[11]

The Confederate Army of Tennessee had worse days in terms of losses than seen at the Battle of Atlanta—but not many. The exact casualty figures for the battle were never officially tallied, forcing an estimate based on the known returns. Hood used two infantry corps and an undetermined number from Wheeler's cavalry corps at Decatur to engage the Yankees. General Hardee's adjutant tallied the total losses for Hardee's corps attacking McPherson's left on July 22 at 3,299 officers and men killed, wounded, or captured during its three hours of attacks from noon until 3:00 P.M. and the second assault of Bald Hill three hours later. The number Hardee calculated may have been underrepresented by his assistant adjutant general when he recounted the estimate twenty-four years later.[12]

Only Cleburne's three brigadiers filed reports that have survived to posterity. Of the 3,500 soldiers engaged from his division that day, 1,388 were forced from the ranks as casualties of war. The 40 percent losses reveal how tenaciously Cleburne's men attacked, both day and night. Maney carried the largest division on the field, four Tennessee brigades in excess of 4,000 soldiers. His casualty totals were posted as 619 killed and wounded, including two brigade commanders. If Maney had close to the same percentage of losses in captured and missing men as did Cleburne (over one-third), then his total casualties for July 22 approached 900 officers and men.[13]

William Walker's division lost its namesake commander, killed on the field, and all three brigade commanders were wounded. Guyton's brigade went through four brigade commanders (Mercer, Barkuloo, Rawls, and Guyton) and lost 165 other officers and men (a number recently claimed as underreported with reasonable justification); thus Mercer's old brigade lost two brigade commanders and at least 185 officers and men. The entire division (Walker's, then Mercer's, including Gist's brigade) likely suffered 500 killed and wounded men as did Bate's division, with the Florida Brigade taking the brunt of the losses in front of the devastating Ohio battery they were forced to charge. Captured and missing Confederates in those two divisions were incredibly high and likely were underreported in Southern documents. The enemy they faced—three brigades of Dodge's corps—reported the capture of 750 Confederates and at least 119 bodies discovered near their defenses. The discrepancy between Union and Confederate claims on missing soldiers may never be resolved, but it suggests that Hardee's losses for July 22 could have climbed 500 men higher than the original suspicious report to a total of 3,800 officers and men killed, wounded, or missing.[14]

Cheatham's corps losses are nebulous. His three divisions initiated their *en echelon* attacks nearly four hours after Hardee's men opened the battle and their assaults were ended in about ninety minutes. These circumstances suggest that his total losses fell considerably below those suffered by Hardee. Three brigades of Clayton's division reported losses of 511 officers and men; the fourth brigade was in reserve and likely had not suffered appreciable losses. Brown's division appears to have tallied up to three times what Clayton suffered. Manigault unofficially claimed 400 losses in his brigade, and "over 1,000" losses for Brown's entire division, a total that was likely between 1,200–1,500 based on scattered reports from regiments in Coltart's and Sharp's brigades. Pure guesswork for Hood's losses at Atlanta is required for Stevenson's division, with only two of its four brigades known to be engaged in front of Bald Hill; it likely lost no more than 100–200 soldiers. Wheeler's cavalry divisions also have no known casualty figures at Decatur. Since he attacked Sprague's XVI Corps brigade there and inflicted more than 250 losses upon the Union defenders, a reasonable assumption is that Wheeler lost more than 300 men because an attacking force usually suffers more losses than the defenders. General Gustavus Smith's Georgia militia division suffered about 50 casualties. Thus, Hood's entire loss for the Battle of

Atlanta and Decatur will never be known with certainty, but a total loss in the range of 5,700–6,300 appears reasonable.[15]

Upward of 10,000 Americans were killed, wounded, or captured fighting for and defending the rolling landscape east of Atlanta on July 22, 1864. The Battle of Atlanta was the deadliest contest of the entire Atlanta campaign. No single day of action in any theater for the remainder of the Civil War would match the carnage of this battle. The battle was the bloodiest day of the last ten months of the war.[16]

Hood ordered 30,000 soldiers into battle of July 22 (two corps plus the Georgia militia) and another 3,000–5,000 to Decatur with Wheeler's divisions. Of this available force, 27,000 to 30,000 men were engaged (three brigades from Cheatham's corps did not enter into combat). Hood's losses equated to nearly 20 percent of his engaged force. The Army of Tennessee took greater losses in both percentages and numbers at Shiloh, Stones River, and, most recently, at Chickamauga, as well as comparable losses at Chattanooga. But this was different—very much so. The Confederate army, which burgeoned with more than 77,000 soldiers at the end of May, was for the first time in this campaign truly weak in numbers. The grand total present for duty the day after the battle was slightly over 50,000 officers and men, but more than a fifth of this force was represented as cavalry. The infantry numbers for all three of his corps dipped below 40,000. Conversely, General Sherman's army group, after the losses at Peachtree Creek and Atlanta, had 75,000 infantry and 90,000 soldiers in all three branches to nearly double Hood's defenders.[17]

Hood's force was weaker in the quality of leadership as it was in its depleted numbers, for the Battle of Atlanta bled an unusual number of generals, colonels, and other regimental officers from his ranks. His corps commanders came through without injury and General Walker was the only division commander killed or wounded, but eight brigade commanders went down during this fight. More than twice as many inexperienced officers—many of them captains—were forced to lead regiments for the first time in the war due to the killing or wounding of the regimental commander who directed them onto the battlefield, or the regimental commander taking over a brigade vacancy during the course of the battle. The brigadier losses included the proven experience of Generals States Rights Gist and Otho Strahl, and up-and-coming talent like Colonels Francis Walker and Samuel Benton.

Noting the loss of 60 Confederate majors, lieutenant colonels, colonels, and generals in Hardee's attacks, the assistant adjutant general of the corps lamented, "The loss in officers, especially field officers, was unparallel and irreparable." Half of those losses were in Cleburne's division. "This day was the most disastrous as to casualties in the career of the division," sighed Cleburne's adjutant, "not so much as to loss of numbers, but that of officers, which was exceptionally heavy, and irreparable, amounting to 30 general, field, and acting field officers alone, not to count company commanders." Regimental commanders who appeared destined to be elevated to brigade command, like Colonel John E. Murray of the 5th/13th Arkansas, instead were being lowered into graves. Brigadier General Daniel Govan somehow survived the battle unscathed, and he could proudly exult how his brigade accomplished more than any other on July 22, but the price paid for the limited achievement was abysmal. All of his commanders of consolidated Arkansas regiments—including Colonel Murray—were killed or wounded in the battle. Worse was the state of his infantry on July 23. Govan could count on a total of 772 effectives; two regiments had less than 70 foot soldiers prepared to fight again.[18]

The Battle of Atlanta wrecked the Confederate Army of Tennessee through and through. Admitting that he was reduced to tears by the sight of the wounded in the army hospital, a brigade staff officer from Maney's division wailed, "Many of the noblest, and most gallant spirits in the Army of Tenn[essee] have been sent off." Too few men and a dearth of talented and experienced commissioned officers to lead them was a direct and devastating result of this battle. No longer would Hood be able to plan a tactical strike with any hope of significant success. Sherman could call in several thousand men from Tennessee and Alabama if he needed them; and as he slowly encircled the city and squeezed the life out of it, Hood's numbers would only shrink. Hood could claim a "partial success" on July 22, but his choice of words was telling. He no longer was confident of dispelling Sherman, as he had been when he took over the army. That opportunity came and went on July 22. Sherman's capture of Atlanta was approaching inevitability.[19]

For three days after the battle the opposing armies of July 22 continued to lick their wounds and adjust to the devastation each had wrought upon the other. The Army of the Tennessee felt reverberations from the battle for days. Colonel William Belknap of the 15th Iowa—who horse-collared 45th Alabama Colonel Lampley during the battle—was commissioned brigadier general for his conduct on the battlefield. The promotion made it inevitable that Belknap would command the Iowa brigade, a result that did not sit well with Colonel William Hall, who for several hours commanded a division and then saw the brigade he led since 1863 earmarked for a former subordinate. Hall resigned from the army in disgust and returned to Iowa to sit out the rest of the war. Charles Walcutt could have been punished for disobeying General Harrow's order to pull back to a second line of defense during the assault against the XV Corps, but Walcutt anchored the position from which to rally and for this he achieved his promotion to brigadier general two weeks later. Upon his commission, Walcutt became the youngest general in the army at the age of twenty-six years.[20]

Another commander was also forced to sit out the rest of the war. General Thomas J. Sweeny could not let go of how undermined he felt during the battle by General Dodge, who refused to delegate through Sweeny and seemingly acted as a corps, division, and brigade commander at the same time during the first hour of the battle. Sweeny despised Dodge and vice versa. About ten days before the battle Dodge attempted to have Sweeny court-martialed for a run-in over the chain of command within the XVI Corps medical departments. Sweeny's disdain for the 4th Division's commander, General John Fuller, was consistent with the long-standing animosities the Irish held against the English. So on Monday, July 25, when Dodge and Fuller happened upon Sweeny at his headquarters tent, they went inside and, in doing so, lit a powder keg.

Sweeny shortened the wick by purposely sitting between Dodge and Fuller and hurling charged remarks about the conduct of affairs during Friday's battle. When Sweeny insinuated that Fuller's inability to hold his line firm (against Gist's assault) severely threatened Sweeny's position east of Fuller, Dodge and Fuller protested in unison. Dodge accused Sweeny of telling tall tales. The wick was completely consumed when Sweeny could no longer control his temper. "You are a God-damned liar, sir!" Sweeny exclaimed to his superior. The epithets continued. "You are a cowardly son of a bitch, sir!" goaded Sweeny, egging Dodge further by protesting, "You are a God-damned inefficient son of a bitch, sir!"

Then the keg exploded. Dodge struck Sweeny in the face. To prove that his one arm was good enough to handle Dodge, Sweeny punched his corps commander in the nose. Fuller joined in and the two division commanders and their superior tussled within the tent as staff officers stood stunned at what was transpiring. Sweeny punched himself out, was swiftly subdued, and led away under arrest. Dodge got the court-martial he sought, replacing Sweeny with Brigadier General John M. Corse. Sweeny's only satisfaction came a few weeks later at the hands of the Confederates when one of them fired a shot that furrowed the top of Dodge's head without penetrating the skull. The wound took Dodge out of field command for the rest of the war.[21]

The change in division command was exceeded by Sherman's desire to settle upon an army commander he could deal with for the rest of the campaign and beyond. General Logan's ascension from regimental colonel within the Army of the Tennessee to major general in charge of the army in just two years was achieved despite his political background as a Democrat, and not because of it. General Grant, when he led the Army of the Tennessee, overturned two attempts by President Lincoln to prevent the promotion of the Democrat, but Logan had responded with sound performances throughout 1863 and the first half of 1864, symbolized by his inspirational leadership at Atlanta. Logan indeed had been a favorite of Grant, but not so with Sherman, whose preference for West Point-educated commanders was known to all. Sherman considered Logan's command of the army as a temporary or interim position while he sought a general with a strong background in logistical training to complete the campaign at the helm of the army.

On July 26 Sherman chose Major General Oliver Otis Howard, the commander of the IV Corps in the Army of the Cumberland. The choice of Howard was not entirely surprising given his West Point education and strong friendship with Sherman, but based on his record and position it was unusual. Howard did not have a strong record of success in the war: He was routed from his position at Antietam and Chancellorsville and unsuccessful in attempted assaults at Resaca and New Hope Church in the Atlanta campaign. Most surprising about the choice of Howard was that the Army of the Tennessee would for the first time be commanded by an outsider, a general who did not have any previous ties within the army, as Grant, Sherman, McPherson, and Logan had.[22]

So, why did Sherman shun Logan in favor of Howard? Sherman offered several reasons over the years, including the strong misgivings of General Thomas, who had difficulties with Logan earlier in the campaign. Sherman also claimed that since Logan was not a West Pointer, he held little interest in and appreciation for logistics (but in fact, as a corps commander Logan displayed a heightened sensitivity to supply issues throughout the campaign).[23]

When Sherman called Logan to headquarters to explain his decision, he revealed to him that he essentially considered the Army of the Tennessee more as a department than a field army. Sherman reported, noting that Logan "thought he ought to have been allowed the command of the army in the field until the end of the campaign; but I explained to him that a permanent department commander had to be appointed at once, as discharges, furloughs, and much detailed business could alone be done by a department commander." Sherman defended his decision for most of his life, only once considering that "I made a mistake at Atlanta."[24] Logan sulked over the decision but immediately returned to command the XV Corps five days after the Atlanta battle, returning Morgan L. Smith to his division, Joseph Lightburn to his brigade, and Colonel Wells Jones back to his regiment, the 53rd Ohio Infantry. So, by July 27, the Army of the Tennessee had a new leader but every single corps had the same commander that led it during the battle of Atlanta and only one new division commander when General Corse replaced General Sweeny.

Conversely, General Hood's army underwent considerable reconstruction as a result of the Battle of Atlanta. The Army of Tennessee had lost only one brigade commander in the ill-fated assault at Peachtree Creek on July 20, but Hood's army was so depleted of officers and foot soldiers on July 22 that the commanding general was forced to consolidate commands and shuffle commanders. So strapped was Hood for quality and experienced commanders that he decided to break up General William Walker's command rather than replace the dead division commander. One brigade went to Bate's division, Rawls's brigade served under Cleburne, and the South Carolinians and Georgians that formerly served under States Rights Gist were then brigaded under the command of Colonel James McCullough in the Tennessee division.

The same brigade and division commanders of Cheatham's corps that led their men off the Atlanta battlefield stayed in command for their next battle, except that they would be reporting to a new corps commander.

Lieutenant General Stephen D. Lee arrived with a mixed record of successes and failures in Mississippi. With his senior rank, he took over Hood's old corps and General Cheatham was returned to his division, while General Maney went back to his brigade, filling a void created by the death of Colonel Francis Walker.

Under those conditions and changes, the Army of Tennessee and the Army of the Tennessee battled again on July 28, just six days after the battle of Atlanta. The latter contest between the two occurred 180 degrees from the first one, 2 miles west of Atlanta near Ezra Church. Hood's grand plan was to isolate a moving portion of the Army of the Tennessee and destroy it, but new corps commander Stephen D. Lee proved overzealous in his first battle while serving under Hood. Lee's corps, the same one led by General Cheatham on July 22, attacked the Union XV Corps, the same opposing forces that clashed at the Troup Hurt house. Contrary to last time the Union men held their ground against repeated assaults by Lee and Alexander P. Stewart's corps (the lone corps not engaged at Atlanta the week before).

The result was a one-sided affair with a disparity of casualties that Kennesaw Mountain could not top. Hood's army suffered 3,000 losses to a mere 632 Union casualties. General John A. Logan again was the field commander of record since his corps fought virtually alone giving him a second victory in six days. That battle reflected the downside of the fighting ability of Hood's army after the Atlanta battle: toothless and desperate assaults that failed to budge an unprepared force from its newly gained position. The outcome seemed inevitable within the first hour of the four-hour contest. When General Sherman was informed of the mass of Confederates hurled upon the Army of the Tennessee at the start of this battle, he responded with such nervous delight that he could not help repeating himself, "That is fine—just what I wanted, just what I wanted. Tell Howard to invite them to attack, it will save us trouble, save us trouble, they'll only beat their brains out, beat their brains out."[25]

Sherman's excited scorn was not directed at the Confederate soldiers, for he freely admitted to his wife four days after the Atlanta battle and two days before Ezra Church, "These fellows fight like Devils and Indians combined, and it calls for all my cunning and strength." Still, Sherman knew that after July 22, Hood could not beat him in an open-field fight and Hood no longer was going to surprise him with night marches through woods. After Ezra Church, Hood's army was down 12,000 fighting men in just a week and a half. Weaker by 20 percent in manpower and immeasurably crippled by voids in leadership at the regimental and brigade level, the Army of Tennessee could not possibly win another battle against Sherman's three armies, even at Ezra Church where just one Union infantry corps became separated from the other six and was forced to fight without the aid of artillery or the protection of earthworks. The Battle of Atlanta started Hood on an inevitable downward spiral.[26]

General Hood had failed to dislodge his opponent in three big battles fought in nine days. The Confederates and the citizens of Atlanta were suffering, but Hood was by and large not blamed for the troubles. His losses in ten *days* of command were approaching the casualties suffered by General Joseph E. Johnston in the previous ten *weeks*. Early in August a member of the 1st Arkansas explained to his parents, "The troops regretted the removal of General Johnston but now they are perfectly satisfied with Gen. Hood. They know he will fight—the Federals will never be able to get Atlanta." Complete concurrence came from others who insisted the morale of the army remained high, confident that Hood would eventually drive Sherman from Georgia.[27]

Others were leery of Hood's aggression. "All that I hear say anything about General Hood say that he is too fond of charging the enemy's works," wrote a Texan to his uncle early in August, "We had rather not charge them, but would rather be charged by them, until our number equals theirs." A horse soldier saw the carnage at Atlanta and surmised that General Hood "gives us evidence of some ability—but at what fearful cost? We have lost 8,000 killed and wounded in the last two or three days. This sort of fighting, unless we meet with some more decided success, will dissipate our army very soon." Even those who were satisfied with General Hood were uncomfortable with his tactics. "We are getting used to being shot at," claimed one of Cleburne's men, "but you may guess there is no fun in it."[28]

No one in the North was seeing any fun in the Georgia campaign either. Sherman's midsummer progress was reported throughout the North exactly as it appeared from a distance—a siege of Atlanta. The three July battle victories received considerable press but the battle victories on the outskirts of Atlanta were muted by disasters elsewhere. On July 24—two days after the Atlanta victory—the last substantial Union force in the Shenandoah Valley was routed by Jubal Early at the Second Battle of Kernstown. Before July closed, Early's men had invaded the North again, this time torching two-thirds of the town of Chambersburg, Pennsylvania. Grant was making no progress at Petersburg and on July 30 (the same day that Chambersburg was nearly burned off the map) a secret operation to blow up the Confederate defense near Petersburg with underground explosives produced another fiasco with the loss of 3,800 Union soldiers who charged into the crater created by the mine explosion. "The effort was a stupendous failure," admitted Grant.[29]

By the middle of August the progress at Atlanta was no longer hailed in the North. To readers of Northern newspapers the battle victories merely appeared as successful repulses of Hood's attacks without any tactical or strategic gain. The appearance was deceiving, for both Sherman and Hood recognized that the diminished Confederate manpower and the failure of Hood to destroy a significant portion of Sherman's department meant that the eventual capture of Atlanta was a fait accompli.

Lincoln came to the conclusion in early August that his time had run out. When a White House visitor informed the president that his reelection bid was likely to fail, Lincoln candidly responded, "You think I don't know that I am going to be beaten, but I do and unless some great change takes place, *badly beaten.*" Hands tied, Lincoln could no longer change the direction of the political ill winds that continuously blew against him, preventing any attempt to push forward with momentum. Political insiders fed Lincoln the bad news of which he was all too aware. "I told Mr. Lincoln that his re election was an impossibility," wrote Thurlow Weed of New York, a top political insider who told another, "Lincoln is gone, I suppose you know as well as I. And unless a hundred thousand men are raised sooner than the draft, the country's gone too." When an Illinois confidant asked Lincoln about his prospects for reelection, Lincoln replied, "Well, I [don't] think I ever heard of any man being elected to an office unless someone was for him."[30]

Perhaps he was exaggerating, but not by much. Lincoln's prospects looked bleak to nearly all. Before August closed, Lincoln set the table to prepare for his defeat. He called a meeting between himself and Frederick Douglass. Lincoln explained to Douglass about his likely defeat and his concern that a Democratic administration would negotiate away the

Emancipation Proclamation to bring the South back to the Union. Concerned that the slaves in the Southern states had yet to be informed that they had been freed two years earlier, Lincoln was assured by Douglass that he would recruit black agents to slip behind opposing lines of armies and "carry the news of emancipation" to prod the slaves of the South to head to the North.[31]

Four days after meeting with Douglas, Lincoln asked his cabinet to sign a statement without reading it, ostensibly concerned that the press would seize and publish its fatalistic contents. The cabinet secretaries did as requested, putting their signatures to the "Blind Memorandum," not knowing that it stated, "This morning, as for some days past, it seems exceedingly probable that this Administration will not be reelected." The statement concluded by promoting the Lincoln administration's support for the incoming president-elect "to save the Union between the election and the inauguration" because Lincoln maintained that the Democrat would be elected under the premise "that he can not possibly save it afterwards." The first statement of Lincoln's memorandum could not be clearer. He was so convinced he would lose the November election that he called for his entire administration's signatures to that effect.[32]

The Democratic National Convention convened in Chicago at the end of August. Lincoln predicted that they would choose a War Democrat on a peace platform or a Peace Democrat on a prowar platform. The delegates followed the former template with Major General George McClelland balloting as the nominee. The platform was a stark contrast to Lincoln's ideals. It branded the war "a failure" and although it supported the Union over a separate Confederacy, it made it clear that it would do so by allowing the Southern states to return with its prewar status intact, including slavery. Lincoln's reelection, indeed his legacy, was entirely dependent on outcomes in the four theaters of offensives.

As the Democrats completed their Chicago convention, Sherman and Hood waged a two-day battle for control of the Macon Railroad south of Atlanta. The Battle of Jonesboro, commenced between the railroad and the Flint River, was the first battle where the Army of the Tennessee and the Army of the Cumberland together fought Hood's army. General Hardee's desperate assaults on August 31, the first day of fighting, against Logan's XV Corps proved a disaster, suffering more than 2,200 casualties to Logan's 154 (plus 18 others from the rest of the Army of the Tennessee). Although crippled by the losses, the Army of Tennessee survived the second day of fighting on September 1, losing the battle but able to retreat southward. Sherman had control of all railroads and roads and had the bulk of his army between Hood's men and Atlanta. The campaign was over as the first Union troops entered Atlanta on September 1, and continued unopposed over the next three days. Triumphant over the success of his hard-fought campaign, Sherman trumpeted a telegram to Lincoln on September 4, "Atlanta is ours, and fairly won."[33]

The timing of the message could not have been more beneficial because it arrived on the heels of the Democrats' war-is-a-failure platform released from Chicago. The Atlanta campaign victory not only ridiculed the Democratic platform (the entire event in Chicago was denigrated as the Copperhead Convention), it immediately breathed life into Lincoln's reelection. His supporters reveled in the game changer. John Nicolay, Lincoln's secretary, crowed that Atlanta "ought to win the Presidential contest for us," and the Union campaign victory had caused "a complete revolution in feeling." Joseph Medill hailed the victory in his *Chicago Tribune* editorial, "Union men! The dark days are over. . . . The Republic is safe!" George Templeton Strong said essentially the same thing in private, telling his diary, "Glorious news this morning—*Atlanta taken at last!*" Noting the political timing, Strong declared it "the greatest event of the war."[34]

Indeed it was. The capture of Atlanta two months before the election was tailor-made to boost Lincoln's prospects as the news carried throughout the North. It also allowed for some of the heroes of the campaign to be excused temporarily from service to campaign for the administration in some of the more disaffected regions of the North. General Blair and General Logan, both War Democrats, as well as other commanders were ordered to the home front to campaign for Lincoln in their respective political spheres of influence or to suppress antiwar violence and intimidation. Logan in particular provided superlative service for Lincoln in his former Congressional district of Southern Illinois, a region where the president had received only 17 percent of the popular vote in 1860. Southern Illinois, nicknamed "Egypt," was and always had been synonymous with Jacksonian Democracy. Arriving in early October as the region's most famous citizen and hailed as "the Hero of Atlanta," Logan brushed away death threats and tirelessly delivered two dozen speeches in five weeks. His singular and unusual effort—a Democrat stumping for a Republican—helped turn Egypt into a pro-Lincoln region (albeit by less than 1,000 votes) and put Illinois safely in Lincoln's corner in November.[35]

The Shenandoah Valley turned from Lincoln's three-year bugaboo into another positive referendum on the war. Major General Philip Sheridan united three armies previously working independently and proceeded to defeat Jubal Early in three battles in four weeks between mid-September and mid-October. By itself, the turnaround in the Shenandoah Valley was unlikely to sway voters to support Lincoln's war effort in the face of stalled campaigns everywhere else on the continent. In conjunction with Sherman's capture of Atlanta, the second-front victory enhanced Lincoln's popularity and assured his victory in November.

The election results were not very close. Lincoln won by 10 percentage points over Democrat George McClellan in the popular vote and crushed him in the Electoral College: 212 to 21. For Lincoln, who was so certain he would lose as to author the "Blind Memorandum" in August, the swift turnaround and election results were his mandate to carry out his prosecution of the war on his two terms: the return of the Southern states into the Union and the end of slavery. Although he was assassinated before the official end of the war, the successes in the field—observed after his second inauguration—assured him that his two goals would be achieved.[36]

Union successes beginning in September reversed Lincoln's fortunes and won his reelection. Had Lincoln lost, states of the Confederacy could still have been restored to the Union, but based on the Democratic platform the re-formed United States would have continued with slavery intact. Under Lincoln's terms, the South would survive but slavery would not. The postwar passage and ratification of the Thirteenth Amendment to the U.S. Constitution wiped out slavery throughout the land, a by-product of Lincoln's victory.

Several campaigns certainly had an impact on the war's outcome. The Maryland campaign of 1862 is such an example, famous for the Battle of Antietam (fought on September 17, 1862) that effectively drove the Confederate army from Northern soil and back into Virginia. The results of the Maryland campaign opened the door for President Lincoln to issue his Emancipation Proclamation; it added the freedom of Southern slaves as a major war measure and assured that the South would have to fight the war without significant aid from antislavery Europe. The devastating Confederate setbacks in the Vicksburg and Gettysburg campaigns together and simultaneously (both campaigns produced Union victories in early July of 1863) put an end to the prospect of the South conquering the North, but none of those Union campaign victories signified an end to the war on Lincoln's two terms.

By the summer of 1864 the overmatched South could still win the war without carrying the conflict to the North and without European intervention. The strategy to defend its territory against simultaneous Union operations was unlikely to enable them to destroy any of those invading Federal armies, but it provided the opportunity to resist them long enough to change the course of the war. The change would come from the ballot box stuffed with papers of repudiation of the administration by a war-weary populace that saw no end in sight unless they ousted their commander in chief. By August no one felt this outcome as inevitable more than President Lincoln himself.

The Atlanta campaign caused the death of Dixie. It was the most important military effort that assured the end of the Confederate States of America (a nation Lincoln refused to recognize in any of his public utterances) and the return of the South to the United States without the institution of slavery. Only Lincoln's reelection made both of those outcomes possible. Had the other late-summer and autumn Union advances and victories still transpired with a stalemate around Atlanta, Lincoln's prospects for reelection would have appeared very dim. Conversely, if the Union campaign victory at Atlanta occurred without resounding victories in the Shenandoah Valley and other theaters in the autumn of 1864, Lincoln's election victory in November would still have been considered probable instead of possible.

All campaigns have a turning point—a moment or a day (or sometimes longer) where the tide turned inevitably in the direction of one side over another. In some instances those campaign turners were perceived almost immediately during the campaign or by the close of it. When General Robert E. Lee ended his Maryland campaign by crossing his army over the Potomac River back to Virginia in September of 1862, the Battle of Antietam was nearly universally recognized as the cause of it. Likewise, one would have to be hard pressed to find anyone during the war or after who could not recognize the Battle of Gettysburg as the reason why Robert E. Lee retreated from his Pennsylvania campaign in July of 1863.

Other military campaigns have turning points that seem impossible to identify. Lieutenant General Ulysses S. Grant's Overland campaign of 1864 was noteworthy for its behemoth, blood-stained battles at the Wilderness, Spotsylvania Courthouse, North Anna, and Cold Harbor. Although those clashes rank as some of the largest in Civil War history, none of them was decisive in itself to force Robert E. Lee back to a siege defense at Petersburg, Virginia. Perhaps the true turning point of the campaign was Grant's decision to turn southward at the Wilderness crossroads the day after his army suffered reeling losses in the two-day Battle of the Wilderness (all previous Union generals had turned tail in the years before rather than continue to press General Lee in Virginia as Grant had decided to do).

Other campaigns did have true and recognizable turning points that could only be detected in hindsight. The Atlanta campaign serves as an example. One day and one battle stood above all others as the decisive day of the campaign—the Battle of Atlanta on July 22, 1864—although few could perceive this at the time it was fought or even during the remainder of their lives. They went to their graves recognizing this battle as the largest and most dramatic one of the campaign, but their surviving letters, diaries, and memoirs fail to reveal that they held it in the highest regard as the day that assured Union victory for the entire campaign.

Perhaps the only man who recognized this day as the immediate turning point was General John Bell Hood. He refused to admit it in his writings or his utterances but his hopes and expectations for the day confirmed this day as the watershed for the campaign. General Hood awoke on the morning of July 22 realizing his ambitious plan to whip Sherman's three armies with one grand battle could make or break his campaign. Rout all three and Hood wins the campaign; roll up and severely wound two of the armies and he still could claim a decisive advantage over Sherman; destroy the Army of the Tennessee and Hood would significantly weaken Sherman and delay the outcome of the campaign indefinitely.

None of that happened. The two "Tennessee" armies fought each other in an eight-hour bloodbath throughout that wickedly hot and just plain wicked Friday. By not removing the Army of the Tennessee from its entrenched position 2 miles east of Atlanta, Hood lost the Battle of Atlanta and all of his proclamations as to the number of men and cannon he captured could not change that outcome. His men would spend the rest of their lives hailing their hard-fought efforts that day but those efforts were in vain, for the stubborn hold of the Union Army of the Tennessee to their positions at the end of the day meant that Hood's bold plan had failed. He was too weak in numbers and experienced officers and Sherman was too wary for Hood to undertake such an offensive again. Sherman could tighten his grip as he encircled Atlanta and sought control of the remaining rail lifelines into the city. After the close of July 22 it was only a matter of time. No one could have understood and appreciated this more clearly than General Hood.

John Bell Hood succumbed to yellow fever in an epidemic in 1879. By the time of his death the site of one of his grandest battles as commander of the Army of Tennessee had begun to slowly dwindle to extinction. By the early 1880s the scars of the Battle of Atlanta were still apparent 2 miles east of the Gate City but the landscape, which still bore the 1864 trench lines and covered remnants of the battle, had already begun to change as suburban communities—including new houses and roads—had begun to grow around it, while most of the homes that dotted that landscape at the time of the battle were already gone. Other major battlefields of the Civil War were also under threat of encroachment. The federal government recognized the importance of battlefield preservation in other contested theaters of the Civil War and would establish five battlefield parks in the 1890s to commemorate the battles of Gettysburg, Vicksburg, Shiloh, Antietam, Chickamauga, and Chattanooga (the latter two preserved in the same military park). The Atlanta battlefield would not be saved by the U. S. government.

It was instead preserved by foreigners. In October of 1885 a team of German artists arrived in Atlanta and struck out to visit the battlefield. They erected a 40-foot wooden platform south of the Georgia Railroad on Moreland Avenue (a north-south street that did not exist during the war). For several weeks they studied the landscape of the battlefield and collected as much information as they could through military reports and reminiscences from citizens and veterans who relayed their information to an interpreter for the Germans. The artists created detailed oil sketches of all the features of the Atlanta battlefield. They were aided by an American artist—Theodore Davis—who bore witness to the battle and created several sketches of it as a staff artist for *Harper's Weekly*; he served as a special advisor to this project.[37]

After several weeks of work on the battle site, the artists returned to the studios of the American Panorama Company in Milwaukee. Throughout the winter and spring of 1886 they created an immense oil painting of the battlefield, one designed to be displayed as a cyclorama by wrapping it inside a circular stage to be viewed from the center. The artists were experienced at creating those works, having created cycloramas of the Franco-Prussian War and—most recently—completing a glorious image of the Missionary Ridge portion of the Battle of Chattanooga. For the Atlanta battle a group of four artists worked on the landscape; four others created the soldiers; and two others were specialized to paint horses. The cyclorama was completed early in the summer of 1886. The oil painting stood 50 feet high, stretched out 400 feet, and weighed over 9,000 pounds.[38]

The Atlanta Cyclorama was as awesome as it was immense. It was first displayed in a specially designed building in Minneapolis in July, just in time to commemorate the twenty-second anniversary of the battle. The painting captured Cheatham's corps breaking through the XV Corps defense near the Georgia Railroad; it stopped the clock there at 4:45 to 5:00 P.M. of the battle day, just as Union reinforcements were rushing to the scene to restore the breached line. It was a spectacular scene: depicting Manigault's troops lined behind haystacks at the Troup Hurt house to repel the counterassault, General Logan galloping toward the maelstrom on his coal black charger while leading a line of staff officers, a line of Confederate troops attempting to storm Bald (Leggett's) Hill from the west, and opposing scenes of soldiers Blue and Gray aiding each other and slaying each other. The cyclorama included General Sherman, the ambulance bearing the body of General McPherson, several division commanders from both sides as well as distant views of Atlanta, Kennesaw Mountain, and Stone Mountain. Completely missing from the vantage point of the cyclorama was the southern half of the battlefield where Hardee's corps assaulted the XVI and XVII corps and where General McPherson was killed in the wooded gap between the two Union corps.[39]

Veterans of the battle mingled within crowds of citizens born before and after the Civil War to gaze at the brilliant recreation of the battle on

THE ATLANTA CYCLORAMA: THE 1886 MEMORIAL OF THE BATTLE OF ATLANTA.

Troops of the XV Corps (foreground) rally to retake their former position from Cheatham's corps in this image from the Atlanta Cyclorama, the immense oil painting of the Battle of Atlanta. The Georgia Railroad runs through a cut in the earthworks on the right. On the left a Confederate courier is gunned down at point-blank range when his spooked horse runs him into the Union line. (Courtesy of the Atlanta Cyclorama & Civil War Museum) canvas. The cyclorama sparked battle and war reminiscences from the soldiers while the glorious image captured the imagination of civilians young and old. From Minneapolis, the cyclorama went on tour as it was displayed for weeks in various American cities beginning with Detroit in the winter of 1886–1887. It was advertised as "Logan's Great Battle" in tribute to General John A. Logan, who had died the day after Christmas 1886.[40]

Veterans completed well planned trips to visit the cyclorama and the battlefield of Atlanta. In the first week of February 1889—nearly a quarter century after the battle—General Grenville Dodge met his former division commander, General John Fuller, in Atlanta and rode out with a sightseeing group of veterans, family members, a photographer, and at least one reporter to visit the contested grounds of yesteryear, a field that had already been commemorated by previous veterans. According to a Cincinnati reporter:

> The party started to explore the battlefield in carriages and on horseback. . . . McPherson's monument was the first point visited. It is simply a cannon pointed heavenward, the muzzle closed by a huge ball and the base resting on a block of Georgia granite. An iron fence encloses it. The monument was erected by the Society of the Army of the Tennessee to mark the spot where General McPherson fell. There is no inscription. The woods about it remain untouched since the day the General . . . yielded his life in this lonely thicket. A tall pine tree stands near. Through its rough bark are several deep cuts, where relic-hunters have searched for bullets. Even the corners of the granite base have been chopped off as mementos of the dead hero.[41]

Dodge, Fuller, and the rest of the party visited Leggett's Hill and the Georgia Railroad, but their main objective was to find the earthworks that had protected their XVI Corps troops, after they were surprisingly attacked by Bate's and Walker's divisions during the first hours of the afternoon of July 22, 1864. The old line was discovered fairly easily and the two completed a task that was interrupted at the start of the battle— they sat down in the field and ate a fried-chicken lunch. Nothing and no one disturbed them this time.[42]

Georgia newspapers reported on statewide attempts to preserve the battlefields of the Atlanta campaign, but the century closed with this plan dying on the vine. Veterans from both sides made their mark on those fields by placing key monuments on the battlefield. The McPherson monument was improved by the U.S. Army Engineers and Confederate veterans erected a monument to commemorate the spot where General William H. T. Walker was killed early in the battle. (Walker was more likely killed one mile northwest of where his monument stands.)[43]

The gradual erosion of the battlefield failed to stop the veterans from visiting Atlanta. Beginning in 1892 those trips were enhanced by the "homecoming" of the Atlanta Cyclorama that arrived from Chattanooga and was essentially swapped with the Missionary Ridge painting that had been displayed in Atlanta and was subsequently sent to Nashville. A tornado swept through central Tennessee and destroyed the Missionary Ridge Cyclorama. The Atlanta Cyclorama was also damaged by fluke weather when a heavy Georgia snowstorm collapsed the roof of the Edgewood Avenue building that housed it and caused significant damage to the valuable work of art. The cyclorama was moved to Grant Park where it was displayed again in 1893. The damage from the roof collapse was eventually repaired—at a cost of $4,000—and the refurbished painting was up again in time for the thirty-fourth anniversary of the battle in 1898. (Surviving more damage and repairs but remaining on display for public viewing for all but two years since the 1890s, the Atlanta Cyclorama entered its third century as the largest oil painting in the world and it is billed as "the longest running show in the United States.")[44]

By 1900 much of the battlefield was not nearly as recognizable by the veterans as it had been for the multitude of aging soldiers who visited the field in years past. None of the houses—headquarters and otherwise— had survived from the previous century, as residential communities had begun to cover the landscape. The population of Atlanta surpassed 150,000 in 1910—fifteen times the number of residents who lived there during the Civil War—that increase naturally threatened the integrity of the battlefield. Kennesaw Mountain National Military Park was established during World War I and state parks salvaged portions of the battlefields of May 1864, but it was too late to preserve the battlefields enveloped by the burgeoning city of Atlanta.

For many of the battle veterans, the stunning visual display of Atlanta Cyclorama offset the failure to preserve the ground depicted by the famous painting. The anniversary of the battle was routinely observed with a large gathering of both Union and Confederate veterans. The thirtieth anniversary saw 2,000 Blue and Gray veterans commingling in Grant Park in 1894; it was a special day for both sides highlighted by speeches, food, and an emotional viewing of the cyclorama. Fewer in number but not in enthusiasm, the veterans met again in harmony several times in the 1900s. Old Southern soldiers carried on in the 1920s and 1930s virtually alone, aided by shorter distances to travel compared to the Union veterans. Eleven aerial bombs—one representing each state of the Confederacy—were fired in an otherwise small ceremony to mark the seventy-fifth anniversary of the battle in the summer of 1939. More significant "fireworks" were set off in Atlanta several months later that year when famous actors Clark Gable and Vivien Leigh appeared in Atlanta in December to promote their movie, *Gone With the Wind,* the award-winning adaptation of Margaret Mitchell's novel of the Civil War in Atlanta. Ms. Leigh and Mr. Gable were escorted to Grant Park for a special viewing of the Atlanta Cyclorama. There, "Scarlett O'Hara" and "Rhett Butler" marveled at the battle image surrounding them. The actress raved, "It is the most wonderful thing I have ever seen."[45]

She was reacting to the visuals of a tremendous painting, but the scene depicted in the cyclorama undervalued the significance of the larger event it portrayed. The Battle of Atlanta was one of the most exciting single-day battles ever fought on American soil, a day that cannot be captured even by one of the most magnificent military paintings ever created. Few days in American military history can match the intensity and drama east of Atlanta on July 22, 1864. It was a battle worthy of a grand painting, a day fitting for annual commemoration, an event requiring needful pilgrimages to its hallowed grounds by survivors, humbled and cursed by memories of what they had witnessed and endured.

Yet it was more than that—much more. The Battle of Atlanta was the turning point in the most impactful campaign of the Civil War. It marked the day that assured Union victory not only for the campaign but also for the most important presidential election in American history—a political event that guaranteed the preservation of the Union, the death of the Confederacy, and the end of enslavement throughout the South.

Indeed, it was the day Dixie died.

* * * * * * * * * * * * * * * * * *

ORDER OF BATTLE
ATLANTA

JULY 22, 1864

∽

UNION
MILITARY DIVISION OF THE MISSISSIPPI
Major General William T. Sherman

ARMY OF THE TENNESSEE
Major General James B. McPherson (k)*
Major General John A. Logan

Chief of Artillery: Captain Andrew Hickenlooper

Escort
4th Company Ohio Cavalry: Captain John S. Foster
1st Ohio Cavalry, Company B: Captain George F. Conn

XV Army Corps: Major General John A. Logan (p), Brigadier General Morgan L. Smith
Chief of Corps Artillery: Major Thomas D. Maurice

1st Division: Brigadier General Charles R. Woods

1st Brigade: Colonel Milo Smith

26th Iowa Infantry: Lieutenant Colonel Thomas G. Ferreby

*Key to the letters in parentheses: (k) killed; (p) promoted; (c) captured; (w) wounded; (s) sick; (mw) mortally wounded; (ds) regiment absent on detached service

30th Iowa Infantry: Lieutenant Colonel Aurelius Roberts
27th Missouri Infantry: Major Dennis O'Connor
76th Ohio Infantry: Colonel William B. Woods

2nd Brigade: Colonel James A. Williamson

4th Iowa: Major Samuel D. Nichols
9th Iowa: Colonel David Carskaddon
25th Iowa: Colonel George A. Stone
31st Iowa: Colonel William Smyth

3rd Brigade: Colonel Hugo Wangelin

3rd Missouri: Colonel Theodore Meumann
12th Missouri: Lieutenant Colonel Jacob Kaercher
17th Missouri: Lieutenant Colonel Francis Romer
29th Missouri: Major Philip H. Murphy
31st Missouri: Lieutenant Colonel Samuel P. Simpson
32nd Missouri: Major Abraham J. Seay

Artillery: Major Clemens Landgraeber

2nd Missouri Light, Battery F: Captain Louis Voelkner
Ohio Light, 4th Battery: Captain George Froehlich

2nd Division: Brigadier General Morgan L. Smith (p), Brigadier General
    Joseph A. J. Lightburn

1st Brigade: Colonel James S. Martin

55th Illinois: Captain Francis H. Shaw
111th Illinois: Major William M. Mabry
116th Illinois: Captain John S. Windsor
127th Illinois: Lieutenant Colonel Frank S. Curtiss
57th Ohio: Lieutenant Colonel Samuel R. Mott
6th Missouri: Lieutenant Colonel Delos Van Deusen
8th Missouri (Company K): Captain Hugh Neill

2nd Brigade: Brigadier General Joseph A. Lightburn (p), Colonel Wells
    S. Jones

83rd Indiana: Captain Benjamin North
30th Ohio: Colonel Theodore Jones

37th Ohio: Major Charles Hipp
47th Ohio: Lieutenant Colonel John Wallace (c), Major Thomas T. Taylor
53rd Ohio: Colonel Wells S. Jones (p), Lieutenant Colonel Robert A. Fulton
54th Ohio: Major Israel T. Moore

Artillery: Captain Francis De Gress

1st Illinois Light, Battery A: Lieutenant Samuel S. Smyth (c)
1st Illinois Light, Battery B: Captain Israel P. Rumsey
1st Illinois Light, Battery H: Captain Francis De Gress

4th Division: Brigadier General William Harrow

1st Brigade: Colonel Reuben Williams

26th Illinois: Lieutenant Colonel Robert A. Gillmore
90th Illinois: Lieutenant Colonel Owen Stuart
12th Indiana: Lieutenant Colonel James Goodnow
100th Indiana: Lieutenant Colonel Albert Heath (ds)

2nd Brigade: Colonel Charles C. Walcutt

40th Illinois: Major Hiram W. Hall
103rd Illinois: Captain Franklin C. Post
97th Indiana: Lieutenant Colonel Aden G. Cavins
6th Iowa: Major Thomas J. Ennis
46th Ohio: Captain Joshua W. Heath (k), Lieutenant Colonel Isaac
    N. Alexander

3rd Brigade: Colonel John M. Oliver

48th Illinois: Colonel Lucien Greathouse (k), Major Edward Adams
99th Indiana: Colonel Alexander Fowler
15th Michigan: Lieutenant Colonel Frederick S. Hutchinson
70th Ohio: Major William B. Brown

Artillery: Captain Henry H. Griffiths

1st Illinois Light, Battery F: Captain Josiah H. Burton
1st Iowa Light Battery: Lieutenant William H. Gay

XVI Army Corps: Major General Grenville M. Dodge

Chief of Corps Artillery: Major William H. Ross

2nd Division: Brigadier General Thomas W. Sweeny

1st Brigade: Brigadier General Elliott W. Rice

52nd Illinois: Lieutenant Colonel Edwin A. Bowen
66th Indiana: Lieutenant Colonel Roger Martin
2nd Iowa: Lieutenant Colonel Noel B. Howard (w), Major Mathew G. Hamill
7th Iowa: Lieutenant Colonel James C. Parrott

2nd Brigade: Colonel August Mersy (w), Lieutenant Colonel Robert N. Adams

9th Illinois (mounted): Lieutenant Colonel Jesse J. Phillips (ds)
12th Illinois: Lieutenant Colonel Henry Van Sellar
66th Illinois: Captain William S. Boyd
81st Ohio: Lieutenant Colonel Robert N. Adams (p), Major Frank Evans

Artillery: Captain Frederick Welker

1st Missouri Light, Battery H: Lieutenant Andrew T. Blodgett

4th Division: Brigadier General John W. Fuller

1st Brigade: Colonel John Morrill (w), Lieutenant Colonel Henry
    T. McDowell

64th Illinois: Lieutenant Colonel Michael W. Manning
18th Missouri: Lieutenant Colonel Charles S. Sheldon
27th Ohio: Lieutenant Colonel Mendal Churchill
39th Ohio: Lieutenant Colonel Henry T. McDowell (p), Major John
    S. Jenkins

2nd Brigade: Brigadier General John W. Sprague

35th New Jersey: Colonel John J. Cladek
43rd Ohio: Colonel Wager Swayne (ds)
63rd Ohio: Lieutenant Colonel Charles E. Brown (w), Major John W. Fouts
25th Wisconsin: Colonel Milton Montgomery (w, c), Lieutenant Colonel
    Jeremiah M. Rusk

Artillery: Captain George Robinson

1st Michigan Light, Battery C: Lieutenant Henry Shier
14th Ohio Light, Battery: Lieutenant Seth M. Laird
2nd United States, Battery F: Lieutenant Albert M. Murray (c)

XVII Army Corps: Major General Francis "Frank" P. Blair Jr.

Chief of Corps Artillery: Lieutenant Colonel Albert M. Powell

Escort: 9th Illinois (mounted infantry), Company G: Captain Isaac Clements

3rd Division: Brigadier General Mortimer D. Leggett

1st Brigade: Brigadier General Manning F. Force (w), Colonel George
  E. Bryant

20th Illinois: Lieutenant Colonel Daniel Bradley
30th Illinois: Colonel Warren Shedd (c), Lieutenant Colonel William C. Rhoads
31st Illinois: Lieutenant Colonel Robert N. Pearson
45th Illinois: Lieutenant Colonel Robert P. Sealy (ds)
12th Wisconsin: Colonel George E. Bryant (p), Lieutenant Colonel James K.
  Proudfit
16th Wisconsin: Colonel Cassius Fairchild

2nd Brigade: Colonel Robert K. Scott (c), Lieutenant Colonel Greenberry F. Wiles

20th Ohio: Lieutenant Colonel John C. Fry (w), Major Francis M. Shaklee
68th Ohio: Lieutenant Colonel George E. Welles (w)
78th Ohio: Lieutenant Colonel Greenberry F. Wiles (p), Major John T. Rainey

3rd Brigade: Colonel Adam G. Malloy

17th Wisconsin: Lieutenant Colonel Thomas McMahon
Worden's Battalion: Major Asa Worden

Artillery: Captain William S. Williams

1st Illinois Light, Battery D: Captain Edgar H. Cooper
1st Michigan Light, Battery H: Captain Marcus D. Elliott
3rd Ohio Light Battery: Lieutenant John Sullivan.

4th Division: Brigadier General Giles A. Smith

Escort: 11th Illinois Cavalry, Company G: Captain Stephen S. Tripp

1st Brigade: Colonel Benjamin F. Potts

53rd Illinois: Lieutenant Colonel John W. McClanahan
23rd Indiana: Lieutenant Colonel William P. Davis
53rd Indiana: Lieutenant Colonel William Jones (k), Major Warner L. Vestal
  (w), Captain George H. Beers.

3rd Iowa (three companies): Captain Pleasant T. Mathes (k), Lieutenant Lewis
   T. Linnell
32nd Ohio: Captain William M. Morris

3rd Brigade: Colonel William Hall

11th Iowa: Lieutenant Colonel John C. Abercrombie
13th Iowa: Colonel John Shane
15th Iowa: Colonel William W. Belknap
16th Iowa: Lieutenant Colonel Addison H. Sanders (c)

Artillery: Captain Edward Spear Jr.

2nd Illinois Light, Battery F: Lieutenant Walter H. Powell (c)
1st Minnesota Light Battery: Captain William Z. Clayton
15th Ohio Light Battery: Lieutenant James Burdick

CONFEDERATE
ARMY OF TENNESSEE
General John B. Hood

Hardee's Corps: Lieutenant General William J. Hardee
Bate's Division: Major General William B. Bate

Orphan Brigade: Brigadier General Joseph H. Lewis

2nd Kentucky: Colonel James W. Moss
4th Kentucky: Lieutenant Colonel Thomas W. Thompson
5th Kentucky: Lieutenant Colonel Hiram Hawkins
6th Kentucky: Colonel Martin H. Cofer
9th Kentucky: Colonel John W. Caldwell

Florida Brigade: Brigadier General Jesse J. Finley

1st/3rd Florida Cavalry (dismounted): Captain Matthew H. Strain
1st/4th Florida: Lieutenant Colonel Edward Badger
6th Florida: Lieutenant Colonel Daniel L. Kenan
7th Florida: Lieutenant Colonel Robert Bullock

Tyler's Brigade: Brigadier General Thomas Benton Smith

4th Georgia Battalion Sharpshooters: Major Theodore D. Caswell

37th Georgia: Lieutenant Colonel Joseph T. Smith
15th/37th Tennessee: Lieutenant Colonel R. Dudley Frayser (w), Captain Matthew Dwyer
20th Tennessee: Lieutenant Colonel William M. Shy
30th Tennessee: Lieutenant Colonel James J. Turner

Walker's Division: Major General William H. T. Walker (k), Brigadier General Hugh W. Mercer

Gist's Brigade: Brigadier General States Rights Gist (w), Colonel James McCullough

8th Georgia Battalion: Lieutenant Colonel Zachariah L. Watters
46th Georgia: Major Samuel J. C. Dunlop (w), Captain Eleazar Taylor
16th South Carolina: Colonel James McCullough (p), Captain John W. Boling
24th South Carolina: Colonel Ellison Capers (w), Lieutenant Colonel Jesse S. Jones

Mercer's Brigade: Brigadier General Hugh W. Mercer (p), Colonel William Barkuloo (s), Lieutenant Colonel Morgan Rawls (w), Lieutenant Colonel Cincinnatus S. Guyton
1st Volunteer Georgia: Colonel Charles H. Olmstead (w), Major Martin J. Ford
54th Georgia: Lieutenant Colonel Morgan Rawls (p), Captain Thomas W. Brantley
57th Georgia: Colonel William Barkuloo (p), Lieutenant Colonel Cincinnatus S. Guyton (p)
63rd Georgia: Major Joseph V. H. Allen

Stevens's Brigade: Colonel George A. Smith (w), Colonel J. Cooper Nisbet (c), Colonel William J. Winn

1st Georgia (Confederate): Captain William J. Whitsitt
1st Georgia Battalion Sharpshooters: Major Arthur Shaaff
25th Georgia: Colonel William J. Winn (p), Major A. W. Smith
29th Georgia: Captain John W. Turner
30th Georgia: Lieutenant Colonel James S. Boynton
66th Georgia Infantry Regiment: Colonel J. Cooper Nisbet (p), Captain Thomas L. Langston

Cleburne's Division: Major General Patrick R. Cleburne

Govan's Brigade: Brigadier General Daniel C. Govan

1st/15th Arkansas: Lieutenant Colonel William H. Martin (w), Captain Felix
    G. Lusk
2nd/24th Arkansas: Colonel Elisha Warfield (w), Lieutenant Colonel Eldridge
    G. Brasher (w), Major Amzi T. Meek
5th/13th Arkansas: Colonel John E. Murray (k), Colonel Peter V. Green
6th/7th Arkansas: Colonel Samuel G. Smith (w), Lieutenant Colonel
    Feaster J. Cameron (w), Major William F. Douglass (w), Captain J. T.
    Robinson
8th/19th Arkansas: Colonel George F. Baucum (w), Lieutenant Colonel
    Anderson Watkins (k), Lieutenant Colonel Augustus S. Hutchison (w),
    Major David H. Hamiter
3rd Confederate: Captain Mumford H. Dixon

Granbury's Brigade: Brigadier General James A. Smith (w), Lieutenant Colonel
    Robert B. Young

7th Texas: Captain J. William Brown
10th Texas: Colonel Roger Q. Mills (w), Lieutenant Colonel Robert B. Young
    (p), Captain John A. Formwalt
6th/15th Texas Cavalry (dismounted): Captain Steven E. Rice (c), Lieutenant
    Thomas L. Flynt
17th/18th Texas Cavalry (dismounted): Captain George D. Manion (w),
    Captain William H. Perry
24th/25th Texas Cavalry (dismounted): Major William A. Taylor
5th Confederate: Major Richard J. Person (c), Captain Aaron A. Cox

Lowrey's Brigade: Brigadier General Mark P. Lowrey

3rd Mississippi Battalion: Lieutenant Colonel John D. Williams (c), Captain
    Thomas P. Connor
5th Mississippi: Lieutenant Colonel John B. Herring
8th Mississippi: Colonel John C. Wilkinson (k), Captain H. W. Crook (w)
32nd Mississippi: Colonel William H. H. Tison (w)
16th Alabama: Lieutenant Colonel Frederick A. Ashford
33rd Alabama: Lieutenant Colonel Robert F. Crittenden
45th Alabama: Colonel Harris D. Lampley (w, c), Lieutenant Colonel Robert
    H. Abercrombie

Cheatham's Division: Brigadier General George E. Maney

Maney's Brigade: Colonel Francis M. Walker (k)

1st/27th Tennessee: Lieutenant Colonel John L. House
6th/9th Tennessee: Colonel George C. Porter
19th Tennessee: Major James G. Deaderick
50th Tennessee: Colonel Stephen H. Colms
4th Tennessee (Confederate): Lieutenant Colonel Oliver A. Bradshaw

Strahl's Brigade: Brigadier General Otho F. Strahl (w), Lieutenant Colonel James D. Tillman

4th/5th Tennessee: Major Henry Hampton
24th Tennessee: Colonel John A. Wilson (w), Lieutenant Colonel Samuel E. Shannon
31st Tennessee: Lieutenant Colonel Fountain E. P. Stafford
33rd Tennessee: Lieutenant Colonel Henry C. McNeill
41st Tennessee: Lieutenant Colonel James D. Tillman (p), Major T. G. Miller (w), Captain A. M. Keith

Vaughan's Brigade: Colonel Michael Magevney Jr.

11th Tennessee: Colonel George W. Gordon
12th/47th Tennessee: Colonel William M. Watkins
13th/154th Tennessee: Major William J. Crook
29th Tennessee: Colonel Horace Rice

Wright's Brigade: Colonel John C. Carter

8th Tennessee: Colonel John H. Anderson
16th Tennessee: Captain Benjamin Randals
28th Tennessee: Lieutenant Colonel David C. Crook
38th Tennessee: Lieutenant Colonel Andrew D. Gwynne (c), Major Hamilton W. Cotter
51st/52nd Tennessee: Lieutenant Colonel John W. Estes

Corps artillery: Colonel Melancthon Smith

Hood's Corps: Major General Benjamin F. Cheatham

Stevenson's Division: Major General Carter L. Stevenson

Brown's Brigade: Colonel Joseph B. Palmer

3rd Tennessee: Lieutenant Colonel Calvin J. Clack
18th Tennessee: Lieutenant Colonel William R. Butler
23rd/45th Tennessee: Colonel Anderson Searcy
26th Tennessee: Colonel Richard M. Saffell
32nd Tennessee: Captain Thomas D. Deavenport

Cumming's Brigade: Brigadier General Alfred Cumming

2nd Georgia State Troops: Colonel James Wilson
34th Georgia: Major John M. Jackson
36th Georgia: Major Charles E. Broyles
39th Georgia: Captain J. W. Cureton
56th Georgia: Colonel E. P. Watkins

Pettus's Brigade: Brigadier General Edmund W. Pettus

20th Alabama: Colonel James M. Dedman
23rd Alabama: Lieutenant Colonel Joseph B. Bibb
30th Alabama: Colonel Charles M. Shelley
31st Alabama: Major George W. Mattison
46th Alabama: Major George E. Brewer

Reynolds's Brigade: Brigadier General Alexander W. Reynolds

54th Virginia: Lieutenant Colonel John J. Wade
63rd Virginia: Captain David O. Rush
58th North Carolina: Captain Alfred T. Stewart
60th North Carolina: Colonel Washington M. Hardy

Hindman's Division: Brigadier General John C. Brown

Deas's Brigade: Colonel John G. Coltart

17th Alabama Battalion Sharpshooters: Captain James F. Nabors
19th Alabama: Lieutenant Colonel George R. Kimbrough
22nd Alabama: Colonel Benjamin R. Hart
25th Alabama: Captain Napoleon B. Rouse
39th Alabama: Lieutenant Colonel William C. Clifton (w), Captain T. J.
    Brannon
50th Alabama: Captain George W. Arnold

Manigault's Brigade: Brigadier General Arthur M. Manigault

10th South Carolina: Colonel James F. Pressley (w)

19th South Carolina: Major James L. White (w), Captain Elijah W. Horne
24th Alabama: Colonel Newton N. Davis
28th Alabama: Lieutenant Colonel William L. Butler
34th Alabama: Colonel Julius C. B. Mitchell

Tucker's Brigade: Colonel Jacob H. Sharp

7th Mississippi: Colonel William H. Bishop
9th Mississippi: Lieutenant Colonel Benjamin F. Johns
9th Mississippi Battalion Sharpshooters: Major William C. Richards
10th Mississippi: Lieutenant Colonel George B. Myers
41st Mississippi: Colonel J. Byrd Williams
44th Mississippi: Lieutenant Colonel R. G. Kelsey

Walthall's Brigade: Colonel Samuel Benton (mw), Colonel William F. Brantly

24th/27th Mississippi: Colonel Robert P. McKelvaine
29th/30th Mississippi: Colonel William F. Brantly (p), Lieutenant Colonel James M. Johnson
34th Mississippi: Captain T. S. Hubbard

Clayton's Division: Major General Henry D. Clayton

Baker's Brigade: Colonel John H. Higley

37th Alabama: Lieutenant Colonel Alexander A. Greene (k)
40th Alabama: Major Ezekiah S. Gulley
42nd Alabama: Captain Robert K. Wells
54th Alabama: Lieutenant Colonel John A. Minter

Holtzclaw's Brigade: Colonel Bushrod Jones

18th Alabama: Lieutenant Colonel Peter F. Hunley
32nd/58th Alabama: Captain John A. Avirett
36th Alabama: Lieutenant Colonel Thomas H. Herndon
38th Alabama: Major Shep Ruffin (w), Lieutenant John C. Dumas

Gibson's Brigade: Brigadier General Randall L. Gibson

1st Louisiana Regulars: Captain W. H. Sparks
13th Louisiana: Lieutenant Colonel Francis L. Campbell
14th Louisiana Sharpshooters Battalion: Major Duncan Buie
16th/25th Louisiana: Lieutenant Colonel Robert H. Lindsay

19th Louisiana: Colonel Richard W. Turner
20th Louisiana: Colonel Leon Von Zinken

Stovall's Brigade: Colonel Abda Johnson

1st Georgia State Line: Lieutenant Colonel John M. Brown (mw),
     Captain Albert Howell
40th Georgia: Captain John F. Groover
41st Georgia: Major Mark S. Nall
42nd Georgia: Captain Lovick P. Thomas
43rd Georgia: Major William C. Lester
52nd Georgia: Captain Rufus R. Asbury

Cheatham's corps artillery (Beckham)

1st division Georgia Militia: Major General Gustavus W. Smith

1st brigade: Brigadier General Reuben W. Carswell

1st Georgia Militia: Colonel Edward H. Pottle
2nd Georgia Militia: Colonel James Stapleton
3rd Georgia Militia: Colonel Q. M. Hill

2nd brigade: Brigadier General Pleasant J. Phillips

4th Georgia Militia: Colonel James N. Mann
5th Georgia Militia: Colonel S. S. Stafford
6th Georgia Militia: Colonel J. W. Burney

3rd brigade: Brigadier General Charles D. Anderson

7th Georgia Militia: Colonel Abner Redding
8th Georgia Militia: Colonel William B. Scott
9th Georgia Militia: Colonel J. M. Hill

4th brigade: Brigadier General Henry K. McCay

10th Georgia Militia: Colonel C. M. Davis
11th Georgia Militia: Colonel William T. Toole
12th Georgia Militia: Colonel Richard Sims

Cavalry Corps: Major General Joseph Wheeler

Martin's Division: Major General William T. Martin

Allen's Brigade: Brigadier General William Wirt Allen

1st Alabama: Lieutenant Colonel D. T. Blakely
3rd Alabama: Colonel James Hagan
4th Alabama: Colonel Alfred A. Russell
7th Alabama: Captain George Mason
51st Alabama: Colonel M. L. Kirkpatrick
12th Alabama Battalion: Captain Warren S. Reese

Iverson's Brigade: Brigadier General Alfred Iverson

1st Georgia: Colonel Samuel W. Davitte
2nd Georgia: Colonel Charles C. Crews
3rd Georgia: Colonel Robert Thompson
4th Georgia: Colonel Isaac W. Avery
6th Georgia: Colonel John R. Hart

Ferguson's Brigade: Brigadier General Samuel W. Ferguson

2nd Alabama: Lieutenant Colonel John N. Carpenter
9th Mississippi: Colonel Horace H. Miller
56th Alabama: Colonel William Boyles
11th Mississippi: Colonel Robert O. Perrin
12th Mississippi Battalion: Colonel William M. Inge

NOTES

INTRODUCTION

[1] Michael Burlingame and John R. Turner Ettlinger, eds., *Inside Lincoln's White House: The Complete Civil War Diary of John Hay* (Carbondale, Ill.: Southern Illinois University Press, 1997), pp. 221–23.

[2] William P. Mellen to Salmon P. Chase, August 10, 1864, in John Niven, ed., *The Salmon P. Chase Papers* Vol. 4 (Kent, Ohio: Kent State University Press, 1997), p. 421.

[3] Lincoln to Grant, June 15, 1864, in John G. Nicolay and John Hay, eds., *Abraham Lincoln: Complete Works* Vol. 2 (New York: Century Company, 1920), p. 533.

[4] Roy P. Basler, ed., *The Collected Works of Abraham Lincoln* Vol. 7 (New Brunswick, New Jersey: Rutgers University Press, 1955), pp. 448–49; *Adam Gurowski, Diary: 1863–'64–'65* (Washington, D.C.: W.H. & O.H. Morrison, 1866), p. 293.

[5] John C. Waugh, *Reelecting Lincoln: The Battle for the 1864 Presidency* (New York: Crown Publishers, 1997), p. 270.

[6] Ibid., pp. 251–54; Albert Castel, *Decision in the West: The Atlanta Campaign of 1864* (Lawrence, Kansas: University Press of Kansas, 1992), p. 361.

[7] Noah Brooks, *Washington in Lincoln's Time* (New York: Century Company, 1895), p. 149.

[8] Manning Force diary, July 12, 1864, Manning Force Papers, Library of Congress, Washington, D.C. (Hereinafter cited as LOC); Sherman to his wife, July 9, 1864, and to Philemon B. Ewing, July 13, 1864, in Brooks D. Simpson and Jean V. Berlin *Sherman's Civil War: Selected Correspondence of William T. Sherman, 1860–1865* (Chapel Hill, N.C.: University of North Carolina Press, 1999), pp. 663, 666.

[9] Marc Wortman, *The Bonfire: The Siege and Burning of Atlanta* (New York: Public Affairs, 2009), pp. 69–75.

[10] Jay Luvaas, "The Atlanta Campaign," in Francis H. Kennedy, ed., *The Civil War Battlefield Guide* (Boston, Mass.: Houghton-Mifflin Co., 1990), pp. 173–77.

[11] July 20, 1864 *Atlanta Daily Appeal* reproduced in "The Rebel Account," *Philadelphia Inquirer,* July 28, 1864, and also in "The War in Georgia," *New York Times,* July 29, 1864.

[12] Lowell quote in Waugh, *Reelecting Lincoln,* p. 296.

CHAPTER 1—CLOSING THE VISE

[1] William W. McCarty diary, July 20, 1864, United States Army Military History Institute, Carlisle Barracks, Pa. (Hereinafter cited as USAMHI); William Hemstreet, "A Remarkable Stroke of Lightning," *Quincy Whig and Republican,* August 5, 1864.

[2] For a history of this army, see the fine work of Steven E. Woodworth, *Nothing but Victory: The Army of the Tennessee, 1861–1865* (New York: Knopf, 2005). Title obtained from Jacob Ritner letter to his wife (see page ix of this source).

[3] United States War Department, *The War of the Rebellion. A Compilation of the Official Record of the Union and Confederate Armies* (Washington, D. C.: Government Printing Office, 1880–1901) (Hereinafter cited as *OR*), 38 (1), pp. 116, 120.

[4] John M. Schofield, *Forty-six Years in the Army* (New York: Century Company, 1897), pp. 125–26.

[5] Elizabeth J. Whaley, *Forgotten Hero: General James B. McPherson* (New York: Exposition Press, 1955), pp. 95, 106–108, 177.

[6] Ibid., pp. 142–44; Lloyd Lewis, *Sherman: Fighting Prophet* (New York: Harcourt, Brace & Co., 1932), pp. 345–46.

[7] McPherson to his mother, April 4, 1864, McPherson Papers, Toledo-Lucas County Historical Society, Toledo, Ohio.

[8] Castel, *Decision in the West,* pp. 121–23, 135–39; Rowland Cox, "Snake Creek Gap, and Atlanta: A Paper Read by Brevet Major Rowland Cox, U.S.V., December 2, 1891," p. 13.

[9] Tamara A. Smith, "A Matter of Trust: Grant and James B. McPherson," in Steven E. Woodworth, ed., *Grant's Lieutenants: From Cairo to Vicksburg* (Lawrence, Kansas: University Press of Kansas, 2001), pp. 161–63.

[10] *OR* 38 (1), pp. 115–16, 120.

[11] Thomas D. Christie to his brother, July 25, 1864, Christie Letters, Minnesota Historical Society, St. Paul, Minn.; J. G. B. to the editor, July 23, 1864, *Canton* (Illinois) *Weekly Register,* August 8, 1864; T. G. T. to the editor, July 26, 1864, *Clinton* (Iowa) *Herald,* August 13, 1864.

[12] F. McC. to the editor, July 26, 1864, *Cedar Valley Times,* August 11, 1864; Charles W. Wills diary, July 19–20, 1864, in Mary E. Kellogg, comp., *Army Life of an Illinois Soldier, Including a Day-by-Day Record of Sherman's March to the Sea* (Globe Printing Company, 1906: Repr. Carbondale, Ill.: Southern Illinois University Press, 1996), pp. 282–83.

[13] William E. Titze diary, July 20, 1864, Titze diary, Abraham Lincoln Presidential Library, Springfield, Illinois (Hereinafter cited as ALPL).

[14] *OR* 38 (5), pp. 196–97, 207.

[15] Ibid., p. 188.

[16] Richard M. McMurry, *John Bell Hood and the War for Southern Independence* (Lincoln, Nebr.: University of Nebraska Press, 1992), pp. 75–93; *OR* 32 (2), p. 763.

[17] Joseph T. Glatthaar, *Partners in Command: The Relationships Between Leaders in the Civil War* (New York: Free Press, 1998) p. 130; Mary Boykin Chesnut, *A Diary From Dixie,* Ben Ames Williams, ed. (Cambridge, Mass.: Harvard University Press, 1980), pp. 371–72; Thomas P. Lowry, *The Story the Soldiers Wouldn't Tell: Sex in the Civil War* (Mechanicsburg, Pa.: Stackpole Books, 1994), p. 157.

[18] Douglas Southall Freeman, *Lee's Lieutenants* Vol. 1 (New York: Charles Scribner's Sons, 1942), p. 198.

[19] Richard M. McMurry, "A Policy So Disastrous: Joseph E. Johnston's Atlanta Campaign," in Theodore P. Savas and David A. Woodbury, eds., *The Campaign for Atlanta & Sherman's March to the Sea* Vol. 2 (Campbell, Calif.: Savas Woodbury Publishers, 1994), pp. 234–38; *OR* 38 (3), p. 679.

[20] Larry J. Daniel, *Soldiering in the Army of Tennessee* (Chapel Hill, N.C.: University of North Carolina Press, 1991), pp. 142–44; Gill to his wife, July 18, 1864, in Bell Irvin Wiley, "A Story of 3 Southern Officers," *Civil War Times Illustrated* (April 1964), p. 33; Martin Van Buren Oldham diary, July 18, 1864, "Civil War Diaries of [Martin] Van Buren Oldham" (University of Tennessee at Martin) http://www.utm.edu/departments/acadpro/library/departments/special_collections/E579.5%20Oldham/text/vboldham_1864.htm.

[21] *OR* 38 (3), pp. 630–31.

[22] *OR* 38 (5), p. 196.

[23] Ibid., p. 194.

[24] Ezra Warner, *Generals in Gray: Lives of the Confederate Commanders* (Baton Rouge, La.: Louisiana State University Press, 1995), p. 333; *OR* 38 (3), pp. 543, 951–52; John W. DuBose, *General Joseph Wheeler and the Army of Tennessee* (New York: Neale Publishing Company, 1912), p. 371; Thomas D. Christie to his brother, July 25, 1864, Christie Letters, Minnesota Historical Society.

[25] John Randolph Poole, *Cracker Cavaliers: The 2nd Georgia Cavalry Under Wheeler and Forrest* (Mercer, Ga.: Mercer University Press, 2000), p. 69; *OR* 38 (5), p. 895; *OR* 52 (1), p. 569.

[26] *OR* 38 (3), p. 102; Wortman, *The Bonfire,* p. 268; Russell S. Bonds, *War Like the Thunderbolt: The Battle and Burning of Atlanta* (Yardley, Pa.: Westholme Publishing, 2009), pp. 115, 434–35 (n. 3); Wallace P. Reed, ed., *History of Atlanta, Georgia: With Illustrations and Biographical Sketches of Some of Its Prominent Men and Pioneers* (Syracuse, N.Y.: D. Mason and Co., 1889), p. 175.

[27] Janet B. Hewett, ed., *Supplement to the Official Records of the Union and Confederate Armies* Vol. 7 (Wilmington, NC: Broadfoot Publishing Co., 1994–1998) (Hereinafter cited as *SOR*), pp. 48, 61.

[28] Matilda Gresham, *Life of Walter Quintin Gresham, 1832–1895* Vol. 1 (Chicago: Rand McNally & Co., 1919), p. 302.

[29] Charles W. Calhoun, *Gilded Age Cato: The Life of Walter Q. Gresham* (University Press of Kentucky, 1988), p. 34; *OR* 38 (3), pp. 579–80, 590.

[30] Gilbert D. Munson, "Battle of Atlanta," *Sketches of War History, Military Order of the Loyal Legion of the United States* (Hereinafter cited as *MOLLUS*), Ohio Commandry, Robert Hunter, ed., Vol. 3 (1890), Reprint (Wilmington, N.C.: Broadfoot Publishing Co., 1991), p. 214; M. D. Leggett, "The Battle of Atlanta: A Paper by General M. D. Leggett, Before the Society of the Army of the Tennessee, October 18, 1883, at Cleveland," p. 2; *OR* 38 (3), pp. 543, 596.

[31] Ibid.; General Blair reported that he sent an order to Leggett to attack the hill but it miscarried. Leggett's and Munson's accounts refute this assertion. Blair may have been attempting to prevent any blame from being cast upon McPherson for delaying the assault until morning.

[32] *OR* 38 (5), p. 197; Sherman to Thomas, July 20, 1864, in Simpson and Berlin, *Sherman's Civil War* p. 670.

[33] *OR* 38 (3), p. 543; *OR* 38 (5), pp. 208, 895–96.

[34] *OR* 38 (3), pp. 218–19.

CHAPTER 2—PRELUDE

[1] *OR* 38 (3), pp. 951–52; *OR* 38 (5), p. 896; W. C. Dodson, ed., *Campaigns of Wheeler and His Cavalry, 1862–1865* (Atlanta: Hudgins Publishing Co., 1899), p. 209; John W. Dubose, *General Joseph Wheeler and the Army of Tennessee* (New York: Neale Publishing Co., 1912), p. 371.

[2] Warner, *Generals in Gray*, pp. 53–54.

[3] Irving A. Buck, *Cleburne and His Command* (Jackson, Tenn.: McCowat-Mercer Press, 1959), p. 232. Cleburne's brigade commander, General Govan, confuses the history by claiming that Adams was killed at 9:30 A.M. (*OR* 38 [3], p. 734.)

[4] *OR* 38 (3), pp. 746, 752.

[5] *OR* 38 (3), p. 361; *SOR* 7, p. 61.

[6] *OR* 38 (3), p. 367.

[7] Ibid.; Foster diary, July 21, 1864, in Norman D. Brown, ed., *One of Cleburne's Command: The Civil War Reminiscences and Diary of Capt. Samuel T. Foster, Granbury's Texas Brigade, C.S.A.* (Austin: University of Texas Press, 1980), pp. 108–109.

[8] Foster diary, July 21, 1864, in Brown, ed., *One of Cleburne's Command*, pp. 108–109; *OR* 38 (3), p. 746.

[9] Turner quote in Larry M. Strayer and Richard A. Baumgartner, eds., *Echoes of Battle: The Atlanta Campaign* (Huntington, West Va.: Blue Acorn Press, 1991), p. 220.

[10] C. C. Reif, "Mortimer D. Leggett," *Journal of the Patent Office Society* Vol. 2 (1919), pp. 543–44.

[11] Leggett, "The Battle of Atlanta," p. 3. The monthly return for June for Leggett's division showed 4,436 officers and men present for duty (*OR* 38 [4], p. 653). One of

those regiments, the 45th Illinois, was not with Leggett on July 21, reducing his strength that day by about 400.

¹² Leggett, "Battle of Atlanta," pp. 3–4; Henry J. Walker, "In Front of Atlanta," *National Tribune* (Hereinafter cited as *NT*), October 11, 1883; Hosea Whitford Rood, *Story of the Service of Company E, and of the Twelfth Wisconsin Veteran Volunteer Infantry* (Milwaukee, Wisc.: Swain & Tate, Co., 1893), p. 309.

¹³ Thomas M. Vincent to General McPherson, July 19, 1864, RG 393 (pt. 1), Letters Received, 1864–1865, Department of the Army of the Tennessee, National Archives, Washington, D.C. (Hereinafter cited as NA).

¹⁴ Charles A. Dana, *Recollections of the Civil War: With the Leaders at Washington and in the Field in the Sixties* (Lincoln, Nebr.: University of Nebraska Press, 1966), p. 68; Thomas J. Key diary, July 21, 1864, in Wirt A. Cate, ed., *Two Soldiers: The Campaign Diaries of Thomas J. Key, C.S.A. December 7, 1863–May 17, 1865 and Robert J. Campbell, U.S.A. January 1, 1864–July 21, 1864* (Chapel Hill, N.C.: University of North Carolina Press, 1938), p. 93.

¹⁵ Walker, "In Front of Atlanta," *NT,* October 11, 1883; Rood, *Story of the Service of Company E,* p. 309.

¹⁶ [Gilbert D. Munson], "A Matter of War History. The Capture and Fortification of Leggett's Hill," *Cincinnati Daily Gazette,* September 12, 1879; Gilbert D. Munson, "Battle of Atlanta," p. 216; A. G. Wray, "Battle of Bald (or Leggett's) Hill, Atlanta, July 27 [21], 1864," *Janesville Daily Gazette,* April 6, 1912.

¹⁷ *OR* 38 (3), p. 752; John Randolph Poole, *Cracker Cavaliers,* pp. 130–31. Most secondary accounts of this action mention only two brigades of cavalry under attack. This is refuted by Wheeler who makes it clear that three brigades were eventually forced back. See *OR* 38 (3), pp. 952.

¹⁸ James M. McCaffrey, ed., *Only a Private: A Texan Remembers the Civil War: The Memoirs of William J. Oliphant* (Houston, Texas: Halcyon Press, 2004), p. 68; James M. McCaffrey, *This Band of Heroes: Granbury's Texas Brigade, C.S.A.* (College Station, Texas: Texas A & M University Press, 1996), pp. 115–16; *OR* 38 (3), pp. 746, 752–53.

¹⁹ A. G. Wray, "Battle of Bald (or Leggett's) Hill," *Janesville Daily Gazette,* April 6, 1912.

²⁰ "Cousin Tom" to the editor, August 4, 1864, in William B. Styple, ed., *Writing and Fighting the Civil War: Soldier Correspondence to the New York Sunday Mercury* (Kearny, N.J.: Belle Grove Publishing Co., 2001), p. 279; Walker, "In Front of Atlanta," *NT,* October 11, 1883.

²¹ Munson, "Battle of Atlanta," p. 216; Walker, "In Front of Atlanta," *NT,* October 11, 1883; Brown, ed., *One of Cleburne's Command,* p. 109.

²² Walker, "In Front of Atlanta," *NT,* October 11, 1883; E. B. Quiner, *The Military History of Wisconsin: A Record of the Civil and Military Patriotism of the State in the War for the Union* (Chicago: Clark & Co., 1866), p. 583.

²³ Marcus D. Elliott to the editor, n.d., in Chapman Brothers, *Portrait and*

Biographical Album of Oakland County, Michigan (Chicago: Chapman Brothers, 1891), p. 819; *OR* 38 (3), p. 753.

²⁴ Munson, "Battle of Atlanta," p. 217.

²⁵ Ibid.; W. S. Ayres, "The Position Held by the Seventeenth Corps, July 22," *NT,* July 23, 1891; *OR* 38 (3), pp. 543, 566.

²⁶ *OR* 38 (3), p. 543; Jack D. Welsh, *Medical Histories of Union Generals* (Kent, Ohio: Kent State University Press, 1996), pp. 308–309.

²⁷ Dana, *Recollections of the Civil War:* p. 66.

²⁸ W. H. Goodreli, "From the Fifteenth," [Des Moines] *Iowa State Register,* August 10, 1864; *OR* 38 (3), pp. 580, 596–97, 601, 605.

²⁹ Ibid.; Munson, "Battle of Atlanta," p. 217; McCaffrey, ed., *Only a Private,* p. 69.

³⁰ *OR* 38 (3), pp. 580, 596–97, 601, 605; H. H. Rood, "Sketches of the Thirteenth Iowa," *MOLLUS-Iowa* Vol. 1 (Des Moines, Iowa: Press of P. C. Kenyon, 1893), p. 148.

³¹ *OR* 38 (3), p. 580; Chapman Brothers, *Portrait and Biographical Album of Oakland County, Michigan,* pp. 819–20; Richard S. Tuthill, "An Artilleryman's Recollection of the Battle of Atlanta," *MOLLUS-Illinois* Vol. 1 (Chicago: A.C. McClurg and Co., 1891), pp. 293, 304–5; McCaffrey, ed., *Only a Private,* p. 70.

³² Quote reproduced in Strayer and Baumgartner, eds., *Echoes of Battle,* p. 219. Confederate losses are estimated and greater than previously considered. General James A. Smith details losses for July 21. (*OR* 38 [3], p. 746) Cleburne's other brigades also sacrificed men that day. Govan's brigade losses were not negligible (see Mark K. Christ, ed., *Getting Used to Being Shot At: The Spence Family Civil War Letters* [Fayetteville, Ark.: University of Arkansas Press, 2002], p. 99). Lowrey's official report states 6 killed (including Colonel Adams) and 42 wounded (*OR* 38 [3], p. 734). The Confederate cavalry also sustained losses that were never officially tallied. For example, one Georgia cavalry regiment suffered 9 losses, including its commander (see Poole, *Cracker Cavaliers,* pp. 131–32). Given that up to fifteen regiments in three cavalry brigades were involved in the initial attack, total losses for the cavalry likely exceeded 50 men and could have approached 100.

³³ F. McC. To the editor, July 26, 1864, *Cedar Valley Times,* August 11, 1864; A. G. Wray, "Battle of Bald (or Leggett's) Hill," *Janesville Daily Gazette,* April 6, 1912; McCaffrey, ed., *Only a Private,* p. 70.

³⁴ Buck, *Cleburne and His Command,* p. 234; Ann York Franklin, comp., *The Civil War Diaries of Capt. Alfred Tyler Fielder, 12th Tennessee Regiment Infantry, Company B 1861–1865* (Louisville, Kentucky: Ann York Franklin, 1996), p. 189; *OR* 38 (5), pp. 898–99. Confederate division strength estimated. See *OR* 38 (3), p. 679.

³⁵ W. F. Beyer and O. F. Keydel, eds., *Deeds of Valor: How America's Civil War Heroes Won the Congressional Medal of Honor* (1903 Reprint: Stamford, Conn.: Longmeadow Press, 1993), p. 383.

³⁶ Franklin, comp, *Civil War Diaries of Capt. Alfred Tyler Fielder,* p. 189; Samuel K. Adams to J. Kebler, July 23, 1864, Manning F. Force Papers, LOC.

³⁷ *OR* 38 (3), pp. 544, 581, 590, 594.

[38] Mamie Yeary, comp., *Reminiscences of the Boys in Gray, 1861–1865* (McGregor, Texas: 1912), p. 656.

[39] Buck, *Cleburne and His Command,* p. 233.

CHAPTER 3—THE PLAN

[1] *OR* 38 (5), p. 899.

[2] T. B. Roy, "General Hardee and the Military Operations Around Atlanta," *Southern Historical Society Papers* (Hereinafter cited as *SHSP*) Vol. 8 (September, 1880), p. 353.

[3] Stephen W. Sears, *To the Gates of Richmond: The Peninsula Campaign* (New York: Ticknor & Fields, 1992), pp. 249, 307, 335, 343. Hood's plan in *OR* 38 (3), p. 631.

[4] Warner, *Generals in Gray,* pp. 124–25; Castel, *Decision in the West,* pp. 28–29, 355–57.

[5] John B. Hood, *Advance and Retreat* (New Orleans, La.: G. T. Beauregard, 1880), pp. 174–75.

[6] Ibid.; *OR* 38 (3), p. 679.

[7] Hood, *Advance and Retreat,* p. 177; *OR* 38 (3), p. 631. The light before dawn appeared at 5:14 A.M.; dawn officially entered Atlanta at 5:42 A.M. on July 22, 1864. See http://aa.usno.navy.mil/cgi-bin/aa_pap.pl

[8] Hood, *Advance and Retreat,* p. 177.

[9] Ibid., pp. 176–78.

[10] Route location and length described in Roy, "General Hardee," p. 356; Wilbur G. Kurtz, "Civil War Days in Georgia: The Death of Major-General W. H. T. Walker," *Atlanta Constitution Magazine,* July 27, 1930.

[11] Russell K. Brown, *To the Manner Born: The Life of General William H. T. Walker* (Mercer, Ga.: Mercer University Press, 2005), pp. 151, 257–58.

[12] Ibid., pp. 12, 263; James S. Robbins, *Last in Their Class: Custer, Pickett and the Goats of West Point* (New York: Encounter Books, 2006), p. 46.

[13] Evidence for this important meeting and its outcome found in *OR* 38 (3), p. 699; Roy, "General Hardee," p. 354; Roy to Cheatham, October 15, 1881, Cheatham Papers, Tennessee State Library and Archives, Nashville. After the battle Hood maintained that Hardee violated his original attack plan (*OR* 38 [3], p. 631), thus denying that he ever adjusted that plan. That the plan was modified as claimed by the aforementioned citations has been convincingly concluded by biographers of Hood and Hardee (see McMurry, *John Bell Hood and the War for Southern Independence,* p. 43, and Nathaniel Cheairs Hughes Jr., *General William J. Hardee: Old Reliable* (Baton Rouge: Louisiana State University Press, 1965), p. 226.

The time of the meeting is estimated based on when the column started.

[14] Nathaniel Cheairs Hughes Jr., *The Civil War Memoir of Philip Daingerfield Stephenson, D. D.* (Conway, Arkansas: UCA Press, 1995), p. 217.

[15] *SOR* (7), p. 100.

[16] *SOR* (7), pp. 80, 100; Roy, "General Hardee," pp. 357–59.

[17] *SOR* (7), p. 100; Hamilton Branch to his mother, July 23, 1864, in Mauriel Phillips Joslyn, *Charlotte's Boys: Civil War Letters of the Branch Family of Savannah* (Berryville, Va.: Rockbridge Publishing Company, 1996), p. 270; Kurtz, "Major General W. H. T. Walker," *Atlanta Constitution Magazine,* July 27, 1930.

[18] Lot D. Young, *Reminiscences of a Soldier of the Orphan Brigade* (Louisville, Kentucky: Courier-Journal Job Printing Co., 1918), p. 90; Kurtz, "Major General W. H. T. Walker," *Atlanta Constitution Magazine,* July 27, 1930.

[19] Hughes, ed., *Civil War Memoir of . . . Stephenson,* p. 217.

[20] Hughes, *General William J. Hardee,* p. 227; *SOR* (7), 100. This lengthy and detailed campaign report of General Bate was submitted with a postscript by the officer transcribing it, claiming it was copied in a hurry "and not with much accuracy." (p. 103). The region can be seen on a detailed Georgia map used by General Hood. See George B. Davis, Leslie J. Perry, and Joseph W. Kirkley, The *Official Military Atlas of the Civil War* (New York: Gramercy Books, 1983), Plate LX.

[21] Van Buren Oldham diary, July 22, 1864, University of Tennessee.

[22] *OR* 38 (5), p. 231. General Leggett claims that two of his men were sent toward Atlanta and came back with the news that Hood's men were attempting to flank them (see Leggett, "The Battle of Atlanta," p. 11). It appears Leggett, writing twenty years later, was influenced by his knowledge of subsequent events, for those pickets would only have been able to see troops heading south, not east. That Sherman believed they were heading to East Point appears to be the response to the intelligence gathered from Leggett's pickets.

[23] *OR* 38 (3), p. 369; Grenville M. Dodge, *The Battle of Atlanta and Other Campaigns, Addresses, Etc.* (Council Bluffs. Iowa: Monarch Printing Company, 1911), p. 40.

[24] Ibid.; William E. Strong, "The Death of General James B. McPherson," *MOLLUS-Illinois,* Vol. 1 (Chicago: A.C. McClurg, 1891), pp. 319–20.

[25] Sherman's order reproduced in Strong, "Death of General James B. McPherson," p. 319.

[26] Ibid., pp. 319–20.

[27] Hughes, *General William J. Hardee,* p. 227; Roy, "General Hardee," p. 365.

[28] Kurtz, "Major General W. H. T. Walker," *Atlanta Constitution Magazine,* July 27, 1930.

[29] Hughes, *General William J. Hardee,* p. 229.

[30] Brown, *To the Manner Born,* pp. 265–66.

[31] Reed, *History of Atlanta,* p. 180; *OR* 38 (3), p. 699.

CHAPTER 4—BEHIND THE LINES

[1] William Tecumseh Sherman, *Memoirs of General W. T. Sherman* (New York: Literary Classics of the United States, Inc., 1990), pp. 544, 548–49.

[2] Strong, "The Death of General James B. McPherson," pp. 320–22.

[3] Stephen Ambrose, *Nothing Like It in the World: The Men Who Built the Transcontinental Railroad, 1863–1869* (New York: Simon & Schuster, 2000), pp. 23–24, 32–33, 86–88.

[4] John Wallace Fuller, "A Terrible Day: The Fighting Before Atlanta July 22, 1864," *NT,* April 16, 1885; *OR* 38 (3), p. 369. General Fuller's report places the meal closer to 1:00 P.M. than noon (see OR 38 [3], p. 475), but this assertion is overwhelmed by evidence that this event took place "within fifteen to twenty minutes of 12 o'clock (noon)." See Dodge, *The Battle of Atlanta,* p. 41.

[5] W. G. Hamrich, "Incidents of the Battle Before Atlanta," *NT,* July 26, 1883.

[6] H. I. Smith, *History of the Seventh Iowa Veteran Volunteer Infantry During the Civil War* (Mason City, Iowa: E. Hitchcock Printer, 1903), p. 153.

[7] William H. Chamberlin, *History of the Eighty-first Regiment Ohio Infantry Volunteers During the War of the Rebellion* (Cincinnati: Gazette Steam Printing House, 1865), p. 132.

[8] "Report of Major-General William Brimage Bate," [July] 30, 1864, *SOR* I (7), pp. 101–102.

[9] Charles B. Wright, *A Corporal's Story: Experiences in the Ranks of Company C, 81st Ohio Vol. Infantry* (Philadelphia: Published by author, 1887), pp. 127–28.

[10] Ibid.; Fuller, "A Terrible Day," *NT,* April 16, 1885; W. H. Chamberlin, "Recollections of the Battle of Atlanta," in Theodore F. Allen, Edward S. McKee, and J. Gordon Taylor, eds., *Sketches of War History 1861–1865, MOLLUS-Ohio* Vol. 6 (Cincinnati: Montfort & Company, 1908), p. 279; Dodge to General W. E. Strong, October 10, 1885, William E. Strong Papers, ALPL.

[11] J. R. Donaldson, "Sweeny's Fighters," *NT,* May 19, 1898; Warner, *Generals in Blue: Lives of the Union Commanders* (Baton Rouge, La.: Louisiana State University Press, 1992), 491–92; Welsh, *Medical Histories of Union Generals,* p. 330; Ronald H. Bailey and the editors of Time-Life Books, *Battles for Atlanta: Sherman Moves East* (Alexandria, Va.: Time-Life Books, Inc., 1985), p. 103; W. M. Sweeny, ed., "Man of Resource. Active Service of Gen. T. W. Sweeny, as Told by His Letters," *NT,* October 17, 1895.

[12] Captain James Compton, "The Second Division of the 16th Army Corps in the Atlanta Campaign," *MOLLUS-Minnesota,* p. 112.

[13] Donaldson, "Sweeny's Fighters," *NT,* May 19, 1898; *OR* 38 (3), p. 418; Sweeny to Bodge, July 30, 1864, in "Man of Resource," *NT,* October 17, 1895.

[14] "Logan in Battle," *Indianapolis Journal,* December 30, 1886; Strong, "The Death of General James B. McPherson," pp. 321–22.

[15] Number is estimated. A claim persists that Bate's entire division at this time had no more than 1,200 men has merit if it is assumed that the number refers to privates only. See Edwin Porter Thompson, *History of the Orphan Brigade* Vol. 2 (Louisville, Kentucky: Lewis N. Thompson, 1898), p. 263. Bate confirms the 1,200 estimate, but implies it was for the two-thirds of his division that attacked the XVI Corps. See "Report of Major-General William Brimage Bate," [July] 30, 1864, *SOR* I (7), p. 102.

¹⁶ The Florida Brigade may have been commanded by Colonel Robert Bullock that day as it is unclear if General Finley had recovered from a wound received earlier in the campaign to take the helm on July 22.

¹⁷ Fuller, "A Terrible Day," *NT,* April 16, 1885; *OR* 38 (3), p. 538.

¹⁸ *OR* 38 (3), p. 538; Woodworth, *Nothing but Victory,* p. 548.

¹⁹ John William Green, *Johnny Green of the Orphan Brigade: The Journal of a Confederate Soldier* (Lexington, Ky: The University Press of Kentucky, 2001), p. 148; Gervis D. Grainger, *Four Years With the Boys in Gray* (Franklin, Ky.: n.p., 1902), p. 19.

²⁰ Ibid.; Donaldson, "Sweeny's Fighters," *NT,* May 19, 1898.

²¹ Ezra J. Warner, *Generals in Blue,* pp. 400–402; *OR* 38 (3), p. 418.

²² Donaldson, "Sweeny's Fighters," *NT,* May 19, 1898; *OR* 38 (3), pp. 468–70.

²³ Strong, "The Death of General James B. McPherson," p. 323.

²⁴ Thompson, *History of the Orphan Brigade,* p. 263; Grainger, *Four Years With the Boys in Gray,* p. 19; Hugh Black to his wife, July 26, 1862, in E. C. Frano, ed., *Letters of Captain Hugh Black to his Family in Florida During the War Between the States, 1862–1864* (Newburgh, Ind.: n.p., 1998), p. 68; *OR* 38 (3), p. 419; Smith, *Seventh Iowa,* p. 153.

²⁵ Thompson, *History of the Orphan Brigade,* p. 263; *OR* 38 (3), p. 419; Smith, *Seventh Iowa,* p. 153; Green, *Johnny Green,* pp. 148–49.

²⁶ H. E. Hayes, "From the 14th Ohio Battery," *Western Reserve Chronicle,* August 17, 1864; Green, *Johnny Green,* pp. 148–49; John McKee diary, July 22, 1864, USAMHI.

²⁷ Green, *Johnny Green,* pp. 148–49; John McKee diary, July 22, 1864, USAMHI; J. R. Donaldson, "Sweeny's Fighters," *NT,* May 19, 1898.

²⁸ Nathaniel Cheairs Hughes Jr., *The Pride of the Confederate Artillery: The Washington Artillery in the Army of Tennessee* (Baton Rouge: Louisiana State University Press, 1997), p. 202.

²⁹ "Report of Major-General William Brimage Bate," [July] 30, 1864, *SOR* I (7), p. 102; Grainger, *Four Years With the Boys in Gray,* p. 19; Thomas D. Christie to Sandy, July 25, 1864, "Civil War Letters of the Christie Family," Minnesota Historical Society, http://www.mnhs.org/library/Christie/letters/transcripts/td640725.html.

³⁰ Hugh Black to his wife, July 26, 1864, in Frano, ed., *Letters of Captain Hugh Black,* p. 68; L. D. Young, "Kentucky Confederate Visits Scenes of Battle and Siege During the Civil War," *Lexington Herald,* May 19, 1912.

³¹ *OR* 38 (3), p. 538; Woodworth, *Nothing but Victory,* p. 548; Typo to the editor, August 13, 1864, *Western Reserve Chronicle,* August 24, 1864.

³² Traditionally, Smith's brigade (often referred to as Tyler's brigade for its former commander) has been placed on the right (north) of the Orphan Brigade in the initial assault against Rice's brigade, but General Rice specifically reported that the Confederates "burst forth from the woods . . . in front of my right." (*OR* 38 [3], p. 418) Here he refers to the Kentuckians but never mentions troops attacking his center or left. The shifting of Union regiments to the southern part of the brigade line is also consistent

with heavy action against the right and lack of pressure against the left. A member of the Orphan Brigade insisted that no more than 1,200 members of Bate's division were engaged on July 22 (see Thompson, *History of the Orphan Brigade,* p. 263); even factoring in straggling this is a nearly unfathomably low number for three brigades and can only be consistent with two small brigades engaged.

[33] Hugh Black to his wife, July 26, 1864, in Frano, ed., *Letters of Captain Hugh Black,* p. 68.

[34] Washington Ives to his sister, August 21, 1864, Ives Papers, Florida State Archives, Tallahassee.

CHAPTER 5—REPULSE

[1] Russell K. Brown, *Our Connection With Savannah: A History of the 1st Battalion Georgia Sharpshooters* (Macon, Ga: Mercer University Press, 2004), p. 112.

[2] Nisbet quote reproduced in Strayer and Baumgartner, eds., *Echoes of Battle,* p. 224; Wright, *A Corporal's Story,* p. 129.

[3] James Compton, "The Second Division of the 16th Army Corps in the Atlanta Campaign," p. 118.

[4] Dodge, *The Battle of Atlanta,* p. 42; *OR* 38 (3), p. 370.

[5] W. M. Sweeny, ed., "Man of Resource," *NT,* October 17, 1895.

[6] Strayer and Baumgartner, eds., *Echoes of Battle,* p. 224.

[7] Thomas J. Shelley, "Atlanta: The Battle of July 22 as Seen by an 81st Ohio Comrade," *NT,* September 15, 1887.

[8] Robert N. Adams, "The Battle and Capture of Atlanta," *MOLLUS-Minnesota* (4th Series), p. 159.

[9] *OR* 38 (3), pp. 370, 454, 463; Typo to the editor, August 13, 1864, *Western Reserve Chronicle,* August 24, 1864; "A Month's History of the 81st Ohio Regiment," (Chillicothe, Ohio) *Scioto Gazette,* August,16, 1864.

[10] Shelley, "Atlanta," *NT,* September 15, 1887; *OR* 38 (3), p. 454; Brown, *Our Connection with Savannah,* p. 113; Wright, *A Corporal's Story,* p. 129; Chamberlin, *History of the Eighty-first Regiment,* p. 132; Adams, "Battle and Capture of Atlanta," p. 159.

[11] Fuller, "A Terrible Day," *NT,* April 16, 1885; *OR* 38 (3), p. 475.

[12] Strayer and Baumgartner, eds., *Echoes of Battle,* pp. 224–25.

[13] Churchill diary, July 22, 1864, in Thomas W. Lewis, ed., "Battle of Atlanta as Told by Colonel Churchill's Diary," *Zanesville* (Ohio) *Sunday Times-Signal,* December 5, 1926.

[14] Eugene W. Jones, *Enlisted for the War* (Hightstown, N.J.: Longstreet House, 1997), p. 180.

[15] *OR* 38 (3), p. 500; Fuller, "A Terrible Day," *NT,* April 16, 1885.

[16] *OR* 38 (3), p. 500.

[17] *OR* 38 (3), p. 492.

[18] *OR* 38 (3), pp. 477–78; Fuller, "A Terrible Day," *NT,* April 16, 1885.

[19] Churchill diary, July 22, 1864, in Lewis, ed.; "Battle of Atlanta," *Zanesville Sunday Times-Signal,* December 5, 1926.

[20] *OR* 38 (3), p. 496.

[21] OR 38 (3), 475–76, 500, 504.

[22] OR 38 (3), 475–76, 496; Fuller, "A Terrible Day," *NT,* April 16, 1885; Churchill diary, July 22, 1864, in Lewis, ed.; "Battle of Atlanta," *Zanesville Sunday Times-Signal,* December 5, 1926.

[23] "The Late Battle," *Georgia Weekly Telegraph,* July 29, 1864; Jack D. Welsh, *Medical Histories of Confederate Generals* (Kent, Ohio: Kent State University Press, 1994), p. 81.

[24] "General W. H. T. Walker and His Division," *Georgia Weekly Telegraph,* September 6, 1867; E[ugene] P. S[pear], "General W. H. T. Walker," *Newman* (Ga.) *Herald,* May 29, 1883; Dodge, *The Battle of Atlanta,* p. 56; *OR* 38 (3), pp. 476–77, 496; Fuller, "A Terrible Day," *NT,* April 16, 1885.

[25] Fuller, "A Terrible Day," *NT,* April 16, 1885; *OR* 38 (3), pp. 373, 476–77. The 64th Illinois casualties represented on these tables will be incurred later in the afternoon.

[26] Warner, *Generals in Gray,* pp. 216–17; Welsh, *Medical Histories of Confederate Generals,* p. 157.

[27] Hamilton Branch to his mother, July 23, 1862, *Charlotte's Boys,* p. 271. Disagreement exists on who initially commanded Mercer's Brigade after General Mercer ascended to command William Walker's division. Charles H. Olmstead of the 1st Georgia Infantry claims in his memoirs that he himself commanded the unit until wounded and replaced by Colonel Barkuloo. See Scott Walker, *Hell's Broke Loose in Georgia: Survival in a Civil War Regiment* (Athens, Ga.: University of Georgia Press: 2005), pp. 161, 164, 271 (n. 20). Olmstead's memoir is challenged by the official report of Colonel Barkuloo, written two months after the battle (see *OR* 38 [3], p. 758–59). Based on the timeline and evidence, Olmstead appears to have been wounded just before General Walker's death, making him a regimental commander at the time, and Barkuloo by attrition ascended to most senior available colonel to move up to brigade command after General Mercer replaced William Walker.

[28] *OR* 38 (3), pp. 758–59; Hamilton Branch to his mother, July 23, 1862, *Charlotte's Boys,* p. 271. Barkuloo incorrectly states that he took over the brigade in the morning, a time he refutes by reporting that the two brigades from the division had already been repulsed when he entered the fight. The confusion on time can only be explained by the fact that Barkuloo wrote the report exactly two months after the battle and since this action swirled close to the noon hour, he was confused about an early afternoon action that he incorrectly believed happened in the late morning, a difference as small as 70–80 minutes.

[29] Robert G. Mitchell to his wife, July 23, 1864, Robert G. Mitchell Papers, Special Collections, University of Georgia.

[30] *OR* 38 (3), pp. 506, 952; David Evans, "The Fight for the Wagons," *Civil War Times Illustrated* Vol. 26, no. 10 (February, 1988), pp. 16–18.

31 *OR* 38 (3), pp. 511, 516, 521, 537.

32 *OR* 38 (3), pp. 508, 521; Philip Roesch Journal, 1862–1865, USAMHI, pp. 17–18.

33 *OR* 38 (3), p. 952; Yeary, *Reminiscences of the Boys in Gray,* pp. 223–24. Neither the fate of the mangled man nor his identity has ever been discovered.

34 Evans, "The Fight for the Wagons," pp. 19–22; Benjamin F. McGee, *History of the 72d Indiana Infantry of the Mounted Lightning Brigade* (LaFayette, Ind.: S. Vater & Co., 1882), p. 352; *OR* 38 (3), pp. 507, 953; Quartus, "From General Sherman's Army," *Daily Toledo Blade,* August 3, 1864.

35 *OR* 38 (3), p. 953.

36 *OR* 38 (3), p. 373. The Union casualties for the three brigades and two batteries of the XVI Corps units facing Bate and Walker total about 580 for the entire day. At least two-thirds of them occurred in that sector of the field in the first seventy minutes of the battle.

CHAPTER 6—SACRIFICE

1 Fuller, "A Terrible Day," *NT,* April 16, 1885; Strong, "The Death of General James B. McPherson," p. 324.

2 *OR* 38 (3), p. 608.

3 A. A. Stuart, *Iowa Colonels and Regiments* (Des Moines, Iowa: Mills & Company, 1865), pp. 237–41.

4 *OR* 38 (3), pp. 594, 608.

5 *OR* 38 (3), pp. 738, 741; Munford H. Dixon diary, July 22, 1864, Munford H. Dixon Papers, Special Collections Library, Duke University.

6 *OR* 38 (3), p. 753; William R. Scaife, *The Campaign for Atlanta.* Fourth Ed. (Cartersville, Ga.: Civil War Publications, 1993), p. 184; Key diary, July 22, 1864, in Cate, ed., *Two Soldiers,* p. 94; T. B. Roy, "General Hardee and the Military Operations Around Atlanta," *SHSP* VIII (August & September, 1880), p. 367.

7 Strong, "Death of General James B. McPherson," pp. 324–25.

8 *OR* 38 (3), pp. 588, 608–11, 738; "The 16th Iowa at Atlanta," *NT,* August 26, 1886; F. McO. to the editor, July 26, 1864, *Cedar Valley Times,* August 11, 1864; Amos Sniff, "The Capture of the 16th Iowa," *NT,* March 27, 1884.

9 *OR* 38 (3), pp. 608–9.

10 William E. Bevins, *Reminiscences of a Private* (privately published, 1913), pp. 57–58.

11 Roy, "General Hardee," p. 364.

12 "John Edward Murray," in Bruce S. Allardice, *More Generals in Gray* (Baton Rouge, La.: Louisiana State University Press, 1995), pp. 173–74; *OR* 38 (3), p. 741.

13 *OR* 38 (3), pp. 538–39, 738; Key diary, July 22, 1864 in Cate, ed., *Two Soldiers,* p. 95. See Davis *Official Military Atlas,* Plate CXXXI, for map showing opposing forces and wagon roads on that region of the battlefield.

14 *OR* 38 (3), pp. 588, 606; X to the editor, July 24, 1864, New Albany (Ind.) *Daily Ledger,* August 5, 1864.

¹⁵ *OR* 38 (3), pp. 588, 602, 604.

¹⁶ "The Civil War Diaries of Mifflin Jennings, 11th Iowa Infantry," http://iagen web.org/civilwar/books/mifflinj.htm.

¹⁷ Amos Sniff, "The Capture of the 16th Iowa," *NT,* March 27, 1884; *OR* 38 (3), 576, 609–11, 738.

¹⁸ *OR* 38 (3), pp. 739–41. Govan's total losses for the day were 499, including casualties incurred from another charge later in the day.

¹⁹ *OR* 38 (3), pp. 609, 662, 747, 749, 751.

²⁰ *OR,* 38 (3), pp. 82, 394–95; Strong, "Death of General James B. McPherson," pp. 325–26, 330, 335.

²¹ *OR,* 38 (3), pp. 82, 395; Strong, "Death of General James B. McPherson," pp. 327, 329–31, 334, 337.

²² Strong, "Death of General James B. McPherson," p. 337.

²³ Ibid., pp. 331–32, 337–38. Most secondary accounts time McPherson's mortal wounding at 2:02 P.M., citing the stopped watch of Lieutenant Sherfy (see Strong, "Death of General James B. McPherson," p. 331) as the chief source of the moment when the general was shot. That cited time is at least fifteen minutes too late and perhaps half an hour based on the time that the northern sector of the Union defense learned of it. For example, a very precise campaign diary kept by Lieutenant Colonel Joseph S. Fullerton, Assistant Adjutant General of the IV Corps, Army of the Cumberland, reveals that the corps headquarters learned of McPherson's death from one of Sherman's staff officers at 2:10 P.M. (See *OR* 38 [1], p. 908.) This third-hand notification three miles from where McPherson was unhorsed would be impossible to convey in under fifteen minutes. Therefore, McPherson must have been mortally wounded at or *before* 1:45 P.M. and Lieutenant Sherfy's watch was damaged at this exact time but did not stop completely until the time showed 2:02 P.M. Ironically, McPherson may have lingered for 10–15 minutes before he expired, although his injured, riderless horse announced his demise almost immediately after he was shot.

²⁴ Fuller, "A Terrible Day," *NT,* April 16, 1885.

²⁵ Ibid.; *OR* 38 (3), p. 477–78, 500.

²⁶ Hickenlooper to William E. Strong, August 7, 1876, Strong Papers, ALPL; Fuller, "A Terrible Day," *NT,* April 16, 1885; *OR* 38 (3), p. 477, 538.

CHAPTER SEVEN—TWO-SIDED FIGHT

¹ *Atlanta Historical Bulletin* Vol. 15 (1970), p. 94. Gartrell would reenter the war as a brigadier general. See Warner, *Generals in Gray,* p. 101.

² Casualty figures obtained from official tabulations and commander reports. See *OR* 38 (3), pp. 550, 596. The sequence of action described in this chapter has been a subject of various interpretations in other works regarding the Atlanta Campaign. I have relied on the report of Giles Smith (*OR* 38 [3], pp. 581–84) and his numbered diagram sequencing the order of attacks (Davis, *Official Military Atlas,* Plate XC, #5). The times when those attacks occurred are estimations based on ac-

tions described in the previous two chapters and from a composite of source material described in this chapter.

[3] *OR* 38 (3), pp. 679, 680.

[4] Castel, *Decision in the West,* pp. 376–77, 381.

[5] Warner, *Generals in Gray,* p. 295.

[6] *OR* 38 (3), p. 582; Davis, *Official Military Atlas,* Plate XC, #5 (3rd and 4th Position).

[7] *OR* 38 (3), pp. 582, 589, 602–603, 606; W. L. Curry, *War History of Union County* (Marysville, Ohio: 1883), p. 46.

[8] Sumner A. Cunningham, *Reminiscences of the 41st Tennessee: The Civil War in the West* (John A. Simpson, ed.) (Shippensburg, Pa.: White Mane Books, 2001), p. 82; *OR* 38 (3); p. 588, Castel, *Decision in the West,* p. 402.

[9] Alfred Fielder diary, July 22, 1864, in Franklin, comp., *The Civil War Diaries of Capt. Alfred Tyler Fielder,* p. 189; *OR* 38 (3), p. 602.

[10] Peter Marchant to his wife, August 4, 1864, "Letters of Captain Peter Marchant, 47th Tennessee Infantry," http://www.geocities.com/bsdunagan/letters.htm; *OR* 38 (3), p. 603.

[11] *OR* 38 (3), pp. 609, 680. The latter page shows the present-for-duty strength of Cleburne's division on July 31 of 4,300 officers and men (numbers that don't include the casualties of July 22). Straggling in Cleburne's division should not have been as severe as it was in Bate's and Walker's, given the much lighter march they had to engage in. Govan claims a strength of 1,000 "effectives" in his brigade at the battle, a number not including officers. Regardless, it can be assumed the average of the remaining two brigades must have been larger, perhaps as many as 1,500 in each, but not less than 1,200 per brigade, an assessment confirmed by Cleburne's assistant adjutant general, who claimed a total of "about" 3,500 carried into action. (See Roy, "General Hardee," p. 367.)

[12] *OR* 38 (3), p. 747; E. E. Nutt, "Fight at Atlanta," *NT,* January 3, 1884.

[13] *OR* 38 (3), p. 280.

[14] *OR* 38 (3), pp. 319, 747; Foster reminiscences, in Brown, ed., *One of Cleburne's Command,* pp. 112–13.

[15] Foster reminiscences, in Brown, ed., *One of Cleburne's Command,* p. 113; *OR* 38 (3), pp. 280, 319, 361, 363–64, 367–68; *SOR* (7), p. 49.

[16] *OR* 38 (3), pp. 342, 353, 730, 747–48, 753–54; "The 15th Mich. at Atlanta," *NT,* February 17, 1887; Timothy W. Doyle, "Gen. McPherson's Death," *NT,* October 6, 1892.

[17] William V. Powell to the Governor of Texas, "An Indianan Wishes to Return a Texas Battleflag," *Houston Daily Post,* May 13, 1900; D. R. Lucas, New *History of the 99th Indiana Infantry* (Rockford, Ill.: Horner Printing Co., 1900), pp. 104–107; *OR* 38 (3), p. 342. For an alternative story on the claim of the capture of the flag of the 17th/18th Texas, see "Return of a Confederate Flag," *Confederate Veteran* Vol. 22, no. 7 (July 1914), p. 302.

[18] Woodworth, *Nothing but Victory,* p. 553.

[19] Key diary, July 22, 1864, in Cate, ed., *Two Soldiers,* pp. 95–96; Scaife, *The Campaign for Atlanta,* p. 184.

[20] Warner, *Generals in Gray,* p. 195; *OR* 38 (3), pp. 732, 735–36.

[21] *OR* 38 (3), pp. 731–32. Lowrey provides an alternate version to his official report in his postwar autobiography, claiming that General Cleburne, not Hardee, had ordered him to enter the battle directly behind Govan's brigade, but Lowrey took it upon himself to penetrate the gap on the right of Govan when the aide delivering Cleburne's orders recognized the existence of the gap and encouraged Lowrey to take advantage of it. See Craig L. Symonds, *Stonewall of the West: Patrick Cleburne and the Civil War* (Lawrence, Kansas: University Press of Kansas, 1998), p. 228. This is a conundrum of two opposing claims made by the same eyewitness. Lowrey's official report is accepted here over his later writings for two reasons: First, Lowrey's claim of taking the initiative and thus more credit for his performance is typical of embellished postwar claims that cannot be refuted by a since-dead witness (in this case, Cleburne); and second, Lowrey filed the report one week after the battle expecting it to be studied by Generals Cleburne and Hardee, his superiors. For Lowrey to officially report that General Hardee—his corps commander—ordered him in behind Govan, if this was not true (as his autobiography suggests), knowing that Hardee was likely to read that false claim, is akin to military suicide and thus defies logic.

[22] Foster reminiscences, in Brown, ed., *One of Cleburne's Command,* pp. 111, 113.

[23] *OR* 38 (3), pp. 606, 732, 748, 750. The assault strength is estimated. Lowrey's report suggests that his brigade was only about 1,200 strong by claiming losses of 578 soldiers—"about one-half the men that were in the charge." Given the half-mile width of this attack line and the ferocity of the attack based on Union accounts, as well as the apparent participation of two regiments of James A. Smith's brigade and Carter's brigade from Maney's division it is implausible to accept fewer than 2,000 Confederates attacking at this stage of the battle. Also noteworthy is the summation of estimates within each of the three brigades places the strength of Cleburne's entire attacking division at 3,000, while Cleburne's AAG claims it was 3,500. The latter is accepted over the former based on the tradition of both North and South to falsely underestimate assault sizes by the participants as a means to enhance their accomplishments and provide an easy explanation for their lack of success.

[24] *OR* 38 (3), pp. 165, 546. Blair complained that Wangelin had only "about 600 or 700 men" in the brigade. Two days earlier, a submitted morning report tallied 978 officers and men present for duty. (See RG 393/2, #5917 "1st Division Consolidated Morning Reports" [XV Army Corps], NA.) Wangelin's regiments each had between 132 and 207 soldiers. Blair's assertion would hold only if one or two regiments remained in their original position—a possibility but without supporting evidence.

[25] E. E. Nutt, "Fight at Atlanta," *NT,* January 3, 1884.

[26] Rood, *Story of the Service of Company E,* p. 317. The exact same quote is also attributed to the colonel of the 68th Ohio. See Myron Loop, "Sounding the Alarm: The

68th Ohio's Trying Time at the Battle of Atlanta," *NT,* December 1, 1898. The latter account was published five years after the former and the 68th Ohio was not on the hill at the start of the two-directional defense; therefore, it is discounted.

[27] Tuthill, "An Artilleryman's Recollection," p. 305.

[28] *OR* 38 (3), pp. 564–65, 607; *OR* 38 (5), p. 318. Leggett's July returns place his force at 3,226 officers and men. The 15th Iowa replaced the 68th Ohio, which was not in line at the start of this assault. Leggett's loses from July 21 have been factored in to reduce this number to close to 3,000. It may have been 10 percent less than this if the monthly returns included the 32nd Ohio, which transferred out of Leggett's division on July 10.

[29] *OR* 38 (3), pp. 732–33; W. S. Ayres, "The 78th Ohio at Bald Hill," *NT,* January 17, 1884; Yeary, ed., *Reminiscences of the Boys in Gray,* p. 22.

[30] *OR* 38 (3), p. 606; Samuel H. M. Byers, *Iowa in War Times* (Des Moines, Iowa: W. D. Condit & Co., 1888), p. 318; F. McC. To the editor, July 26, 1864, *Cedar Valley Times,* August 11, 1864; F. Y. Hedley, *Marching Through Georgia: Pen-Pictures of Every-Day Life* (Chicago: Donohue, Henneberry; 1890), pp. 157–58; Frank P. Delany, "Leggett's Hill," *NT,* November 9, 2008; William W. Belknap, *History of the Fifteenth Regiment Iowa Veteran Volunteer Infantry* (Keokuk: R. B. Ogden & Son, 1887), pp. 350, 371–72.

[31] Frank P. Delany, "Leggett's Hill" *NT,* November 9, 2008; the casualty figures for the 38th Tennessee are unrecorded. The 45th Alabama tallied 132 casualties (all named in "List of Casualties in 45th Ala. Reg.," *Columbus* [Ga.] *Daily Sun,* July 30, 1864). This was estimated as half of the attacking strength. See http://www.tarleton.edu/~kjones/alinf.html#45th-Inf.

[32] James H. Wilson, ed., *Life and Services of Brevet Brigadier-General Andrew Jonathan Alexander, United States Army* (New York: 1887), p. 129; Samuel K. Adams to Peter Force & J. Kebler, July 23, 1864, Force papers, LOC.

[33] Chapman Brothers, *Portrait and Biographical Album of Oakland County, Michigan,* pp. 819–20; Tuthill, "The Battle of Atlanta," pp. 293, 302, 304–5.

[34] Grenville Dodge to William E. Strong, October 10, 1885, Strong Papers; *OR* (38) 3, pp. 560–61; Chester G. Higbee, "Personal Recollections of a Line Officer," *MOLLUS-Minnesota,* pp. 315–16; Henry Wilson to Lincoln, September 5, 1864, Abraham Lincoln Papers, LOC.

[35] W. S. Ayres, "The 78th Ohio at Bald Hill," *NT,* January 17, 1884; *OR* 38 (3), p. 732; "Cousin Tom" to the editor, August 4, 1864, in Styple, ed., *Writing and Fighting the Civil War,* p. 279; Tuthill, "The Battle of Atlanta," p. 304.

[36] E. E. Nutt, "Fight at Atlanta," *NT,* January 3, 1884; Yeary, ed., *Reminiscences of the Boys in Gray,* p. 6; *OR* 38 (3), pp. 556, 732.

[37] Henry McDonald story told by his brother. See G. B. McDonald, "History of the 30th Illinois Veteran Volunteer Regiment of Infantry," http://home.comcast.net/~30il/mcdonald.html, p. 29. (Reproduced from a 1916 memoir published in the *Sparta News.*)

[38] J. L. Brown, "The 78th Ohio in Close Quarters," *NT,* February 21, 1884; Tuthill, "The Battle of Atlanta," p. 305.

[39] *OR* 38 (3), pp. 732–33.

[40] Key diary, July 22, 1864, in Cate, ed., *Two Soldiers,* p. 96.

[41] Yeary, ed., *Reminiscences of the Boys in Gray,* p. 19.

[42] OR 38 (3), pp. 969–70.

CHAPTER 8—BLOODY DIVERSION

[1] Sherman, *Memoirs of General W. T. Sherman,* p. 551.

[2] Hood, *Advance and Retreat,* pp. 179–81.

[3] *OR* 38 (3), p. 631.

[4] Henry O. Dwight, "How We Fight at Atlanta," *Harper's New Monthly Magazine* Vol. 29 (October, 1864), p. 665. For the twenty-minute lull, see Leggett's report in *OR* 38 (3), p. 565.

[5] Jeffrey C. Weaver, *54th Virginia Infantry* (Lynchburg, Va.: H. E. Howard, 1993), p. 121; Jeffrey C. Weaver, *63rd Virginia Infantry* (Lynchburg, Va.: 1991), p. 62; Reynolds's strength estimated from one regiment from a late-June calculation. See Weaver, *54th Virginia,* p. 117.

[6] *OR* 38 (3), pp. 970–71.

[7] *OR* 38 (3), pp. 280, 342, 355; T. W. Connelly, *History of the Seventieth Ohio Regiment from Its Organization to Its Mustering Out* (Cincinnati, Ohio: Peak Bros., 1902), p. 95. Cumming's involvement in the contest is derived entirely from casualties specific to July 22. See "Regiment Casualty Analysis" (34th, 36th, 39th, 56th Georgia Infantry) in *American Civil War Research Database,* http://www.civilwardata.com. A diary from a member of the 39th Georgia provides evidence that they saw no action that day. See Brenda Phillips, ed., *Personal Reminiscences of a Confederate Soldier Boy* (Milledgeville, Ga.: Boyd Publishing Co., 1993), p. 53.

[8] *OR* 38 (3), pp. 285, 342.

[9] Tri-monthly returns for Stevenson's division show an "effective" strength that diminished by only thirty-six men from July 20 and July 31, 1864. (See Peter W. Alexander Papers, Rare Books and Manuscript Department, Columbia University; provided to the author by Keith S. Bohannon.) Note: the effective totals—4,069 and 4,033—underrepresent some battle losses that are compensated by soldiers who returned from absences. The "effectives" do not count officers and therefore also underrepresent present-for-duty strength by at least 500. See *OR* 38 (3), pp. 679–80.

[10] David S. Heidler and Jeanne T. Heidler, eds., *Encyclopedia of the American Civil War: A Political, Social, and Military History* (New York: W. W. Norton & Co., 2000), p. 294; Manigault quote reproduced in Castel, *Decision in the West,* p. 338; Augustus C. Buell, *History of Andrew Jackson* Vol. 2 (New York: Charles Scribner's Sons, 1904), p. 381.

[11] *OR* 38 (3), pp. 778–79; R. Lockwood Tower, ed., *A Carolinian Goes to War: The Civil War Narrative of Arthur Middleton Manigault, Brigadier General, C.S.A.* (Co-

lumbia, S.C.: Published for the Charleston Library Society by the University of South Carolina Press, 1983), p. 226.

¹² *OR* 38 (3), pp. 223, 235, 250; Tower, ed., *A Carolinian Goes to War,* p. 226; C. I. Walker, *Rolls and Historical Sketch of Tenth Regiment, So. Ca. Volunteers in the Army of the Confederate States* (Charleston, S. C.: Walker, Evans & Cogswell, 1881), p. 113.

¹³ Allen Daniel Candler and Clement Anselm Evans, eds., *Georgia: Comprising Sketches of Counties, Towns, Events, Institutions, and Persons, Arranged in Cyclopedic Form* Vol. 2 (of 3) (Atlanta, Ga.: State Historical Association, 1906), p. 326; Wilbur G. Kurtz, "At the Troup Hurt House," *Atlanta Constitution Magazine,* January 25, 1931, p. 4.

¹⁴ *OR* 38 (3), pp. 139, 147.

¹⁵ *OR* 38 (3), p. 195; "Report of Major Thomas Davies Maurice," *SOR* 7, pp. 48–49.

¹⁶ Lewis F. Lake, "My War Service as a Member of 'Taylor's Battery'" (1888), Lewis F. Lake Papers, ALPL; "From Chicago Battery A (A Private Letter)," *Chicago Tribune,* August 4, 1864; *OR* 38 (3), p. 262; "The Late Battles in Georgia," *Chicago Tribune,* August 10, 1864.

¹⁷ Wilbur G. Kurtz, "At the Troup Hurt House," pp. 4–5.

¹⁸ Tower, ed., *A Carolinian Goes to War,* pp. 226–27; *OR* 38 (3), p. 787; Walker, *Tenth Regiment,* p. 114.

¹⁹ George W. Bailey, *A Private Chapter of the War (1861–5)* (St. Louis, Mo.: G. I. Jones and Co., 1880), p. 4.

²⁰ De Gress to Major Thomas Maurice, July 22, 1864, in "Report of the Battle of Atlanta," *Blue & Gray Magazine* 11 (April, 1994), p. 29; *OR* 38 (3), p. 188.

²¹ Tower, ed., *A Carolinian Goes to War,* p. 227; *OR* 38 (3), p. 787; Gill to his wife, July 23, 1864, in Wiley, "A Story of 3 Southern Officers," *Civil War Times Illustrated* (April, 1964), p. 33.

²² *OR* 38 (3), p. 779. Strength estimated obtained by comparing returns of July 10 and 31. See *OR* 38 (3), pp. 679–80.

²³ *OR* 38 (3), p. 779; J. G. B. to the ed., July 23, 1864, *Canton Weekly Register,* August, 8, 1864; Committee of the Regiment, *The Story of the Fifty-fifth Regiment Illinois Volunteer Infantry in the Civil War* (W. J. Coulter; 1887), pp. 338–39; Dunbar Rowland, ed., *Publications of the Mississippi Historical Society, Centenary Series,* Vol. 1 (Jackson, Miss.: Mississippi Historical Society, 1916), pp. 574–76.

²⁴ Committee of the Regiment, *The Story of the Fifty-fifth Regiment,* p. 339; *OR* 38 (3), pp. 285, 778–79.

²⁵ *Atlanta Constitution,* July 20, 1898; Albert Castel, *Tom Taylor's Civil War* (Lawrence, Kansas: University Press of Kansas, 2000), pp. 246–47; Tower, ed., *A Carolinian Goes to War,* pp. 226–27.

²⁶ Lewis F. Lake, "My War Service as a Member of 'Taylor's Battery'" (1888), Lewis F. Lake Papers, ALPL; "From Chicago Battery A (A Private Letter)," *Chicago Tribune,* August 4, 1864; *OR* 38 (3), p. 262; "The Late Battles in Georgia," *Chicago Tribune,* August 10, 1864.

27 Gary Ecelbarger, *Black Jack Logan: An Extraordinary Life in Peace and War* (Guilford, Conn.: Lyons Press, 2005), p. 130; Hotaling quote reproduced in "A Great War Picture," *Freeport County* (Minn.) *Standard,* July 21, 1886.

28 Lewis F. Lake, "My War Service as a Member of 'Taylor's Battery'" (1888), Lewis F. Lake Papers, ALPL; "From Chicago Battery A (A Private Letter)," *Chicago Tribune,* August 4, 1864; *OR* 38 (3), p. 262; "The Late Battles in Georgia," *Chicago Tribune,* August 10, 1864.

29 Tower, ed., *A Carolinian Goes to War,* p. 230.

30 "A Great War Picture," *Freeport County* (Minn.) *Standard,* July 21, 1886; Ecelbarger, *Black Jack Logan,* p. 129.

31 *OR* 38 (3), p. 246; William Bakhaus, "The Battle of Atlanta," *The Ohio Soldier,* April 27, 1889; Castel, *Tom Taylor's Civil War,* pp. 247–48.

32 *OR* 38 (3), pp. 210, 224, 787; Tower, ed., *A Carolinian Goes to War,* pp. 227–29; A. B. Crummel, "De Grasse's [sic] Battery," *NT,* September 10, 1885; De Gress to Maurice, July 22, 1864, "Report of the Battle of Atlanta," p. 29.

33 Committee of the Regiment, *The Story of the Fifty-fifth Regiment,* p. 339; *OR* 38 (3), p. 29.

34 Reuben Williams, "Memories of War Times," *Warsaw* (Ind.) *Daily Times,* December 12, 1903.

35 Ibid.; James B. Swan, *Chicago's Irish Legion: The 90th Illinois Volunteers in the Civil War* (Carbondale, Ill.: Southern Illinois University Press, 2009), p. 150.

36 Walker, *Tenth Regiment,* p. 115; *OR* 38 (3), pp. 280–81, 779.

37 Leggett, "Battle of Atlanta," p. 18.

38 *OR* 38 (3), p. 872; William Titze diary, July 22, 1864, ALPL.

CHAPTER 9—A HUMAN HURRICANE ON HORSEBACK

1 "From Georgia," Burlington *Weekly Hawkeye,* July 23, 1864.

2 J. W. Long, "Flanking Johnston: The Army of the Tennessee on the Move," *NT,* September 13, 1888.

3 Letter excerpted in Gary L. Scheel, *Rain, Mud & Swamps: The Story of the 31st Missouri Volunteer Infantry* (Pacific, Missouri: Plus Communications, 1998), pp. 358–59.

4 Leggett quote in "Resolutions on General Logan," Society of the Army of the Tennessee, *Report of the Proceedings of the Society of the Army of the Tennessee, at the Twentieth Meeting, Held at Detroit, Mich., September 14th and 15th, 1887* (Cincinnati, Ohio: Published by the Society, 1893), p. 541.

5 Jacob D. Cox, *Atlanta* (New York: Charles Scribner's Sons, 1882), p. 171; *OR* 38 (2), pp. 516–17; *OR* 38 (3), p. 26; *OR* 38 (5), pp. 230–31, 317; Dodge, *The Battle of Atlanta,* p. 60.

6 *OR* 38 (3), p. 26, 195.

7 *OR* 38 (3), pp. 195, 203–205, 451, 679–80, 819–20.

8 Bailey, *A Private Chapter of the War,* pp. 8–9.

[9] Gill to his wife, July 23, 1864, in Wiley, "A Story of 3 Southern Officers," p. 33; John R. Windham, "A Johnny Reb Speaks," *NT,* March 4, 1897. Gill misspelled his sergeant's surname as "Nabors."

[10] *SOR* 7, pp. 118, 127.

[11] Wilber G. Kurtz, "The Broken Line and the DeGress [sic] Battery," *Atlanta Constitution Magazine,* February 8, 1931.

[12] *SOR* 7, pp. 127–29; Wilmer Kurtz, "Civil War Days in Georgia," *The Atlanta Constitution Magazine,* January 25, 1931. Charles W. Wills diary, July 25, 1864, in Mary E. Kellogg, comp., *Army Life of an Illinois Soldier* (Carbondale, Ill.: Southern Illinois University Press, 1996), p. 285. Abda Johnson vehemently denied the spade incident to Wilmer Kurtz, even though he reported it officially right after the battle, naming McGinnis in his summary.

[13] *SOR* 7, pp. 119–124; Tower, ed., *A Carolinian Goes to War,* p. 228. It should be noted that Colonel Jones placed his brigade strength at "678 muskets, the remainder being on the picket line" (see *SOR* 7, p. 119). This is a common mode for Confederate reports that enumerates privates and not officers of companies (up to 3 men), and regiments (up to 3 men). The 900 estimate is for rank and file for the brigade and the picket line, adding in an estimate of 2 commissioned officers per company and one per regiment for each of the four regiments to make an equal comparison with Union strength reports.

[14] *OR* 38 (1), p. 74; *OR* 38 (2), pp. 516–17, 572, 617; *OR* 38 (5), p. 319.

[15] *OR* 38 (3), p. 174; Williams, "Memories of War Times," *Warsaw* (Ind.) *Daily Times,* December 12, 1903.

[16] Tower, ed., *A Carolinian Goes to War,* p. 228; *SOR,* pp. 119, 122–23.

[17] "Several Reminiscences. Stories Told of Incidents in Gen. Logan's Career," *Chicago Tribune,* December 27, 1886; William Bakhaus, "The Battle of Atlanta," *The Ohio Soldier,* April 27, 1889; John S. Bosworth, "July 22, 1864: Gallantry of Logan, Giles A. Smith and Others on That Terrible Day," *NT,* August 7, 1884.

[18] Leggett, "Battle of Atlanta," pp. 18–19; *OR* 38 (3), p. 319.

[19] D. Q. M., "Letter From Atlanta," (Princeton, Ill.) *Bureau County Republican,* September 1, 1864; "A Veteran," "Who Recaptured the De Gres [sic] Battery in the Battle Before Atlanta?" *NT,* June 28, 1883; G. L. Childress, "Degrasse's [sic] Battery," *NT,* September 9, 1885; Adams, "The Battle and Capture of Atlanta," pp. 156–57.

[20] Thomas J. Shelley, "Atlanta," *NT,* September 15, 1887.

[21] *OR* 38 (3), pp. 305, 342–43, 348, 355–56, 778–80.

[22] *OR* 38 (3), pp. 217–18.

[23] Committee of the Regiment, *The Story of the Fifty-fifth Regiment,* p. 341.

[24] *SOR* (38), pp. 122–23, 127; Gill to his wife, July 23, 1864, in Wiley, "A Story of 3 Southern Officers," p. 33.

[25] Thomas J. Shelley, "Atlanta," *NT,* September 15, 1887; "81st Ohio" [William E. McReary], "DeGress's [sic] Battery," *NT,* July 5, 1888; De Gress to Maurice, July 22, 1864, "Report of the Battle of Atlanta," *Blue & Gray Magazine,* pp. 29–30.

[26] Ibid.; "Capture of the DeGress [sic] Battery—The Question Settled," *NT,* July 19, 1883.

[27] "A Great War Picture," *Freeport County Standard,* July 21, 1886; Lake, "My War Experience," Lewis F. Lake Papers, ALPL, pp. 9–10; "A Handsome Record of a Chicago Boy," *Chicago Tribune,* August 10, 1864.

[28] Gill to his wife, July 23, 1864, in Wiley, "A Story of 3 Southern Officers," p. 33.

[29] *Sixteenth Annual Reunion of the Association of the Graduates of the United States Military Academy* (East Saginaw, Mich.: Evening News, 1885), p. 88; Thomas McCunniff, "De Gress's Battery," *NT,* February 2, 1888; Oliver Otis Howard, "The Battles About Atlanta," *Atlantic Monthly Magazine* (October–November, 1876), p. 395.

[30] *OR* 38 (1), p. 74; *OR* 38 (3), pp. 139, 147.

[31] *OR* 38 (3), pp. 139–41.

[32] Walker, *Tenth Regiment,* pp. 115–16; *OR* 38 (3), p. 118. Manigault placed the casualties for Brown's division over 1,000. Clayton's losses are tallied for his three most active brigades (see *SOR* 38, pp. 120, 126, 129).

CHAPTER 10—DESPERATION

[1] Davis, Perry, and Kirkley, *Official Military Atlas of the Civil War,* Plate LVI (No. 6), Plate LXII (No. 3).

[2] *OR* 38 (3), pp. 547, 565, 573, 583; W. S. Ayres, "The 78th Ohio at Bald Hill," *NT,* January 17, 1884.

[3] Higbee, "Personal Recollections of a Line Officer," p. 322; Munson, "Battle of Atlanta," pp. 224–28.

[4] Edmund E. Nutt, "Twentieth Ohio at Atlanta," *The Ohio Soldier,* July 28, 1894; E. E. Nutt, "Fight at Atlanta," *NT,* January 3, 1884; W. L. Wade, "Bald Knob," *NT,* July 3, 1884; N. D. Brown, "Who Held Bald Hill?" *NT,* August 28, 1884.

[5] *OR* 38 (5), p. 219. This revealing dispatch, published in the Official Records, has been neglected partly because it was misdated by Blair as "July 21." Although it was corrected to July 22 upon its transcription, it was compiled chronologically with the previous day's correspondences in the official publication.

[6] "General M. P. Lowrey. An Autobiography," *SHSP* XVI (1888), p. 372; Joslyn, ed., *Charlotte's Boys,* p. 271; *OR* 38 (3), pp. 732, 754, 759.

[7] "General M. P. Lowrey. An Autobiography," *SHSP* XVI (1888), p. 372; Brown, ed., *One of Cleburne's Command,* p. 114; *SOR* 7 (1), p. 103; *OR* 38 (3), pp. 732–39.

[8] *OR* 38 (3), pp. 739, 754; Will Thomas Hale and Dixon Lanier Merritt, *A History of Tennessee and Tennesseans* Vol. 7 (Chicago and New York: Lewis Publishing Co., 1913), p. 2100; Sam R. Watkins, *Co. Aytch, Maury Grays, First Tennessee Regiment* (Nashville, Tenn.: Cumberland Presbyterian Publishing House, 1882), p. 151.

[9] *OR* 38 (3), p. 759.

[10] Walker, *Hell's Broke Loose in Georgia,* p. 167; Watkins, *Co. Aytch,* p. 153; James R. Fleming, *The Confederate Ninth Tennessee Infantry* (Gretna, La.: Pelican Publishing Co., 2006), pp. 117–18.

[11] *OR* 38 (3), p. 166.

[12] *OR* 38 (3), pp. 600, 739–41, 749; F. P. Cander, "Before Atlanta, and the Part That the Eleventh Iowa Played There," *NT,* November 8, 1883.

[13] *OR* 38 (3), p. 741; Dixon diary, Duke University, July 22, 1864. Captain Bourne's enlistment and regimental information available at: http://www.tngennet.org/civil war/csainf/csa15.html; http://www.couchgenweb.com/civilwar/3rdinf_regt.html.

[14] Ibid.; Byers, *Iowa in War Times,* p. 319; *OR* 38 (3), pp. 599–600; W. L. Wade, "Bald Knob," *NT,* July 3, 1884. Wade, the Iowan (Company G), learned Bourne's name, rank, and unit during a burial detail the next day, but inadvertently altered his name twenty years later as "Capt. F. A. Bohn, Co. B, 3d battalion, CSA."

[15] *OR* 38 (3), pp. 740–41.

[16] *OR* 38 (3), pp. 739–40; Fleming, *The Confederate Ninth Tennessee Infantry,* p. 119.

[17] Chapman Brothers, *Portrait and Biographical Album of Oakland County, Michigan,* p. 820.

[18] Munson, "Battle of Atlanta," p. 228; Fleming, *The Confederate Ninth Tennessee Infantry,* pp. 119–20; Oldham diary, July 24, 1862.

[19] Munson, "Battle of Atlanta," p. 228.

[20] Joslyn, *Charlotte's Boys,* p. 271; "The Story of the 54th Georgia's Flag," in *Richmond Whig,* August 24, 1864.

[21] *OR* 38 (3), pp. 754, 756.

[22] Christopher Losson, *Tennessee's Forgotten Warriors: Frank Cheatham and His Confederate Division* (Knoxville, Tenn.: University of Tennessee Press, 1989), p. 183; E. E. Nutt, "Fight at Atlanta," *NT,* January 3, 1884.

[23] Dwight, "How We Fight at Atlanta," p. 666; W. S. Ayres, "The 78th Ohio at Bald Hill," *NT,* January 17, 1884; E. E. Nutt, "Fight at Atlanta," *NT,* January 3, 1884.

[24] J. P. Ross, "July 22, 1864," *NT,* April 14, 1892.

[25] Leggett, "The Flag of the Seventy-eighth," http://www.ohiocivilwar.com/stori/ 78flag.html; Dwight, "How We Fight at Atlanta," p. 666; Leggett, "Battle of Atlanta," p. 27.

[26] Eli Detwiler letter published in *Aledo Weekly Record,* August 24, 1864; "The Battle Flag of the Thirtieth Illinois . . . ," *Journal of the Illinois State Historical Society* Vol. 4 (April, 1911–January, 1912), pp. 493–96; McDonald, History of the 30th Illinois, *Sparta News,* 1916, transcribed on http://home.comcast.net/~30il/mcdonald .html.

[27] Captain Elliott quote in Chapman Brothers, *Portrait and Biographical Album of Oakland County, Michigan,* p. 820.

[28] Edmund E. Nutt, "Twentieth Ohio at Atlanta," *The Ohio Soldier,* July 28, 1894; E. E. Nutt, "Fight at Atlanta," *NT,* January 3, 1884; W. L. Wade, "Bald Knob," *NT,* July 3, 1884; *OR* 38 (3), pp. 594–95, 600.

[29] *OR* 38 (3), pp. 747, 750.

[30] Cander, "Before Atlanta," *NT,* November 8, 1883; Edmund E. Nutt, "Twentieth

Ohio at Atlanta," *The Ohio Soldier,* July 28, 1894; George Mercer diary, July 22, 1864, in Walker, *Hell's Broke Loose in Georgia,* p. 168; *OR* 38 (3), pp. 740, 754.

³¹ William J. Worsham, *Old Nineteenth Tennessee Regiment, C.S.A.* (Knoxville, Tenn.: Paragon Printing Co., 1902), p. 129; Castel, *Decision in the West,* p. 409; *OR* 38 (3), pp. 741, 756. Worsham states a brigade loss of 140 (p. 129). This figure appears suspiciously low based on the ferocity of their fight on the knoll, particularly when the killed and wounded (not including captured) of Maney's division exceeded 600 and Walker's brigade was more imperiled than the other three brigades of the division. (See "Grand Summary of Casualties in Cheatham's Division," Cheatham Papers, TSLA.)

³² *OR* 38 (3), pp. 550, 600; Wesley Craig to the editor, July 25, 1864, *Warren* (Ohio) *Chronicle,* August 10, 1864; Detwiler letter, *Aledo Weekly Record,* August 24, 1864; George E. Welles, "List of Casualties in 68th O.V.I," *Daily Toledo Blade,* August 2, 1864; John P. Ross to the editor, July 23, 1864, (Cambridge, Ohio) *Guernsey Times,* August 4, 1864; Ayres, "The 78th Ohio at Bald Hill," *NT,* January 17, 1884.

³³ *OR* 38 (5), p. 232.

³⁴ *OR* 38 (5), p. 900; *New York Herald,* July 29, 1864.

³⁵ William F. Neubert to Guido Marx, July 25, 1864, *Daily Toledo Blade,* August 2, 1864.

CHAPTER 11—IMPACT

¹ R. C. Carden, "The Old Confederate's Story," *Boone* (Iowa) *Independent,* May 31, 1912, http://bellsouthpwp.net/C/a/CanCofHist/coffee/carden.htm; William P. Howell, "History of the 25th Alabama Infantry Regiment," Alabama Department of Archives and History, Montgomery, Alabama, http://home.earthlink.net/~sdriskell/25th/25th.htm; Fuller, "A Terrible Day," *NT,* April 16, 1885; Henry O. Dwight Sketch Album, Ohio Historical Society, Columbus, Ohio.

² Foster reminiscences, July 23, 1864, in Brown, ed., *One of Cleburne's Command,* p. 115.

³ F. G. De F., "From the Army of Tennessee," *Columbus Daily Sun,* July 29, 1864; Black to his wife, July 26, 1864, in Frano, ed., *Letters of Captain Hugh Black,* p. 68.

⁴ Yeary, *Reminiscences of the Boys in Gray,* p. 809; Key diary, July 23, 1864, in Cate, ed., *Two Soldiers,* p. 99; Fleming, *The Confederate Ninth Tennessee Infantry,* p. 122; William Jennings diary, July 23, 1864, http://www.rootsweb.ancestry.com/~ialcgs/mifflinj.htm.

⁵ Yeary, *Reminiscences of the Boys in Gray,* pp. 85, 586.

⁶ *OR* 38 (3), p. 373. The list shown on this page is confusing because the 64th Illinois losses are incorrectly placed as "Total" for the brigade. The error appears to be corrected in the "Grand Total" line at the bottom of the list. General Leggett reported the present-for-duty strength of the Army of the Tennessee at 27,593 on July 20 (Leggett, "Battle of Atlanta," p. 27), but this number apparently included two brigades of men not present on July 22.

⁷ *OR* 38 (3), p. 118.

[8] *OR* 38 (3), p. 550; *OR* 38 (4), p. 653; *OR* 38 (5), p. 318.

[9] Whaley, *Forgotten Hero*, p. 164.

[10] Ibid., pp. 167, 169–70.

[11] *OR* 38 (1), pp. 115–16; *OR* 38 (3), pp. 28–29; *OR* 38 (4), p. 316; *OR* 38 (5), p. 651.

[12] T. B. Roy, "General Hardee and the Military Operations Around Atlanta," p. 367. Roy, Hardee's chief of staff, claims this oddly exacting figure came from a letter Hardee wrote just two days after the battle, a letter yet to be discovered. The number is so close to the number of 3,297 killed and wounded (captured and missing not included) cited by the Medical Director of the Army of Tennessee for the month of July (see "Letters, Orders and Circulars Sent and Received, Medical Director's Office, Army of Tennessee," War Department Collection of Confederate Records, RG 109, NA) to appear more than a coincidence. Perhaps Roy confused the figures when he wrote his piece in 1880. A modern detailed and thorough analysis of Hardee's total losses on July 22 suggests casualty figures of 4,500 (see Brown, *To the Manner Born*, pp. 277–78). That estimate is rejected as it appears the modern analysis was victim of a simple mathematical error that counted Walker's full division loss to that of just one brigade and appears to have overestimated the losses in Bate's division. Regardless, if the 3,299 is erroneous, a total casualty count for the corps between 3,300 and 3,800 is as close an estimate that can be obtained until more evidence comes to light.

[13] *OR* 38 (3), pp. 733, 741, 748; Maney's killed and wounded division totals summarized in "Grand Summary of Casualties in Cheatham's Division," Cheatham Papers, TSLA.

[14] Brown, *To the Manner Born*, p. 278. This author's claim of 4,500 losses for Hardee is rejected, and Hardee's claim of 3,299 is suspicious. See endnote #12 on this page.

[15] *SOR* 7, pp. 119–129; Tower, ed., *A Carolinian Goes to War*, p. 229.

[16] The Third Battle of Winchester (September 19, 1864) and the Battle of Franklin (November 30, 1864) were single-day contests with casualties approaching 9,000 in each battle. Both fell below the number of losses at Atlanta.

[17] *OR* 38 (1), p. 116; *OR* 38 (3), p. 680.

[18] Roy, "General Hardee and the Military Operations Around Atlanta," p. 367; Buck, *Cleburne and His Command*, p. 243; OR 38 (3), pp. 740–41.

[19] Losson, *Tennessee's Forgotten Warriors*, p. 183; Hood, *Advance and Retreat*, p. 181.

[20] Stuart, *Iowa Colonels and Regiments*, p. 238; Warner, *Generals in Blue*, p. 535.

[21] Stephen Davis, "The General's Tour—Atlanta Campaign: Hood Fights Desperately," *Blue & Gray Magazine* Vol. 6, #6, (August, 1989), p. 26. The enmity between Dodge and Sweeny was long-standing. See Leslie Anders, "Fisticuffs at Headquarters: Sweeny vs. Dodge," *Civil War Times Illustrated*, Vol. 15, no. 10 (February, 1977), pp. 8–15.

[22] *OR* 38 (5), p. 266; Castel, *Decision in the West*, p. 418.

23 Dodge reminiscence reproduced in Mrs. John A. Logan, *Reminiscences of a Soldier's Wife: An Autobiography* (New York: Charles Scribner's Sons, 1913), pp. 171–72; "Address of General W. T. Sherman," Society of the Army of the Tennessee, *Proceedings of the Society of the Army of the Tennessee at the Twentieth Meeting* (Cincinnati: Published by the Society, 1893), pp. 471–72.

24 *OR* 38 (5), p. 272; "A Noble Man," *Los Angeles Times,* August 1, 1897.

25 Castel, *Decision in the West,* pp. 424–36.

26 Sherman to his wife, July 26, 1864, in Simpson and Berlin, eds., *Sherman's Civil War,* p. 671.

27 Alexander Spence to his parents, August 10, 1864, in Christ, ed., *Getting Used to Being Shot At,* p. 97; Daniel, *Soldiering in the Army of the Tennessee,* pp. 145–46.

28 Hosea Garrett to his uncle, August 5, 1864, Special Collections, Atlanta History Center; Daniel, *Soldiering in the Army of the Tennessee,* p. 146; Alexander Spence to his parents, August 10, 1864, in Christ, ed., *Getting Used to Being Shot At,* pp. 97–98.

29 Ulysses S. Grant, *Memoirs and Selected Letters* (New York: Literary Classics of the United States, 1990), p. 613.

30 Waugh, *Reelecting Lincoln,* pp. 262, 264; Don E. Fehrenbacher and Virginia Fehrenbacher, eds., *Recollected Words of Abraham Lincoln* (Stanford, Calif.: Stanford University Press, 1996), p. 441.

31 Frederick Douglass, *Life and Times of Frederick Douglass* (Hartford, Conn.: Park Publishing, 1882), pp. 434–35.

32 David Herbert Donald, *Lincoln* (New York: Simon & Schuster, 1996), p. 529.

33 Quote in *OR* 38 (5), p. 777. These famous six words are embodied within a 350-word dispatch from Sherman to Major General Henry Halleck.

34 Michael Burlingame, *Abraham Lincoln: A Life* Vol. 2 (Baltimore, Md.: John Hopkins University Press, 2008), p. 688; Waugh, *Reelecting Lincoln,* p. 297.

35 Special Orders No. 212, September 20, 1864, Logan Papers, LOC; Ecelbarger, *Black Jack Logan,* pp. 191–95.

36 Waugh, *Reelecting Lincoln,* p. 354.

37 "Atlanta on Canvass," *Atlanta Constitution,* October 20, 1885; Wilbur G. Kurtz, *The Atlanta Cyclorama: The Story of the Famed Battle of Atlanta* (City of Atlanta, 1954), pp. 24–25.

38 "What You Will Find at the Atlanta Cyclorama & Civil War Museum," and "Painting the Cyclorama," printed by the Atlanta Cyclorama & Civil War Museum, Atlanta, Ga.

39 Kurtz, *The Atlanta Cyclorama,* pp. 13–23. Traditionally, this cyclorama supposedly debuted in 1887, but contemporary evidence easily refuted this to place its opening to July of 1886 in Minnesota. See "A Great War Picture: The Panorama of Atlanta Recently Placed on Exhibition in Minneapolis" (Albert Lea, Minn.) *Freeport County Standard,* July 21, 1886

40 Kurtz, *The Atlanta Cyclorama,* pp. 24, 27. Tradition claims that General Logan commissioned the painting for $43,000 to boost his vice presidential candidacy in

1884. This is easily refuted by the fact that Logan was too strapped financially for such an extravagant expense and that no one would reasonably believe that the cyclorama could be studied and painted in the few months of Logan's vice presidential candidacy in 1884 (he was not selected on the ticket with James G. Blaine until May and the painting would have done little to aid him unless it was released before the end of the summer). A more reasonable "correction" of the tradition is that Logan's wealthy supporters commissioned the work to support a potential presidential bid in 1888. Contrary to another tradition, Logan was alive when the cyclorama was first put on display in Minneapolis, but no evidence exists that he ever saw the completed work.

[41] "Talk of the Day," *Atlanta Constitution,* February 4, 1889; "Atlanta's Battle Field. Union Officers Exploring the Old Lines," *Cincinnati Commercial Tribune,* February 9, 1889.

[42] "Atlanta's Battle Field. Union Officers Exploring the Old Lines," *Cincinnati Commercial Tribune,* February 9, 1889.

[43] The McPherson marker standing today is markedly different from the one placed by the Society of the Army of the Tennessee in 1877. The base is more elaborate than the original and no cannonball plugs the upward facing cannon barrel. For a picture of the original, see Thomas H. Martin, *Atlanta and Its Builders: A Comprehensive History of the Gate City of the South* Vol. 1 (Atlanta, Ga.: Century Memorial Publishing Co., 1902), p. 402. The monument that stands today may be an entirely different cannon barrel than the 1877 original. The William Walker monument was placed based on one eyewitness testimony of his death, a suspect account challenged by several contemporary sources that place his death an hour or so later than tradition and with Gist's brigade (near the current Walker Park in East Atlanta). For the story of the monument see Kurtz, "Civil War Days in Georgia: Major-General W. H. T. Walker," *Atlanta Constitution Magazine,* July 27, 1930.

[44] "What You Will Find at the Atlanta Cyclorama & Civil War Museum," and "Painting the Cyclorama," printed by the Atlanta Cyclorama & Civil War Museum, Atlanta, Ga.; "The Battle of Atlanta Is Here," *Atlanta Constitution,* February 12, 1892.

[45] "The Blue and Gray," *Atlanta Constitution,* July 23, 1894; "Firing of 11 Bombs Will Mark Battle of Atlanta Observance," *Atlanta Constitution,* July 22, 1939; "Clark Gable and Vivien Leigh Marvel at Cyclorama," *Atlanta Constitution,* December 16, 1939.

BIBLIOGRAPHY

MANUSCRIPTS
Abraham Lincoln Presidential Library, Springfield, Illinois.
   Lewis F. Lake Papers
   William E. Strong Papers
   William E. Titze diary
Columbia University, Rare Books and Manuscript Department, New York.
   Peter W. Alexander Papers
Duke University, Special Collections Library, Durham, North Carolina.
   Munford H. Dixon Papers
Florida State Archives, Tallahassee.
   Washington Ives Papers
Library of Congress, Manuscript Division, Washington, D.C.
   Manning F. Force Papers
   Abraham Lincoln Papers
   John A. Logan Papers
Minnesota Historical Society, St. Paul, Minnesota.
   Christie Letters
National Archives, Washington, D.C.
   RG 109: "Letters, Orders and Circulars Sent and Received, Medical Director's Office, Army of Tennessee," War Department Collection of Confederate Records.
   RG 393 Letters Received, 1864–1865, Department of the Army of the Tennessee
Ohio Historical Society, Columbus, Ohio.
   Henry O. Dwight Sketch Album
Tennessee State Library and Archives, Nashville.
   Cheatham Papers

Toledo-Lucas County Historical Society, Toledo, Ohio.
    McPherson Papers
University of Georgia, Special Collections, Athens, Georgia.
    Robert G. Mitchell Papers
United States Army Military History Institute. Carlisle Barracks, Pennsylvania.
    William W. McCarty diary
    John McKee diary
    Philip Roesch Journal, 1862–1865

BOOKS

Allardice, Bruce S. *More Generals in Gray.* Baton Rouge, La.: Louisiana State University Press, 1995.

Ambrose, Stephen E. *Nothing Like It in the World: The Men Who Built the Transcontinental Railroad, 1863–1869.* New York: Simon & Schuster, 2000.

Bailey, George W. *A Private Chapter of the War (1861–65).* St. Louis, Mo.: G. I. Jones and Co., 1880.

Bailey, Ronald H. and the editors of Time-Life Books. *Battles for Atlanta: Sherman Moves East.* Alexandria, Va.: Time-Life Books, Inc., 1985.

Basler, Roy P., ed. *The Collected Works of Abraham Lincoln.* 8 vols. New Brunswick, New Jersey: Rutgers University Press, 1953–55.

Belknap, William W. *History of the Fifteenth Regiment Iowa Veteran Volunteer Infantry.* Keokuk, Iowa: R. B. Ogden & Son, 1887.

Bevins, William E. *Reminiscences of a Private.* Privately published, 1913.

Beyer, W. F. and O. F. Keydel, eds. *Deeds of Valor: How America's Civil War Heroes Won the Congressional Medal of Honor.* Stamford, Conn.: Longmeadow Press, 1993.

Bonds, Russell S. *War Like the Thunderbolt: The Battle and Burning of Atlanta.* Yardley, Pa.: Westholme Publishing, 2009.

Brooks, Noah. *Washington in Lincoln's Time.* New York: The Century Company, 1895.

Brown, Norman D., ed. *One of Cleburne's Command: The Civil War Reminiscences and Diary of Capt. Samuel T. Foster, Granbury's Texas Brigade, C.S.A.* Austin: University of Texas Press, 1980.

Brown, Russell K. *Our Connection With Savannah: A History of the 1st Battalion Georgia Sharpshooters.* Macon, Ga: Mercer University Press, 2004.

Brown, Russell K. *To the Manner Born: The Life of General William H. T. Walker.* Mercer, Ga.: Mercer University Press, 2005.

Buck, Irving A. *Cleburne and His Command.* Jackson, Tenn: McCowat-Mercer Press, 1959.

Buell, Augustus C. *History of Andrew Jackson.* 2 vols. New York: Charles Scribner's Sons, 1904.

Burlingame, Michael, *Abraham Lincoln: A Life.* 2 vols. Baltimore, Md.: John Hopkins University Press, 2008.

Burlingame, Michael and John R. Turner Ettlinger, eds. *Inside Lincoln's White House: The Complete Civil War Diary of John Hay*. Carbondale, Ill.: Southern Illinois University Press, 1997.

Byers, Samuel H. M. *Iowa in War Times*. Des Moines, Iowa: W. D. Condit & Co., 1888.

Calhoun, Charles W. *Gilded Age Cato: The Life of Walter Q. Gresham*. University Press of Kentucky, 1988.

Candler, Allen Daniel and Clement Anselm Evans, eds. *Georgia: Comprising Sketches of Counties, Towns, Events, Institutions, and Persons, Arranged in Cyclopedic Form*. 3 vols. Atlanta, Ga.: Staten Historical Association, 1906.

Castel, Albert. *Decision in the West: The Atlanta Campaign of 1864*. Lawrence, Kansas: University Press of Kansas, 1992.

Castel, Albert. *Tom Taylor's Civil War*. Lawrence, Kansas: University Press of Kansas, 2000.

Cate, Wirt A., ed. *Two Soldiers: The Campaign Diaries of Thomas J. Key, C.S.A. December 7, 1863–May 17, 1865 and Robert J. Campbell, U.S.A. January 1, 1864–July 21, 1864*. Chapel Hill, N.C., University of North Carolina Press, 1938.

Chamberlin, William H. *History of the Eighty-first Regiment Ohio Infantry Volunteers During the War of the Rebellion*. Cincinnati: Gazette Steam Printing House, 1865.

Chapman Brothers. *Portrait and Biographical Album of Oakland County, Michigan*. Chicago: Chapman Brothers, 1891.

Chesnut, Mary Boykin. *A Diary From Dixie* (Ben Ames Williams, ed.). Cambridge, Mass.: Harvard University Press, 1980.

Christ, Mark K., ed. *Getting Used to Being Shot At: The Spence Family Civil War Letters*. Fayetteville, Ark.: University of Arkansas Press, 2002.

Committee of the Regiment. *The Story of the Fifty-fifth Regiment Illinois Volunteer Infantry in the Civil War*. Clinton, Mass.: W. J. Coulter, 1887.

Connelly, T. W. *History of the Seventieth Ohio Regiment From Its Organization to Its Mustering Out*. Cincinnati, Ohio: Peak Bros., 1902.

Cox, Jacob D. *Atlanta*. New York: Charles Scribner's Sons, 1882.

Cunningham, Summer A. *Reminiscences of the 41st Tennessee: The Civil War in the West*. (John A. Simpson, ed.) Shippensburg, Pa.: White Mane Books, 2001.

Curry, W. L. *War History of Union County*. Marysville, Ohio: 1883.

Dana, Charles A. *Recollections of the Civil War: With the Leaders at Washington and in the Field in the Sixties*. Lincoln, Nebr.: University of Nebraska Press, 1966.

Daniel, Larry J. *Soldiering in the Army of Tennessee*. Chapel Hill, N.C.: University of North Carolina Press, 1991.

Davis, George B., Leslie J. Perry, and Joseph W. Kirkley. *The Official Military Atlas of the Civil War*. New York: Gramercy Books, 1983.

Dodge, Grenville M. *The Battle of Atlanta and Other Campaigns, Addresses, Etc.* Council Bluffs, Iowa: Monarch Printing Company, 1911.

Dodson, W. C., ed. *Campaigns of Wheeler and His Cavalry, 1862–1865*. Atlanta, Ga.: Hudgins Publishing Co., 1899.

Donald, David Herbert. *Lincoln*. New York: Simon & Schuster, 1996.

Douglass, Frederick. *Life and Times of Frederick Douglass*. Hartford, Conn.: Park Publishing, 1882.

DuBose, John W. *General Joseph Wheeler and the Army of Tennessee*. New York: Neale Publishing Company, 1912.

Ecelbarger, Gary. *Black Jack Logan: An Extraordinary Life in Peace and War*. Guilford, Conn.: Lyons Press, 2005.

Fehrenbacher, Don E. and Virginia Fehrenbacher, eds. *Recollected Words of Abraham Lincoln*. Stanford, Calif.: Stanford University Press, 1996.

Fleming, James R. *The Confederate Ninth Tennessee Infantry*. Gretna, La.: Pelican Publishing Co., 2006.

Franklin, Ann York, comp. *The Civil War Diaries of Capt. Alfred Tyler Fielder, 12th Tennessee Regiment Infantry, Company B 1861–1865*. Louisville, Kentucky: Ann York Franklin, 1996.

Frano, E. C., ed. *Letters of Captain Hugh Black to his Family in Florida During the War Between the States, 1862–1864*. Newburgh, Ind.: Published by the author, 1998.

Freeman, Douglas Southall. *Lee's Lieutenants: A Study in Command*. 3 vols. New York: C. Scribner's Sons, 1942–44.

Glatthaar, Joseph T. *Partners in Command: The Relationships Between Leaders in the Civil War*. New York: Free Press, 1998.

Grainger, Gervis D. *Four Years With the Boys in Gray*. Franklin, Ky.: Published by the author, 1902.

Grant, Ulysses S. *Memoirs and Selected Letters*. New York: Literary Classics of the United States, 1990.

Green, John William. *Johnny Green of the Orphan Brigade: The Journal of a Confederate Soldier*. Lexington, Ky: The University Press of Kentucky, 2001.

Gresham, Matilda. *Life of Walter Quintin Gresham, 1832–1895*. 2 vols. Chicago: Rand McNally & Co., 1919.

Gurowski, Adam. *Adam Gurowski, Diary: 1863–'64–'65*. Washington, D.C.: W.H. & O.H. Morrison, 1866.

Hale, Will Thomas and Dixon Lanier Merritt. *A History of Tennessee and Tennesseans*. 8 vols. Chicago and New York: Lewis Publishing Co., 1903–1913.

Hedley, F. Y. *Marching Through Georgia: Pen-Pictures of Every-Day Life*. Chicago: Donohue, Henneberry, 1890.

Heidler, David S. and Jeanne T. Heidler, eds. *Encyclopedia of the American Civil War: A Political, Social, and Military History*. New York: W. W. Norton & Co., 2000.

Hewett, Janet B., ed. *Supplement to the Official Records of the Union and Confederate Armies*. 100 vols. Wilmington, NC: Broadfoot Publishing Co., 1994–1998.

Hood, John B. *Advance and Retreat*. New Orleans, La.: G. T. Beauregard, 1880.

Hughes, Nathaniel Cheairs Jr. *General William J. Hardee: Old Reliable.* Baton Rouge: Louisiana State University Press, 1965.

Hughes, Nathaniel Cheairs Jr. *The Civil War Memoir of Philip Daingerfield Stephenson, D. D.* Conway, Arkansas: UCA Press, 1995.

Hughes, Nathaniel Cheairs Jr. *The Pride of the Confederate Artillery: The Washington Artillery in the Army of Tennessee.* Baton Rouge: Louisiana State University Press, 1997.

Jones, Eugene W. *Enlisted for the War.* Hightstown, N.J.: Longstreet House, 1997.

Joslyn, Mauriel Phillips. *Charlotte's Boys: Civil War Letters of the Branch Family of Savannah.* Berryville, Va.: Rockbridge Publishing Company, 1996.

Kennedy, Francis H., ed. *The Civil War Battlefield Guide.* Boston, Mass.: Houghton-Mifflin Co., 1990.

Lewis, Lloyd. *Sherman: Fighting Prophet.* New York: Harcourt, Brace & Co., 1932.

Logan, Mrs. John A. *Reminiscences of a Soldier's Wife: An Autobiography.* New York: Charles Scribner's Sons, 1913.

Losson, Christopher. *Tennessee's Forgotten Warriors: Frank Cheatham and His Confederate Division.* Knoxville, Tenn.: University of Tennessee Press, 1989.

Lowry, Thomas P. *The Story the Soldiers Wouldn't Tell: Sex in the Civil War.* Mechanicsburg, Pa.: Stackpole Books, 1994.

Lucas, D. R. New *History of the 99th Indiana Infantry.* Rockford, Ill.: Horner Printing Co., 1900.

McCaffrey, James M., ed. *Only a Private: A Texan Remembers the Civil War. The Memoirs of William J. Oliphant.* Houston, Texas: Halcyon Press, 2004.

McCaffrey, James M. *This Band of Heroes: Granbury's Texas Brigade, C.S.A.* College Station, Texas: Texas A & M University Press, 1996.

McGee, Benjamin F. *History of the 72d Indiana Infantry of the Mounted Lightning Brigade.* LaFayette, Ind.: S. Vater & Co., 1882.

McMurry, Richard M. *John Bell Hood and the War for Southern Independence.* Lincoln, Nebr.: University of Nebraska Press, 1992.

Nicolay, John G. and John Hay, eds. *Abraham Lincoln: Complete Works.* 10 vols. New York: Century Company, 1920.

Niven, John ed. *The Salmon P. Chase Papers.* 5 vols. Kent, Ohio: Kent State University Press, 1993–1998.

Phillips, Brenda, ed. *Personal Reminiscences of a Confederate Soldier Boy.* Milledgeville, Ga.: Boyd Publishing Co., 1993.

Poole, John Randolph. *Cracker Cavaliers: The 2nd Georgia Cavalry Under Wheeler and Forrest.* Mercer, Ga.: Mercer University Press, 2000.

Quiner, E. B. *The Military History of Wisconsin: A Record of the Civil and Military Patriotism of the State in the War for the Union.* Chicago: Clark & Co., 1866.

Reed, Wallace P., ed. *History of Atlanta, Georgia: With Illustrations and Biographical Sketches of Some of Its Prominent Men and Pioneers.* Syracuse, N.Y.: D. Mason and Co., 1889.

Robbins, James S. *Last in Their Class: Custer, Pickett and the Goats of West Point*. New York: Encounter Books, 2006.

Rood, Hosea Whitford. *Story of the Service of Company E, and of the Twelfth Wisconsin Veteran Volunteer Infantry*. Milwaukee, Wisc.: Swain & Tate, Co., 1893.

Rowland, Dunbar, ed. *Publications of the Mississippi Historical Society, Centenary Series*, Vol. 1 (Jackson, Miss.: Mississippi Historical Society, 1916.

Savas, Theodore P. and David A. Woodbury, eds., *The Campaign for Atlanta & Sherman's March to the Sea: Essays on the American Civil War in Georgia, 1864*. 2 vols. Campbell, Calif.: Savas Woodbury Publishers, 1992–1994.

Scaife, William R. *The Campaign for Atlanta*. Fourth Ed. Cartersville, Ga.: Civil War Publications, 1993.

Scheel, Gary L. *Rain, Mud & Swamps: The Story of the 31st Missouri Volunteer Infantry*. Pacific, Missouri: Plus Communications, 1998.

Schofield, John M. *Forty-six Years in the Army*. New York: Century Company, 1897.

Sears, Stephen W. *To the Gates of Richmond: The Peninsula Campaign*. New York: Ticknor & Fields, 1992.

Sherman, William Tecumseh. *Memoirs of General W. T. Sherman*. New York: Literary Classics of the United States, Inc., 1990.

Simpson, Brooks D. and Jean V. Berlin. *Sherman's Civil War: Selected Correspondence of William T. Sherman, 1860–1865*. Chapel Hill, N.C.: University of North Carolina Press, 1999.

Sixteenth Annual Reunion of the Association of the Graduates of the United States Military Academy. East Saginaw, Mich.: Evening News, 1885.

Smith, H. I. *History of the Seventh Iowa Veteran Volunteer Infantry During the Civil War*. Mason City, Iowa: E. Hitchcock Printer, 1903.

Society of the Army of the Tennessee. *Report of the Proceedings of the Society of the Army of the Tennessee, at the Twentieth Meeting, Held at Detroit, Mich., September 14th and 15th, 1887*. Cincinnati, Ohio: Published by the Society, 1893.

Strayer, Larry M. and Richard A. Baumgartner, eds. *Echoes of Battle: The Atlanta Campaign*. Huntington, West Va.: Blue Acorn Press, 1991.

Stuart, A. A. *Iowa Colonels and Regiments*. Des Moines, Iowa: Mills & Company, 1865.

Styple, William B., ed. *Writing and Fighting the Civil War: Soldier Correspondence to the New York Sunday Mercury*. Kearny, N.J.: Belle Grove Publishing, Co., 2001.

Swan, James B. *Chicago's Irish Legion: The 90th Illinois Volunteers in the Civil War*. Carbondale, Ill.: Southern Illinois University Press, 2009.

Symonds, Craig L. *Stonewall of the West: Patrick Cleburne and the Civil War*. Lawrence, Kansas: University Press of Kansas, 1998.

Thompson, Edwin Porter. *History of the Orphan Brigade*. 2 vols. Louisville, Kentucky: Lewis N. Thompson, 1898.

Tower, R. Lockwood, ed. *A Carolinian Goes to War: The Civil War Narrative of Ar-*

thur Middleton Manigault, Brigadier General, C.S.A. Columbia, S.C.: University of South Carolina Press, 1983.

United States War Department. *War of the Rebellion. A Compilation of the Official Records of the Union and Confederate Armies.* 128 vols. Washington, D. C.: Government Printing Office, 1880–1901.

Walker, C. I. *Rolls and Historical Sketch of Tenth Regiment, So. Ca. Volunteers in the Army of the Confederate States.* Charleston, S. C.: Walker, Evans & Cogswell, 1881.

Walker, Scott. *Hell's Broke Loose in Georgia: Survival in a Civil War Regiment.* Athens, Ga.: University of Georgia Press, 2005.

Warner, Ezra J. *Generals in Blue: Lives of the Union Commanders.* Baton Rouge, La.: Louisiana State University Press, 1992.

Warner, Ezra J. *Generals in Gray: Lives of the Confederate Commanders.* Baton Rouge, La.: Louisiana State University Press, 1995.

Watkins, Sam R. *Co. Aytch, Maury Grays, First Tennessee Regiment.* Nashville, Tenn.: Cumberland Presbyterian Publishing House, 1882.

Waugh, John C. *Reelecting Lincoln: The Battle for the 1864 Presidency.* New York: Crown Publishing, 1997.

Weaver, Jeffrey C. *54th Virginia Infantry.* Lynchburg, Va.: H. E. Howard, 1993.

Weaver, Jeffrey C. *63rd Virginia Infantry.* Lynchburg, Va.: H. E. Howard, 1991.

Welsh, Jack D. *Medical Histories of Confederate Generals.* Kent, Ohio: Kent State University Press, 1994.

Welsh, Jack D. *Medical Histories of Union Generals.* Kent, Ohio: Kent State University Press, 1996.

Whaley, Elizabeth J. *Forgotten Hero: General James B. McPherson.* New York: Exposition Press, 1955.

Wills, Charles W. *Army Life of an Illinois Soldier, Including a Day-by-Day Record of Sherman's March to the Sea.* Mary E. Kellogg, comp. Carbondale, Ill.: Southern Illinois University Press, 1996.

Wilson, James H. *Life and Services of Brevet Brigadier-General Andrew Jonathan Alexander, United States Army.* New York: Published by author, 1887.

Woodworth, Steven E. *Nothing but Victory: The Army of the Tennessee, 1861–1865.* New York: Knopf, 2005.

Woodworth, Steven E., ed. *Grant's Lieutenants: From Cairo to Vicksburg.* Lawrence, Kansas: University Press of Kansas, 2001.

Worsham, William J. *Old Nineteenth Tennessee Regiment, C.S.A.* Knoxville, Tenn.: Paragon Printing Co., 1902.

Wortman, Marc. *The Bonfire: The Siege and Burning of Atlanta.* New York: Public Affairs, 2009.

Wright, Charles B. *A Corporal's Story: Experiences in the Ranks of Company C, 81st Ohio Vol. Infantry.* Philadelphia: Published by author, 1887.

Yeary, Mamie, comp. *Reminiscences of the Boys in Gray, 1861–1865.* McGregor, Texas: Published by compiler, 1912.

Young, Lot D. *Reminiscences of a Soldier of the Orphan Brigade.* Louisville, Kentucky: Courier-Journal Job Printing Co., 1918.

ARTICLES AND MONOGRAPHS

"The Battle Flag of the Thirtieth Illinois," *Journal of the Illinois State Historical Society* Vol. 4 (April, 1911–January, 1912), pp. 493–96.

"General M. P. Lowrey. An Autobiography," *Southern Historical Society Papers* XVI (January–December, 1888), pp. 365–76.

"Report of the Battle of Atlanta," *Blue & Gray Magazine* 11 (April, 1994), pp. 28–31.

"Return of a Confederate Flag," *Confederate Veteran* Vol. 22, no. 7 (July 1914), p. 302.

Adams, Robert N. "The Battle and Capture of Atlanta," *Glimpses of the Nation's Struggle: Papers Read Before the Minnesota Commandery of the Military Order of the Loyal Legion of the United States, 1892–1897.* (4th Series) St. Paul, Minn.: H. L. Collins, 1898, pp. 144–163.

Anders, Leslie. "Fisticuffs at Headquarters: Sweeny vs. Dodge," *Civil War Times Illustrated* Vol. XV, no. 10 (February, 1977), pp. 8–15.

Atlanta Historical Bulletin Vol. 15 (1970), p. 94.

Chamberlin, W. H. "Recollections of the Battle of Atlanta," in Theodore F. Allen, Edward S. McKee, and J. Gordon Taylor, eds., *Sketches of War History 1861–1865, Papers Prepared for the Commandery of the State of Ohio, Military Order of the Loyal Legion of the United States.* Vol. 6 (Cincinnati: Montfort & Company, 1908), pp. 276–86.

Compton, James. "The Second Division of the 16th Army Corps in the Atlanta Campaign," *Glimpses of the Nation's Struggle: Papers Read Before the Minnesota Commandery of the Military Order of the Loyal Legion of the United States, 1892–1897.* Vol. 30 (St. Paul, Minn.: Review Publishing Co., 1903), pp. 103–23.

Cox, Rowland. "Snake Creek Gap, and Atlanta: A Paper Read by Brevet Major Rowland Cox, U.S.V., December 2, 1891.

Davis, Stephen, "The General's Tour—Atlanta Campaign: Hood Fights Desperately," *Blue & Gray Magazine* Vol. 6, no. 6 (August, 1989).

Dwight, Henry O. "How We Fight at Atlanta," *Harper's New Monthly Magazine* Vol. 29 (October. 1864), pp. 663–66.

Evans, David. "The Fight for the Wagons," *Civil War Times Illustrated* Vol. 26, no. 10 (February, 1988), pp. 16–18.

Higbee, Chester G. "Personal Recollections of a Line Officer," *Glimpses of the Nation's Struggle: Papers Read Before the Minnesota Commandery of the Military Order of the Loyal Legion of the United States, 1892–1897.* (4th Series) St. Paul, Minn.: H. L. Collins, 1898, pp. 313–28.

Howard, Oliver. "The Battles About Atlanta," *Atlantic Monthly Magazine* Vol. XXXVIII (October–November, 1876), pp. 385–99, 559–67.

Kurtz, Wilbur G. "At the Troup Hurt House," *Atlanta Constitution Magazine,* January 25, 1931.

Kurtz, Wilbur G. "The Broken Line and the DeGress [sic] Battery." *Atlanta Constitution Magazine,* February 8, 1931.

Kurtz, Wilbur G. "Civil War Days in Georgia: Major-General W. H. T. Walker," *Atlanta Constitution Magazine,* July 27, 1930.

Leggett, M. D. "The Battle of Atlanta: A Paper by General M. D. Leggett, Before the Society of the Army of the Tennessee, October 18, 1883, at Cleveland."

Munson, Gilbert D. "Battle of Atlanta," *Sketches of War History, 1861–1865. Papers read Before the Ohio Commandry of the Military Order of the Loyal Legion of the United States. 1888–1890.* Edited by Robert Hunter. Published by the Commandery. Vol. 3. Cincinnati, Ohio: Robert Clarke and Company. 1890, pp. 212–30.

Rood, H. H. "Sketches of the Thirteenth Iowa," *War Sketches and Incidents. as Related by Companions of the Iowa Commandery, Military Order of the Loyal Legion of the United States, Published by the Commandery.* Vol. 1. Des Moines: Press of P. C. Kenyon, 1893, pp. 115–56.

Roy, T. B., "General Hardee and the Military Operations Around Atlanta," *Southern Historical Society Papers* Vol. 8 (September, 1880), pp. 337–87.

Strong, William E. "The Death of General James B. McPherson," *Military Essays and Recollection:, Papers Read Before the Commandery of the State of Illinois, Military Order of the Loyal Legion of the United States.* Vol. 1 Chicago: A.C. McClurg, 1891, pp. 311–44.

Tuthill, Richard S. "An Artilleryman's Recollection of the Battle of Atlanta," *Military Essays and Recollections: Papers Read Before the Commandery of the State of Illinois, Military Order of the Loyal Legion of the United States.* Published by the Commandery. Vol. 1. Chicago: A.C. McClurg and Co. 1891, pp. 293–310.

Wiley, Bell I. "A Story of 3 Southern Officers," *Civil War Times Illustrated* Vol. 3, no. 1 (April 1964), pp. 26–34.

SOLDIERS' LETTERS/DIARIES PUBLISHED IN NEWSPAPERS

"Capture of the DeGress [sic] Battery—The Question Settled," *National Tribune,* July 19, 1883.

"81st Ohio" [William E. McReary], "DeGress's [sic] Battery," *National Tribune,* July 5, 1888.

"The 15th Mich. at Atlanta," *National Tribune,* February 17, 1887.

"From Chicago Battery A (A Private Letter)," *Chicago Tribune,* August 4, 1864.

"From Georgia," Burlington *Weekly Hawkeye,* July 23, 1864.

[Gilbert D. Munson], "A Matter of War History. The Capture and Fortification of Leggett's Hill," *Cincinnati Daily Gazette,* September 12, 1879.

"A Month's History of the 81st Ohio Regiment," (Chillicothe, Ohio) *Scioto Gazette,* August, 16, 1864.

"The 16th Iowa at Atlanta," *National Tribune*, August 26, 1886.

A Veteran, "Who Recaptured the De Gres [sic] Battery in the Battle Before Atlanta?," *National Tribune*, June 28, 1883.

J. G. B. To the editor, July 23, 1864, *Canton* (Illinois) *Weekly Register*, August 8, 1864.

F. G. De F., "From the Army of Tennessee," *Columbus Daily Sun*, July 29, 1864.

D. Q. M., "Letter From Atlanta," (Princeton, Ill.) *Bureau County Republican*, September 1, 1864.

F. McC. To the editor, July 26, 1864, *Cedar Valley Times*, August 11, 1864.

T. G. T. To the editor, July 26, 1864, *Clinton* (Iowa) *Herald*, August 13, 1864.

X. To the editor, July 24, 1864, New Albany (Ind.) *Daily Ledger*, August 5, 1864.

Ayres, W. S., "The 78th Ohio at Bald Hill," *National Tribune*, January 17, 1884.

Ayres, W. S., "The Position Held by the Seventeenth Corps, July 22," *National Tribune*, July 23, 1891.

Bakhaus, William, "The Battle of Atlanta," *The Ohio Soldier*, April 27, 1889.

Bosworth,, John S., "July 22, 1864: Gallantry of Logan, Giles A. Smith and Others on that Terrible Day," *National Tribune*, August 7, 1884.

Brown, J. L., "The 78th Ohio in Close Quarters," *National Tribune*, February 21, 1884.

Brown, N. D., "Who Held Bald Hill?" *National Tribune*, August 28, 1884.

Cander, F. P., "Before Atlanta, and the Part That the Eleventh Iowa Played There," *National Tribune*, November 8, 1883.

Childress, G. L., "Degrasse's [sic] Battery," *National Tribune*, September 9, 1885.

Craig, Wesley, to the editor, July 25, 1864, *Warren* (Ohio) *Chronicle*, August 10, 1864.

Crummel, A. B., "De Grasse's [sic] Battery," *National Tribune*, September 10, 1885.

Detwiler, Eli, *Aledo Weekly Record*, August 24, 1864.

Delany, Frank P., "Leggett's Hill," *National Tribune*, November 9, 2008.

Donaldson, J. R., "Sweeny's Fighters," *National Tribune*, May 19, 1898.

Doyle, Timothy W., "Gen. McPherson's Death," *National Tribune*, October 6, 1892.

Fuller, John Wallace, "A Terrible Day: The Fighting Before Atlanta July 22, 1864," *National Tribune*, April 16, 1885.

Goodreli, W. H., "From the Fifteenth," (Des Moines) *Iowa State Register*, August 10, 1864.

Hamrich, W. G., "Incidents of the Battle Before Atlanta," *National Tribune*, July 26, 1883.

Hayes, H. E., "From the 14th Ohio Battery," *Western Reserve Chronicle*, August 17, 1864.

Hemstreet, William, "A Remarkable Stroke of Lightning," *Quincy Whig and Republican*, August 5, 1864.

Lewis, Thomas W., ed., "Battle of Atlanta as Told by Colonel Churchill's Diary," *Zanesville* (Ohio) *Sunday Times-Signal*, December 5, 1926.

Long, J. W., "Flanking Johnston: The Army of the Tennessee on the Move," *National Tribune*, September 13, 1888.

Loop, Myron, "Sounding the Alarm: The 68th Ohio's Trying Time at the Battle of Atlanta," *National Tribune*, December 1, 1898.

McCunniff, Thomas, "De Gress's Battery," *National Tribune*, February 2, 1888.

Neubert, William F., to Guido Marx, July 25, 1864, *Daily Toledo Blade*, August 2, 1864.

Nutt, E. E., "Fight at Atlanta," *National Tribune*, January 3, 1884.

Nutt, Edmund E., "Twentieth Ohio at Atlanta," *The Ohio Soldier*, July 28, 1894.

Powell, William V., to the Governor of Texas, "An Indianan Wishes to Return a Texas Battleflag," *Houston Daily Post*, May 13, 1900.

Quartus, "From General Sherman's Army," *Daily Toledo Blade*, August 3, 1864.

Ross, J. P., "July 22, 1864," *National Tribune*, April 14, 1892.

Ross, John P. to the editor, July 23, 1864, (Cambridge, Ohio) *Guernsey Times*, August 4, 1864.

Shelley, Thomas J., "Atlanta: The Battle of July 22 as Seen by an 81st Ohio Comrade," *National Tribune*, September 15, 1887.

Sniff, Amos, "The Capture of the 16th Iowa," *National Tribune*, March 27, 1884.

Typo to the editor, August 13, 1864, *Western Reserve Chronicle*, August 24, 1864.

S[pear], E[ugene] P., "General W. H. T. Walker," *Newman* (Ga.) *Herald*, May 29, 1883.

Sweeny, W. M., ed., "Man of Resource. Active Service of Gen. T. W. Sweeny, as Told by His Letters," *National Tribune*, October 17, 1895.

Wade, W. L., "Bald Knob," *National Tribune*, July 3, 1884.

Walker, Henry J., "In Front of Atlanta," *National Tribune*, October 11, 1883.

Welles, George E., "List of Casualties in 68th O.V.I," *Daily Toledo Blade*, August 2, 1864.

Williams, Reuben, "Memories of War Times," *Warsaw* (Ind.) *Daily Times*, December 12, 1903.

Windham, John R., "A Johnny Reb Speaks," *National Tribune*, March 4, 1897.

Wray, A. G., "Battle of Bald (or Leggett's) Hill, Atlanta, July 27 [21], 1864," *Janesville Daily Gazette*, April 6, 1912.

Young, L. D., "Kentucky Confederate Visits Scenes of Battle and Siege During the Civil War," *Lexington Herald*, May 19, 1912.

OTHER NEWSPAPERS CITED

Atlanta Constitution, July 20, 1898.

Atlanta Daily Appeal, July 20, 1864.

Chicago Tribune, August 10, 1864.

Chicago Tribune, December 27, 1886.

Columbus (Georgia) *Daily Sun,* July 30, 1864.

Freeport County (Minnesota) *Standard,* July 21, 1886.

Indianapolis Journal, December 30, 1886.

Los Angeles Times, August 1, 1897.

Georgia Weekly Telegraph, July 29, 1864.

Georgia Weekly Telegraph, September 6, 1867.
New York Herald, July 29, 1864.
New York Times, July 29, 1864.
Philadelphia Inquirer, July 28, 1864.
Richmond Whig, August 24, 1864.

WORLD WIDE WEB

American Civil War Research Database: http://www.civilwardata.com.

"Civil War Diaries of [Martin] Van Buren Oldham" (University of Tennessee at Martin): http://www.utm.edu/departments/acadpro/library/departments/special_collections/E579.5%20Oldham/text/vboldham_1864.htm.

"Letters of Captain Peter Marchant, 47th Tennessee Infantry": http://www.geocities.com/bsdunagan/letters.htm.

"The Civil War Diaries of Mifflin Jennings, 11th Iowa Infantry": http://iagenweb.org/civilwar/books/mifflinj.htm.

"The Flag of the Seventy-eighth": http://www.ohiocivilwar.com/stori/78flag.html.

G. B. McDonald, "History of the 30th Illinois Veteran Volunteer Regiment of Infantry": http://home.comcast.net/~30il/mcdonald.html.

"Complete Sun and Moon Data for One Day": http://aa.usno.navy.mil/data/docs/RS_OneDay.php.

"Tennesseeans in the Civil War": http://www.tngennet.org.

"3rd Confederate Infantry Regiment": http://www.couchgenweb.com/civilwar/3rdinf_regt.html.

R. C. Carden, "The Old Confederate's Story," *Boone* (Iowa) *Independent,* May 31, 1912. http://bellsouthpwp.net/C/a/CanCofHist/coffee/carden.htm.

William P. Howell, "History of the 25th Alabama Infantry Regiment," Alabama Department of Archives and History, Montgomery, Alabama. http://home.earthlink.net/~sdriskell/25th/25th.htm.

INDEX

Soldiers and military units are identified by (USA) for Union and (CSA) for Confederate. Italic page numbers refer to illustrations.